The Sage and the People

THE SAGE AND THE PEOPLE

The Confucian Revival in China

SÉBASTIEN BILLIOUD

AND

JOËL THORAVAL

OXFORD
UNIVERSITY PRESS

OXFORD

UNIVERSITY PRESS

Oxford University Press is a department of the University of
Oxford. It furthers the University's objective of excellence in research,
scholarship, and education by publishing worldwide.

Oxford   New York
Auckland   Cape Town   Dar es Salaam   Hong Kong   Karachi
Kuala Lumpur   Madrid   Melbourne   Mexico City   Nairobi
New Delhi   Shanghai   Taipei   Toronto

With offices in
Argentina   Austria   Brazil   Chile   Czech Republic   France   Greece
Guatemala   Hungary   Italy   Japan   Poland   Portugal   Singapore
South Korea   Switzerland   Thailand   Turkey   Ukraine   Vietnam

Oxford is a registered trademark of Oxford University Press
in the UK and certain other countries.

Published in the United States of America by
Oxford University Press
198 Madison Avenue, New York, NY 10016

Originally published in French by CNRS Éditions © 2014
© Oxford University Press 2015
Original title of work: *Le Sage et le peuple: Le renouveau confucéen en Chine*

Library of Congress Cataloging-in-Publication Data
Billioud, Sébastien.
[Sage et le peuple. English]
The sage and the people : the confucian revival in China /
Sébastien Billioud and Joël Thoraval.
pages cm
Includes bibliographical references and index.
Translation of: Le sage et le peuple.
ISBN 978–0–19–025814–6 (pbk. : alk. paper) —
ISBN 978–0–19–025813–9 (cloth : alk. paper)
1. Neo-Confucianism—China.   2. Religion and politics—China—History—21st century.
3. Philosophy—China—History—21st century.   I. Thoraval, Joël.   II. Title.
B127.N4B5513 2015
181'.112—dc23
2014050103

1 3 5 7 9 8 6 4 2
Printed in the United States of America
on acid-free paper

Contents

Acknowledgments

THIS BOOK IS primarily based on field research carried out between 2005 and 2013. The project was supported by the Chiang Ching-kuo Foundation within the framework of an international research program titled *The Confucian Revival in Mainland China: Forms and Meanings of Confucian Piety Today*. Some financial support was also granted by the French Centre for Research on Contemporary China (CEFC, Hong Kong). We are very thankful to both these institutions.

We are especially indebted to Vincent Goossaert, David Ownby, and Ji Zhe who took the time to read part or the totality of the original French manuscript of the book and gave us their thoughtful comments. Our gratitude also goes to Maurice Godelier who encouraged us throughout this project and published the French edition of this volume in his series (Bibliothèque de l'anthropologie) at CNRS Editions, Paris.

This book benefited a lot from discussions with colleagues and friends, among whom were the participants of the Chiang Ching-kuo Foundation project: Chen Bisheng, Chen Ming, Chung Yun-ying, Guillaume Dutournier, Gan Chunsong, Ishii Tsuyoshi, Ji Zhe, Nakajima Takahiro, David Palmer, Anna Sun, and Wang Chien-chuan. We also thank Stephen Angle, Daniel A. Bell, Jean-François Billeter, Chen Na, Anne Cheng, Philip Clart, Deng Xinnan, Silvia Elizondo, Fan Lizhu, Thomas Fröhlich, Philip J. Ivanhoe, Paul Katz, John Lagerwey, Li Shiwei, John Makeham, Thierry Meynard, Peng Guoxiang, Axel Schneider, Suenari Michio, Wang Shouchang, Frédéric Wang, Watanabe Hiroshi, and Xiao Yang. Guillaume Dutournier, Chung Yun-ying, and Mr. Wang Pao-Tzong helped us by providing some of the pictures included in this book. Finally, we are also grateful to the whole team at Oxford University Press: Cynthia Read, Marcela Maxfield, Michael Durnin, Eswari Maruthu, and Alyssa Bender.

Preliminary research results were published in *China Perspectives* between 2007 and 2009. We thank the journal for its authorization to use and reproduce part of this material (Billioud: "*Jiaohua*: The Confucian Revival Today as an Educative Project," *China Perspectives* 2007, no. 4 [2007]: 4–20; Billioud and Thoraval: "*Anshen liming* or the Religious Dimension of Confucianism," *China Perspectives* 2008, no. 3 [2008]: 88–106; "*Lijiao*: The Return of Ceremonies Honouring Confucius in Mainland China," *China Perspectives* 2009, no. 4 [2009]: 82–99). Finally, appreciative acknowledgments are also due to *Oriens Extremus* for the authorization to use sections of the paper written by Billioud in 2010 ("Carrying the Confucian Torch to the Masses: The Challenge of Structuring the Confucian Revival in the People's Republic of China," *Oriens Extremus* 49 [2010]: 201–224).

The Sage and the People

Introduction

THE SPECIFIC AMBITION of this book crystallizes in its very title—*The Sage and the People*. In recent years, the "revival of Confucianism" in China has generated an impressive literature. However, whereas normative works or commentaries of discourses are many, studies dedicated to the reappropriation or reinvention of popular practices remain much more scarce. They precisely constitute the core of this book, itself the product of both a question and a surprise.

The question resulted from a previous phase of our research dedicated to the impressive creation in twentieth-century China of a modern philosophy inspired by Confucianism.[1] Whereas in the 1990s discourses claiming a Confucian identity still largely remained confined to academia, it was nevertheless clear that such a specialization and transformation of an ancient and multifaceted tradition in pure "thought" was only the consequence of a recent—and maybe only temporary—historical evolution. It was also clear that after the loosening of state grip in the post-Mao era the Confucian tradition would necessarily generate new developments within the Chinese population. The mere perception of such an objective trend clearly demanded a switch in disciplinary approach. In brief, philosophical questioning had to be complemented with sociological and anthropological fieldwork.

---

1 See Joël Thoraval, "Idéal du sage, Stratégie du philosophe: Introduction à la pensée de Mou Zongsan," in Mou Zongsan, *Spécificités de la philosophie chinoise*, 7–60 (Paris: Éditions du Cerf, 2003); Sébastien Billioud, *Thinking through Confucian Modernity: A Study of Mou Zongsan's Moral Metaphysics* (Leiden and Boston, MA: Brill, 2012); Sébastien Billioud and Joël Thoraval, eds., "Regards sur le politique en Chine aujourd'hui," special issue, *Extrême-Orient Extrême-Occident* 31 (2009).

The surprise came with one of the specific forms of these recent developments, when in 2007 we met in Shandong province ordinary people attempting to collectively reinvent practices and words that would enable them to directly interact with ancient sages. In Zoucheng, not far away from the city of Qufu, homeland of Confucius and his linage, workers, technicians, craftsmen, former peasants, primary school teachers, and low-ranking cadres attempted to reconstruct in a deserted temple—and far away from political and academic authorities—elements of sacrificial rituals. Two chapters of this book (8 and 9) are dedicated to this micro event and its intertwinement with a broader context.

In order to understand the originality of this direct relation, "in the space of the people" (*minjian* 民間), to the figure of Confucius and his disciples and, by the same token, to assess the novelty of the very idea of a "popular Confucianism" (*minjian rujia* 民間儒家), one needs first to underscore why such a phenomenon shares little with the many previous discourses that also pointed to a return of "Confucianism."[2] The phenomena that we intend to study here are neither schools of thought, nor mere reconstructions of previously existing social structures, nor local manifestations of official ideology or politics.

Differences with Previous Debates about the Return of Confucianism

It is well known that the collapse of the imperial order in 1911 translated in the name of a modernizing nationalism into a century of destruction, marginalization, and radical transformation for whole segments of Chinese cultural tradition. The action of political elites of both the nationalist (Guomindang) and Communist parties combined to give to Western observers the feeling that Confucian tradition had gradually died

---

2 The very category of Confucianism generates numerous difficulties. The Western word primarily results from the European science of religion that developed from the nineteenth century onwards: Confucianism was understood as a philosophical or religious doctrine of an eponymous figure, in the same vein as Christianism, Mohammedanism, or Buddhism. This notion does not correspond to the Chinese word *ru* 儒 (and its derivatives: *ruxue* 儒學, *rujia* 儒家, *rujiao* 儒教, etc.). It gives to this tradition a definition that is either too vast—since Confucius commented on a number of ancient Chinese texts "Confucianism" is sometimes mixed up with classical culture—or sometimes too narrow—when one forgets that *ru* and "ruism" existed before Confucius. See Nicolas Zufferey, *To the Origins of Confucianism: The Ru in Pre-Qin Times and During the Early Han Dynasty* (Berne: Peter Lang, 2003).

out: Despite the persistence of symbols emptied of their original significations, Confucianism would be primarily relegated to the museum.[3] Such a pessimistic diagnosis, formulated among others by American historian Joseph Levenson, was contested on several occasions between the 1950s and the 1990s when developments taking place first in Taiwan, Hong Kong, and Singapore (and the United States) and then in the mainland itself reflected a certain vitality of the Confucian legacy. However, one needs to underscore here that the encounter between the sage and the people observed in the 2000s does not share much with the different kinds of hypotheses formulated so far in order to explain the perpetuation or the resurgence of Confucianism in China.

First, it is not a school of thought whose ultimate promoters would be scholars or public intellectuals. The most impressive reaction to the aforementioned thesis of an ineluctable demise of Confucian tradition was the development of a philosophical movement called "contemporary neo-Confucianism" (*dangdai xinrujia* 當代新儒家). It emerged in China during the republican era and developed after 1949 in Hong Kong and Taiwan, where it translated into a remarkable philosophical production. A manifesto signed in 1958 by prominent figures such as Mou Zongsan 牟宗三 (1909–1995) and Tang Junyi 唐君毅 (1909–1978) asserted strongly the vitality of Confucianism. Philosophical systems were elaborated in a clear opposition to Western philosophy in order to emphasize the ethical dimension of the Confucian legacy understood as a way of wisdom and a life doctrine (*shengming de xuewen* 生命的學問). However, it is noteworthy that these new metaphysical discourses largely inspired by Song- and Ming-dynasty neo-Confucianism were primarily produced by scholars employed in modern universities. Thus, this novel thought was somewhat cut off from its former material basis. The language game of modern philosophy took precedence over ancient collective and bodily practices (meditation, rituals, etc.). Historian Yu Yingshi spoke about these neo-Confucian thinkers—and of contemporary Confucianism in general—as a "lost" or "wandering" soul (*youhun* 遊魂), severed from the institutional body to which it was previously intimately linked.[4] In a way,

3 Joseph R. Levenson, *Confucian China and Its Modern Fate*, 3 vols. (London: Routledge and Kegan Paul, 1965).

4 Yu Ying-shih 余英時, "Xiandai ruxue de kunjing 現代儒學的困境" [The Predicament of Modern Confucianism], in *Xiandai ruxue lun* [On Contemporary Confucianism], (River Edge, NJ: Global Publishing Co., 1996), 159–164. This text generated numerous objections. In a new foreword, Yu attempted to clarify the meaning of the expression to avoid

practices studied in this book may be considered to be forms of "reincarna-tion" or "reincorporation" of such a soul. However, bodies that become again both individually and collectively vehicles for this ancient thought are nei-ther bodies of former scholar-officials nor of modern intellectuals: Ordinary people are appropriating the teachings of the sage and their ambition is not doctrinal, but primarily practical. Whereas some of the activists acknowledge masters and feel the need to insert themselves into spiritual genealogies, whether real or imaginary, most of the developments of the 2000s are in both their intention and their concrete realizations extremely different from the philosophical Confucianism prevailing in previous decades.

Second, these new developments, despite their popular dimension, can-not be mixed up with another broad phenomenon that began to affect the countryside after the end of the Maoist era: The reconstruction of tradi-tional structures and practices still existing in pre-Communist China. Such a reconstruction became possible at the end of the 1970s thanks to Deng Xiaoping's reform and opening policy. It started quickly, though with strong geographical differences. The ancient lineages that were traditionally well developed in Southeast China attempted to reestablish part of their com-mon legacy: Ancestral temples (*citang* 祠堂), lineage cemeteries, genealogies (*jiapu* 家譜), and so on. At the same time, villagers revived cults of all kinds of local deities. However, the reconstruction of lineage practices remained partial and sometimes fragile (lineages and their properties normally can-not have any legal status) in a social context where striking differences between cities and the countryside were still maintained by the adminis-trative residence-permit (*hukou* 戶口) system.[5] This revival was remarkable enough to be documented by detailed anthropological fieldwork focusing on the transformations of the kinship structures or popular religion.[6] From the

---

possible misunderstandings (ibid., i–ix). Makeham also used the expression as a title for his detailed overview of Confucianism in academic discourses: John Makeham, *Lost Soul, "Confucianism" in Contemporary Chinese Academic Discourse* (Cambridge, MA: Harvard University Press, 2008).

5 The revival of lineages continues to take place in the 2000s and the 2010s, sometimes in a striking way; see chapter 9.

6 The situation of the 1980s presented specific features due to the radical changes of state policy after the Maoist period. In a context characterized by the lack of legal framework and some degree of liberalization leaving enough room to all kinds of initiatives, changes in religious behaviors went along with the emergence or reemergence of new collective groups, whether associated with ethnicity (nationalities) or with kinship (lineages); Joël Thoraval, "Religion ethnique, religion lignagère: sur la tentative d'islamisation d'un lignage Han de Hainan," *Études chinoises* 10, nos. 1–2 (1991): 9–75.

end of the 1990s it was nevertheless affected by the development of the market economy and its consequences in terms of migrations. At a time when the urban population started to increase swiftly at the expense of village life, kinship relationships and religious practices also needed—and still need—to adapt to this new context.[7]

The encounter that takes place in the 2000s between the sage and the people sharply differs from this situation, in at least two ways. First, villagers involved in ancestor cults or in the revival of lineages do not necessarily feel any need to claim a Confucian identity. Values such as "filial piety" or rituals to dead ancestors belong to a broader and more composite whole that is none other than Chinese culture.[8] To the contrary, for new Confucian activists, affiliation to a tradition reconstructed around Confucius and/or the tradition Confucius symbolizes has a special meaning that we later try to analyze. Second, the social context in which these activists operate is extremely different from the one of Deng Xiaoping's era: Mobility within society has increased tremendously. Some of the activists recall their rural background while sharing the way of life of new urbanites. Whereas their projects are carried out in the name of Confucius or the Confucian tradition, this is often done far away from their local roots, whether of kinship or local territory. Generalization is impossible and counterexamples exist, but this new brand of Confucianism is partly deterritorialized and uprooted. In spite of its modest origins, it is also part of the Internet age and some of the initiatives are based on the construction of potentially boundless networks.[9]

---

7 Michael Szonyi, "Lineages and the Making of Contemporary China," paper presented at the conference "Modern Chinese Religion: Values Systems in Transformation, 1850–Present," December 13, 2012, 9–14.

8 Such a situation impacted the visibility of Confucianism at that period of time. See Joël Thoraval, "The Anthropologist and the Question of the 'Visibility' of Confucianism in Contemporary Chinese Society," *China Perspectives* 23 (1999): 65–73.

9 This relative deterritorialization or even dematerialization of new national networks is not contradictory or incompatible with the existence, at the same time, of multiple local traditions about the way to approach the Confucian legacy. Fieldwork provided us with the opportunity to observe how Confucian commitments—though national in the scope of their projected activities—are also often well rooted in local territories and history. Some activists from Shanxi province could participate in activities organized in Shandong, but they tended to introduce the characteristics of their specific brand of Confucianism. China's largest temple dedicated to Guandi, god of war but also of merchants (among other meanings), is located in Xiezhou in the southern part of Shanxi province. Local Confucian activists insist on that point and on the fact that their province is also the birthplace of Xunzi and of ancient general Guan Zhong: "Our spirit is more 'martial' (*wu* 武) than the 'civil' (*wen* 文) spirit of Shandong, birthplace of Confucius"; Field observation, Shanxi, 2010.

Last, "popular" Confucian movements of the 2000s cannot be ana-lyzed as if they were simply the result of an ideology imposed from the top. They are not the consequence of a discourse promoted by the party-state and its representatives in elite circles. A good example of official ideol-ogy emphasizing the benefits of "Confucian ethics" was the discourse on so-called Asian values that appeared in the 1980s and the 1990s in East and Southeast Asia. It is necessary to give a short explanation about this context to show how little it shares with the current situation. Based on an experi-ence of economic growth and political stability, for instance in Malaysia and Singapore, these discourses originated from officials, journalists, and scholars questioning the relevance of applying to their own societies val-ues perceived as "Western" ones, such as the philosophy of human rights or the principles of democratic individualism. In that context, and contrary to a popularized version of Max Weber's sociology, "Confucianism" was introduced not as an obstacle but as a beneficial factor illuminating the rise of an Asian brand of capitalism.[10] In retrospect, the impact of such an ideological discourse on Mainland China was limited: It contributed to disseminating the idea of a new type of modern authoritarianism among political Chinese elites of the Deng Xiaoping era. It also stimulated reflec-tions about global ethics among neo-Confucian philosophers. Finally, it facilitated the reception of the work of Max Weber in academia, with the ambition to go beyond dogmatic Marxism.[11] However, the theories that emerged at the periphery of the Chinese mainland played only a somewhat marginal role and China was not really impacted by a discourse that aimed at "reimagining Asia." The reason was in fact simple: When modernizing models celebrating Asian values flourished, China's development was not sufficient to take part in this trend; by contrast, after its economic growth began to skyrocket, China no longer needed these explanatory models. It was thanks to its own resources and within itself that it could shape a "Chinese model." Between a nation now confident in its own power—if not in the universal validity of its own model—and a global stage on which

10 There is a huge literature on the topic. See for instance David Camroux and Jean-Luc Domenach, eds., *Imagining Asia: The Construction of an Asian Regional Identity* (London: Routledge, 1997), and Mizoguchi Yuzô 溝口雄三 and Nakajima Mineo 中嶋嶺雄, *Jukyô runessansu wo kangaeru* 儒教ルネッサンスを考える [Reflections on the Confucian Renaissance] (Tokyo: Daishûkan shoten, 1991).

11 On the reception of Max Weber in China, see Liu Dong, "The Weberian View and Confucianism," *East Asian History* 25–26 (2003): 191–217.

it can exert its influence, there is little room left for a modern version of "asiatism."[12]

Therefore, it is within a national framework that an official ideology with a seemingly traditional accent emerged in the 2000s.[13] In fact, there is an obvious simultaneity between a kind of discourse emanating from the party-state and the expansion of grassroots initiatives. However, inferring too much from such a coincidence might be ill founded. Projects launched by the authorities to cherry-pick and rehabilitate specific aspects of the cultural tradition (that could for instance serve as resources for moral and educational indoctrination) only very partially overlap with the objectives and activities of Confucian activists.[14] Those activities do not relate to any abstract ideology but consist in practical projects in which the properly Confucian ideals play a pivotal role. Enterprises carried out in the name of popular Confucianism share indeed little with official projects. Nevertheless, they might anticipate future evolutions in society considering a rather new phenomenon—the increasing involvement by part of the elites in the Confucian revival of the 2010s. In any case, before questioning the link between politics and popular Confucianism—which will be done later in this work—the latter must be understood in its own spirit and dynamics.

What Is So New about "Popular Confucianism"?

The starting point of this study of "the sage and the people" is not a general reflection about contemporary China or Confucianism but concrete field experience and observation of the encounter of individuals coming from

---

12 See the volume edited by Pan Wei, one of the main theoretician of a "Chinese model" (*Zhongguo moshi* 中國模式) at the end of the 2000s. Pan Wei 潘維, ed., *Zhongguo moshi: jiedu renmin gongheguo de liushi nian* 中國模式,解讀人民共和國的 60年 [The Chinese Model: Decoding 60 Years (of History) of the People's Republic] (Beijing: Zhongyang bianyi, 2009).

13 This situation became particularly blatant during the 2000s. However, some scholars already emphasized that this trend existed in the 1990s. See Jean-Philippe Béja, "The Rise of National-Confucianism?" *China Perspectives* 1995, no. 2 (1995): 6–12.

14 For a detailed analysis of these issues and of the program of cultural development included in the eleventh five-year plan see Sébastien Billioud, "Confucianism, 'Cultural Tradition' and Official Discourses in China at the Start of the New Century," *China Perspectives* 2007, no. 3 (2007): 50–65.

popular backgrounds with the figure of Confucius or, beyond him, with a Confucian life ideal that they attempt to appropriate and put in practice.

Three preliminary questions had to be raised for this research: (1) What does the often-claimed label of "popular Confucianism" really mean? (2) In which historical continuity is it possible to understand a movement that is first and foremost striking because of its novelty? (3) In which directions of experience could this movement develop?

One should immediately mention the reason why the very notion of "popular Confucianism" may seem unusual or even paradoxical. In this book, this expression is the translation of a notion, if not a slogan, that activists often claim for themselves: *minjian rujia*, that is, Confucianism "in the space of the people." The very notion of *minjian* combines in an ambiguous way two different dimensions: The first one is administrative, since *minjian* may designate nonofficial activities carried on outside the party-state apparatus—which does not mean out of its control. The second one is more sociological and refers to ordinary people. Therefore, according to the context, the notion of *minjian* might be alluded to in reference or opposition to the state or in reference or opposition to the elites. To some extent, this book is also, at least implicitly, a reflection on this issue that is discussed again overtly in the epilogue.

Beyond the specific context of the 2000s, the very idea of "popular Confucianism" may sound surprising for at least two sets of reasons. To begin with, the emergence of such a movement is not without a link to all the destructions that took place after the demise of the empire. If the very idea of ritual celebration of Confucius by workers may sound odd, it is also because Confucius temples (or Temples of culture, *wenmiao* 文廟) used to be the preserve of scholars-literati. They were an institution that maintained tight relationships with the examination system and a ritual system characteristic of the imperial order. Commoners did not have access to those temples. The very fact that technicians, employees, workers, or peasants may now take possession of Mencius or Confucius temples in order to carry out rituals therefore constitutes some sort of transgression. And the fact that some of them still perpetuate—in spite of their dreams to restore an ancient tradition—a symbolic and bodily language typical of the Maoist era simply reinforces the visibility of such a paradox.

However, the existence of a "popular Confucianism" may seem counterintuitive for another reason, namely the importance of modern scientific categories and disciplinary fields. Thus, religious anthropology that now needs to deal with a Chinese space deeply affected by political transformations of the twentieth century sometimes prefers to ascribe a "popular" dimension to representations and practices perceived as independent from an orthodoxy that used in the past to be embodied by the state and a cast of scholars-literati. Daoism in particular has been celebrated as a, if not *the* popular religion in China, thus opposing a Confucian order itself associated with a bureaucracy and an elite eager to impose their values upon society.[15] From this perspective there is a perception that Confucianism should not "by essence" be considered "popular." There is no room here for a detailed discussion of this issue, which would require prior clarifications concerning the use of modern Western categories.[16] However, one can only notice the extent to which practices traditionally associated with Confucian classics—such as ancestor cults—have for centuries permeated the whole of the social structure, from the elites to the villagers. A differentiation between "the people" and the elite can be contemplated only if one takes into account a common, that is, shared cultural background that challenges rigidly imposed categorizations. In any case, it is noteworthy that recent anthropological fieldwork carried out in Taiwan in the realm of religious practices contributed to a more general reflection about the forms and meaning of a possible "popular Confucianism."[17] How could recent movements developing in the People's Republic of China (PRC) in the 2000s be linked to these phenomena and thus reinscribed in certain forms of historical continuity? Answering this question requires that one turns to a second pivotal issue: The link with history and memory but also the invention and the creativity of these movements.

---

15 For a well-argued example of such a perspective, see John Lagerwey, *China: A Religious State* (Hong Kong: Hong Kong University Press, 2010), 1–17. The book opposes in Chinese history—though with nuances—on the one hand a horizontal and spatial perspective focusing on Daoist masters, local gods, and the people and, on the other hand, a vertical and temporal perspective centered upon the relationship to ancestors, Confucian elites, and imperial bureaucracy. A kind of essential precedence, logical or historical, is accorded to the first perspective. In such a view, ordinary people, at the grassroots level, are seen to have kept, up to now, special affinities with the religious universe of Daoist masters (even though the latter have their own esoteric teaching). By contrast, natural heirs of "rationalistic" scholars-literati in today's society are identified with communist bureaucrats. Be that as it may, this is not to deny, beyond its popular roots, the existence of a more elitist tradition of Daoism embodied by a specific bureaucracy that disappeared at the end of the imperial era. On Daoist elites, see Vincent Goossaert, "Bureaucratie, taxation et justice: Taoïsme et construction de l'État au Jiangnan (Chine), XVIIe–XIXe siècle," *Annales Histoire, Sciences Sociales* 4 (2010): 999–1027.

16 Chapter 5 encompasses a discussion about modern categories.

17 See for instance Philip Clart, "Confucius and the Mediums: Is There a Popular Confucianism?" *T'oung Pao* 89 (2003): 1–38.

This broad issue can be tackled from two sides, taking into account both the specificities of the sociological context of the 2000s and the recollection and reinterpretation of collective memory.

One could first wonder to what extent social circumstances of the 2000s could have contributed to fashion this "popular Confucianism." The aforementioned encounter in Zoucheng involved people from a variety of backgrounds gathering for a common ritual project. Inquiring into the initiatives taken by these protagonists also means questioning the status ascribed to individuals in an overall social situation that differs from both the Mao and the Deng Xiaoping eras.

To put things bluntly—maybe taking the risk of oversimplification—the effect of what could be called the Maoist project was to coercively organize the passage from one type of collective life into another type: The individual, though formally acknowledged in his rights, was torn up from ancient ("feudal") communities so as to be assigned to new (socialist) collectives. One could simply give an example that is not without impact on the transformation of "Confucian" ritual practices: The 1950 marriage law intended to abolish former patriarchal links of the "old society" and promote the individual choice of spouses supposed to be free and equal in rights. However, the objective was also to reinsert them, without further delay, into new collective control structures (work unit, collectives, production teams, etc.). Any form of individualism was reined in before it could develop. Of course, such a narrative should not be taken too literally since it downplays both the emancipation processes that had already begun during the republican era[18] and the capabilities of initiative and negotiation of individual behaviors, whether in traditional communities (families, lineages, local communities) or in the new collectives implemented under communist rule.

Contrary to the Maoist period, it is well known that Deng Xiaoping's reform policy translated into massive decollectivization, an opening to international influences and some degree of market economy. During the 2000s, it is possible to follow anthropologist Yan Yunxiang and posit that processes of "individualization" of behaviors became stronger; however, in a social environment that became increasingly mobile and uncertain, they went along with new forms of association and the creation of a number

18 On the evolution of individual behaviors—between legal codes and reality—in the context of weddings, see Philip Huang, *Code, Custom, and Legal Practice in China: The Qing and the Republic Compared* (Stanford, CA: Stanford University Press, 2001), 180–200.

of interpersonal networks.[19] During this decade and up to now, popular Confucianism has developed in a context often described—both in official discourses and within the population—as a time of moral crisis driven by egoism and its manifestations: the cult of money (*baijinzhuyi* 拜金主義), self-ishness at the expense of justice (*jian li wang yi* 見利忘義), neglect of the com-mon good and development of private desires (*sun gong fei si* 損公肥私), and so on. Recurrent scandals (avian flu, contaminated milk, gutter oil, sales of all kinds of fake goods, etc.) as well as increasing distrust between people have been perceived as manifestations of a growing anomy in Chinese society.[20] However, these destructive tendencies have also been somewhat counterbal-anced by a reverse trend focusing on the promotion of "things collective," for instance exemplified by the religious revival or the development of voluntary and disinterested commitments in society.[21] People and projects associated with Confucianism are also part of this countercurrent.

But which resources and historical precedents can they mobilize in order to fuel their hopes for the creation of a new collective body and, by the same token, a new communion with ancient sages and reinvigo-rated solidarities between people? In the 2000s the scope of collective memory has been considerably enlarged compared to previous decades, successfully integrating entire strata of a past previously forgotten or marginalized. The period is no longer the same as the 1980s, when one could for instance observe in scholarly circles an opposition between Western-inspired "modernity" and a "tradition" (*chuantong*) considered dark and confused. Before 1989, "tradition" represented both an impe-rial past, deemed immobile and despotic, and the authoritarianism of the Maoist era, often denounced as a great leap into new forms of "feudal-ism."[22] By contrast, from the 1990s onwards people's perception of the

---

19 Yan Yunxiang, *The Individualization of Chinese Society* (London: Berg, 2009). Yan's book provides a number of highly stimulating studies about many aspects of post-Maoist society, from kinship to economic behaviors. This book has a strong methodological orientation—it consists of a discussion, from a Chinese perspective, of sociologists Beck and Giddens's theses about the issue of "individualization." This orientation constitutes both its strength and its limits.

20 A stimulating anthropological reflection based on avian flu and behaviors in the context of a "catastrophe" can be found in Frédéric Keck, *Un monde grippé* (Paris: Flammarion, 2010).

21 On these themes see Arthur Kleinman et al., *Deep China: The Moral Life of the Person. What Anthropology and Psychiatry Tell Us about China Today* (Berkeley: University of California Press, 2011).

22 A famous documentary of the time, *River Elegy* (He Shang 河殤), inspired by a book by Su Xiaokang 蘇曉康, introduces a country with sharp contrasts: A "blue," coastal, dynamic,

imperial past changed and became endowed with a much more positive meaning. This situation could be observed in all segments of society, far beyond scholarly circles. It gave birth to a phenomenon of reappropriation of strata of the past that could be encountered in mass culture, official discourses, and academia, with a rising interest in "national studies" (*guoxue* 國學).[23] For the Chinese population, reference to tradition ceased to be something abstract: "Cultural tradition" was no longer a dream but translated into a repertoire of very concrete objects, symbols, or ways of behaving that were reappropriated or reinvented—from traditional arts to vestimentary fashion—within a much more opened and consumerist daily culture.

This being said, it will only be possible in this book to emphasize the partial and fragmented dimension of historical resources mobilized in the 2000s by Confucian activists. Moreover, the recollection and reinterpretation of collective memory is far from consensual and often remains highly disputed. Of course, the broadening of people's "horizon of expectations" compared to the Maoist period and its political grip on society also impacts the "field of experience" of new generations rediscovering various strata of the past.[24] But the whole process remains fragmented and selective. A good example of this unequal treatment or reappropriation of memory is the republican era of the 1920s and the 1930s. Whereas the work of famous Confucian intellectuals of this period such as Liang Shuming or Xiong Shili are published and commented on in scholarly circles, the history of "redemptive societies" that gave Confucianism of the time a massive popular dimension remains largely neglected. However, we shall see later that the various popular dimensions of Confucianism in the republican era may help to anticipate some of the undertakings carried out "in the space of the people" in the 2000s and that they sometimes also echo the activities of organizations developing in Taiwan. Transformations of historical perception take place in an ongoing and quick way. They also affect more recent

---

and opened China was opposed to a "yellow" country, since the yellowish color of loess, so typical of inner China, was associated with things backward, traditional, and conservative. The "blue" China was the one of necessary economic and political reforms, whereas the yellow one implicitly pointed to "conservative" communism. See Joël Thoraval, "La tradition rêvée: Réflexions sur *L'Élégie du fleuve* de Su Xiaokang," *L'Infini* 30 (1990): 146–168.

23 See Arif Dirlik, ed., "The National Learning Revival," special issue, *China Perspectives* 2011, no. 1 (2011), dedicated to national studies.

24 These concepts are borrowed from Koselleck, *Vergangene Zukunft, Zur Semantik geschichtlicher Zeiten*, 349–375.

periods such as the Maoist era that becomes increasingly severed from lived experience of part of the population and thus generates new reconstructions and new veils of amnesia.[25] Let us add that historical memory is of course a disputed realm that is also impacted by debates within Chinese society: After a century of antitraditionalist nationalism it would have been surprising not to see—in reaction against the reappearance of references to the sage—concurrent revival of new types of anti-Confucianism.[26]

What are the main orientations of the new "popular Confucianism"? In this study, we focus on three dimensions that also constitute the three parts of the book. To avoid feeling constrained by Western categories and the implicit meanings they convey, at least for a Western readership, we have chosen to turn to Chinese categories. Part I is called *jiaohua* 教化. This notion is made up of the two characters "educate" (*jiao*) and "transform" (*hua*). It does not simply point to the acquisition of knowledge but to a deeper transformation and shaping process of the self, but above all, of the others, thanks to education. Chapters 1 to 3 explore the meaning and the evolution of educational enterprises launched by Confucian activists as well as their specific relationship to classical texts.

---

25 For Republican China, see Zhang Qiang and Robert Weatherley, "The Rise of Republican Fever in the PRC and its Implications for CCP Legitimacy," *China Information* 27, no. 3 (November 2013): 277–300. For Maoist China, Sebastian Veg, ed., "Mao Today: A Political Icon for an Age of Prosperity," special issue, *China Perspectives* 2012, no. 2 (2012).

26 A symptom is the debate that opposed in 2007 liberal advocates of a "cultural renaissance" (*wenhua fuxing* 文化復興) and traditionalist—and Confucianism-inspired—promoters of a "moral reconstruction" (*daode chongjian* 道德重建). See Liu Junning 劉軍寧, "Zhongguo, ni xuyao yi chang wenyifuxing! 中國,你需要一場文藝復興" [China, You Need a Renaissance!], *Nanfang Zhoumou* 南方週末, December 7, 2006, B15; Shu Qinfeng, "Zhongguo zhen de xuyao yi chang wenyifuxing 中國真的需要一場文藝復興" [China Really Needs a Renaissance], *Liaowang Zhoukan* 瞭望周刊, December 28, 2006, 74–76; Qiu Feng 秋風, "Zhongguo xuyao wenyifuxing hai shi bie de yundong? 中國需要文藝復興還是別的運動?" (Does China Need a Renaissance or Another Movement?), *Nanfang Zhoumou* 南方週末, December 21, 2006, 15B; Qiu, "Zhongguo xuyao daode chongjian yu shehui jianshe yundong 中國需要道德重建與社會建設運動" [China Needs a Movement of Moral Reconstruction and Social Construction], *Nanfang Zhoumou*, February 8, 2007, 15B"; Qiu, "Daode chongjian, shehui jianshe yu geti zunyan 道德重建,社會建設與個體尊嚴" [Moral Reconstruction, Social Construction and Dignity of the Individual], *Nanfang Zhoumou*, January 18, 2007, 29D; Cui Weiping 崔衛平, "Women de zunyan zaiyu yongyou jiazhi lixiang lixiang 我們的尊嚴在於擁有價值理想" [Our Dignity Stems from the Fact that We Have an Ideal in the Realm of Values], *Nanfang Zhoumou*, January 11, 2007, B14; Li Jing 李靜, "Geren de jingshen chengshu yu Zhongguo wenyi fuxing 個人的精神成熟與中國文藝復興" [Spiritual Maturity of the Individual and Chinese Renaissance]. *Nanfang Zhoumou*, January 25, 2007, B15; "Wenyifuxing haishi daode chongjian? 文藝復興還是道德重建?" [Renaissance or Moral Reconstruction?], *Zhongguo xinwen zhoukan* 中國新聞週刊, January 22, 2007, 2 [op-ed].

Anshen liming 安身立命 has been the notion that we have selected to encapsulate the array of issues discussed in part II. The expression designates a quest for inner peace and, at the same time, the concern for individual or collective destiny and this, in reference to ultimate values. It is a particularly interesting category since it makes it possible to encompass a large spectrum of activities: Whereas some of them are openly "religious," others refuse or are simply indifferent to such a label. Starting with the description of specific itineraries our study attempts afterwards to show the relative fluidity of categories originally borrowed from the West and often used to describe new Confucianism-inspired projects. Finally, we discuss the possibility of institutionalizing brands of Confucianism explicitly claiming a religious dimension.

Part III of the book addresses the "teaching of rites", that is, *lijiao* 禮教, and enables us to discuss a number of issues ranging from religion to politics. Our departure point is the local situation in Shandong province mentioned above and the organization in the city of Qufu of ceremonies in order to celebrate Confucius's birthday. The main issue that we address is the fate of Confucian ritualism today, between the ancient legacy of local rituals and the creation of new "popular" practices (chapters 7 to 9).

Exploring the multifaceted phenomena emerging in the 2000s obliged us to adopt a cross-disciplinary approach, using the tools and insights of sociology, anthropology, history, and even, to a lesser extent, political science. The initial orientation of this work, however, was anthropological and we therefore felt the need to complement our core enquiry with a more general and anthropological question (chapter 10). Considering that the tradition labeled Confucianism belongs to a vast shared Chinese cosmology that gradually contributed to shaping Chinese culture, how could our research on Confucianism contribute to analyzing the contemporary fates of this cosmology that used to integrate the visible and invisible dimensions of a same universe? This ultimate question is discussed by exploring state-sponsored cults both in the PRC and in Taiwan. It ends with a few hypotheses about transformations of the relationship between the religious and the political—or, in other words, about the "politico-religious" or "theologico-political" questions—in two different societies of the vast sinicized world.

We started this research project in the middle of the 2000s. Considering its relatively long time frame, a number of people, projects, and activities we initially began to study evolved over time. An epilogue briefly introduces the situation in 2014 and suggests possible evolutions for the years ahead.

PART I

Jiaohua *(教化)*

The Confucian Revival in China as an Educative Project

I

Confucian Education during the Twentieth Century

A RETROSPECTIVE OUTLOOK

EDUCATION UNDOUBTEDLY CONSTITUTES one of the realms where the revived reference to Confucianism is particularly visible. Among the many symptoms of this new situation, it suffices to mention the development of a large "classics reading movement," the rediscovery of ancient educational institutions, or the enrollment of scores of business people in so-called *guoxue* classes.

The phenomenon at stake here has two main dimensions that are well reflected in the traditional expression *jiaohua* 教化. This conveys a meaning of both "education-transformation" of the self and "shaping of the other." Beyond the mere acquisition of knowledge, all sorts of projects—realistic and utopian—crystallize in this idea and aim at asserting the future role in China of a reappropriated traditional culture.

This reactivation of a *jiaohua* associated with a Confucian *ethos* needs to be recontextualized, taking into account the general fate of Confucian education since the end of the empire.

In 1905, China abandoned the appointment of scholars-literati to official positions based on an examination system that had turned the mastery of Confucian classics into a tool of imperial ideology. This small revolution actually completed a long-lasting process that had been promoted by reformers within the imperial system since the end of the nineteenth century and that had already led to the suppression of the *shuyuan* 書院 or traditional

Confucian academies.[1] It was then considered that the emergence of a "rich and powerful" country required the integration of a number of features of Western modernity, including a more utilitarian and technical approach to education. The 1911 revolution brought about an overall transformation of the educational system and the new republican government immediately decided to suppress the study of classical texts within the curriculum.[2]

The demise of the imperial system was a watershed in the history of education in China and brought about an irreversible rupture to the centrality of Confucianism. The significance of this rupture is sometimes overlooked by Confucian revivalists today. However, while they look for pedagogical inspiration in traditional practices, their concrete projects also remain in continuity with the history of the republican era. Indeed, contrary to a classical antitraditional narrative that prevailed during the twentieth century, due to specific features of Chinese nationalism, the modern transformation of the educational system encountered some significant degree of resistance, including within the modernizing camp. One of the benefits of the current emergence of "traditional" forms of education is precisely that it enables a more sophisticated retrospective on a period that was certainly more complex and full of potential developments than what a certain progressive narrative used to expound. Many projects took place from the end of the empire in order to preserve classical learning and self-cultivation traditions. They translated into attempts to perpetuate ancient institutions or to preserve certain ways of studying classical texts. Of this somewhat "minor" history it is now necessary to provide a brief overview since it illuminates the genealogy of the current "Confucian revival" in its educational dimension.

The Paradoxical Fate of Traditional Institutions during the Twentieth Century

The restructuring of the educational system at the end of the empire and during the republican era did not completely put an end to the promotion of Confucianism-inspired *jiaohua*. Some established institutions such as

---

1 For a detailed overview of educational reforms at the end of the empire, see William Ayers, *Chang Chih-tung and Educational Reform in China* (Cambridge, MA: Harvard University Press, 1971).

2 Suzanne Pepper, *Radicalism and Education Reform in Twentieth-Century China: The Search for an Ideal Development Model* (Cambridge: Cambridge University Press, 2000), 61.

sishu 私塾 (traditional schools) continued to operate out of sheer necessity, since a full-fledged transition toward a modern educational system was practically impossible during the first half of the twentieth century. Other projects aimed at perpetuating institutions such as Confucian academies while adapting them to a changing time. Finally, *jiaohua* activities could also become integrated within new types of organizations.

Traditional Schools or *Sishu*

The label "traditional schools," or *sishu*, makes it possible to encompass a group of extremely diverse institutions promoting forms of teaching primarily based upon the inculcation of Confucian classics to children (and above all, to young boys). By the end of the empire, attending a *sishu*—which could have been operated by a scholar, by one or several families, or by a lineage or in a village—was considered a preliminary step in order to be accepted in academies that were themselves some sort of preparatory school for the imperial examination system. Such traditional schools existed both in cities and in the countryside. A 1923 survey carried out in Nanjing indicates the presence of around 500 *sishu* in the city. Another survey carried out at the beginning of the 1930s in the countryside underlines that around 66.5 percent of educated males had been schooled in *sishu*.[3] All in all, educational reforms of the republican era proved unable to put an end to the traditional schooling system and replace it with modern-style institutions.

No specific qualification was required to teach in or operate a *sishu*. Teachers—generally one per school—often came from the ranks of candidates who had been unsuccessful in imperial examinations or, after 1905, from those of the sacrificed generation that had prepared in vain for the abolished examinations.

An oral-history work carried out by Stig Thøgersen in Zouping (Shandong province) and based on a collection of interviews with people who attended *sishu* in the pre-1949 period provides some insight into the way these traditional schools were operated.[4] Probably like in most Chinese *sishu* at that time, teaching methods relied heavily on rote memorization

---

3 Pepper, *Radicalism and Education Reform*, 77.

4 Stig Thøgersen, *Country of Culture. 20th Century China Seen From the Village Schools of Zouping* (Ann Arbor: University of Michigan Press, 2002).

by pupils of primers and other classical texts. In general, teachers started with ancient primers such as the *Classic in Three Characters* (*Sanzi jing*), the *Name of the One Hundred Families* (*Baijia jing*), or the *Text in One Thousand Characters* (*Qianzi wen*) that had largely been used since the Song dynasty (960–1279).[5] Then, they could use the Four Books and even sometimes the Five Classics.[6] In rare cases, some lessons were also dedicated to arithmetic. Pedagogical methods were rudimentary and seemingly homogeneous across different *sishu*: In the morning, the teacher would read a text without providing complementary explanations. More often than not, pupils would not understand its meaning but would repeat it over and over again during the rest of the day in order to be able to recite it the day after. In sum, learning mainly meant memorizing. Those who could not manage to do so underwent harsh physical punishments—and cases of beaten students are mentioned.[7] The general "children-shaping scheme" was largely inherited from the social-control scheme of the late empire. This being said, interviewees do not necessarily keep bad memories of their *sishu* education. Some mentioned that they learned how to behave properly (*zenme zuo ren* 怎麼做人), whereas others underscore that they became mature and responsible persons. More generally, considering that many of those who would later become educators were originally trained prior to 1949 in *sishu*, this type of education—at least formally—was not without influence later on in the People's Republic of China.[8]

Confucian Academies or Shuyuan

Whereas *sishu* education could endure in republican China due to the difficulty of modernizing the educational system, the few Confucian academies still operating at that time generally resulted from the deliberate will

---

5 For a detailed historical overview of primers, see Bai Limin, *Shaping the Ideal Child: Children and Their Primers in Late Imperial China* (Hong Kong: Chinese University Press, 2005).

6 The Four Books and Five Classics are fundamental texts of literati culture and of the examination system in China. The Five Classics are: *The Book of Changes* (*Yijing*), *The Book of Odes* (*Shijing*), *The Book of Documents* (*Shujing* or *Shangshu*), *The Book of Rites* (*Liji*), and the annals of *Spring and Autumn* (*Chunqiu*). In the twelfth century, four texts (the Four Books) were extracted: The *Analects* of Confucius, the *Mencius*, the *Great Learning* (*Daxue*), and the *Doctrine of the Mean* (*Zhongyong*). Commented upon by scholars like Zhu Xi 朱熹 (1130–1200), they played an important role in Song-dynasty neo-Confucianism.

7 Thøgersen, *Country of Culture*, 20–26.

8 Thøgersen, *Country of Culture*, 19–20.

of their initiators to perpetuate a model different from the new university system.

Academies played a fundamental role in education in China for more than a thousand years. They were strongly developed during the Song dynasty, especially under the influence of neo-Confucian scholars such as Zhu Xi.[9] They were established by lineages to educate their members and train them to sit for imperial examinations, by Confucian masters, and, especially starting with the Ming dynasty, by the authorities.[10] In the sixteenth century, under the influence of scholars such as Wang Yangming 王陽明 (1472–1529), academies also had an objective of promoting a more general access to education. All through their history they experienced tensions between the ideals of self-cultivation and preparation for official examinations, between integration in the public sphere and resistance against the authorities during times of crisis.[11] By the end of the nineteenth century there were about four thousand academies at various administrative levels, from districts to prefectures.[12]

The end of the academies was the result of the modernization of education at the end of the empire, of the demise of the examination system, and, more generally from 1911 onward, of the emergence of a new political

---

9 For a synthetic overview of the history of academies, see Li Hongqi (Thomas H. C. Lee) 李弘祺, "Shuyuan, chuantong xueshu de zhongxin 書院, 傳統學術的中心" [The *Shuyuan*, Centres of the Traditional Academic World], in *Zhongguo wenhua de zhuancheng yu chuangxin* 中國文化的傳承與創新 [Innovation and Transmission within Chinese Culture], ed. Wang Shouchang 王守常 and Zhang Wending 張文定, 355–364 (Beijing: Beijing daxue chubanshe, 2006). For the relationship between state policy and private initiative, see Alexander Woodside, "The Divorce between the Political Center and Educational Creativity in Late Imperial China," in *Education and Society in Late Imperial China, 1600–1900*, ed. Benjamin A. Elman and Alexander Woodside, 458–492 (Berkeley: University of California Press, 1994). See also Chen Wenyi 陳雯怡, *You guanxue dao shuyuan* 由官學到書院 [From Official Schools to Academies] (Taipei, Lianjing, 2004). Chen's book provides a good overview of the state of research on academies. There have been many discussions and divergences regarding the creation of the first *shuyuan*. See for instance Li Caidong 李才棟, *Zhongguo shuyuan yanjiu* 中國書院研究 [Research on the Academies in China] (Nanchang: Jiangxi gaoxiao chubanshe, 2005).

10 Lee reports that during the Ming dynasty 60 percent of the academies were established thanks to government initiative. Thomas H. C. Lee, "Academies: Official Sponsorship and Suppression," in *Imperial Rulership and Cultural Change in Traditional China*, ed. Frederik P. Brandauer and Chun-chieh Huang (Seattle: University of Washington Press, 1994), 126.

11 Ibid., 119. This was for instance the case of the Dongling academy in the seventeenth century. See also Jacques Gernet, *L'intelligence de la Chine: Le social et le mental* (Paris: NRF Gallimard, 1994), 112.

12 Pepper, *Radicalism and Education Reform*, 51.

system. However, and contrary to the situation that prevailed for official examinations, academies were never criticized harshly, and abandoning them was not the consequence of much deliberation.[13] During the 1920s, at a time when the bulk of these institutions was already dismantled, academies became the focus of what would nowadays be called a slight "fever" (re 熱), that is, some sort of temporary enthusiasm for a given topic.[14] Paradoxically, a number of Westernized intellectuals who had fiercely fought against the ancient order openly lamented their demise. In 1923, Hu Shi 胡適 (1891–1962), one of the most influential figures of the May 4th Movement, explained that "abandoning the academies was actually very unfortunate for our country. The voluntary spirit of study perpetuated for around one thousand years will not reappear again."[15] There were many, like him, who hoped that some form or other of the spirit prevailing in academies would remain in the new Western-inspired university system.[16] The young Mao Zedong himself expressed some nuanced viewpoint about academies, emphasizing their positive sides. He obviously did not think about the Confucian content of the teachings but rather about formal aspects, especially the knowledge transmission methods that could not be separated from relationships being built between masters and students and that favored an atmosphere of freedom and enjoyment of things studied.[17]

Beyond formal aspects, a number of attempts to revive academies and Confucianism-inspired education took place during the first half of the

---

13 Chen Pingyuan 陳平原, *Daxue hewei* 大學何為 [Why the University?] (Beijing: Beijing daxue chubanshe, 2006), 5.

14 Ibid., 3.

15 Ibid., 12.

16 Ibid., 6.

17 Pepper, *Radicalism and Education Reform*, 98. Mao's interest in the academies as institutions, as well as "socialist self-cultivation" advocated by Liu Shaoqi, has been considered by some Chinese intellectuals as the manifestation of a so-called sinicization or confucianization of Marxism, that is, the pervasive continuity of a number of intellectual, behavioral, or organizational schemes inherited from the imperial past. On this topic, see Li Zehou 李澤厚, *Makesizhuyi zai Zhongguo* 馬克思主義在中國 [Marxism in China] (Hong Kong: Mingbao chubanshe, 2006), 44, or Jin Guantao 金觀濤, "Dangdai Zhongguo Makesizhuyi de rujiahua 當代中國馬克思主義的儒家化" [The Confucianization of Marxism in Contemporary China], in *Rujia fazhan de hongguan toushi* 儒家發展的宏觀透視 [Overall Perspective on the Development of Confucianism], ed. Tu Wei-ming 杜維明, 152–183 (Taipei: Zhengzhong shuju, 1988).

twentieth century. The so-called three great *shuyuan* of republican China, opened by representatives of the contemporary Confucianism movement at the end of the 1930s, were probably the most emblematic of these enterprises.[18] Institutions established by Ma Yifu 馬一浮 (1883–1967) and Zhang Junmai 張君勱 (1886–1969) can be taken as examples in that they reflect a different conception of the possible role of academies in postimperial China.

Probably the most traditional of these new institutions, the Return to Nature Academy (Fuxing shuyuan 復性書院), was opened in 1939 by Ma Yifu in Leshan, Sichuan province. This project was implemented within the context of the Sino-Japanese war that started in 1937 and of the withdrawal of the nationalist government in Chongqing. Ma Yifu's path is representative of a period of transition, doubts, and of complex and changing relationships to Confucianism.[19] Considered a child prodigy, Ma became at fifteen a laureate of the provincial examinations. Because of his proficiency in several foreign languages, he was assigned for a while to the Qing Embassy in the United States before advancing his studies in literature and philosophy in Germany and Japan. Back in China, he chose for a while to live a somewhat secluded life, writing and translating, delving into Daoism, Buddhism, and art (he is actually still remembered as a famous calligrapher). He also befriended prominent figures of the time such as Li Shutong 李叔同 (1880–1942) and Feng Zikai 豐子愷 (1898–1975). Without participating in the 1911 revolution he nevertheless supported Sun Yat-sen. In the same way as many intellectuals of the time, it was China's difficult situation that prompted him in the 1920s to turn to Confucianism and to open a traditional-style academy.[20]

In a society that he considered first and foremost to be governed by utilitarianism, Ma Yifu's project was to train a group of young people. The emphasis was not simply on their intellectual developments but primarily on a path of self-cultivation supposed to enable everyone to return to their innate nature. This aim was to revive an ideal of wisdom traditionally central in academies, even if it was often neglected due to the preparation for the imperial examination. His teaching was primarily based on "national

---

18 The three "great *shuyuan*" were those opened by Ma Yifu and Zhang Junmai (discussed later in this chapter) and by Liang Shuming in Beipei (Chongqing area).

19 On Ma Yifu's career, see Chen Rui 陳銳, *Ma Yifu yu xiandai Zhongguo* 馬一浮與現代中國 [Ma Yifu and Contemporary China] (Beijing: Zhongguo shehui kexue chubanshe, 2007).

20 Ibid., 168–171.

studies" (*guoxue* 國學)—that is, on Chinese disciplines—and more specifically on the study of "six arts" (*liu yi* 六藝) or "six classics" (*liu jing* 六經).[21] Sciences and foreign languages were excluded from this curriculum. This academy was apolitical and governed according to regulations inspired by Buddhism. Ma Yifu's ambition was to try to reach a financial balance while preserving its independence. This was far from easy considering that Ma largely relied on Chiang Kai-shek's personal financial support. Ma tried to attract to his academy some prominent intellectual figures of the time, such as neo-Confucian thinker Xiong Shili, master of well-known scholars Mou Zongsan and Tang Junyi. However, fundamental divergences between the two men regarding their conceptions of education made this collaboration impossible. In Xiong's opinion, Ma Yifu's exclusive emphasis on students' moral nature (*dexing* 德性) did not really take into account the country's real needs: training a generation of students able to contribute to social reform by means of virtuous action.

It was a somewhat different conception of the role of a Confucian academy for modern times that Zhang Junmai and philosopher Zhang Dongsun 張東蓀 (1886–1973) had in mind when they set up their National Culture Academy (Minzu wenhua shuyuan 民族文化書院) in 1938 in Dali, Yunnan. Zhang Junmai was also a representative of "contemporary Confucianism" and an original figure of republican China's intellectual and political life. Deeply involved in important intellectual debates,[22] he also established with Zhang Dongsun a political party that was supposed to emerge as a "third force" between the Communist Party and the Guomindang. In their academy, they had the ambition of reviving

---

21 After the Spring and Autumn period (722–481 BC), the six arts were assimilated with the Six Classics, that is, with *The Books of Documents, Odes, Changes, Rites*, and *Music* (the last disappeared under the Qin dynasty, hence the usual reference to Five Classics), as well as the *Spring and Autumn Annals*. These texts are interpreted and referred to by Ma Yifu in the metaphysical and speculative spirit of what is being called "Song studies" and not from a "Han studies" approach. The latter tends to emphasize a more accurate (and rigid) exegetic perspective. On Ma Yifu and the six arts, see Deng Xinwen 鄧新文, *Ma Yifu liu yi yi xin lun yanjiu* 馬一浮六藝一心論研究 [Research on Ma Yijiu's Theory of Heart/Mind and the Six Arts] (Shanghai: Shanghai guji chubanshe, 2008).

22 In 1923, Zhang Junmai initiated a debate on "science and life" and was opposed to scholars such as Hu Shi and Chen Duxiu 陳獨秀 (1879–1942), the latter one of the founders in 1921 of the Chinese Communist Party. Against what he considered to be an idolatrous embrace of science, Chen asserted the primacy of a *Weltanschauung* likely to provide individuals and society with an ethical orientation. See Lee Ming-huei, *Der Konfuzianismus im modernen China* (Leipzig: Leipziger Universitätsverlag, 2001), 34–37.

the classical *shuyuan* institution while adapting it to combine what they believed to be a Western focus on knowledge with a Chinese concern for self-cultivation and morals. Molding students' character and instilling virtues in them were means enabling them to take enlightened decisions. However, the philosophy behind the academy was to promote an open institution engaged with the modern world. Therefore, the curriculum also included the study of major European thinkers. Beyond Confucianism, promotion of morality also meant advocating a patriotic spirit and its attributes: Knowledge of Chinese history, understanding the rule of law, and the meaning of citizenship.[23] Devoted to a cultural renaissance project (*wenhua fuxing*) the academy would thus draw inspiration from a variety of resources.

All in all, the few academies that were reconstructed in republican China had only a very limited impact. The dramatic situation of the country did not make it possible for them to endure, develop, or inspire other projects, and in the end they could manage to train only a handful of students. After 1949, it became necessary to turn to China's margins to observe the perpetuation of a humanistic spirit of self-cultivation based on Confucian classics. New Asia College (Xinya shuyuan 新亞書院), founded in 1950 in Hong Kong by Qian Mu 錢穆 (1889–1990) and Tang Junyi, preserved for a while the ideal of an academy in tune with modernity. Acquisition of knowledge and development of the individual were thus equally encouraged. However, with its integration in 1963 within the Chinese University of Hong Kong it would gradually lose its identity and comply with the university model of the British colony.[24] Most of the projects that were ambitious to revive traditional academies were initiated by scholars usually associated with the so-called contemporary Confucianism movement. Whereas the movement is often remembered as a purely intellectual

---

23 These elements are introduced in Roger B. Jeans, *Democracy and Socialism in Republican China: The Politics of Zhang Junmai* (Lanham, MD: Rowman and Littlefield, 1997), 83–87.

24 See for example Cheung Chan Fai, "Tang Junyi and the Philosophy of General Education," in *Confucian Tradition and Global Education*, ed. Wm. Theodore de Bary (Hong Kong: Chinese University Press, 2007), 59ff. On the early history of the New Asia College, see Qian Mu 錢穆, *Shiyou zayi* 師友雜憶 [Remembering Teachers and Friends] (Taipei: Dongda tushugongsi, 1983). A volume of articles and speeches provides some insight into Qian Mu's enterprise as an educator at the head of the college. Qian Mu, *Xin Ya yiduo* 新亞遺鐸 [Past Echoes of the Xinya Academy] (Beijing: Sanlian shudian, 2004). See also Grace Ai-ling Chou, *Confucianism, Colonialism and the Cold War: Chinese Cultural Education at Hong Kong's New Asia College* (Leiden and Boston, MA: Brill, 2011).

enterprise (or a set of purely intellectual enterprises), it is necessary to underscore that its representatives consistently committed themselves to the realization of practical social projects, even though the latter were not always successful in the troubled context of republican China.

In brief, although traditional academies largely disappeared at the beginning of the twentieth century, some isolated enterprises managed to preserve lines of continuity: They nowadays constitute sources of inspiration for Confucian activists in a completely novel context. But republican China also enabled attempts to perpetuate Confucian education under completely new forms. It is possible to illustrate this phenomenon basing ourselves on two examples: The development of specific organizations aiming at disseminating Confucian values broadly within society and the rural reconstruction project of Liang Shuming 梁淑溟 (1893–1988).

Rethinking the Role of Confucianism in New Educational Spaces

The academic community recently focused its attention on a massive phenomenon that deeply impacted republican China but remained for a long time little studied. The end of the empire provided a very favorable ecology for mass organizations aiming at disseminating core Confucian values through the study of classical texts, self-cultivation, and elements of ritualism. In fact, they managed to attract some of the five million literati who remained without any institutional attachment after the end of the empire and the demise of Confucianism as a state ideology directly opening career paths.[25] The now widely used category encompassing these organizations is that of "redemptive societies." It was originally coined by historian Prasenjit Duara and extensively discussed afterwards.[26] The mere idea of redemption immediately points to the religious dimension of these organizations. In fact, beyond Confucianism, many of them inherited from

---

25 Vincent Goossaert and David A. Palmer, *The Religious Question in Modern China* (Chicago and London: University of Chicago Press, 2012), 95.

26 On the category of "redemptive society," see Prasenjit Duara, *Sovereignty and Authenticity, Manchukuo and the East Asian Modern* (Lanham, MD: Rowman and Littlefield, 2003), 89–129; Goossaert and Palmer, *Religious Question in Modern China*, 91–108; David Ownby, *Falun Gong and the Future of China* (Oxford: Oxford University Press, 2008), 24–44; Ownby, "Redemptive Societies in China's Long Twentieth Century," in *The Modern Chinese Religion, 1850–Present*, ed. Vincent Goossaert (Leiden and Boston, MA: Brill, 2015, forthcoming).

a syncretistic and millenarian tradition typical of the end of the empire. Among the most famous societies one could mention the Teaching of the Observance of Principle (Zailijiao 在理教), the Way of Anterior Heaven (Xiantiandao 先天道), the Society for the Study of Morals (Daode xueshe 道德學社), the Society of the Common Good (Tongshanshe 同善社), the Society for Universal Morality (Wanguo daodehui 萬國道德會), the Dao Academy (Daoyuan 道院), the Way of Pervading Unity (Yiguandao 一貫道), and so on.[27] Taking into account the magnitude of their development, they could probably be considered the main form of organized Confucianism in republican China.[28]

The very category of "redemptive society" raises a number of difficulties due to its extremely general character. Differences are indeed deep between, on the one hand, "new religions" venerating a variety of deities, offering precise views of the world and the underworld, a sophisticated cosmogony and cosmology, a millenarian eschatology, and so on—exemplified by an organization like the Yiguandao—and, on the other hand, societies whose primary mission was the promotion of Confucian ethics and education in this world (and the Society for Universal Morality is maybe a representative of this second group).[29] It is true that, beyond their diversity, all these organizations contributed to the promotion of a certain Confucian *ethos*, especially through promoting the reading of classics. Therefore, it is relevant to include them within this general overview of Confucian education during the twentieth century. However, this diversity should not be forgotten when analyzing current developments taking place within the Confucian revival. Whereas some ancient religious societies nowadays operate again in Mainland China, activities of other Confucian groups need to be understood in continuity with organizations that developed during the republican period and were primarily characterized by their promotion of morality rather than by otherworldly concerns.

Apart from redemptive societies, other educational Confucian projects developed during the republican period. They include a large-scale

---

27 Goossaert and Palmer, *Religious Question in Modern China*, 93ff; David A. Palmer, "Chinese Redemptive Societies and Salvationist Religions," *Minsu Quyi* 172, no. 1 (2011): 24–28.

28 Palmer, "Chinese Redemptive Societies and Salvationist Religions," 55.

29 Palmer underscores the existence of two different types of redemptive societies while also indicating that they were quite close in Republican China. Palmer, "Chinese Redemptive Societies and Salvationist Religions," 55–58.

enterprise of rural reconstruction initiated by Liang Shuming and largely centered on the school institution.

Liang Shuming was a major figure of republican China and another key representative of contemporary neo-Confucianism. Inspired both by Confucianism and Buddhism (see chapter 4), and the author of numerous books, he was also an activist involved in the reconstruction of his country. One of his educational projects was to set up a *shuyuan* in the Chongqing region. But he was deeply committed to rural reconstruction and launched various projects in Guangdong, Henan, and Shandong provinces. He also took part in the political life of his time, advocating like Zhang Junmai a "third way" for China. Today, the name of Liang Shuming is a pervasive reference within the ranks of Confucian revivalists. To some extent, he perpetuates in contemporary China the ancient ideal of unity of knowledge and action.

In 1931, Liang launched with the support of the nationalist authorities a wide scheme of countryside reconstruction that ended only in 1937 with the Japanese invasion. At that time around seventy of Shandong's 107 districts were directly or indirectly affected by this project.[30] Liang's ambition was to contribute to China's social and cultural renovation starting from the countryside. He implemented new forms of socioeconomic organization while promoting a Confucian *ethos*. The inspiration stemmed from ancient historical experiments and more specifically from an institution that can be traced back to the Song dynasty, the *xiangyue* 鄉約 or community compact. This institution encouraged cooperation between villagers, and, starting from the Ming dynasty, it was also instrumental in the peasants' indoctrination by imperial ideology.

Liang Shuming's action was aiming at "the emergence of gentlemen (*junzi* 君子) within the masses," and the "spiritual progress" of villagers was an essential part of his project.[31] It was to be monitored by local cadres, themselves trained in a rural reconstruction institute and also in charge of the dissemination of technical knowledge applicable to agriculture. Villages were reorganized around a central institution—the school, whose missions were enlarged to the point where it was used as a substitute for

---

30 Guy Alitto, "Rural Reconstruction during the Nanking Decade: Confucian Collectivism in Shantung," *China Quarterly* 66 (1976): 216. The rural reconstruction enterprise is also studied in Alitto, *Last Confucian: Liang Shu-ming and the Chinese Dilemma of Modernity* (Berkeley: University of California Press, 1986), 192–278.

31 Alitto, *Last Confucian*, 206–210 (207 for the quote).

governmental and administrative institutions. Such a "schoolification of society" (*shehui xuexiaohua* 社會學校化) would gradually transform the countryside into a broad collective Confucian school.[32] It is significant that people nowadays involved in rural reconstruction projects ("new socialist countryside") rediscover experiments carried out by Liang in the 1930s. Some scientific literature is being published and some practical projects claim a link with this republican heritage.[33]

Classical Texts within Curricula and Their Social Impact in Republican China: A Brief Overview

In the previous sections, the emphasis was put on the modern and contemporary fate of Confucian education from the perspective of peculiar institutions, be they perpetuated or reinvented. It is now time to complement this preliminary presentation with a brief introduction to debates and political decisions related to the reading of classics within the overall context of modernized school curricula.

Confucianism and School Curricula

From the very end of the empire to the advent of the Peoples' Republic of China in 1949, the situation of and importance ascribed to classical texts in the school system fluctuated tremendously, reflecting the changing appreciations of various political regimes toward Confucianism. It is difficult to provide an accurate and comprehensive picture of the situation

---

32 Ibid., 248.

33 Stig Thøgersen, "Revisiting a Dramatic Triangle: The State, Villagers, and Social Activists in Chinese Rural Reconstruction Projects," *Journal of Current Chinese Affairs* 38, no. 4 (2009): 9–33. Wu Shugang and Tong Binchang, "Liang Shuming's Rural Reconstruction and its Relevance for Building the New Socialist Countryside," *Contemporary Chinese Thought* 40, no. 3 (2009): 39–51. Practical projects currently carried out sometimes directly refer to Liang Shuming. This is for instance the case of the Beijing-based Liang Shuming Rural Reconstruction Center (Liang Shuming xiangcun jianshe zhongxin). See Wang Zhensheng, "L'influence de la théorie de la reconstruction rurale de Liang Shuming dans la société chinoise actuelle," MA thesis (East Asian studies), University Paris-Diderot, 2012. However, even though the name Liang Shuming is nowadays often quoted in the context of rural projects, further research would be necessary to understand to which extent elements of Confucian education promoted in the 1930s are also promoted today.

due to the political divisions that affected China during the republican period. For instance, warlord control of some of the provinces enabled the local promotion of Confucianism in ways that differed greatly from what could be observed in Beijing or Nanjing.

Whereas reforms implemented in the name of modernization during the last decade of the empire brought to an end a number of Confucian institutions—academies in 1901 or the civil examination system in 1905—the central dimension of Confucianism was nevertheless still emphasized by the ruling dynasty. The importance of the "three bonds" (*san gang* 三綱: loyalty of the subject to his sovereign, filial obedience of the son to his father, subjection of the wife to her husband) and the "five cardinal relationships" (*wu chang* 五常: benevolence, righteousness, propriety, moral wisdom, and trust) was reaffirmed as the foundations of imperial ideology. At around the same time, in 1906, ceremonies honoring Confucius were elevated to the rank of supreme sacrifices, at the same level as those rendered to Heaven and Earth. In such a context, reading Confucian classics was also broadly encouraged. In schools, modern disciplines (science and technology, etc.) remained in a subsidiary position vis-à-vis the Four Books and Five Classics, and Confucian ethics continued to be at the core of the curriculum. Discussing regulations enacted in 1904, Zheng Yuan shows that courses dedicated to the study of classics and to moral self-cultivation (*xiushen* 修身) still represented 47 percent of the time spent in elementary schools by children aged six to eleven and 39 percent of the time spent by children aged eleven to fifteen. These statistics do not point here to *sishu* education but only to modern schools. Although these percentages tend to decrease for more advanced pupils they nevertheless remain extremely significant.[34]

The republic was proclaimed in January 1912 and Cai Yuanpei 蔡元培 (1868–1940) became minister of education. The study of classical Confucian texts immediately disappeared from the curricula, while veneration of Confucius in schools was also abolished. Self-cultivation teachings were the only ones to be preserved in a spirit that combined the perpetuation of Confucian values such as filial piety with new values such as the undertaking spirit, love for one's community and the motherland, and so

---

34 Zheng Yuan, "Status of Confucianism in Modern Chinese Education, 1901–49: A Curricular Study," in *Education, Culture & Identity in Twentieth-Century China*, ed. Glen Peterson, Ruth Hayhoe, and Yonglin Lu (Ann Arbor: University of Michigan Press, 2001), 196.

on.[35] These radical changes, far from embodying the definite demise of Confucianism within the school system rather reflected a growing tension that ran across the whole of republican China between, on the one hand, a will to reform (be it inspired by Western liberalism or soviet Russia) and, on the other hand, a temptation to continue to have recourse to classical texts as tools of moralization and social control.

Sun Yat-sen briefly occupied the position of president of the new republic, but was replaced in February 1912 by Yuan Shikai 袁世凱 (1859–1916). In 1914 and 1915 several regulations ascribed a central position to Confucianism in the educational realm, both in self-cultivation and in Chinese-language textbooks. At the same time, the study of classical texts was reintroduced into the curriculum. This new turn cannot be dissociated from Yuan Shikai's political ambitions and especially from his 1915 failed attempt to restore the imperial order.[36] After Yuan's death in 1916—and in a context already influenced by the "New Culture Movement" (*xin wen-hua yundong* 新文化運動) that would later on mingle with the May 4th Movement, Confucian education in schools was once more abolished and the use of vernacular language encouraged. One can simply recall here that Confucian texts were of course written in a classical language and that the promotion of vernacular language also implied a specific political agenda. As for self-cultivation, it was replaced by patriotic education courses.[37]

The ambition to revive forms of classics-based education would, however, not vanish. The first reason is that Confucianism remained a political tool for warlords controlling entire segments of the Chinese territory. This was for instance the case of Yan Xishan 閻錫山 (1883–1960) in Shanxi province during the 1920s.[38] The second reason is that evolving political

---

35 Ibid., 203.

36 Yuan Shikai gradually promoted a number of elements associated with Confucianism, such as the sacrifice to Heaven performed in Beijing in 1914. In 1915, he was convinced that Chinese people would be ready to accept an imperial restoration and he bestowed on himself the title of emperor in December of the same year. In March 1916, hostility and a number of defections within his own party convinced him to give up his plan without having been enthroned.

37 Zheng, "Status of Confucianism in Modern Chinese Education," 205–207.

38 Donald G. Gillin, "Portrait of a Warlord: Yen His-shan in Shansi Province, 1911–1930," *Journal of Asian Studies* 19, no. 3 (1960): 299–301.

circumstances would generate new attempts to use Confucianism as an instrument of social and ideological control.

In 1926, the nationalists headed by Chiang Kai-shek launched from their base in Guangdong province the so-called Northern Expedition (*beifa* 北伐), whose aim was to defeat the warlords occupying the northern Chinese territory. They first took Nanjing where the government set up its headquarters (1927) and later on conquered Beijing (1928). Cai Yuanpei, who was a strong advocate of a strict separation between education and politics, had to resign, whereas the need to link party ideology with education was emphasized. Under the influence of Dai Jitao 戴季陶 (1891–1949) the role of Confucianism as a theoretical substrate of the three principles of the people was also affirmed.[39] In 1929, Confucianism was formally reincorporated at all levels within school curricula.[40] This was the beginning of a process that would develop further during the subsequent years. Curricular reforms that took place in 1932 and 1933 stressed the necessity to promote traditional Chinese ethics, filial piety, and, more generally, obedience to the parents, the eldest, and the authorities. Four traditional-sounding central values were particularly emphasized: propriety (*li* 禮), righteousness (*yi* 義), honesty (*lian* 廉), and "sense of shame" (*chi* 恥).[41] Along with a whole set of "Confucianesque symbolism," particularly blatant in schools, these values would later occupy a pivotal role within the ideology of the New Life Movement (*Xin shenghuo yundong* 新生活運動). The latter was launched in 1934 and largely inspired by military discipline: It primarily aimed at shaping behavioral standards and civic responsibility of the citizens.[42]

---

39 See for instance Herman Mast III and William G. Saywell, "Political Ideology of Tai Chi-t'ao," *Journal of Asian Studies* 34, no. 1 (1974): 73–98. "The three principles of the people" (*sanminzhuyi* 三民主義) is a formula that captions Sun Yat-sen political thought and his ideas about nationalism (*minzuzhuyi* 民族主義), democracy (*minquanzhuyi* 民權主義), and people's well-being (*minshengzhuyi* 民生主義). See Marie-Claire Bergère, *Sun Yat-sen* (Paris: Fayard, 1994), 400–450.

40 Zheng, "Status of Confucianism in Modern Chinese Education," 208–209.

41 Ibid., 210–211.

42 Nedostup, *Superstitious Regimes: Religion and the Politics of Chinese Modernity* (Cambridge, MA: Harvard University Press, 2009), 263–271. On the New Life Movement see Arif Dirlik, "The Ideological Foundations of the New Life Movement," *Journal of Asian Studies* 34, no. 4 (1975): 945–980. Jennifer Oldstone-Moore, "The New Life Movement of Nationalist China: Confucianism, State Authority and Moral Formation," PhD diss., University of Chicago, UMI Microform 9959107, 2000.

The 1934 Debate on Classics Reading

It is within the context of the beginning of the New Life Movement that a broad debate on the necessity to read classical texts took place in 1934 in the *Education Journal* (*Jiaoyu zazhi* 教育雜誌). The importance of this debate has been compared with that of the movement to promote Confucianism as a state religion by Kang Youwei and his disciple Chen Huanzhang (see chapter 5).[43] The seventy-two contributions to the journal, far from reflecting unanimously the prevailing ideology of the time, offer an overview of extremely different attitudes to traditional texts and the way to tackle them. Among the most apologetic essays—that do not constitute the bulk of the texts—one finds for instance a document written by He Jian 何健 (1887–1956). He Jian, who was a warlord in Hunan province between 1929 and 1936, largely promoted—in the same way as Chen Jitang 陳濟棠 (1890–1954) in Guangdong province—Confucianism-inspired education in the territories that he was controlling. His contribution highlights the importance of a country's "national character" (*guominxing* 國民性). Starting to learn Confucian classics during primary school was for him the best possible means to inculcate children with cardinal values such as filial piety (*xiao* 孝) or loyalty (*zhong* 忠). Whereas reading a selection of excerpts would be sufficient for some of the classics, he posited that the *Classic of Filial Piety* (*xiaojing* 孝經) or the Four Books should be studied in their entirety.[44] The study of classical texts advocated by conservatives largely stemmed from a denunciation of the moral collapse of society and of the conviction that only a restoration of the "Way of Confucius and Mencius" (*Kong Meng zhi Dao* 孔孟之道) could save the country.[45]

The position of the conservatives was fiercely criticized by many contributors to the debate. This was for instance the case of former minister of education and president of Peking University Cai Yuanpei, for whom classics should primarily be studied at university depending on one's major or, to a lesser extent, at secondary and high schools, but in a very limited way and within the framework of an introduction to classical language.

---

43 A book published in 2008 offers a compilation and some analysis of these debates. Gong Pengcheng 龔鵬程, ed., *Dujing you shenme yong* 讀經有甚麼用 [What Is the Use of Reading the Classics?] (Shanghai: Shanghai renmin chubanshe, 2008). For a comparison with the movement of promotion of a state religion, see 419.

44 Ibid., 38–41 (text by He Jian).

45 Ibid., 423.

Learning classics at school was for him "without any advantage and damaging" (*wu yi er you sun* 無益而有損): Not only were classical texts much too abstract for children but they also conveyed a number of values disconnected from modern life—such as an asymmetrical relationship between the sovereign and his subjects, or between genders.[46] Among the other critical voices, some denounced the "sacred character" ascribed to classics by their advocates and "the religious attitude adopted while reading them." They also explained that these texts were irrelevant for instilling moral standards in young people.[47] They specifically criticized the process of shaping children obliged to memorize (*jisong* 記誦) texts that they could definitely not understand. Against warlords' and Guomindang's politics associating classics reading and veneration of Confucius (*zun Kong du jing* 尊孔讀經), some contributors emphasized that these two dimensions should absolutely be dissociated and that it was essential to read ancient texts with a critical mind. Their position was in fact in line with the famous maxim of Qing-dynasty scholar Zhang Xuecheng 章學誠 (1738–1801) positing that "all (six) classics are history" (*liu jing jie shi* 六經皆史).[48] According to Zhang, classical texts were not the crystallization of an eternal wisdom that could be embraced as such at any time, but texts embedded in specific social and historical configurations whose appropriation could therefore only be the object of a critical process.

The debates that took place during the 1930s as well as the perpetuation or renewal of some educative institutions provide some background information, enabling us to get a better understanding of *jiaohua* enterprises that are nowadays carried out in Mainland China in the name of Confucius. Current developments are in fact connected with segments of republican history and its tensions: Tension between shaping the child and a liberal education; tension between the authoritarian *jiaohua* of the citizen and ideals of construction of the self anchored in modern and humanistic Confucianism; finally, tension between intellectual and practical ways of relating to reappropriated Confucian texts.

---

46 Ibid., 135–137 (text by Cai Yuanpei).

47 Ibid., 138 (text by Cai Yuanpei), 422.

48 Ibid., 141 (text by Hu Buan), 426.

The New Institutionalization
of Confucian Education

WHAT FORMS CAN the Confucian aspiration to a "transformation of the self and others" (*jiaohua*) take in today's China when facing an educational institution established in a rigid manner during the Maoist era? In the 2000s a variety of different strategies can be observed. Educative practices based on Confucianism may consider the modern institution of schools and universities as either an ally or an adversary.

Three types of strategies can consequently be observed: Those that assert themselves within the very space of these institutions, those that deliberately try to establish rival institutions, and those that attempt to divert or add a new educative vocation to existing nonacademic organizations within society. The underlying question in each instance is to determine the resulting relationship with the official institutional order: Complementarity, rivalry, or substitution?

Challenges within the Academic Institution

Since the start of the new century, strong movements have emerged to criticize China's main university models inherited from the twentieth century: the liberal Western model that appeared at the beginning of the last century but became hegemonic after the May 4th Movement; and the Communist model, inspired for a time by the Soviet Union, but reformulated by Chinese socialism and the specific requirements of Maoist ideology. Nowadays, appeals for a "renaissance of Confucianism" within academia express a variety of sometimes contradictory orientations, ranging from internal institutional reforms, aimed at the student body and the intellectual community, to militant activities that use the university as a base but are directed at society at large. To illustrate these two dimensions, we shall examine the case of the People's University (Renda) and of Peking University (Beida) during the 2000s.

Confucianism within the Academic Institution: The Case of the People's University

Initiatives undertaken at the beginning of the 2000s within the People's University to support "traditional culture" were all the more significant given that right from its inception during the Sino-Japanese War this institution was closely connected to the Communist Party. Its main purpose was to train ideologically reliable cadres to serve the government and the party. In 2001, Renda became the first Chinese university to erect a monumental statue of Confucius on its campus (Figure 2.1), and the following year it established an Institute for Confucian Research (*Kongzi yanjiuyuan* 孔子研究院), with generous operating funds. This testified to the shift of the Communist Party line toward a selective and critical reappropriation of traditional culture.

But discussions with various players in this enterprise revealed the complexity of the situation, not only because these initiatives met with resistance from cadres trained in Marxist-Leninist ideology, but also because the true meaning of these orientations remained the subject of different and sometimes contradictory interpretations.

According to one of the directors of the *Kongzi yanjiuyuan* interviewed in 2007, the university found itself in a national context where two different movements are developing:

> There is an academic movement (*xueshu yundong* 學術運動) that only affects scholars. Its objective is to go beyond such disciplines as philosophy, which was not possible before. The second movement is social (*shehui yundong* 社會運動). It aims to promote confidence in one's own culture and attends to the question of the spiritual life (*jingshen shenghuo* 精神生活) in the context of the material development of society. The movement for children to study the classics is also a sign—what the education system cannot be responsible for falls under the ambit of the "space of the people" (*minjian*).

FIGURE 2.1 Statue of Confucius on the campus of Renda.
© Sébastien Billioud.

Two institutes founded by Renda give a better picture of the stratified nature of the problem. In the second half of the 2000s, the Institute of National Studies (*guoxueyuan* 國學院) was still controversial. Its primary intellectual objective was to compensate for the fragmentation resulting from the application of Western disciplinary logic to the study of traditional Chinese culture, and to allow students to expand their study of "literature" or "philosophy" to training in philology and historical disciplines as well. This reasonable aspiration to a more comprehensive access to classic knowledge fell victim not so much to concerns over the danger of nationalist ideologization[1] as to the problem of official validation: In 2007, authorization for the awarding of master's degrees (and a fortiori doctorates) was still not resolved. The second institute, the *Kongzi yanjiuyuan*, whose president is philosophy historian Zhang Liwen, aims to organize as well as manage research on Confucian culture (the constitution of a "Confucian canon," *Ruzang*, more or less in competition with a similar enterprise at Beida, is one of its projects), but also to encourage the teaching of traditional culture to nonspecialist students.

The official attitude toward Confucius remained relatively ambiguous, reflecting the divergences that existed within Renda itself:

> The official line is the one previously defined by Zhang Dainian: Confucius is neither praised nor criticized, he is studied. But some young specialists would like to go a step further. For them, Confucius is not an ordinary man, but a sage or a saint: His teachings are not only the object of academic research but also of research on the Way and the destiny of Man (*rendao de yanjiu* 人道的研究). Nevertheless, there is also opposition to this approach.[2]

Starting with the Academic Institution to Disseminate Confucianism into Chinese Society

Academic institutions are pivotal for those expecting a new role for Confucianism in today's China since they interact broadly with society: The targets of scholars involved in the promotion of Confucianism are no longer simply regular students but a much wider audience. The most striking manifestation of this intellectual activism is the flourishing training programs offered to businessmen by Chinese universities (Beida and Tsinghua played a pioneering role in the capital due to the high caliber of their faculties). For instance, since 2003, different

---

1 The danger of nationalist ideologization exists since classical knowledge was not "national" but purported to be universal. It was the creation of national studies (*kokugaku*) by Japanese nationalism that contributed, as a reaction, at the beginning of the last century, to the rise of Chinese "national studies" (*guoxue*). In opposing Western knowledge, these studies were partially unfaithful, in their principle, to the largely universalist inspiration of the Confucian tradition.

2 Interview, Beijing, March 2007.

faculties of Peking University (the Philosophy Department, the Academy of Chinese Culture, *Zhongguo wenhua shuyuan* 中國文化書院) have joined forces to organize "national study classes" (*guoxueban* 國學班) for company managers and cadres employed in governmental *danwei* (work units). They take the form of well-organized intensive training courses that are remunerated accordingly.[3] The majority of the businessmen (*qiyejia* 企業家) come from other provinces, sometimes far from the capital. The classes are not lectures but rather commented readings of classical texts, including not only the Confucian classics but also the *Yijing* and Sunzi's *Art of War*, as well as Daoist and Buddhist texts. The sessions we were able to attend in 2006 did not include any nationalist ideology and focused on familiarizing the participants with classical language and culture.

This kind of direct experience makes it possible to go beyond overly simplified assessments. Naturally, the entrepreneurs may satisfy their own professional objectives, and the instructors receive remuneration and recognition not easily available these days in the field of literary disciplines. But the majority of these business people have relatively little interest in the virtues of "Chinese-style management" (as practiced and exemplified by the Southeast Asian Dragons during the 1980s). In some cases, they are uneducated entrepreneurs who have succeeded by dint of hard work, but many also have fancy degrees and a fashionable life-style. One needs to underscore here the sociological diversity of the profiles that can be encountered in these classes. The presence of modern and elegant young ladies, who are well integrated in society's mainstream, brings us far away from usual clichés about what a "standard Confucian" is supposed to be (male, conservative, etc.). In any case, all these entrepreneurs and cadres share a common desire for this training, which is quite expensive, even though they are *already* "successful." Their motivations are primarily personal. Some want to acquire a "high culture" they could not have access to due to the special circumstances of the Maoist era. Some others find in these classes resources for some existential or spiritual self-fulfillment that can also be accompanied by meditative and introspective practices or by a social (not-for-profit) commitment. The sincerity and the pleasure that dominate these exchanges reveal a state of

---

3 At Beida in 2006, businessmen enrolled for a year-long series of courses lasting three or four days each month at a cost of 26,000 RMB. A cycle lasting two years is also offered.

mind that goes far beyond purely pragmatic utilitarianism, even though these gatherings and the friendship relationships they generate also provide the opportunity to develop networks of relations (*guanxi*) and, in some cases, joint business projects.

One of the consequences of these *guoxue* classes for entrepreneurs and official cadres is the production of new types of master-disciple relationships. Thus, we could for instance meet in Anhui or Shanxi province entrepreneurs who had attended classes at the Academy of Chinese culture (located on the Peking University campus) and who acknowledged some of the professors they met in Beijing as their masters. It was under the advice of their masters that these entrepreneurs consequently involved themselves in local operations to promote Confucianism. While these cases are encountered often enough to be mentioned here, generalization remains nevertheless impossible. Besides idealistic enterprises supported by professors eager to contribute to a reappreciation of the Confucian heritage we also have—and often in the same universities—*guoxue* programs whose aim is primarily commercial and that do not generate at all the same transmission process.

In any case, for the minority of activists or intellectuals committed to spreading Confucian values, the present-day university functions not only as a training ground for the student population but also as a solid base for educative enterprises in society at large. It has become apparent, however, that the modern institution is not really suited to these new objectives. Hence the proliferation in the 2000s of structures that can be extremely diverse but share a similar aspiration: Promoting beyond university campuses, in society, elements of Confucian education.

Creating New Educational Structures: Between Complementarity and Substitution

Presently, the most original initiatives of reconstruction of a Confucian education come from outside the university institution. In this section, the focus is not on pedagogical experimentation (discussed in chapter 3) but on the degree of tension that new projects maintain with society, its mainstream values and institutions, be they educational or governmental. We observe a sort of continuum between the initiatives taken in the shadow of local authorities, those taken in collaboration with them, and finally those that try to be as autonomous as possible. After a discussion of projects focusing on children and sometimes offering alternatives to the official school system, we explore other enterprises, this time aiming at promoting Confucianism in society at large.

Children Education: The "Classics Reading Movement" (*shao'er dujing* 少兒讀經) and the Revival of Traditional Schools

The so-called "children classics reading movement" is a phenomenon that developed massively during the 2000s and that constitutes one of the most visible dimensions of the reactivation of Confucian references within society. Different figures are given about the number of participants in the movement but it is difficult to crosscheck them. Several million children at least are involved and "classics reading classes" (*dujingban* 讀經班) are burgeoning all over the country (Figures 2.2, 2.3).[4]

The movement originally developed thanks to the action of a number of well-known Confucian activists, such as Taiwanese professor and educator Wang Caigui (see Box 2.1, Figure 2.4) and philosopher Jiang Qing 蔣慶 (b. 1953) who is also the founder of a traditional academy located in Guizhou province. It also benefited from the support of *guoxue* masters such as Nan Huaijin 南懷瑾 (1918–2012).

The development of the classics reading movement was facilitated by the involvement of a variety of different actors: Commercial companies disseminating classics among plenty of other items, religious organizations,[5] circles of activists, or large broadcasting corporations. Thus, CCTV has now for years been proposing an extremely successful program titled Baijia jiangtan 百家講壇 (Forum of the One Hundred Schools) where Confucian classics are largely promoted. Among the texts introduced to wide audiences in the course of genuine "broadcast

---

4 Figures sometimes mentioned are impossible to crosscheck and are problematic since the ones who give them are also engaged in the movement and are therefore far from neutral in their assessments. Estimates—which should therefore be taken with great caution—range from ten to one hundred million children. In comparison, classical texts such as the *Analects* of Confucius nowadays sell millions of copies (the figure of ten million copies is mentioned for Yu Dan's annotated edition of the *Analects*). Related television programs also attract millions of people.

5 Among the most active organizations promoting the reading of Confucian texts, the most active ones are certainly the Buddhist organizations. However, they are by no means the only ones. Sectarian movements or "new religious movements," such as the Yiguandao that operate in an underground way in Mainland China, are also instrumental in the promotion of Confucian texts. This point is discussed later in the book.

FIGURE 2.2 A poster promoting the reading of the classics by children. The inscription on the right asks: "Have you read the *Analects* of Confucius?"
© Sébastien Billioud.

jiaohua sessions,"[6] one finds for instance the *Rules of the Disciple* (Dizigui 弟子規), the *Classics of Filial Piety* (Xiaojing 孝經), and the *Analects*. In any case, the desire to delve into the classics is first of all a popular phenomenon that needs to be understood within the context of

---

6 In his work on the program Baijia jiangtan, Fabrice Dulery mentions a "*jiaohua* par les ondes."

FIGURE 2.3 This poster promoting the reading of the classics proclaims: "Marching forward with the Classics, becoming friend with the Sages." The first of the volumes presented on the poster encompasses three famous texts of the Confucian corpus: *The Great Learning, The Doctrine of the Mean,* and *The Classic of Filial Piety.* © Sébastien Billioud.

reappropriating the strata of the past. More often than not, it develops under various forms besides the school system and does not constitute an alternative to compulsory education.

In the course of fieldwork carried out in Guangzhou, we were able to observe three different institutional forms of classics reading sessions.

BOX 2.1

Portrait of an Activist: Wang Caigui 王財貴

Born in 1949, Wang Caigui is today retired from the academic system after a career in various Taiwanese universities. His is both a prominent actor of the classics reading movement in Taiwan and an emblematic figure of the popular Confucian revival that started in China in the 2000s. A disciple of famous philosopher Mou Zongsan, Wang chose to dedicate his energy to the promotion of a Confucian education, thus largely enabling "contemporary neo-Confucianism"—of which he is an heir—to acquire a new social dimension, the importance of which is only starting to be understood. To some extent, the action of Wang Caigui is the complement at the grassroots level of the endeavors of philosopher Tu Wei-ming, another disciple of Mou Zongsan, to promote Confucianism in elitist circles and at a more institutional level (UNESCO, parliament of religions, and so on).

In Taiwan, Wang Caigui organizes his activities with the support of a private foundation. These activities are numerous and include collective classics reading sessions, workshops for teachers and even a national classics reading contest.* One of Wang's decisive contributions to the promotion of

FIGURE 2.4 Wang Caigui. Courtesy of Guillaume Dutournier.

(continued)

BOX 2.1 Continued

the classics in Taiwan and, by extension, all over Asia, is to have been able in the 1990s to convince the Yiguandao 一貫道 (The Way of Pervading Unity), probably the largest Chinese redemptive society (see chapter 6) to adopt his method to read the classics for the training of its adepts and for its missionary activity.** However, Wang Caigui insists that he is not a Yiguandao member but only a Confucian.***

In Mainland China where he often travels, Wang Caigui has now developed a dense and solid network of disciples who convey his message and promote his method (discussed in chapter 3). The registration of millions of children in all sorts of classics reading classes is partly linked to his action.

While Wang primarily promotes the learning of classics in society, he also strongly encourages the opening of traditional schools of a *sishu* type in which could be brought up a new generation of Confucians.

* See Dutournier, "Les écoles familiales en Chine continentale et à Taiwan," 182–183.

** See Billioud, "Le rôle de l'éducation dans le projet salvateur du Yiguandao," "Religion, éducation et politique en Chine moderne," ed. Ji Zhe, special issue, *Extrême-Orient Extrême-Occident* 33 (2011): 216–222.

*** Interview, Taizhong (Taiwan), 2008.

Within an ordinary public school, one of the professors managed to convince the director that it was interesting to offer each week to the pupils a classics reading course on the top of the standard curriculum. This is an illustration of a pattern that will be found again in this book: Confucian activists employed in the public system (here, the educational system; elsewhere, governmental structures) often facilitate Confucianism-related activities from the inside.[7] The second form of classics promotion takes place in one of Guangzhou's main Buddhist temples, the Guangxiao si 光孝寺 (Figure 2.5). Each week, on Saturday afternoon, around two hundred children gather in an annex of the main temple in order to study primarily Confucian classics.[8] Many come from families that do not have any special relationship to the Buddhist faith. The organizers explain that "these sessions introduce texts that are resources for all Chinese people;

---

7 Field observation, Guangzhou, 2007.

8 The children mainly study Confucian texts (*The Rules of the Disciple, The Great Learning,* the *Analects*). Laozi's *Daodejing* is also introduced. By contrast, there is nothing about Buddhist sutras in this context. Field observation and interview, Guangzhou, 2011.

FIGURE 2.5 Buddhist temples can also be used to disseminate Confucian classics in society. This is the case in Guangzhou's Guangxiao temple.
© Sébastien Billioud.

they have no religious content."[9] Finally, our Guangzhou fieldwork also led us to the outskirts of the city and the premises of a little local company active in the remedial and extracurricular education industry. Its director, Mr. C., organizes each day a short classics reading class for children of the neighborhood (Figure 2.6).[10]

The three cases briefly alluded to here reflect the variety of the ways Confucian texts are nowadays promoted to children. It is nevertheless possible to highlight a number of common features. First, the benefits ascribed to the classics are always underscored by both parents and activists: Classics learning is supposed to provide children with a new relationship to the Chinese language and their own culture, thus contributing to their intellectual development. Moreover, it strengthens memorization and concentration abilities. Children also learn to behave properly (*zenme zuo ren* 怎麼做人) in the most varied situations. Second, these three ways of promoting classics are not-for-profit and carried out by volunteers. It is important to highlight

9 Interview, Guangzhou, 2011.

10 Field observation, Guangzhou, 2008.

FIGURE 2.6 Local association for the promotion of classical texts. It was established by a local entrepreneur active in the education industry.
© Sébastien Billioud.

this point since the "classics fever" is sometimes condemned as a whole by its detractors, who emphasize the commercial nature of many enterprises. While this commercial dimension cannot be denied, it should nevertheless not constitute the only way of analyzing this phenomenon. Finally, these three cases do not present any tension with the mainstream of Chinese society or with the authorities: The first takes place in a very ordinary primary school; the second, in an authorized and duly registered place of worship; as for the third initiative, it was taken by an entrepreneur who is also working closely with local authorities. In other words, the promotion of Confucian texts on the margins of the compulsory educational system is transparent, authorized, and in some instances even encouraged.

Some other projects claiming a Confucian identity are more difficult to implement. The reemergence of traditional schools, or *sishu*, whose persistence in republican China was emphasized in chapter 1 certainly constitutes one of the striking phenomena of the first decade of the new century. However, one should also immediately mention that the scope of the phenomenon is extremely limited and that it remains completely marginal if we consider the magnitude of the classics reading movement as a whole. Providing figures is no easy tasks but there were probably no more than a few thousand—or, at most, a few tens of thousands—children enrolled in *sishu* by the end of the 2000s. The movement was embryonic when we started our fieldwork in 2004 and gradually developed afterwards. It seems to be currently difficult for activists to significantly increase the magnitude of their operations and materialize ambitious projects that they have been nurturing for years—some of them, indeed, planned to train thousands of pupils.[11] We maybe now reach the limits of the *sishu* model in the PRC context. However, the reason why *sishu* education today really matters is less linked to its weight in Chinese educational system than to the fact that it might produce new generations of Confucian activists. Considered from this perspective, the aforementioned figures become much more significant. Activists who engage themselves today in social action in the name of Confucius were brought up and trained in the socialist system. They rediscover and reformulate a tradition toward which they nevertheless remain in a real position of exteriority. What will be the relation to history, society, and the outside world in general of people living in today's China but fashioned during their whole childhood by the incorporation of Confucian classics? What will even be their relationship to Confucianism and modernity? Answers to these questions certainly depend on the type of *sishu* education. In this respect, ongoing experimentations are far from homogenous and there is no unique model.

---

11 Interviews, Taiyuan and Beijing, June 2010. Some activists who managed to successfully operate medium-sized *sishu* (from thirty to 100 pupils) prepared ambitious expansion plans. Thus, we heard in 2010 about a project in Shandong province that was supposed to have the capacity to enroll up to 3,000 students. It seemed at that time that concrete operations were to start soon. In 2012, there was however little progress in its implementation. Interview, Beijing, 2012.

The case of small private schools (*sishu*) founded in the Pearl River Delta with support from officials of a district (*qu*) in the jurisdiction of Dongguan city provides some insight into the situation of institutions opened in complementarity with the compulsory educational system. This case also demonstrates the role personal initiatives can play at a local level. A young woman in her thirties, now in charge of cultural affairs in the local government and eager to promote traditional culture in an industrial city, experienced a real "pedagogical revelation" after she heard about the methods of Taiwanese educator and philosopher Wang Caigui and later had the chance to meet him:

> This is a real cultural desert, says this energetic young woman from the north, and pollution is not only atmospheric. It is urgent to propagate traditional culture. The reading of the classics we encourage should be done on a volunteer basis and not for commercial purposes. They should be based on individual initiatives.[12]

Making the most of her position within the local government, she managed, from the inside, to convince the hierarchy that it would be interesting to promote a classical education to young children aged three to six before they entered the compulsory system. In a section of a park commemorating the virtues of Ming-dynasty general Yuan Chonghuan, two classes are held for children of three and four years old. Every day, three sessions are dedicated to the "reading of the classics" (in other words, reciting for memorization), and two others to basic knowledge and good behavior (small rituals of respect toward teachers and so on). The movement is presented as "popular" (*minjian*), but it is the commitment of local cadres that has made it possible first that the authorities have become more tolerant of instruction presented as "extracurricular interest classes" (*kewai xingqu ban* 課外興趣班) anticipating the entry in the standard educational system; and second that they even provide classrooms free of charge (Figure 2.7).[13]

---

12 Interview, Dongguan, 2007.

13 The existence of this cultural park makes it possible to present this small school as a "Garden of national studies of the Great Harmony" (according to the homonymy that makes the word "yuan" a park instead of an academy). Lodging is also provided for twenty children sent by families interested in traditional culture or moral instruction; in 2007, they paid 600 RMB per month. The first text studied by these very young children is the *Dizigui*, a text from the Qing dynasty outlining the duties of the student. Three masters provide instruction for each class.

FIGURE 2.7 A small *sishu* opened with the support of Dongguan municipality (Guangdong province).
© Sébastien Billioud.

The situation in Dongguan is that of a *sishu* openly supported by the authorities and established in complementarity with the compulsory school system. However, an increasing number of projects are now devised and often implemented that substitute for compulsory education: This of course raises the question of their official recognition and of the applicable legal framework. A first answer was given in 2006 with the so-called Mengmutang case.[14] Located in Shanghai, the Mengmutang *sishu* was forbidden by local authorities. A protest movement developed that involved both parents and teachers. After a negotiation process, local authorities indicated that "schools not falling under compulsory education" could apply for registration as "*minban* 民辦 schools," that is, as schools operated by the people. Such an opportunity was thus given to Mengmutang,

---

14 The information we provide here on the Mengmutang is based on the research carried out by Guillaume Dutournier, "Les écoles familiales en Chine et à Taïwan: Triple regard sur un traditionnalisme éducatif," in *Religion, éducation et politique en Chine moderne*, ed. Ji Zhe, special issue, *Extrême-Orient Extrême-Occident* 33 (2011): 184–186.

and by extension to other *sishu*, but without, however, addressing precisely the status of classical schools, which were therefore not recognized as a specific category of institution. Dutournier notices that requirements for the opening of *minban* schools are strictly defined. Basing himself on an extensive survey carried out in Hunan province (in both urban and rural areas), he underscores that the rudimentary infrastructures of most local *sishu*, as well as their very basic pedagogical organization, would make it very difficult for them to satisfy these stringent requirements.[15] In fact, most of the *sishu* established today operate in a very unclear legal environment and they have to find artifices or transitory solutions to legalize their activity. In some cases, they have no choice but to operate in a completely underground way. Four examples will illustrate the variety of the situations that can be encountered.

In the far outskirts of Beijing city, the Sihai Kongzi shuyuan 四海孔子書院 (Confucius Academy of the Four Seas), which we will call here *sishu* 1, is nowadays one of China's most famous classical schools (Figures 2.8–2.12). The academy—the prestigious term *shuyuan* was preferred to the one of *sishu*—is located in modern Western-style houses. Opened in 2006, it was in 2010 a boarding school for around one hundred pupils.

The founder of *sishu* 1, Mr. F., is a man in his forties who comes from a modest countryside family of Hunan province. A great admirer of Liang Shuming ("Liang is our idol"[16]), he has been one of the pioneers in China of the massive dissemination of classics reading books and leaflets for children. His commitment to Confucianism was fueled by numerous readings (starting with the *Analects*), a number of encounters, and an awareness of the problems and contradictions at work in China today, whose symptoms are for him "the unbridled development of capitalism and Christianity." Only a "Confucian renaissance" would make it possible to contain such a disastrous situation. Given that "it will not be possible to revive Confucianism by means of religion," he considers that the only alternative is "to start with education." Lamenting that the current legal framework hinders the smooth development of Confucianism-inspired institutions, he hopes that a solution will be found, especially "if the government uses

---

15 Ibid., 185n59.

16 *Liang Shuming shi women de ouxiang.*

FIGURE 2.8 One of the buildings of *sishu* 1 (Beijing).
© Sébastien Billioud.

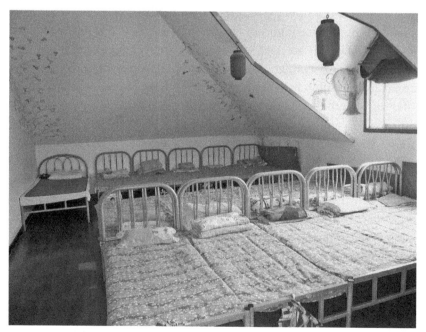

FIGURE 2.9 A dormitory in *sishu* 1 (Beijing).
© Sébastien Billioud.

FIGURE 2.10 Pupils enrolled in *sishu* 1 (Beijing).
© Sébastien Billioud.

FIGURE 2.11 A break in *sishu* 1 (Beijing).
© Sébastien Billioud.

FIGURE 2.12 Calligraphy classroom in *sishu* 1 (Beijing).
© Sébastien Billioud.

Confucianism to counter the development of Christianity."[17] In the meantime, he needs to adapt to the existing situation:

> We are today in a situation of legal vacuum (*feifa* 非法) that should
> clearly be differentiated from an illegal situation (*weifa* 違法). Sihai
> Kongzi shuyuan is currently registered only as a "training school"

---

17 Interview, Beijing, 2010.

(*peixun xuexiao* 培訓學校) and cannot produce any formal school-ing certification (*xueli* 學歷).[18]

Whereas, in theory, Mr. F.'s "academy" cannot serve as a substitute for the compulsory school system, this is in fact what it practically does, enter-taining excellent relationships with local authorities and making the most of their tolerance. The absence of any official accreditation does not deter many parents from enrolling their children in the school.

I do not need to devote much effort to finding interested parents. They come to see me.[19]

This situation can be explained by the strong disillusionment of many par-ents vis-à-vis the compulsory school system. The latter is strongly criticized for its purely instrumental dimension—preparation for exams—and its lack of emphasis on a true and meaningful formation of the individuals. However, the favorable situation of *sishu* 1 can in no way be generalized: In many other places, the absence of official accreditation really constitutes a major hin-drance to attracting prospective students due to the difficulty of later enter-ing the compulsory education or university system. Moreover, difficulties in recruiting students are sometimes also worsened by expensive tuition fees.

Good relationships with the authorities also helped two educators—a father and his daughter, both Beida alumni—to create a traditional school in a rural district of the Taiyuan municipality in Shanxi province.[20] Once again this traditional school (which we will call *sishu* 2), though named Beida Academy of Enlightened Children, corresponds much more to a *sishu* than to a *shuyuan* (academy). Suffice it to mention that the children registered in the school when we conducted our survey were aged from three to ten years old. The institutional affiliation of this *sishu* reflects well the way many Confucianism-related activities currently develop in China. In 2010, it was administratively positioned under a "Shanxi Committee for Education Based on Chinese Classics" itself supervised by an "Association of Shanxi province for the study of contemporary Confucianism." The creation of this associa-tion by local authorities resulted from the internal lobbying of local cadres who were at the same time Confucian activists. Not only did they manage to get their project authorized, but some of them were also appointed to the

---

18 Interview, Beijing, 2010.

19 Interview, Beijing, 2010.

20 Survey carried out in 2010 in Shanxi province.

management of the project, thus benefitting from a quasi-official organization for the promotion of Confucianism in the province. In contrast to the situation that we were able to observe in Dongguan, local authorities did not invest in *sishu* 2 and simply authorized it. But as in Dongguan, we face a situation where a project linked to Confucianism is facilitated by the presence of Confucian activists within the system. Thanks to their support, this project enjoys a degree of official recognition and avoids the problematic situation of tension between the institutional and political environment.

Despite this implicit or even quasi-official support from the authorities, this project nevertheless remains a private and autonomous enterprise implemented by two individuals who present themselves as independent educators. Since the school's target remains the education of children—some of them old enough to be sent to school—it also constitutes an alternative to the compulsory educational system. Materially, the school is located in the countryside, in the middle of fields, on a piece of land that was given by the director of a big farm (*nongchang laoban* 農場老伴). It remains relatively small in scale (less than two dozen children) and is made up of a single building incorporating all the facilities: Classrooms, canteen, and dormitories, since the *sishu* is a boarding school. While only primary school pupils were registered in the school in 2010, the ambition of the founders is to accompany the children when they grow and to open the equivalent of middle and high school classes. This would of course imply a gradual increase in the number of children with new, younger pupils arriving each year.

Sishu 2 is not the only structure operated by the two Beida alumni. In Taiyuan, another school hosts a hundred children, this time in an urban environment.[21] Mr. L., the director, sees himself as a pioneer devising a new educational model in today's China, even though he acknowledges that many of his influences come from educators of the republican era (quotes from Tao Xingzhi 陶行知 could for instance be found on the walls of the school[22]). We will explore later the pedagogical issues. Suffice it to mention here the obvious experimental dimension of this project. The dream of Mr. L. and his daughter is that their experimentation could be studied and appropriated by other educators: Its large-scale

---

21 At the time we carried out our survey the Taiyuan school was moving to larger premises and we could therefore not visit it.

22 Along with James Yen (Yan Yangchu 宴陽初) and Liang Shuming, Tao Xingzhi (1891–1946) was one of the prominent educators attempting to articulate educational reforms during the republican era. He was also involved in several concrete projects aiming at associating education with rural reconstruction.

FIGURE 2.13 The building of *sishu* 3 (outskirts of Taiyuan, Shanxi province).
© Sébastien Billioud.

development (*daliang de fazhan* 大量的發展) would offer to a large
number of children an education that would be more useful, balanced,
and fulfilling than what is available today in the compulsory system.

The link with the authorities is sometimes weaker than what we
mentioned for *sishu* 1 and 2. It is now time to briefly introduce *sishu* 3,
which was also opened in the outskirt of Taiyuan by two businessmen,
Mr. W. and Mr. L. (Figure 2.13). Born in the early 1970s, they undertook some
educational projects after their "discovery" of Confucianism (see Box 2.2).

Their project is the result of an extremely critical analysis of the compulsory educational system:

> In the current educational system, the more the children study,
> the stupider they become. . . . They become "bananas" [yellow out-
> side, white inside] and they no longer know why they are Chinese.
> We have nothing against the West (*bu paichi xifang* 不排斥西方), but
> we really expect our children to become Chinese.[23]

---

23 Interview, outskirts of Taiyuan, 2010.

BOX 2.2

Portraits of Activists: Mr. L. and Mr. W. (Sishu 3)

The itineraries of Mr. L. and Mr. W. make it possible to establish a link with the first part of this chapter, since they both attended a *guoxue* class in a university located in Beijing and even took as a master one of the professors they met in that context. We have here a dynamic: From simple participants to the "Confucian revival" movement, these two men gradually turned into convinced activists. Contrary to the two Beida alumni of *sishu* 2—who are somewhat the products of the Chinese scholarly aristocracy perpetuating an ancient elitist tradition of social and educative commitment—not much predestined them to play the role of educators.

Born in a countryside village of Shanxi province, Mr. L. stopped his studies after middle school and was once employed as a worker in a steel-producing state-owned enterprise before "jumping into the sea" (*xiahai* 下海), that is, leaving his company to start a private business. This experience was materially a success but it also generated all kinds of worries and concerns (*fannao* 煩惱, *jiaolü* 焦慮). "Then, I started to ponder the situation," he says, alluding both to an introspective process and to the situation of society in general ("everyone is only busy making money"). Because of all these new sets of questions, he started to study psychology and to enroll in a *guoxue* class. He attended the courses during three years and had the chance "to meet several masters." More importantly, the discovery of Confucian classics made him feel that he had finally found some sort of direction for his life (*wo ganjue ziji de shengming you suo guisu* 我感覺自己的生命有所歸宿).

Mr. W. was also born in the countryside into a family of poor peasants. He managed with much effort to study Chinese medicine at university. Introducing his itinerary, he emphasizes its philosophical and spiritual dimensions: For a long time, he adopted the Marxist worldview and had a real faith in dialectical and historical materialisms. Experiencing afterwards a period of doubt and professional instability ("I was carrying cement in Dongguan"), he became interested in the middle of the 1990s in the Christian faith after an encounter with a priest with whom he shared a room for several months in a presbytery. "There is something true in Christianity (*zhe ge daoli shi dui de* 這個道理是對的), but I never managed to really believe. Believing in God was too much in contradiction with the materialist worldview that I had embraced for years." At the beginning of the 2000s,

(continued)

BOX 2.2 Continued

he read for the first time the *Analects* of Confucius, that he now calls "the true bible of Chinese people." This reading was a revelation: "When I read the *Analects* I was particularly impressed by the excerpt where Confucius recommends to keep some distance with ghosts and spirits. We do not need to care about what happens when we are dead. Let us simply carry out our daily tasks. I immediately felt that such a teaching was for me." At the same period of time, he started a garment business that soon flourished, changing his material situation dramatically and facilitating his commitment to the promotion of Confucianism.

The beginning of Mr. W.'s educational commitment took place in 2005 after he watched a DVD explaining Wang Caigui's pedagogical approach to classical texts and children's education. Convinced that Wang's method was a real breakthrough, he invited him to Taiyuan and opened a classics reading class. It was only three years later, in 2009, that he established the *sishu* 3, with Mr. L. In the vein of *sishu* 1 and 2, *sishu* 3 also offers an alternative to the compulsory education system. In 2010, one year after its opening, twenty-nine children aged three to twelve were enrolled with full boarding. The school was legally registered but as a kindergarten (*youeryuan* 幼兒園).[24] Ten professors and educators were at that time taking care of the children. The whole structure (premises, boarding, employees) requires heavy investments and in 2010 the two founders did not break even, in spite of high tuition fees of 30,000 RMB per year and per child. They expect to reach a financial equilibrium in following years when the number of children increases: In fact, their challenge is not only to enroll extra students each year but also to accompany those already studying in the *sishu* for the rest of their school curriculum, that is, until they are eighteen years old.[25] In any case, finding parents ready and able to spend a large

---

24 "We had no other means of getting official registration. We could not present ourselves as an "academy" or as a classical school (*xuetang* 學堂)." Interview, Taiyuan, 2010.

25 The founders mentioned that children wishing to transfer to the standard education system can do so when they are twelve, when their overall level would make it possible.

amount of money for such an education is no easy task. But this is not the only difficulty:

> Parents whose wish is to prepare their children to pass the exams are not ready to come to our school. We have to find parents who share our conceptions of education.[26]

Those "conceptions" refer both to a pedagogical approach and to the school's target. We discuss pedagogical issues in chapter 3. As for the targets, they point to what the children will do later, after they finish their *sishu* education:

> They will engage in self-cultivation, regulate their families, govern the country and pacify the universe (*xiushen qijia zhiguo ping tianxia* 修身齊家治國平天下).[27]

This answer is a direct quote from a major Confucian text, *The Great Learning (Daxue)*, that celebrates a continuum between government of the self, of one's family, and of political affairs. It primarily means that thanks to their classical education children will engage in lifelong self-cultivation that will be beneficial to their families—the role of families in society is often underscored by Confucian activists—and, beyond, that will also be useful for their professional activities. But this answer can also be understood in a more implicit way: The future Confucians who are trained in this school will later commit themselves, each at his own level, to social reform. The two founders' underlying appreciation of the current situation of Chinese society (moral crisis, etc.) is gloomy, and there is little doubt that at their modest level they wish to contribute to its improvement.[28] This projection in the future reflects some degree of tension with the social environment. However, this tension is much more obvious in *sishu* 4.

---

26 Interview, Shanxi, 2010.

27 Interview, Shanxi, 2010.

28 It might be useful to distinguish the situation of this school (in which the founders' most ambitious expectations crystallize) from the situation of other educative projects also undertaken by Mr. L. and Mr. W. For instance, they also promote classics reading in a Taiyuan primary school. Forty minutes of classics reading take place each day with the support of the directors of the school. Sixteen hundred pupils take part in these activities. Mr. W. explains that "this is positive and we involve ourselves in this project hoping that the whole society

Sishu 4 provides some insight into a more fundamentalist dimension of Confucian education. This *sishu*—the label is here used by the activists—is much more modest in size than what we have been discussing so far. Located in a rented flat in a high-rise Shenzhen building, it was cofounded by five families for their young children. Parents work in different sectors: A mother operates a restaurant; another is a white-collar executive in a foreign company; one of the fathers is a high-ranking officer in the People's Liberation Army. The *sishu* operates in a completely underground way and totally as a substitute for compulsory education. No registration whatsoever was made and activists do not care much about the legal environment. One of the mothers bluntly explains her position: "the authorities enact the laws that they want, I live the life that I want."[29] There is complete mistrust of society at large, which is considered totally "polluted" (*wuran* 污染). Facing this dramatic situation, parents share the opinion that classics should be used to protect the children from pernicious outside contamination. Such an isolation has a strong sectarian flavor in the sense commonly ascribed to this term in the West. It is also highly paradoxical considering that one of the traditional functions of *sishu* education was the socialization of children. Besides, one should also emphasize that children of *sishu* 4 are not considered by their parents as "their" children (*bu shi women de* 不是我們的), but as the children "of the nation, the people, mankind." The objective of *sishu* 4 is nothing less than the production of saints able to regenerate China. One of the mothers even emphasized that she intended to give birth to two more children "in order to have two more Confucians."[30]

The cases that we have introduced so far reflect the extreme diversity of the ways classical education for children is currently revived, reinvented, or recreated by Confucian activists. The institutionalization of their projects takes place in a gray area, between complementarity and substitution. When substitution is on the agenda, it proceeds not only from a

---

will discover the classics, but this remains nevertheless superficial (*biaomian de* 表面的)." Another project launched by the two associates is oriented toward children of poor family backgrounds who are unable to pay high tuition fees. It consists of a school opened in the countryside. Whereas registered children study the classics intensively, the compulsory education curriculum is also respected. Consequently, this school obtained the accreditation of the local education bureau. Interview, Taiyuan, 2010.

29 Interview with Mrs. X., forty years old, Shenzhen, 2007.

30 Interview with Mrs. M., Shenzhen, 2007.

reaction against the compulsory educational system, but also sometimes from a reaction against society and its prevailing values. Whereas in its most liberal forms—exemplified here by *sishu* 2—the establishment of a traditional school results from a concern to promote a more fulfilling and humanistic education model, in its most extreme forms (*sishu* 4) it proceeds from a radical social critique and a quasi messianic vision of Confucianism understood as a salvation path for the country, if not for the whole world. The tension with both the legal and educational system and the usual goals of compulsory education (acquisition of the knowledge to integrate oneself in society, molding of the socialist citizen) then reaches a climax.

It is necessary to finish with a few words about terminology. Among the cases discussed above, only two schools—the small *sishu* opened in Dongguan and *sishu* 4—claim the label *sishu*. We have used it as a convenience, since it traditionally points to a model of education given to small children on the basis of classical texts. The three other schools present themselves either as *xuetang* 學堂 (study hall, *sishu* 3) or as academies, or *shuyuan* (*sishu* 1 and 2), even though, in the latter case, they share little with traditional Confucian academies. In fact, the term *shuyuan* nowadays becomes in China an extremely unclear and ill-defined category, likely to encompass the most diverse institutions. It is often selected for its prestigious historical connotations.

Adult Education: *Jiaohua* Organizations and Academies

Projects promoting Confucian education within revived or reinvented traditional educative structures (*xuetang* and academies) independent from official institutions are not limited to the children. They also target young people and adults. This section provides some insights into this phenomenon with two examples: The Yidan study hall (Yidan xuetang 一耽學堂, Figure 2.14) and the Pinghe academy (Pinghe shuyuan 平和書院).

The Yidan xuetang is an organization founded in 2001 by a Peking University alumnus, Pang Fei (see Box 2.3, and Figure 2.15), in collaboration with other students from universities located in Beijing.[31]

31 For a more comprehensive presentation of the Yidan xuetang, see Sébastien Billioud, "Confucian Revival and Emergence of *Jiaohua* Organizations: A Case Study of the Yidan Xuetang," *Modern China* 37, no. 3 (2011): 286–314.

FIGURE 2.14 The headquarters of the Yidan xuetang in Beijing.
© Sébastien Billioud.

BOX 2.3

Portrait of an Activist: Pang Fei 逄飛, *Founder of the Yidan Xuetang*

Pang Fei was born in 1973 into Shenyang in a working-class family. He spent his childhood and teenage years in Shenyang before going to Changchun and later to Beijing for his studies. He graduated from Peking University's department of philosophy with a master's degree dedicated to the concept of truth in the history of Western philosophy. Whereas an academic career seemed to be an attractive path, he abandoned the idea of doing a PhD in order to establish the Yidan xuetang. This turn probably resulted both from the fact that philosophy was never for him a mere intellectual endeavor and from an awareness of the gap separating his ideals from prevailing values in society's mainstream (and probably also in Peking University): "Everyone wants to become capable, to progress, to obtain honors and positions, but for me these aspirations generate only confusion and foolishness in the way people see the world" (*Yidan xuetang chendu gongzuo bu*, 2008). "Seeing the

(continued)

BOX 2.3 Continued

FIGURE 2.15 Pang Fei, the director of the Yidan xuetang.
© Sébastien Billioud.

world as it is" does not require for him philosophical speculations but a reori-entation of the way we see things and, by extension, a self-transformation. He mentions that he "wants to live as an ordinary man" (*zuo yi ge putongren* 做一個普通人). This anti-intellectualistic attitude actually became one of the ten "golden rules" of the Yidan xuetang. Any social renaissance first requires for Pang Fei a moral renaissance of the subject or the self. Such a renaissance requires self-cultivation (based on classical texts) and, through volunteering, a disinterested commitment to the others.

While the Yidan xuetang largely inscribes itself in the Confucian heri-tage as much for the texts it promotes as for certain rituals carried out in temples to honor Confucius, Pang Fei insists that what is at stake today is not the promotion of a given school of thought but the renaissance of the individual (*ren de fuxing* 人的復興). One should beware of all kinds of episodic "fevers" such as the classics reading movement or the "national studies craze" (*guoxue re* 國學熱). One's actions should be deeply anchored in duration and the long term, not in short-lived phenomena.

Interviews, Beijing, 2004, 2006, 2008, 2012.

Strategically located next to Peking University but outside the actual campus, this nongovernmental organization is primarily involved, on the basis of volunteering, in the promotion of traditional culture and classics reading in society. Since its creation at the beginning of the 2000s, it has initiated all kinds of projects: Several thousand volunteers carried out punctual actions all across China in which half a million people participated.[32] The term *xuetang* or study hall was chosen to reflect the ambition—at least at the beginning of the project—to gradually reconstruct a network of institutions (schools and academies) offering premises to study classical culture and experience some forms of community life, also including little rituals (Figure 2.16). It seems that practical difficulties, whether financial, administrative, or human, relegated this institutional target to a secondary priority even though a traditional school could be opened in Zuozhou, Hebei province.[33] The Yidan xuetang has two main kinds of involvement. The first one—which became the main one in recent years—is the early reading of Confucian classics. It consists in sending groups of volunteers into the main parks of Chinese cities in the early morning in order to collectively read the classics, inviting passersby to join them. Other forms of classics reading could additionally take place in schools, companies, or the media, so as to introduce the benefits of the classics to a large audience. The second type of involvement focuses on the creation of a core of volunteers sharing common activities: training sessions, small rituals (for instance to honor Confucius), study trips, and so on.

The nature of this organization could be formally defined as amphibious:[34] Although it benefits from the support of prominent intellectuals and a precarious but legal official status,[35] its orientation is opposed to the essential

---

32 Interview, Beijing, 2010. These figures cannot be crosschecked and should therefore be taken with caution.

33 In fact, this traditional school already existed in the "Wenchang hall" of the city and somehow associated itself with the Yidan xuetang一耽學堂. See *Yidan xuetang tongxun tongxun* 一耽學堂通訊 [Yidan Xuetang's Information Letter], issue 11 (2006), and Yidan Xuetang, *Xiandai yishu xuanchuan ziliao* 現代義塾宣傳資料 [Promotional Material of Tradition-Inspired Modern Schools], VCD published by the organization.

34 On the "amphibious" character of "civil society" in China, see Ding Xueliang, "Institutional Amphibiousness and the Transition from Communism: The Case of China," *British Journal of Political Sciences* 23, no. 3 (1994): 293–318.

35 Administratively, the Yidan xuetang is accountable to a work unit called the Chinese Association for the International Promotion of Science and Peace (*Zhongguo guoji kexue yu heping cujinhui* 中國國際科學與和平促進會), which in turn is registered with the Ministry of Civil Affairs (*Minzhengbu* 民政部). The leaders of the organization are well aware that due to the fact that they promote sets of values in society their activities might potentially be considered subversive by the authorities. Therefore, they take all kinds of measures to prevent

FIGURE 2.16 Little altar to honor Confucius at the Beijing headquarters of the Yidan xuetang.

© Sébastien Billioud.

possible problems from happening. On the one hand, the organization constantly embraces the policies of the authorities. Thus, writings published by the Yidan xuetang often praise public actions undertaken to promote virtue, to create proximity between elites and the people, and so on. See for instance *Yidan xuetang tongxun* no. 4, 1; no. 6, 1; no. 7, 1; no. 8, 1; and Yidan xuetang, *Peiyang minzu jingshen, jiangou hexie shehui—Yidan xuetang zhongyang jingshen xuexi gangyao* 培養民族精神,建構和諧社會,一耽學堂中央精神學習綱要 [Nurturing National Spirit, Constructing a Harmonious Society, Presentation of the Yidan Xuetang's Study of the Spirit Promoted by Chinese Central Authorities] (unpublished material distributed by the Yidan Xuetang). High dignitaries of the regime are often quoted. In 2006, Pang Fei for instance dedicated an article to the "spirit of central authorities" (*zhongyang jingshen*

spirit of the modern university in either the liberal or communist mode. The "national renaissance" (*minzu de fuxing* 民族的復興) to which it is committed requires a "cultural renaissance" (*wenhua de fuxing* 文化復興) that questions the nature of certain basic paradigms of Western knowledge and pedagogy:

> We know that the schools and models of contemporary teaching grew out of a movement of urbanization and professional associations dating from the end of the Middle Ages in Europe. It is a system based on knowledge and the transmission of techniques, an educative mechanism dedicated to rapid and industrialized fabrication of "intellectual products." So it is important to take into account that we are faced with an instrumental rationality with no relation to a spiritual life. The result is a huge carnival of knowledge, and not the transmission of wisdom.[36]

This demand for of a kind of "wisdom" (*zhihui* 智慧) as opposed to "knowledge" (*zhishi* 知識) is an element common to many movements in the "Confucian renaissance." For Pang, considering the inertia of teaching establishments and the conformist tendencies of the elites attached to Western models, the "space of the people" (*minjian*) has become the point of departure for an educational regeneration:

> As limited as I may be, I think the system of spreading the spirit of Chinese culture is tied to a disciple–master relationship and to a form of oral transmission, in the way a father teaches a son. This should be undertaken within society by the system of academies and study halls. Modern university and educative systems modeled on those of the United States and Europe are completely incapable of this. Education in China today suffers from a similar shortcoming, which it cannot overcome. Because the essential spirit of Chinese culture is anchored in civil society and the masses, it is only by using concrete methods and local situations as a point of departure that we can return to our roots in order to look toward new horizons

---

中央精神), praising "harmonious society," "scientific development," "the new socialist countryside," and so on. On the other hand, the Yidan xuetang always takes great care to offer some high degree of transparency about its activities. Finally, one should also note that a number of young volunteers are also party members.

36 *Yidan xuetang tongxun*, no. 5, 1.

and perpetuate the ideals of wisdom. This is the most critical issue in China today. On such a foundation, a cultural renaissance can be built and, if it occurs, there will be a national renaissance.[37]

In its educative spirit as well as in its vision of the "people," we may observe the ambiguous nature of the Yidan xuetang's relationship to the university institution. While its long-term ideal distances it from the type of rationality that governs the university, it nevertheless continues to depend on permanent exchanges with the academic community whose validity it questions. The classes it managed to organize in Guangzhou can also be seen at the fringes of Sun Yat-sen University: Propagative activities and volunteer work also bring together educators who are well established in their institutions, from primary school teachers to professors in university philosophy departments. However, the propositions advanced by the Yidan xuetang's leadership do not always receive unanimous acceptance and are sometimes the object of divergent interpretations.[38]

In a way that parallels what was mentioned before about children's education and *sishu* schooling, another step toward becoming autonomous is made when the structure established by the adepts of a "Confucian renaissance" acquires not only its very own locality but also the permanent elements of community life. In the 2000s, this situation nevertheless remains scarce and many of the entities claiming a *shuyuan* identity are informal groups gathering disciples around a master in order to study and exchange. More often than not, their gathering places, when they are real—one of the striking phenomena is the proliferation of virtual academies on the Internet—do not have the logistical and organizational characteristics of ancient academies or even of the projects that emerged in republican China. Some projects, however, try to go further. This is for

---

37 *Yidan xuetang tongxun*, no. 4, 1.

38 Pang Fei's talent for inspiration and organization has developed a network in Guangzhou that brings together very different personalities: volunteer activists, students, employees. A philosophy professor thus made a clear distinction between the spirit of self-training and moral renaissance, of which he approved, and the scientific and democratic values to which he remained attached (interview, December 2006). We rediscovered this phenomenon everywhere that the Yidan xuetang operates. The individuals engaged in this organization are far from having homogeneous opinions on social and political issues. Moreover, the management of Yidan xuetang does not seem to require such unanimity, but emphasizes concrete action and self-cultivation.

instance the case of an institution in Guangdong that calls itself an academy, the Pinghe shuyuan 平和書院.

Founded in 2005 in Zhuhai by a young professional who trained as a scientist and then went on to head a successful commercial language school, this institution originally occupied two vast apartments in a large modern compound. Its founder, who studied in the United States and turned to "Confucianism" after a period of belief in Bahá'ism, combined a spirit of enterprise and association with successful Cantonese businessmen with a visionary conception devoid of erudition. He was open in a rather undefined way to the religious and political as well as the educative aspects of Confucianism. Even though he had no academic credentials, he maintained friendly relations with professors known for their cultural conservatism, such as Jiang Qing, the main theoretician behind "political Confucianism." One of the academy's apartments served as a workplace for study or meetings, which were sometimes accompanied by simple rituals, while the other served as a guesthouse for boarders staying for varying lengths of time. The academy employed several people on full-time and part-time bases. They shared an enthusiasm for spreading Confucian teachings, even though their backgrounds varied widely: A former schoolmaster in charge of organizing ceremonies (births, marriages, etc.) in the region; a management specialist responsible for promoting the theory of good "human relations" (*lunli* 倫理) in the businesses community; a teacher specializing in English but who also propagates "*Han* clothing";[39] and a computer engineer who focused on the academy's website and the many relationships developing now on the Internet among supporters of a "Confucian renaissance." The Pinghe shuyuan, funded by donations and the resources of its directors, could be considered a "private" institution, but was nevertheless an official member of the Association for Research on Traditional Culture (*Chuantong wenhua yanjiuhui*), which is registered with a department of the local government.[40]

---

39 The so-called movement of Han garb (*Hanfu yundong* 漢服運動) developed in big Chinese cities in the 2000s. Hundreds—in some cases thousands—of young people paraded in the streets in traditional dress and numerous discussions took place on Internet forums about this topic.

40 This type of institution remains fragile. Our initial visit to the Pinghe shuyuan was made in 2006. When we finished our survey in 2010, Mr. Hong mentioned that he was intending to close the structure in Zhuhai—which has since been done—and open a new one in Hangzhou. In fact, it seems that he is now convinced that a Confucian revival needs other kinds of institutions than academies created *ex nihilo*. He intends to root his enterprises

Appropriating New Spaces to Promote Confucian Education: Companies and Official Institutions

By combining idealist activism with economic realism, the academy somewhat echoes new vectors of Confucian educative engagement: firms and companies in general (*gongsi*). Sometimes they are motivated by commercial considerations or social strategy, but more often than not it is out of conviction and personal commitment that businessmen and women add an educative and cultural vocation to their economic enterprise.

Somehow, this situation has given rise to a crucial legal problem. It is difficult in China to receive official legal status when establishing a private institution whose activities cover a quite a wide area, including social, cultural, and even religious dimensions.

It is significant that a convert to Wang Caigui's pedagogical methods, the director of one of the main Chinese companies specializing in the distribution of audiovisual material for reciting and memorizing the classics by children[41] insists on the fact that his company is not primarily commercial: "The model of an NGO would have been more suitable for us, but officially we can only be recognized as a company (*gongsi*)."[42] This company develops its activities on a national scale by supporting small schools attracted to its programs, organizing competitions of reading classics (*Lun Yu* reading clubs), and lobbying for official recognition of its objectives. It also shares with the new *xuetang* and *shuyuan* the practice of applying to itself the educational and moral principles it promotes: The twenty or so employees of the company start their workday by reciting the classics and participating in a weekly discussion group.

To this legal context is also added a change in attitudes in the economic sphere, where the traditional model of *rushang* 儒商, the "literary merchant," has undergone an unexpected modern evolution. This traditional notion, which described the development in the Ming dynasty of a closer

---

in traditional structures such as lineages and local associations while ascribing them new function. We come back to this situation in an epilogue to this book in order to question new developments taking place at the beginning of the second decade of the new century.

41 *Ertong jingdian songdu gongcheng.*

42 Interview, Beijing, June 2006. One could legitimately ask to what extent such a claim does not hide primarily commercial motivations. There are probably various reasons behind this enterprise: Its clear business dimension is not incompatible with the staff's genuine interest in promoting the classics.

relationship between merchants and the milieus of Confucian scholars,[43] is a sort of multivocal term in today's China, sometimes the subject of jokes, but also a strategy for social recognition.[44] But the businessman who takes on (or more aptly said, since the term is considered flattering, does not refuse) such a title does not do so merely to augment his economic success with the symbolic capital of reputation. For some, it expresses a responsibility and commitment that is part of the daily life of their companies. In Guangzhou, for instance, the head of a prosperous educational company (*jiaoyu jituan* 教育集團) is a realistic man aware of contemporary intellectual issues. Though he rejects the religious and political aspects of Confucianism, he upholds the message of moral instruction promoting independence of character (*renge de duli* 人格的獨立) and "existential" education (*shengming de jiaoyu* 生命的教育). While he affects a liberal attitude, he does not hesitate to provide his thousands of employees with courses in national studies (*guoxue*), distributing bonuses to encourage the best students.[45]

Although it is always difficult to determine whether ambition takes precedence over personal commitment, certain experiences suggest a genuine missionary vocation arising within some *gongsi* (companies). This was the case for a young woman from Dongbei who experienced an existential crisis that led her to Buddhism. The manager of a restaurant in Shenzhen, she developed a commitment to Confucianism that led her to systematically proselytize her employees as well as some of her clients and their families. Her passion as an autodidact goes beyond organizing classes for children to recite the classics, and she gives great importance to the training and personal well-being of her employees, some of whom have experienced the hardships of working in factories in the Dongguan region. This is a significant albeit atypical case of a small business with a

---

43 About the emergence of this new "merchant spirit," see Yu Ying-shih 余英時, *Zhongguo jinshi zongjiao lunli yu shangren jingshen* 中國近世宗教倫理與商人精神 [Religious Intra-Mundane Ethics and the Spirits of Merchants in China] (Taipei: Lianjing, 1987), 99–166.

44 A training institute called Rushang at Zhejiang University tries to give management students an indispensable complementary course on the subject of commercial ethics. According to its director, "The mentality of these young MBA graduates is often horrendous, and their ignorance of elementary rules of behavior (without even mentioning economic life) is a considerable liability" (interview, Qufu, October 2007).

45 Interview, Guangzhou, December 2006.

communitarian vocation dedicated to an almost messianic degree to the ideal of a "Confucian renaissance."[46]

Apart from companies, governmental structures and state-controlled entities sometimes also surprisingly become vectors of promotion of Confucian education. Thus, the party school offered in 2006 in Beijing courses dedicated to "the fundamental spirit of classical Chinese philosophy," which was warmly welcomed by the "student-cadres."[47] One professor at the party school explains:

> From the opium war until today, classical culture only suffered from attitudes of negation and critique (*pipan fouding de taidu* 批判否定的態度). This is not normal. We start again to pay attention to it. . . . The party school has to get along with societal changes. Nobody opposed these courses even though at the beginning people had to adapt to this idea (*you yi ge mohe de guocheng* 有一個磨合的 過程).[48]

The organization of this course benefited from the support of the leadership of the party school and the course was also attended by high-ranking officials. The success of the initial lectures gave birth to the creation of a "series of courses on traditional culture" (*chuantong wenhua xilie* 傳統文化系列), whose spirit is somewhat to establish some sort of Marxist and Confucian synthesis:

> Marxism remains today the mainstream, but we need to acknowledge our national culture. We need to combine (*jiehe* 結合) Confucian thought and Marxism and the latter even needs to further sinicize in order to further develop.[49]

---

46 Interviews, Shenzhen, December 2006.

47 The party school has implemented a rating course system. In 2007, the course on "the fundamental spirit of classical Chinese philosophy" was rated the best of the whole year. More than 200 students chose it. According to our informant, most of the "student cadres" would be in favor of the promotion of Confucianism. Interview with a party school professor, Beijing, 2009.

48 Interview, Beijing, 2009.

49 Interview, Beijing, 2009.

How is it practically possible to combine Confucianism and Marxism? How is this combination presented to "students-cadres" at the party school? The method consists of introducing some texts and topics of traditional philosophy and afterwards to show their relevance to a discussion of current issues. Then, Marxist theory is used to show that the same kinds of conclusions can be drawn to solve a given problem, even though the two doctrines are completely different:

> It is for instance possible to discuss Confucian environmental philosophy (*rujia de shengtai zhexue* 儒家的生態哲學) and the idea of a harmonious relationship with nature, and afterwards to link them to the notions of "ecological civilization" (*shengtai wenming* 生態文明) and sustainable development that are promoted by the party.[50]

As a matter of course, this spirit of synthesis is often emphasized by governmental structures organizing activities linked to traditional culture. We could for instance observe this in the city of Bangbu 蚌埠, Anhui Province, at the occasion of an event organized by local authorities on the theme of the "harmonious society." The slogan of the central authorities made it possible, thanks to local cadres sympathetic to the Confucian cause and to Confucian activists involved in the city's urban renovation project, to organize a one-day training program, during which an array of local cadres (employed in a variety of different departments of the local government) attended a lecture given by a university professor—himself Confucian activist—on classical Confucian texts and their relevance to a harmonious contemporary social context.[51] Some public structures

---

50 Interview, Beijing, 2009. This is a description reported by an informant associated with the party school. We did not attend the courses ourselves.

51 Field observation, Bangbu, 2005. The mobilization of local cadres around one of the few scholars strongly involved in the *minjian* revival in the middle of the 2000s illustrates how the creation of equivocal spaces enables textual interpretations that share little with the official vulgate. Thus, the famous sentence of the *Analects* of Confucius (13:23, translated by R. Ames and H. Rosemont Jr. [New York: Ballantine, 1998]): "Exemplary persons seek harmony not sameness; petty persons, then, are the opposite" (君子和而不同,小人同而不和), was commented upon in a much more democratic way. The emphasis was put on the fact that "unification of thought" that was emblematic of the Maoist era had to give way to harmony and that a prerequisite for harmony was the possibility of expressing a plurality of opinions. (It is noteworthy that this comment was formulated before the start of the official campaign promoting a harmonious society later in the same year.)

do not necessarily take so many precautions in the way they synthetize various ideological resources and narratives. Thus, in one of the Internet subsidiaries of CCTV, employees were asked in 2009 to wear ties with a Confucius logo during their working hours and, more importantly, one of the criteria for the recruitment of new employees was their ability to integrally memorize the *Rules of the Disciples* (*Dizigui*).[52]

Governmental structures and state-controlled entities illustrate with new examples one of the points we have already alluded to: Confucian activists are often well integrated within the official system. In a quantitative study that he dedicates to them, Kang Xiaoguang shows that 41 percent of the people studied in his sample are Communist Party members.[53] However, in all the cases that we have discussed so far, the embrace of Confucianism was never a top-down policy. A more detailed presentation of the different cases where Confucianism is promoted within official work-unit (*danwei*) would reveal that in each case the practical promotion of a "Confucianism-inspired education" or of Confucian textual references is the result of complex internal processes. It is the activists employed in governmental structures who introduce Confucian education, convince colleagues and leaders of its importance, negotiate with them possibilities of disseminating it, gain new colleagues to their cause, and so on. Confucianism is making relative headway within the state apparatus because of a sort of "trickling effect": Sympathy for this cause is gradually built thanks to internal proselytizing. This situation should nevertheless be considered cautiously. Whereas fieldwork indicates some gradual progress of Confucian ideas over the years, the magnitude of this interest in Confucianism is far from clear and, no global picture being available, its developments should not be exaggerated.

We thus see the variety of solutions for reviving Confucian teachings through institutional structures that sometimes appear in very unexpected forms. But whether it is in the context of universities rethinking and broadening their educational vocation, of new institutions inspired by classic models, or of businesses taking responsibility for educative functions, these militant movements exist in a new context without which

---

52 Field observation, Beijing, 2009.

53 Kang Xiaoguang, "A Study of the Renaissance of Traditional Confucian Culture," in *Confucianism and Spiritual Traditions in Modern China and Beyond*, ed. Fenggang Yang and Joseph Tamney, 54–56 (Leiden and Boston, MA: Brill, 2012).

the rapidity and scale of their commitments would be unthinkable—the means of communication made possible by the Internet. In fact, no "Confucian" organization of any importance is without its own website, sometimes visited daily by thousands of Internet users.[54] A variety of opinions about Confucianism and its possible role for China, including in the political realm, can even sometimes be read on official websites.[55] The Internet, moreover, has become the main tool for isolated activists who are just starting out. From Shenzhen to Qufu, one may witness the effectiveness of these virtual networks, these "immaterial academies," in organizing discussions as well as activities in common with participants from all regions of China.[56]

Having thus presented a picture of the multiplicity of forms taken by the "Confucian revival" in the context of educative projects, we may now focus our attention on one of the dominant features of this educational revival in the 2000s: its paradoxical anti-intellectualism.

---

54 Among the main websites dedicated to the revival of Confucianism, we may cite Yuandao, Guoxue luntan (http://bbs.guoxue.com), Huaxia fuxing (http://hxfx.net), Confuchina (http://confuchina.com), rujia wang (http://rujiazg.com), zhongguo dangdai ruxue wang (http://cccrx.com), Zhongguo guoxue wang (http://chinaguoxue.net), Confucius 2000 (a more academic site), and so on.

55 See for instance the website of the Party School (http://www.ccps.gov.cn), or the website of Xuexi shibao (http://www.studytimes.com.cn). For more accurate examples drawn from these websites, see Billioud, "Confucianism, 'Cultural Tradition' and Official Discourses at the Start of the New Century," 60–62.

56 Interviews, Qufu, March and October 2007; Shenzhen, December 2006. The proliferation of Confucianism-related websites reflects the diversity of the interests for Confucianism. However these sites are not always important and they sometimes cannot be sustained for long. Our surveys were carried out between roughly the end of 2004 and 2013. Quite a number of the websites we initially followed no longer exist.

3

A Modern Anti-Intellectualism

THE BODY, THE CHILD, THE PEOPLE

THE ASPIRATION FOR a revival of Confucian education has now been introduced in its institutional dimensions. In this chapter, we attempt to explore it further, starting with concrete practices that are promoted in today's society.

The most striking feature of educative practices observed during field-work was what could be termed their anti-intellectualism. This new attitude translates into a sort of suspicion toward intellectual speculations and a certain caution regarding the possible role that could be played by intellectuals in the current revival. This prominent trend of the 2000s is all the more remarkable in that it contrasts with one of the prevailing fates of Confucianism during the twentieth century, that is, its transformation in intellectual enterprises taking place to a large extent in Western-style universities. The epitome of the transformation of Confucianism in modern intellectual discourses was probably the contemporary neo-Confucian movement embodied by scholars such as Mou Zongsan who proposed impressive theoretical systems in a direct dialogue with Western modern philosophy. Despite their own critical attitude toward the hegemony of Western thought, it is noteworthy that these scholars were themselves the heirs of the intellectual and pedagogical revolution generated by the creation of Western-style academic institutions. In sum, their worldviews were determined by the May 4th Movement and importantly influenced by the overall aspiration for modern science and democracy that they shared to a large extent.

One of the underlying questions raised by new educational practices carried out in the name of Confucianism is the reinterpretation of a grand modernization narrative. Such a narrative, which also turned into a state doctrine, celebrated the emancipatory values of the Western educational and pedagogical approach that prevailed massively during the twentieth century, be it in its liberal or communist form. "Popular Confucianism" now promotes concrete educational models directly challenging this paradigm. Its anti-intellectualism is both the exploration of sets of new practices on the margin of the official system and a retrospective reflection on ancient Chinese patterns of knowledge transmission. From this perspective this movement is worthy of careful study independently from the variable scope of its practical realizations.

Three dimensions of this anti-intellectualism can be distinguished and are articulated around three elements: The body, the child, and the people.

In Opposition to the Theoretical: The Body

The motto of Yidan xuetang, "Less talk, more action," reflects in general terms the deep suspicion of the theoretical that characterizes the current revival of Confucianism. Self-transformation is not an intellectual operation and even if the text is assuredly one of its vehicles, it must engage the whole person, including the body. The Yidan xuetang organizes regular sessions of morning readings of classic texts (like *The Great Learning*) in small groups in parks where passersby are welcome to join. The sessions, generally lasting fifty minutes, start with a series of gymnastic exercises:

> These exercises are derived from ancient practices of self-cultivation, which we have simplified and modified and which we continually try to improve. Their purpose is to relax the body and the mind, to regulate breathing.[1]

The small groups alternate different modes of reading (reading by the coordinator to the other members, collective, alternating, or solitary reading; varying rhythms, emphasizing slowness, etc.). These methods make it possible to take into account the variety of origins and levels of the participants while stimulating their pleasure of learning as they steep themselves

---

1 *Yidan xuetang tongxun*, no. 9, 2.

in texts in different ways.² The goals of these readings are explained in the following terms:

> One of the objectives of the morning reading is to unify our knowl-
> edge with our actions (*zhi xing he yi* 知行合一), so it is appropriate
> not to read more than one chapter of the *Analects* of Confucius each
> week. We read and reread it so as to learn it by heart and be able to
> recite it. Establishing a connection between our daily lives and pas-
> sages of the *Analects* in this gentle way allows them to truly inner-
> vate our lives. The second objective is to cultivate our nature—if we
> spend a little more time and go to a place with a wide panorama, a
> pleasant landscape, and start with a session of physical exercises,
> and if we also choose a slow reading rhythm to give us a sense of
> the eternal, all of these things serve mainly to purify our hearts,
> cultivate our natures, and strengthen our "overflowing vital energy"
> (*hao ran zhi qi* 浩然之氣).³
>
> Continuing to read the classics in the morning can enable our
> negative [literally "muddy"] energy to purify itself. This energy
> (*qi* 氣) and our spiritual dimension (*shen* 神) reach a state of per-
> ception and serenity. Not only does our body strengthen itself, but
> we obtain access to greater authenticity and a fuller, more unified
> form of humanity. From the classics, we become aware of the roots
> of our culture, and we are surprised to discover that the ancients
> were confronted with the same problems we are, even if in different
> forms. Since they remain identical nonetheless, we can draw from
> the classics wisdom that is still effective. Through this daily exercise
> of reading, we enter into daily exchanges with the sages.⁴

These testimonies are not intended as theoretical explanations, but as a sharing of and reflection upon the actual experience of self-transformation, which originates in the body. The process is that of *incorporation* of the text, an experience of savoring and impregnation, facilitated by physi-cal exercises, breathing, and slowness. These testimonies include an attempt to suggest explanations of what is experienced (purification of

---

2 Ibid.

3 Ibid.

4 Ibid.

"muddy energy," evocation of authenticity and of access to a fuller form of humanity, etc.). But what really matters is the emphasis on temporary access to another state (perception, serenity) and the more lasting feeling of self-transformation, which is not an act of faith, but a real experience, accessible to everyone. These experiences are nourished by a back-and-forth movement between daily life and texts that are constantly repeated and thus progressively memorized. For most people we met, the effectiveness of this process was self-evident.

Texts are literally "incorporated" in the course of a self-cultivation process. However, this relation to the body is sometimes even intensified when self-cultivation is being ascribed a therapeutic dimension. Among the documents, both texts and videos, disseminated by the Yidan xuetang we find a DVD introducing a number of healing techniques based on morality. These techniques are introduced by someone presented as a "peasant" from Heilongjiang province named Mr. Liu Yousheng 劉有生 (b. 1939). He claims inheritance from an important figure of the religious landscape during the republican period, Wang Fengyi 王鳳儀, whose writings are in fact also reedited and published by the Yidan xuetang. Both Wang and Liu were actually associated with the Association for Universal Morality (Wanguo daodehui 萬國道德會), one of the prominent redemptive societies of the republican era mentioned in chapter 1. It is only gradually that we could perceive the importance in today's context of the historical link between current organizations such as the Yidan xuetang and a republican heritage. This link is far from conspicuous, but it is of a crucial importance for a contextualization of current developments within the larger picture of the transformations of Confucianism across a century.[5]

Wang Fengyi, also called Wang the Good (Wang Shanren 王善人), was an uneducated peasant who managed at age thirty-five to cure himself of a very serious illness. He then became aware of his healing abilities.[6] After

---

5 Links between Wang Fengyi and the Universal Morality Society are well known. See Duara, *Sovereignty and Authenticity*, 113. Goossaert and Palmer, *Religious Question in Modern China*, 96–97. For the links between Liu Yousheng and the Universal Morality Society see Luo Jiurong 羅久蓉, Qiu Huijun 丘慧君, and Zhou Weipeng 周維朋, Cong Dongbei dao Taiwan, Wanguo daodehui xiangguan renwu fangwen jilu 從東北到台灣—萬國道德會相關人物訪問紀錄 [From the Northeast to Taiwan: Compilation of Interviews with Figures Associated with the Wanguo Daodehui], 139–141 (Taipei: Zhongyang yanjiuyuan jindaishi yanjiusuo, 2006).

6 Song Guangyu dedicated an article to Wang Fengyi and his healing methods: Song, "Wang Fengyidexinglijiangbing王鳳儀的性理講病"[WangFengyi'sDiscourseonIllnessBasedon[His Conceptions] of Nature and Principle], in *Zongjiao wenhua lunwen ji* 宗教文化論文集, 214–241

a period dedicated to healing people, he developed a true system of "therapeutic *jiaohua*" based on the distinction between what we are ascribed when we are born (nature, heart/mind, body), our behavioral characteristics (five elements commanding our "response" to things affecting us in the world: metal, wood, water, fire and earth), and our means of interaction with the world (will, intention, heart/mind, body). Taiwanese scholar Lin Anwu 林安悟 pointed out that it might correspond to a popular and practical development of Song and Ming speculative Confucianism (literally "of the school of heart/mind and nature": *xin xing zhi xue* 心性之學).[7] There is no need here to delve into Wang Fengyi's teaching and its neo-Confucian roots. Suffice it to mention that the healing dimensions of self-cultivation were regularly emphasized in neo-Confucian writings. During the Song dynasty, a scholar-official as famous as Sima Guang 司馬光 (1019–1086) underscored for instance that harmony and equilibrium obtained by the means of ritual practice were instrumental in preventing diseases.[8]

The leader of the Yidan xuetang, Pang Fei, explains in the following way how he understands Wang Fengyi's methods:

> When Mr. Wang Fengyi talks about ethics, evokes nature (*xing* 性) and principle (*li* 理), and addresses the issue of nurturing and transforming the conditions of one's body and heart/mind (curing disease by focusing on nature and principle), his fundamental focus is on how to act in a good way so that each person rectifies him- or herself. If people manage to rectify themselves, then they will reach centrality and harmony and will be less the victims of the "five poisons" (*wu du* 五毒), namely resentment (*yuan* 怨), hate (*hen* 恨), irritation (*nao* 惱), anger (*nu* 怒), and worries (*fan* 煩). The five poisons provide favorable conditions for the appearance and development

(Yilan: Foguang renwen shehui xueyuan, 1999). See also Billioud, "Confucian Revival and the Emergence of *Jiaohua* Organizations," 303–305.

7 Lin Anwu 林安梧, "Yinyang wuxing yu shen xin zhiliao—Yi Wang Fengyi shi'er zi xin-chuan wei hexin de zhankai 陰陽五行與身心治療—以王鳳儀'十二字薪傳'為核心的展開" [Yin-Yang, Five Elements and Therapy of the Body and Mind: Developments Based on Wang Fengyi's Twelve Characters Transmission]. In *Zhongguo zongjiao yu yiyi zhiliao* 中國宗教與意義治療 [Chinese Religions and Therapies Based on the Meaning of Things], ed. Lin Anwu 林安梧, 211–241 (Taipei: Mingwen shuju, 1996). This article is dedicated to the study of Wang Fengyi's system.

8 Philip Clart, "The Concept of Ritual in the Thought of Sima Guang," in *Perceptions of Antiquity in Chinese Civilization*, ed. Dieter Kuhn et Helga Stahl, 250–252 (Heidelberg: Edition Forum, 2008).

of diseases and therefore unaffected people get affected, whereas those only suffering from small diseases develop big ones. Diseases grow in the flesh but roots are within heart/mind.[9]

As far as science is concerned, we have to acknowledge that it is not almighty. It is not by simply pushing a button that everything will immediately find its order. In our life pivotal elements are inner changes, what we construct and achieve based on our heart/mind and nature. Therefore, Wang Fengyi discusses the transformation of our nature (*hua xing* 化性), as does the Song-dynasty thinker Zhang Zai 張載, . . . when he mentions that "the great advantage in learning is that one can transform one's inner state."[10]

For Pang Fei, healing diseases is not the central point, but a prolongation of self-cultivation practices characterized by a continuum between the teaching of the sages, through their texts, our internal transformations enabling us to escape from the "five poisons" and finally our body and its vitality.

The "antitheoretical" relationship to Confucian texts may sometimes translate into a more emotional dimension than the well-articulated quest for "centrality" and "harmony" permeating Pang Fei's discourses and the Yidan xuetang's practices. To illustrate such a phenomenon, let us mention the case of a group gathering regularly since 2005 within the premises of Taiyuan's temple of culture (*wenmiao*) (Figure 3.1). Their objective is to read collectively in the open air the *Rules of the Disciples* (*Dizigui*).[11] The person in charge of this small group, Mrs. S., is a retired accountant in her sixties. She introduces herself as the disciple of the director of a traditional culture training center located in Anhui province and of the master of this director, the famous and venerable Buddhist Master Jingkong 淨空法師. She embraced the Buddhist faith very early, influenced by the writings of *guoxue* Master Han Huaijin, and she remained afterwards a vegetarian. However, she always found it difficult to understand the meaning of speculative Buddhist sutras. This is the reason why she turned to Confucianism and to the *Rules of the Disciple* that

9 Yidan xuetang 一耽學堂. *Yidan xuetang bangongshi xinwen jianbao* 一耽學堂辦公室新聞簡報 [Information Bulletin of the Yidan Xuetang], no. 6 (2009), no page number (distributed through an electronic mailing list). This short excerpt and the following one have been published in Billioud, "Confucian Revival and the Emergence of *Jiaohua* Organizations," 304.

10 *Yidan xuetang bangongshi xinwen jianbao*, no. 6 (2009), no page number.

11 Field observation, Shanxi, 2010.

FIGURE 3.1 Collective reading of the *Dizigui* in Taiyuan's temple of culture.
© Sébastien Billioud.

she discovered thanks to her masters (Box 3.1). In 2010, she was in charge of a group of around ten "volunteers" (*yigong* 義工) helping her to promote the teaching of this text. Activities consist of weekly group readings and exchanges (*fenxiang* 分享). There are usually around thirty participants, of all ages and conditions. Sessions begin with three big bows (*san jugong* 三鞠躬) in front of Confucius's statue, followed by around twenty minutes of slow and collective reading. Then, one of the participants comments upon the text. Mrs. S. insists on the fact that these readings are devoid of intellectual ambition:

> The *Rules of the Disciple* seems to be such an easy text! However, I have been reading it for six years now. We have to understand the real meaning of what we learn and carry it out in a serious way.[12]

The little group focuses on this single text, a simple one but on which wisdom is nevertheless supposed to crystallize. Therefore, Mrs. S. believes

---

12 Interview, Taiyuan, 2010.

BOX 3.1

The Rules of the Disciple 弟子規 *(Dizigui)*

The *Rules of the Disciple* is a short text used for the education of children that became highly popular and widely distributed during the Qing dynasty. Written under the reign of Emperor Kangxi (r. 1661–1722) by an obscure scholar named Li Yuxiu 李毓秀, it encapsulates in short three-character sentences the most important behavioral rules toward the other, including the master. It is totally rooted in the Confucian tradition and draws its inspiration partly from the *Analects* of Confucius. The sentences of the first part (titled: At home, be filial; *ru ze xiao* 入則孝) give a flavor of what the text looks like:

Fu mu hu ying wu huan 父母呼,應勿緩
Fu mu ming xing wu lan 父母命,行勿懶
Fu mu jiao xu jing ting 父母教,須敬聽
Fu mu ze xu shun cheng 父母責,須順承

When parents call you, reply promptly
When parents give you instructions, act and do not dawdle
When parents teach you something, listen to them respectfully
When parents complain about you, obey and accept their scolding

Along with the *Classics of Filial Piety* (*Xiaojing* 孝經) and other texts, the *Dizigui* plays today a pivotal role in the classics learning movement by children, but even more broadly. Thus it has been for instance reported that this text has been used by a police superintendent in the Beijing area so as to settle problems of juvenile delinquency. The *Dizigui* has also been the focus of CCTV program *Baijia jiangtan* 百家講壇 (Lecture Room).*

*On this point, see Duléry, Conférences, usages du passé et propagande.

that there is no need to use other texts and speaks ironically about all those learning the classics by rote:

What's the need? Isn't the only important thing to know how to carry out what we have learnt?

The awareness of the importance of what is being read generates within the group a strong emotional intensity. Thus, during the exchange sessions between the participants—when the latter publicly express their progress and difficulties—not infrequently everyone ends up crying.[13]

The importance of emotions—in contrast with theoretical speculations—is also often prevalent in a phenomenon frequently encountered in the course of fieldwork: The promotion of a Confucian education largely based on music. Historically, music and rites were often combined since they shared harmony as a common foundation. More generally, music has always been enhanced in Chinese culture.[14] As is well known, one of the six great Confucian classics—today lost—was dedicated to music, and music, along with rites, archery, charioting, calligraphy, and mathematics was one of the "six arts" (liu yi 六藝), that is, one of the pillars of classical education. Music was supposed to provide some mediation making it possible both to interiorize cosmic order and to exteriorize the state of inner equilibrium attained by the sage.[15]

The use of music nowadays takes different forms. Thus, in a recreated place of worship in the city of Shenzhen (see chapter 6), a room is dedicated to music and a number of guqin (古琴, a sort of Chinese zither) are put at the disposal of the "adepts" who regularly come to practice. In some of the sishu introduced in chapter 2, music is also pervasive, whether as background sound or as self-cultivation practice for children.[16] Let us now mention the case of a society opened in Xi'an, whose objective is the promotion of aesthetic and moral education for children but also for young students.[17] This society was founded in 2000 by Mrs. Deyin 德音, a young woman employed in a government office who had already been involved in the promotion of classics reading for children. Encouraged by Wang Caigui, she began to research and gather material on music, which had

---

13 This strong emotional dimension characterized by deep weeping can be encountered in the most diverse religious groups, from the Chinese "born again" to the Yiguandao.

14 See the pages dedicated by Lévi to music: Jean Lévi, Confucius (Paris: Pygmalion, 2002), 206–215.

15 Ibid., 208.

16 Sometimes—e.g., in sishu 4—the musical sound is omnipresent throughout the day, especially during the long hours of classics memorization. One may wonder to what extent the environment thus created does not ascribe to music—heard and not performed—a function of normalization and molding that would be the antithesis of the "natural impulsions in their spontaneity and freshness" mentioned by Jean Lévi in his Confucius, 210.

17 This development is based on Ji Zhe's article "Educating through Music: From an 'Initiation into Classical Music' for Children to Confucian 'Self-Cultivation' for University Students," China Perspectives 2008, no. 3 (2008): 107–117.

been for her a life-long interest. The focus of her research was how music could embody the culture of sages and men of virtue.[18] This resulted in the production of a textbook of initiation into Chinese classical music, accompanied by original recordings. The crux of her method is not the transmission of musical knowledge but a gradual impregnation process enabling "silent transformations" within the individual by musically nurturing his or her natural moral dispositions. Beyond Xi'an, Deyin's method was used to train hundreds of masters countrywide thanks to a long-term cooperation with the Confucian studies institute of Renmin University. She even obtained official recognition since her program of initiation into classical music was incorporated into the Tenth Five-Year Plan (2001–2005). Her activities could also develop in the direction of the universities thanks to the support of the China Charity Foundation.[19]

Deyin's action emphasizes an "ethical-aesthetic" approach to education. Beyond intellectualism, she calls for all the resources of the body, of perception, and of emotions to inspire children and students and invite them to exert "natural values" such as benevolence (*ren* 仁) or to "extend their innate moral knowledge" (*zhi liangzhi* 致良知). In so doing, she echoes aforementioned practices that left aside speculations and accumulation of knowledge and insists on the need to appropriate texts by the means of slow reading and exercises, on the therapeutic value of self-cultivation, and on the benefits of emotionally sharing one's feelings when reading words of the sages.

In sum, reconstructions of Confucian education often aim at transforming the whole person starting with the body. The body may be the one of the adult, but more often than not it is the one of the primary target of this transformation enterprise: The child.

Transformation of the Other: The Child

As already mentioned, the classics reading movement (*shao er dujing*) is one of the most prominent features of the current reappropriation of traditional culture. This movement is developing in very different contexts: Lucrative schools where pupils attend a few complementary courses on top of compulsory education; public (i.e., government-run) schools,

---

18 Mrs. Deyin was especially interested in the guqin's "sounds of virtue." For a detailed explanation, see Ji, "Educating through Music," 109–112.

19 Ibid., 113–114.

where the pedagogical team manages to include classics reading sessions within the curriculum; *jiaohua* organizations; informal neighborhood or friendly societies inviting a tutor; reactivated traditional or pre-Maoist educational structures (*sishu, shuyuan, xuetang*); temples (and particularly Buddhist temples); companies; governmental structures. The overall phenomenon tends to be massive.

The role of a Taiwanese disciple of Mou Zongsan, Wang Caigui, has already been emphasized and it is possible to notice that his name is a pervasive reference in activist circles. Wang is both a key actor of the practical promotion of classics reading and a "theoretician" of education. In the following sections, we first introduce the methods he advocates, since they in a way constitute a sort of matrix for a variety of different enterprises. Afterwards, we come back to some of the enterprises introduced in chapter 2 and attempt to show that even though Wang is inspirational his methods remain critically appropriated and give birth to very different pedagogical projects.

Theories of Wang Caigui

Wang Caigui's classics learning method is frontally opposed to a "modern education" said to be primarily inspired by "American utilitarianism" and founded on the primacy of the child (*ertong zhongxin benwei* 兒童中心本位). He identifies three main characteristics of the educational approach he condemns:

(1) Selected textbooks follow a "principle of assimilation." This means that they are based on the children's understanding ability and on a progressive approach. They first tackle what is superficial and easy before things deep and difficult. They provide only the amount of knowledge that a child can understand.

(2) Educational objectives embrace a "utilitarian principle": A child is given only knowledge that he [practically] needs in his life.

(3) Teaching methods are governed by a "principle of interest:" One adapts to the interests developed by the child. [The underlying postulate is that] he will only learn well things he is interested in.[20]

---

20 Wang Caigui 王財貴, "Ertong jingdian songdu de jiben lilun 兒童經典誦讀基本理論" [Basic Theory of Classics Reading by Children], in *Jingdian daodu shouce* 經典導讀手冊 [Introductory Handbook for the Reading of Classics] (Beijing: Beijing shifan daxue yinxiang chubanshe, 2005), 4.

Wang Caigui fiercely criticizes this pedagogy and, more generally, a whole philosophy of education directly inspired by authors such as John Dewey. The "principle of assimilation" that he condemns is rooted for him in an artificial distinction between inculcating knowledge and shaping the child. The emphasis put on the child's understanding ability stems from a restrictive perspective on knowledge that excludes from the educational realm spiritual uplift and *Bildung* of the character. The "utilitarian principle" is also criticized since it assimilates education with immediate usefulness, thus neglecting the inculcation of values that will in fact be useful when the child becomes an adult. As for the "principle of interest," it relies on the unverifiable assumption that children would not be interested in what they do not understand.[21]

Wang Caigui's approach claims to be overarching. Not only should children acquire knowledge, but they should also develop their natural dispositions (*xingqing de xuexi* 性情的學習), nurture their aesthetic sensibility, and open themselves to "eternal" (*yongheng de* 永恆的) teachings, that is, to the wisdom of the classics.[22] His method does not negate the necessity of a gradual learning process that would take into account the age of the children and their related abilities.[23] However, he does not consider these abilities merely from the perspective of an intellectual ability to understand. As far as he is concerned, the development of a child undergoes four successive phases. The second phase—on which the classics reading movement focuses—encompasses children from four to thirteen years old. Characterized by a very strong capacity to memorize and a fairly weak capacity for comprehension, this phase stresses the accumulation of basic knowledge that will serve the children throughout their lives, even if they are not able to understand it for the time being. This knowledge, which aims to nourish "the moral intelligence of the sages" and "cultivate the rectitude of the heart/mind, of nature, and of action," consists of the progressive assimilation of the classics, "starting with the most difficult and going toward the simpler" (*cong nan dao yi* 從難到易); in other words going in the opposite direction of comprehension ease. It is only much later, as their capacity to understand develops progressively, that the classics

---

21 Ibid.

22 Ibid., 5–7. Wang mentions "eternal books" (*yongheng de shu* 永恆的書).

23 Ibid., 4–10. In the same textbook see also the anonymous (though inspired by Wang Caigui) text "Wanmei de rencai, rensheng si jieduan jiaoyu linian," 1–3.

become intelligible resources for these children, illuminating their daily lives, their acts, and their choices.

Wang Caigui's conceptions of education and classics reading have strong historical roots.[24] Jacques Gernet, in a study on early education of children based on texts from the Song to the Qing dynasties, explains that: "Chinese authors are very careful to specify the ages in terms of the development of the child." The role of memory before puberty is emphasized: For Lu Shiyi 陸世儀 (1611–1672), "children under fourteen have not been troubled by sexual feelings, have good memories, and little comprehension."[25] Thus, it is necessary to take advantage of the extreme malleability of these years—especially before ten—to instill basic teachings. But Gernet also shows that alternative theories regarding the necessity of making children understand the content of the texts also existed. Though Xie Zhaozhe 謝肇淛 (1567–1624) insisted on the benefits of rote learning without comprehension, others such as Wang Yun 王筠 (1764–1854) were extremely critical of this approach.[26] The rather marked dissociation of learning from comprehension that is often found among contemporary Confucians is not, therefore, necessarily legitimized by historical precedent. In any event, there seemed to be a common emphasis on the importance to be given to texts considered the most precious. Cheng Duanli 程端禮 (1271–1345), followed by Lu Shiyi, maintain that commentaries should be set aside for concentration on the Four Books and the Five Classics, the cornerstones of the Confucian body of work.[27]

---

24 Many studies have been made of the education of children and of the methods of learning Chinese classics. See, for instance, the writing of Thomas H. C. Lee on the Song, or more recently, the important work by Bai, *Shaping the Ideal Child.*

25 Jacques Gernet, " L'éducation des premières années (du XIe au XVIIe s.)," in *Education et instruction en Chine,* ed. Christine Nguyen Tri and Catherine Despeux; vol.1, *L'éducation élémentaire* (Paris and Louvain: Editions Peeters, 2003), 38.

26 Jacques Gernet translates a text by Wang Yun: "The students are human beings, not dogs or pigs. Learning texts by heart without explaining their meaning is like reciting sutras or chewing on a piece of wood"; ibid., 42. In the same spirit, Gernet shows that Qing author Tang Biao 唐彪 is also extremely critical of mechanical learning, whereas Wang Rixiu 王日休, from the late North Song dynasty, maintains that children should be given an explanation of the texts they learn by heart.

27 Ibid., 37.

Classics Learning Pedagogy: A Few Cases

Wang Caigui's idea, according to which one should build upon a child's abilities at each age, permeates the classics reading movement. However, one should nevertheless stress that memorization is less an objective than a consequence. The children are generally not pushed to retain for the sake of recitation, but constant repetition of the texts (*nian* 念) results in the children ultimately memorizing them with increasing ease, to the point where they can recite (*beisong* 背誦) long passages and sometimes even complete texts.[28] Surprisingly, this is often the case for "Western classics" as well: Several times, we heard children recite entire sonnets of Shakespeare, which they had memorized through phonetic Chinese transcriptions and recordings, without speaking a single word of English (Figure 3.2). Parents and teachers all emphasize the joyful and playful dimension associated with the reading sessions (*le zai qi zhong* 樂在其中), a point that was nevertheless far from always obvious in the course of fieldwork.[29] The diametrically opposite example constantly cited is the teaching of mathematics in the modern education system, where children are considered to have difficulty assimilating knowledge that is not useful (either professionally or for personal development), and which is beyond their abilities.[30] The reading of the classics is also frequently accompanied by the teaching of "rites," which are most often little rules of behavior (greeting adults with a slight bow, dressing neatly, being tidy, etc.) modeled on the precepts of thinkers such as Zhu Xi, who, like other neo-Confucian reformers, insisted on the importance of having children acquire physical habits and better control of themselves.[31]

These general features are quite recurrent. However, as far as pedagogy is concerned there are significant differences between the various kinds of

---

28 As noted by Jacques Gernet, the term *du* 讀 (used in the expression *dujing*) carries the double meaning both of reading and rote learning; ibid., 41.

29 Historically, many authors have underlined the extremely disagreeable nature of this mechanical method of learning, even when they were genuinely convinced of its effectiveness. This was for example the case of Xie Zhaozhe. The monotonous and mechanical tone of the children reading the classics that we often—but not always—encountered in the course of fieldwork did not really make the joyful character of these sessions blatant.

30 The teaching of mathematics, while very strongly promoted in China, is denounced vigorously by Wang, "Ertong jingdian songdu de jiben lilun," 8–9.

31 Ibid., 25.

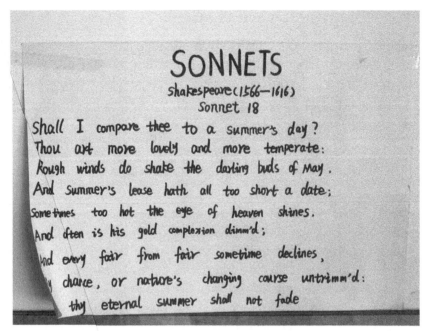

SONNETS
Shakespeare (1566—1616)
Sonnet 18

Shall I compare thee to a summer's day?
Thou art more lovely and more temperate:
Rough winds do shake the darling buds of May.
And summer's lease hath all too short a date;
Sometimes too hot the eye of heaven shines.
And often is his gold complexion dimm'd;
And every fair from fair sometime declines,
chance, or nature's changing course untrimm'd:
thy eternal summer shall not fade

FIGURE 3.2 A sonnets by Shakespeare on the wall of *sishu* 3.
© Sébastien Billioud.

Confucianism-inspired educational enterprises, and Wang Caigui's theories are appropriated in extremely different ways.

Reading sessions organized for children on the top of compulsory education are often rudimentary. This is for instance the case in Guangzhou, with daily classics reading organized by a local society for the children of a neighborhood. Pupils are lined up in a room and for fifteen minutes chant an excerpt of a classical text until they know it by heart. The tone is usually monotonous and mechanical, the rhythm often fast, in marked contrast to the deliberate cult of slowness practiced by the young participants of the Yidan xuetang. No explanation whatsoever is given about the text and the overall impression to the outside observer is that of a somewhat military rigidity. The approach is completely different in Guangzhou's Guangxiao temple. Sessions begin with a reminder about the importance of reading classics with a "quiet heart" and participants start with a time of "quiet sitting" (*jingzuo* 靜坐). Children and their parents are invited to sit straight, to put their hands on their thighs, and to close their eyes. After a few minutes, while everyone remains in the same position, a teacher tells a little moral story and the assembly is invited to slowly open their eyes and massage their face. The children are then asked a few questions about the content of the story. Answers are spontaneous and respectful (one bows in front of the teacher before answering), followed each time by applause. The next step is a collective reading of a text—when we visited the temple, it was the *Rules of the Disciples*. Volunteers go around the room to help children switching off and to make sure that bodies remain straight. At the end of the reading phase, a short explanation about the meaning of the text is given by one of the teachers.[32]

A somewhat similar pedagogical concern can be found among the adepts in charge of organizing classics reading classes in a Hong Kong Yiguandao place of worship (*fotang*). Whereas the absolute necessity to inculcate classical texts to the children is asserted, Wang Caigui's method is deemed too radical: It would not sufficiently take into account the well-being of the children so that classics reading become for them an immediately flourishing experience. During the weekly readings (one and a half hours in the temple, on the top of which one should add a daily time of reading at home), a quiet atmosphere is first created with smooth classical Chinese music in order to enable the children to calm down (Figure 3.3). Excerpts read collectively are not long and chosen each time in three different texts: Ruptures in the rhythm make it easier to have the children's full attention. The next sequence, twenty minutes long, is a time to "speak about what one has in one's heart" (*tanxin shijian* 谈心时间), during which role playing is used to illustrate how moral features could be nurtured. A relaxing time with a few recreational activities (drawing, handicraft, etc.) ends up the session.[33]

The cases mentioned so far only relate to *dujingban* 讀經班, that is, to classics reading classes organized besides normal school activities. It is now time to return to the situation of the four *sishu* introduced in chapter 2 and more specifically to the pedagogy they advocate. Two prevailing and broadly shared features, largely inspired by Wang Caigui, can be emphasized. On the one hand, these *sishu* have the ambition to provide an education of the whole person, as opposed to the simple transmission of knowledge supposed to characterize compulsory education. On the other hand, classical texts are instrumental in reaching such a goal. This being said, obvious differences also remain between these four projects.

---

32 Field observation, Guangzhou, 2011.

33 Field observation, Hong Kong, 2010. On Yiguandao education see Billioud, "Le rôle de l'éducation dans le projet salvateur du Yiguandao," especially 218–219.

FIGURE 3.3 Classics reading in a Yiguandao temple in Hong Kong under a portrait of Confucius.

© Sébastien Billioud.

Education of the whole person is promoted in the four schools against the absolute antimodel, that is, the compulsory education system. As was previously mentioned, for the directors of *sishu* 3 (Taiyuan), pupils become "increasingly stupid" in this system.[34] For one of the young mothers who opened *sishu* 4 (Shenzhen):

> Compulsory educations destroys the children's thinking abilities. They are force-fed with mathematics and become the opposite of gentlemen (*junzi* 君子) and sages.[35]

The "production" of gentlemen, sages if not saints, able to take over the highest responsibilities in society, is a discourse that can often (but not always) be heard, even if not necessarily with the same intensity. It is obvious in *sishu* 4 but also perceptible, to a lesser extent, in *sishu* 1 (Beijing) and 3.

---

34 Interview, Taiyuan, 2010.

35 Interview, Shenzhen, 2007.

We did not hear it in *sishu* 2 (Shanxi, Taiyuan's rural district). However, the necessity of moral—and not only intellectual—education, of something useful during the whole life, is a recurrent feature everywhere. The director of *sishu* 2 explains his position in the following way:

> The child that we educate here is not simply a child who studies but also a child who lives and develops feelings.[36] We want to develop his rectitude (*yang zhengqi* 養正氣).

The idea of nurturing children's moral and behavioral rectitude (*yang zheng, yang zhengqi*) is an ancient one. During the Ming dynasty, Lü Desheng 呂得勝 (who passed away in 1568) indicated that this was precisely the objective of education.[37] For the people in charge of *sishu* 2 for whom the priority is not the production of Confucian sages but the experimentation of an educational model relevant to China's future, nurturing such a rectitude demands a comprehensive and multifaceted education of the child. Therefore, reading Confucian classics can in no way be the only pedagogical approach and they are quite critical about Wang Caigui's method: "Wang Caigui hopes that the children will know the classics off by heart, but our approach is much more comprehensive (*quanmian* 全面)." For Mr. L., the most important thing is to preserve the child's balance: "He needs to sleep enough and play. Children who cannot play well are not clever." The emphasis put on such a dimension is not new and can be found in the writings of scholar-literati such as Wang Yangming 王陽明 (1472–1529), who laments that poetry is being neglected, or Lü Desheng, who underscores the playful dimension of singing. As for Mr. L., amusement requires for him physical activities, since development of the body (*ti neng* 體能) is considered a prerequisite to the development of moral intelligence (*zhi neng* 智能). Amusement can also be found in the contact with nature, all the more so in that *sishu* 2 is located within a farm. Children actually also learn how to grow fruit and vegetables, a situation that also exists in *sishu* 1. Besides classics learning, this *sishu* also encourages children to practice calligraphy (Way of writing, *shudao* 書道, rather than Art of writing, *shufa* 書法) as well as physical activities. In *sishu* 3, it is music that is considered a source of both pleasure and moral awakening.

---

36 Interview, Shanxi, 2010.

37 Gernet, "L'éducation des premières," 24–25.

Among the four *sishu* discussed here, it is probably *sishu* 2 that ascribes the least importance to the classics. Classics need to be fostered, but along with a whole set of other activities likely to contribute to a sound development of the child. The three other schools consider memorization a priority, but with some differences, and whereas there is little doubt that directors of *sishu* are all inspired by Wang, they do not necessarily openly recognize this influence.[38] In any case, in all these schools classics are ascribed some sort of peculiar performative function that sometimes entails an almost magical dimension in the fields of knowledge, sociability, and wisdom.

In all the four *sishu*, the benefits of classics reading for the acquisition of knowledge are underlined. Mr. L. (*sishu* 2) explains that:

> If we look at the content, what is being taught in the official education system is much too basic. Eighty percent of the students at the bachelor level (*benke*) at university do not have the level of an eight-year-old child in our school.[39]

For Mr. W. (*sishu* 3), reading classics entails three main benefits for the children: It increases their capabilities of memorization (*jiyili* 記憶力), understanding (*lijieji* 理解力), and concentration (*zhuanzhuli* 專注力) (Box 3.2). The increase in the ability to memorize is not difficult to understand given the intensive training of the children. In *sishu* 1, pupils are supposed to read each of the great classical texts up to a thousand times.[40] In that context, the development of an ability to concentrate is no surprise either: Not only do the children memorize texts, but their lives are also well disciplined and in some cases largely cut off from society's mainstream. As for their recreational time, it is also closely supervised—one does not waste time surfing the Internet in a *sishu*. But these contextual elements do not prevail in Mr. W.'s speech. His conception of the benefits provided by classics, including concentration, seems to be primarily linked to *a real faith in the powers* of classical texts: The performative dimension ascribed

---

38 Mr. F. of *sishu* 1 mentions that he has no master but the emphasis both on memorization and aesthetics echoes Wang's theories. In *sishu* 3, Mr. W. also insists that children may start very early on with the most difficult texts. The woman in charge of *sishu* 4 explains that Wang Caigui is her master.

39 Interview, Taiyuan, 2010.

40 Interview, Beijing, 2010.

BOX 3.2

Importance of Reading the Classics and Vacuity of the Knowledge Acquired in the Compulsory School System

In order to illustrate the importance of reading the classics, the founders of *sishu* 3 presented us with the following demonstration:

"Imagine," says Mr. W, "that we take two five-year-old children and that we require from each of them that they memorize a different text. The first text, that I now write on the left on the blackboard (see Figure 3.4), reflects the kinds of things usually taught in the compulsory education system. The second text, on the right, is the kind of text that children learn in our school."

FIRST TEXT (INTRODUCED AS THE ARCHETYPE OF TEXTS STUDIED IN THE NORMAL EDUCATIONAL SYSTEM)

Which animal has a long tail? Which animal has a short tail? Which animal has a tail that looks a bit like an umbrella? The monkey has a long tail. The rabbit has a short tail. The squirrel has a tail that looks a bit like an umbrella.

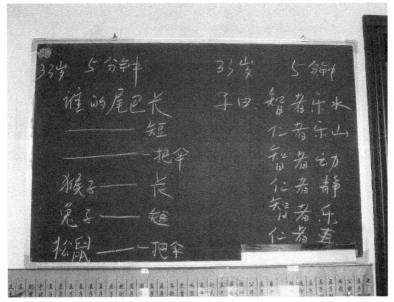

FIGURE 3.4 The importance of reading the classics: A demonstration in *sishu* 3.
© Sébastien Billioud.

BOX 3.2 Continued

SECOND TEXT (REPRESENTATIVE OF CLASSICS-BASED
SISHU EDUCATION): AN EXCERPT OF THE *ANALECTS*
OF CONFUCIUS (6:23)*

The Master said:

> *The wise** enjoys water*
> *Those authoritative in their conduct enjoy mountains*
> *The wise are active*
> *The authoritative are still*
> *The wise find enjoyment*
> *The authoritative are long-enduring*

"When the children are in their thirties what will be left of the five minutes they spent learning these texts? There will be nothing valuable left for the person coming from the compulsory education system. But the one who memorized this excerpt of the *Analects* will be able to understand it and this will make him think. And what about the situation when they become old? The person who learnt the *Analects* will look like a venerable sage. As for the one who will mumble at ninety that the monkey has a long tail and the rabbit a short one, everyone will believe that he has turned senile! The tragic point about the compulsory education system is that, in its spirit, it is based on the rote learning of things as useless as the size of the monkey's tail or that of the rabbit."

* Ames and Rosemont, *Analects of Confucius.*

** The character *zhi* 智 that can be seen written on the blackboard in Figure 3.4 differs from the original *zhi* 知 character in the *Analects* 6:23.

---

to classics reading (i.e., the fact that classics reading transforms children and increases their abilities) largely stems from such a faith. As for the increase in the understanding ability of the children and in their capacity to analyze problems, it is especially interesting since one would not spontaneously associate these capabilities with a form of education that, in its most extreme forms, does not seem to ascribe much room to intellectual autonomy and critical thinking. However, Mr. W. insists that the development of understanding capabilities is obvious if one looks at the way children enrolled in *sishu* 3 perform in mathematics:

Aged nine, children have already acquired, thanks to the classics, some good memorization, concentration, and understanding abilities. It then becomes possible to give them some mathematics textbooks. We give them a first textbook and ask them to read it within five days. Afterwards, they receive a second textbook to which they dedicate seven days. Finally they are given a third textbook that keeps them busy for ten days. They read approximately twenty pages per day. They need to write down things that they do not understand and may discuss them with other pupils. But in any case, they need to keep on reading since difficulties are thus gradually solved. Teachers do not interfere. If some children find that mathematics are too difficult, they leave them aside for a while and study more classical Chinese (*wenyanwen*).[41]

It would be difficult to find pedagogical approaches to teaching mathematics that would be more clashing with Western methods—or with current Chinese methods—than this one. The discourse about mathematics in this *sishu* is not devoid of paradoxes. On the one hand, the centrality of this subject in the compulsory curriculum is fiercely criticized since it is considered both useless and difficult to understand. For *sishu* educators, the extreme importance ascribed to mathematics in China does not make sense. On the other hand, reading classical texts seems to make it possible to overcome any difficulty encountered. The child educated in "holy texts" (the *Analects* are considered "the Bible of the Chinese"[42]) is supposed to develop an intellectual agility capable of solving the most complex problems. In *sishu* 3, this assertion is linked to a precise method for delving into the classics. Besides memorization, Mr. W. insists on the necessity to teach the etymology of Chinese characters. The study of *jiaguwen* (甲骨文), the ancient oracular scriptures, is supposed to develop the children's capabilities of imagination and logical thinking due to their visual and "pictographic" properties. However, in *sishu* 4, where the critical discourse about mathematics resembles the one of *sishu* 3, it is simply the impregnation of classical texts that is supposed to provide the children with superior wit so that in the end anything remains possible for them.

---

41 Interview, Taiyuan, 2010.

42 Interview, *sishu* 3, Taiyuan, 2010.

Apart from the realm of knowledge, classics are also ascribed a real efficacy in the field of sociability. This can be observed in a more or less blatant way in the different schools. In the most open, *sishu* 2, one can at least point to a reasonable optimism, since humane qualities nurtured in this type of education are supposed to facilitate relationships with others. But in the most radical *sishu* 4 the performativity ascribed to classical texts almost reaches a magical dimension. It was previously mentioned that this school maintained an extreme degree of tension with its environment. Since the rule is to protect the children from any form of "outside pollution," children lack opportunities to interact with and face the real world. For the initiator of this *sishu*, this remains a secondary issue, unlikely to generate problems later. The wisdom of the classics will boost children's abilities to integrate themselves (*hequn* 合群) into society. Furthermore, classics learning (i.e., memorization) is supposed to lead children to some sort of inner state where they manage to spontaneously respond to all that affects them in the way advocated by the classics. The lives of people educated in *sishu* should "become like a classic" (literally, *wo shi jingdian* 我是經典: "I am a classic").[43] These ancient texts become the vehicles of all kinds of expectations and their gradual appropriation is considered a practical way towards a supreme state of sagehood or saintliness.

The valorization of classical texts and of their intrinsic efficacy also has the following consequence: While activists may rightfully refer to historical tradition in legitimizing their practices, the emphasis is deliberately placed on direct literal access to ancient texts without any kind of interpretive mediation. Pushing aside exegetes and commentators, and along with them the whole hermeneutic tradition that was an important part of Confucian teaching—even though one could rightly object that this tradition was primarily lively in academies and not in *sishu*—presents a more general problem: The possible development in today's China of a specific form of "Confucian fundamentalism." Besides, the absolute primacy of classics reading may also have an unexpected effect in the most radical schools:[44] A complete withdrawal of the figure of the master. Thus, in *sishu* 4, "masters" selected by the parents were young girls in their early twenties without any university education. Their main qualification was that they gave value to self-cultivation and therefore presented some guarantees of

---

43 Interview, Shenzhen, 2007.

44 This of course does not apply to all the schools.

morality. In that context, the charisma traditionally associated with the figure of the master disappears in front of the efficacy that faithful parents ascribe to the memorization of texts. Such a situation is completely different from the one prevailing in some of the structures organizing courses for adults where, by contrast, one can observe the prominent position of charismatic masters and the reconstruction of quasi-spiritual lineages.

The disappearance in some situations of the figure of the master is not without relation to a last dimension of the new anti-intellectualist Confucianism: Its constant reference to the people.

Confucianism away from the Elites: The People

The actual revival of Confucianism has broad popular roots. Many activists come from modest backgrounds, peasant or working-class. Pang Fei, the charismatic director of Yidan xuetang, is one example; we have already mentioned his openly acknowledged working-class background. Today, activists who create Confucian websites, organize reading groups of the classics in society, invite employees to read the classics in their enterprises, and even open schools, are often from similar backgrounds. They have not necessarily attended universities, and their rediscovery of Confucian tradition follows very different paths.[45] It is clear that this phenomenon, on the whole, is not a top-down movement led by an academic or politically institutionalized "elite" (*jingying* 精英): In the 2000s, it is a popular endeavor (*pingmin* 平民) in both origin and vocation. In addition to the activists, supporters, and sympathizers of this movement, who are sometimes recruited from more privileged classes of society (students, cadres, and members of the business community), there are also large numbers of ordinary employees and workers.[46]

Thus, during a discussion group about traditional culture and Confucianism at the Shenzhen restaurant mentioned above, about fifty or so people in the audience came from modest backgrounds and various age groups. Among them were workers, owners of small businesses, and

---

45 We do not have comprehensive statistics on the social origins of the Confucian activists, but we have observed the frequency of this phenomenon during many extensive interviews with activists in various regions of China.

46 Our study has been carried out for the most part in urban and periurban areas, and further field investigation should complement it to obtain a better understanding of the situation in the rural areas.

restaurant employees (waiters, a cook). Some with "peasant household registration" (*nongmin hukou* 農民戶口) had come to look for work in the city, whereas others had jobs as manual laborers for government enterprises. Several told us they had become dedicated to the practice of daily readings of the *Analects* of Confucius, going so far as to memorize them in classical—not vernacular—Chinese. They openly expressed their pleasure at having access to this form of culture, and regret at not having done so earlier. We observed comparable phenomena in other cities and contexts.[47]

What are the references for this kind of "Confucianism for the masses"? Rarely are they scholarly academic treatises. Direct access to the ancient texts is the priority; when commentaries are taken into account, it is primarily to shed light on the relationship between the teachings of the sages and concrete daily life. The role of Nan Huaijin, a specialist and propagator of Buddhism who went to Taiwan as a refugee in 1949, is important in this respect. His works have been very popular on the mainland ever since 1990, as much on account of his personality as for his personalized reading of the classics (including Confucian ones), which for many people constitute an entry into traditional culture. In a somewhat comparable spirit, the Yidan xuetang recently edited three works from the late Qing dynasty ascribed to Wang Fengyi, introduced as a peasant who "gained awareness of The Way" (*wu dao* 悟道).[48] We mentioned earlier the name of Wang, who was involved in one of the largest redemptive societies of the republican era. In his introduction to these works, Pang Fei stresses the fact that Wang never had any formal education and that his wisdom was above all grounded in life experience: "This rural language he uses," declares Pang, "is the language of life." In other words, the teaching originates from the common people and returns to the common people. It avoids the detour made by the sophisticated discourse of the so-called elite. It is the diffusion

---

47 Popular Confucianism often means to be "useful" and applicable in resolving concrete problems. The meeting to which we have just referred dealt for the most part with the positive role that traditional culture could play in educating children. For this reason, it was centered on sharing experiences, each person revealing his problems, and the coordinator of the session offered solutions. There is even a Confucian website calling itself *shijian ruxue*, "Practical Confucianism."

48 Wang Fengyi 王鳳儀, *Cheng ming lu* [vol. 1: On the Brilliance of Authenticity]; *Du xing lu* [vol. 2: On a Firmly Established Practice] (Changchun, Jilin sheying chubanshe, 2003); *Jiating lunli jiangyanlu* [vol. 3: On Family Morality] (Beijing: Yishu yu renwen kexue chubanshe, 2006).

of this rediscovered tradition among the masses that will enable a renaissance of culture and the nation.

More broadly speaking, the relationship between the "people" and the "elite" no longer offers the neat simplicity that still characterized it in the 1980s, when intellectuals, united in a widely shared vision of their role as defenders of the "Enlightenment," spontaneously considered themselves to represent the superior interests of a nation faced with the authoritarianism of political and ideological power. The former model of the "universal intellectual" was replaced by much more diversified figures: Independent academics, media intellectuals, think tankers, militants committed to the recognition of specific rights, and so on. The relationship of the intellectual to the "people" evolved to the same degree as his relationship to the state. In this we can see tensions that were unthinkable before: The idea of the "intellectual against the people" (and the reverse) has now become a perfectly acceptable model.

Intellectuals with different qualifications who consider themselves part of the Confucian revival sometimes diverge in their critical assessment of the manifestations of "popular Confucianism." Some radical cultural conservatives extol the virtues of authoritarian confucianization controlled by an elite who would take into account both national interests and cultural tradition.[49] Some other intellectuals are critical of the vulgarization of teaching and the populist derivations they can produce. Thus Peng Guoxiang 彭國翔, a Tsinghua (now Zhejiang University) professor, cautioned at the end of 2006 against the risk of "narrow nationalism," which he considered "the kiss of death" for Confucianism.[50] Accordingly, he called for a serious study of the Confucian tradition in view of its authentic "reestablishment" (*chongjian ruxue chuantong* 重建儒學傳統). Naturally, this serious study is subject to the intellectual credentials of those who speak in the name of Confucianism. The expression of the ambiguous relationship between the "Confucian" intellectual and popular movements is particularly clear in a veritable social phenomenon—the reading of the classics by Yu Dan 于丹.

---

49 See for instance Kang Xiaoguang 康曉光, *Renzheng, Zhongguo zhengzhi fazhan de di san jiao daolu* 仁政：中國政治發展的第三條道路 [Benevolence-Based Politics: The Third Way of Chinese Political Development] (Singapore: Global, 2005).

50 Peng Guoxiang 彭國翔, "Ruxue fuxing de shensi 儒學復興的慎思" [Pondering over the Confucian Revival], *Ershiyi shiji jingji baodao* 二十一世紀經濟報道, December 18, 2006, 34–35.

A professor of media studies, Yu Dan is not a specialist of Confucianism. In October 2006, Central Television (CCTV) invited this charismatic woman to introduce the *Analects* of Confucius in the context of one of its popular TV programs (*Baijia jiangtan*). The result was a lively presentation of the text accompanied by commentaries that emphasized personal experience and daily life. The program has been a triumphant success, and the book based on it has sold millions of copies. Reactions to this phenomenon, however, vary widely. Some prominent intellectuals supported Yu Dan. For instance, a discussion article by philosopher Li Zehou 李澤厚 pointed out that "her contribution was to reawaken an interest in the classics."[51] He described Yu's role as not that of an intellectual but of a preacher or an evangelist (*budaoshi* 布道師) who serves as a bridge between the elite and the common people.[52] Li Zehou also explained that the religious dimension of Confucianism has certainly been well presented by the scholarly works of contemporary Confucianists such as Mou Zongsan, but that the complexity and abstract nature of their formulations limit their effect on society. What was openly acknowledged here was the inevitable and desirable division of tasks between the scholar and the media popularizer. The intellectual historian Ge Zhaoguang 葛兆光 also recognized certain positive aspects of the phenomenon, but went on to emphasize the responsibility of the elites for the presentation and the popular diffusion (*tongsuhua* 通俗化, *pujihua* 普及化) of the classics. He felt they should have better control of the difficult art of vulgarization "in order to progress in concert with the general population, and not be pulled down by it."[53] Many academic criticisms, however, pointed out errors committed by Yu in her interpretation of the texts and the superficiality of her analyses. For her detractors, Yu was simply not qualified to express herself on the subject. In an effort to have her book withdrawn, ten doctoral candidates signed a widely circulated petition in which they denounced the betrayal of the teachings of the old master and the way he was being thrown into the pasture of the ignorant masses.

---

51 Li, "tamen shi jingying he pingmin zhijian de qiaoliang," *Nanfang Zhoumo* 南方週末, March 22, 2007, 28 (interview).

52 Ibid., *jingying yu pingmin zhijian de qiaoliang* 精英與平民之間的橋樑.

53 Ge Zhaoguang 葛兆光, "Ge Zhaoguang: yao gongtong tisheng bu neng jiti chenlun 葛兆光: 要共同提升, 不能集體沈淪" [Ge Zhaoguang: We Need to Progress Together, We Cannot Sink Together]. *Nanfang Zhoumo* 南方週末, March 22, 2007, 28 (interview).

During the 2000s the two poles of the Confucian revival—*pingmin* 平民 (common people) and *zhishi jingying* 知識精英 (intellectual elites)—gave the impression of not communicating much with each other. There are, of course, areas of mutual permeability, and many intellectuals now participate in the current movement of *ruxue fuxing* (Confucian revival). This is particularly apparent in the revival of the classic institution within the university and this trend was probably reinforced at the end of the 2000s. A number of university professors also currently support the idea of social and educative commitment inspired by Confucianism and going beyond the narrow horizon of their professional obligations. But this new trend, however, should not prevent us from stressing the gap, during the first decade of the new century, between the academic world, which hardly anticipated the strong resurgence of interest in cultural tradition, and segments of the general population that progressively re-appropriated certain dimensions of this tradition. If some intellectuals maybe played a central role during the initial phase of this movement, they were "grassroots scholars" (*caogen xuezhe* 草根學者) not employed by university institutions but by ordinary schools, government offices, or companies. More often than not it was out of personal interest that they delved into texts and their commentaries, reading about intellectual and social history, and, for some of them, following scholarly debates. Gradually embracing a Confucian worldview, they were happy to share it with others, friends, family, or sometimes colleagues, or to involve themselves in local societies for the promotion of culture or education. Along with Confucian activists involved within the system—with whom they sometimes carried out joint projects—these grassroots scholars, who are not necessarily visible, were and are still pivotal components of the current Confucian revival.

The local dimension of popular or grassroots Confucianism requires a few comments regarding a recurrent narrative about the Chinese countryside in the circles of Confucian activists.

For some, the soil and the peasant world are invested with a strong "mystique" or imaginary dimension. The project of reconstructing Chinese civilization based on the countryside thus makes Liang Shuming a tutelary figure for these reinvented genealogies. The example of barely educated peasants gaining access to wisdom and illumination from their own experience, far removed from intellectual pedantry, is for instance held up as a model for the Yidan xuetang. In view of this, it is not surprising that the movement invites its participants to return to the countryside, in particular by arranging field trips. Since they don't have the means to organize truly structured activities in the countryside, this orientation mainly serves as a rite of initiation—plunging into the peasant world and striding along country paths becomes for these young urbanites a much more tangible, almost physical, experience of the Chinese civilization of their dreams.

For many activists, the countryside is considered the cradle of Chinese culture and, by extension, of Confucianism. Furthermore, it is also often described or dreamed of as the place where this tradition could be preserved by the people. Here, Confucianism in no way means an intellectual enterprise but rather an *ethos* and a number of practices that could be perpetuated both throughout the vicissitudes of Chinese modern history and in spite of the individualization and Westernization of current society.

Aged thirty-four, Mr. Q. works as an independent journalist for a local Shanxi newspaper. Besides, he is also active in a cultural society where he teaches a course on the *Analects*. A typical representative of the grassroots intellectuals mentioned above, he was born into a peasant family. At fourteen, he discovered traditional culture after he purchased an introduction to the thought of Zhu Xi. The reading of this book was for him some sort of shock:

> I was struck to discover how one could introduce those deep truths with just a few words. This book was infinitely more precious than all my school textbooks.[54]

He then began to read a lot: The *Analects*, Xunzi ("a man from Shanxi province!"), Mencius, as well as a number of major neo-Confucian texts of the Song and Ming dynasties. He describes this phase as the one when he became aware of the links between Confucian thought and the prevailing values of the rural society he was living in:

> People from the countryside refer each day to these values without knowing much about them.[55] They permeate their lives and are

---

54 Interview, Taiyuan, 2010.

55 *Baixing riyong er bu zhi* 百姓日用而不知.

celebrated under a variety of different forms. For instance, in our village there have always been operas, through which values of loyalty (*zhong* 忠) or filial piety (*xiao* 孝) were encouraged. Music also plays an important role for instance during major ceremonies (funerals, weddings, . . .). And at the very foundation of Confucianism there are rites such as those that have always been organized in our place to honor "the two deities"[56] even during the Japanese invasion or during the Cultural Revolution. Customs never disappeared, even during the Cultural Revolution. They can survive independently from politics (*duli yu zhengzhi* 獨立於政治). People in the countryside have absorbed Confucianism, this is a faith that we all share (*gongtong de xinyang* 共同的信仰).[57]

These explanations are highly representative of at least one kind of pervasive discourse on the countryside. Confucianism is associated with a general system of traditional values that informs the daily life of village people. From this perspective, much more than academic discourses, the countryside becomes the symbolical source of a Confucianism that needs to be reconstructed and promoted.

Concluding Remarks about Confucian Education in the 2000s

In the 2000s, China experienced a number of educational enterprises claiming some forms of Confucian identity. They were remarkable due to their variety and their quick development.

They can be analyzed both as a reaction and as a creative process.

Their reactionary dimension is visible in concrete projects carried out in direct opposition to progressive pedagogical conceptions inherited from the May 4th period. In some of our interviews with Confucian activists (who were sometimes but not always influenced by Wang Caigui) the rejection of highly influential educational ideals promoted by John Dewey during the republican era—child psychology, science education, the role of the master, school as an experimental and democratic community, and so

---

56 Local cult: *liang ge niangniang* 兩個娘娘

57 Interview, Taiyuan, 2010.

on—was striking.[58] More generally, such a perspective challenges the position of the twentieth-century "Chinese enlightenment" regarding values prevailing in the transmission of knowledge and perpetuation of culture.

However, these new movements also display a large amount of creativity thanks to their active, inventive, and unpredictable exploration of new forms of education that are not necessarily forms of indoctrination. The fact that these initiatives often emanate from the "people" (however this term may be interpreted) indicates that they are not purely ideological phenomena that can be reduced to mere political instrumentalization or the invention of a new cultural market. In its most elaborated forms, this is certainly a minority movement, but the motivations of the activists are profound and might anticipate future developments.

We have undertaken this analysis of the present aspirations of a "Confucian revival," taking into consideration its educative dimension, because this particular dimension can be expressed with relative freedom in the official institutional area—or in a calculated relationship of distance from it. But the educative practice is naturally part of a larger cultural context. "Self-transformation" also carries the hope of being able to justify such an enterprise by referring to values that transcend the worldly, and to receive some kind of official recognition from government authorities: Religion, to which we now turn, is necessarily on the horizon of such ambitions.

58 For an overview of the Chinese reception of Dewey's pedagogical thinking over the twentieth century, see Barbara Schulte, "The Chinese Dewey: Friend, Fiend and Flagship," in *The Global Reception of John Dewey's Thought: Multiple Refractions through Time and Space*, ed. Rosa Bruno-Jofre and Jürgen Schriewer, 83–115 (London: Routledge, 2012). On the importance of Dewey's visit in China, see Jessica Ching-Sze Wang, *Dewey in China, to Teach and to Learn* (Albany, GA: SUNY Press, 2007), and Barry Keenan, *The Dewey Experiment in China* (Cambridge, MA: Harvard University Asia Center, 1977); On the contemporary significance of debates about Dewey and pragmatism see Joël Thoraval, "La tentation pragmatiste dans la Chine contemporaine," in *La pensée en Chine aujourd'hui*, ed. Anne Cheng, 103–134 (Paris: Folio, 2007).

PART II

Anshen Liming *(安身立命)*

The Religious Dimension of Confucianism

In the context of the rediscovery of a multifaceted Confucianism during the first decade of the new century, what is the meaning of emerging aspirations about and references to a properly religious dimension of Confucianism? Given the abolition of the imperial cult of Heaven, the transformation of traditional academies in modern teaching institutions, the decline of ancestral worship, and the conversion of Confucius temples (or temples of culture, *wenmiao*) into touristic sites, it is legitimate to wonder whether Confucianism-inspired religiosity might not be today more imaginary than real. Beyond commemoration of ancient ritual heritage or utopian dreams about possible ritual restoration, how significant are current narratives about a religious Confucianism?[1]

In fact, modern enterprises claiming a relationship to such a prestigious past can be understood only within the background of a hundred years of dramatic history, during which social transformations and Western influences impacted the whole religious field. A century of massive destructions has now left enough room for a number of ongoing reconfigurations: They provide some evidence of the difficulties generated by the reference to the modern Western concept of religion within a Chinese cultural context.[2]

---

1 The more general issue of the contemporary fate of ancient Chinese cosmology is discussed in chapter 10.

2 See Vincent Goossaert, "L'invention des 'religions' dans la Chine moderne," in *La pensée en Chine aujourd'hui*, ed. Anne Cheng, 185–213 (Paris: Gallimard, 2007); Goossaert and Palmer, *Religious Question in Modern China*. Anna Sun, *Confucianism as a World Religion: Contested Histories and Contemporary Realities* (Princeton, NJ: Princeton University Press, 2013).

One might today ask how it is possible to identify within the current upheavals in Chinese society phenomena that could reveal an aspiration to a religious revival of Confucianism. The fieldwork conducted for this study provides only imperfect answers to this question. In fact, within a social environment deeply influenced by the religious policy of the authorities, it might be useful to temporarily suspend the use of familiar categories of the sociology of religion to pay empirical attention to a body of discourses and practices that remain ambiguous due to their multiple meanings and the rapid societal changes affecting them.

Some insight into these new circumstances is provided by the symptomatic proliferation of references to the multivocal term *xin* 信 (trust). A pervasive narrative laments the absence or decline of this value within social interactions today while ascribing to it a variety of different meanings from "trust" to "belief."[3]

For example, a worker coming from Hubei province and employed in one of the new industrial centers of the Pearl River Delta by a Dongguan-based shoe manufacturer one day decides to resign. Shortly afterwards, he is offered an opportunity to work in a restaurant opened by a young woman embracing Confucian ideals. In such an environment, he finds a daily fulfillment by reading every morning, alone or together with other colleagues, the *Analects* of Confucius. He explains:

> The working conditions were hard in that factory. However, the problem was not material: I made more money than now. But in that factory, people had only money in mind and there was no trust (*xin*). I am much happier here.[4]

At the other end of the social scale—still in Guangdong province—an entrepreneur embracing the ideal of a Confucian revival also emphasizes the importance of trust, within his company, where employees are

---

3 Many analyses go in that direction. Thus, for Ci Jiwei, the justice crisis currently existing in Chinese society first translates into a lack of trust and can be understood as a collapse of reciprocity: It is no longer expected from other members of society that they should abide by standards of social coexistence and people take into account the incapacity of the state to impose those standards; Ci Jiwei, "La crise morale dans la Chine post-maoïste," *Diogène* 221 (2008): 32.

4 Interview, Shenzhen, June 2007.

encouraged to find in the classics inspirations for their lives, or within the broader social and economic environment.

Tracing the variety of contexts where the notion is invoked, it would be possible to outline a "general economy" of *xin* that would build upon both Chinese cultural tradition and the imperatives of the new capitalist society. Thus, one could emphasize three possible realms of such a virtue: The dimension of "trust" that instills social interactions, the dimension of "credit" that is expressed in economic relationships, and the dimension of "creed" that permeates religious relations in general. It is within such a context that the category of the "religious" applied to some aspects of the current Confucian vogue would find its specificities and limits.

This part of the book focuses on three dimensions of a multifaceted quest that the popular expression *anshen liming* 安身立命 encapsulates well. This expression is useful considering that the label "religion" is sometimes considered inadequate, if not irrelevant, by Confucian activists to describe their activities. It refers to the aims or ultimate concerns of human life and points both to a search for inner peace and a concern for a destiny, whether personal or sometimes collective.[5] In order to unveil the depth of a personal experience rooted in Confucian religiosity, the particular and complex itinerary of a businesswoman converted to Confucianism is first depicted. Understanding the meaning ascribed to the notion of religion then requires positioning this personal experience within the broader and shifting context of categorizations (religion, philosophy, science) that for long were taken for granted but that are now increasingly challenged not only in elite circles but also more broadly in society. Finally, in order to provide some insights into explicit and carefully devised projects aiming at granting an official and institutional recognition to Confucianism, we examine several attempts carried out in that direction and that aim at: (1) Transforming, *unus inter pares*, Confucianism into a specific religion in line with the other authorized religions in the PRC; (2) incorporating Confucianism within other syncretistic traditions; (3) promoting Confucianism as a state religion; (4) understanding Confucianism as a Chinese model of "civil religion."

---

5 On this notion see the collective volume Huo Taohui 霍韜晦, ed., *Anshen liming yu dongxi wenhua* 安身立命與東西文化 [*Anshen liming* and Eastern and Western Cultures] (Hong Kong: Fazhu chubanshe, 1992). On the link between this notion and that of "ultimate concerns" (*zhongji guanhuai* 終極關懷), see pp. 31, 42, 81. Mou Zongsan explains that "in the end, *anshen liming* point to our own inner heart/mind (*neixin* 內心)" (6).

4

"The Varieties of Religious Experience"

IN THE NEW city of Shenzhen, not much distinguishes the vegetarian restaurant of Mrs. D. from other establishments, apart maybe from its name, which alludes to "the Spring and Autumn of Poetry and Ritual." It is only through a friend or someone sharing the commitment of its owner that one can access what happens to be a little base of Confucian proselytizing. Visitors are warmly welcome by an enthusiastic woman in her forties, ready to share her personal odyssey and collective experience with a surprising combination of lucidity and fervor.[1]

Her story entails a series of dramatic events that follow a pattern often encountered in various types of religious experiences: An illusory happiness, a phase of downfall, and, ultimately, a painful access to salvation. At stake for us here is to understand the peculiar role played by the reference to Confucianism in this context.

The historical background of her youth was the end of the Maoist period—at fourteen, she joined a dancing troupe of the People's Liberation Army—and the transition to a new society after the reforms of the Deng era. In her own words:

> I come from an uneducated military family in Liaoning Province. My parents belonged to a generation that experienced only strug-gle. But what are the benefits of struggle—struggle between

---

1 All interviews with Mrs. D. in this chapter were conducted in Shenzhen in June 2007.

brothers, struggle between those on the top and those at the bottom? Today, my parents still belong to this generation of people revering Mao Zedong. The spiritual life (*jingshen shengming* 精神生命) of this generation has been destroyed. They have no peace of mind.

At age twenty she left the army and went to several cities in order to find some work. Her independent and entrepreneurial spirit could make the most of the opportunities offered by the flourishing market economy of the 1990s. She started as a simple waiter in a restaurant and, at twenty-five, became its director, joining by the same token the coveted category of people with over 10,000 RMB of monthly income. However, this easy life generated dissipation and anxiety:

> I had all possible material goods, but my life was a hell. I went wild, committed lots of mistakes you know. . . . When one has no education, no religion, no capacity of behaving in a really humane way (*zuo ren* 做人), but lots of money, one can easily go wild. . . . Usually, when someone commits a crime or a sin (*fanzui* 犯罪), he also repents (*chanhui* 懺悔), right? Not me. I couldn't care less. My life was out of control and I was incapable of any rational thinking (*lixing de sikao* 理性的思考). I realized that money would not solve all my problems and I indulged in all sorts of superstitions (*mixin* 迷信).

It was an encounter with Buddhism that enabled her to get out of this phase of dereliction. A Buddhist adept made her understand that she was heading toward her ruin: "It is as if you were dead, but you can live a new life. I cannot help you now, you first need to read Buddhist sutras."

> For three years, I have lived the life of a Buddhist (*jiaotu* 教徒) and I really became different from the others. I understood that bad deeds (*eguo* 惡果) originated from a bad heart (*exin* 惡心). Buddhism can turn people living in confusion into enlightened people. I read the sutras alone, but because of my life experience, I could understand them. Buddhism is not a religion. It does not command but teaches. Whereas we ask things from a God, we don't ask anything from the Buddha. Buddhism is a high wisdom that teaches the path

toward awakening or sagehood (*chengfo chengsheng* 成佛成聖). The ordinary man can become a Buddha: This is no superstition, but a real transformation.

This rupture marked the beginning of a new existence that could hardly be understood by her family and friends:

Today, I have nothing, no car or fixed income. I am not concerned about money and my parents believe that I have lost my mind. I don't care.

However, this Buddhist experience constituted only a first phase of what looks like a redemption: It is Confucianism that ascribed to her life a direction that she now considers to be a definite one. Her embrace of Confucianism started with a discovery of Wang Caigui's teachings on a CD originally purchased for her daughter. Wang began afterwards to play a pivotal role in her life. She had the chance to meet him in 2004 and would afterwards commit herself to a mission of disseminating Confucian wisdom among children and, more generally, in society. In her restaurant, she organizes classics reading classes for children and her employees, while customers and friends—themselves often parents with young children—are regularly invited to participate in conferences about Confucian education.

However, her commitment to Confucianism goes far beyond a mere educative project. From her encounter with Wang Caigui, she realized that Confucian teaching is relevant in a more general way for the destiny of humanity (*renlei de mingyun* 人類的命運):

If Confucianism were only a particular doctrine (*yi men* 一門) or just another ideology, it would not be worth studying. It is not simply a doctrine for scholars, but the path by which humanity can find refuge (*renlei guisu de fangxiang* 人類歸宿的方向). There are no racial or religious limits to Confucianism: It can solve the world's problems!

In spite of its singularity, Mrs D.'s experience provides an opportunity to question what could be called the properly religious dimension of Confucianism.

Confucianism and Conversion

It is difficult to characterize Mrs D.'s adhesion to Confucianism other-wise than as a conversion, since it implies a radical reorientation of her worldview and a reconfiguration of her value system. Her perspective on society, that is, the way she sees or understands it, is no longer that of the mainstream of Chinese people, reflected in the attitude of her parents, pri-marily concerned about material issues. Moreover, society has become for her the place of a "task" to be accomplished since her entire commitment aims at improving it by promoting around her—within her own family, among customers and employees—the way of Confucius.[2] Such a situ-ation is often encountered among entrepreneurs who feel invested of a social responsibility and consider Confucianism to be a tradition likely to contribute to the common good.

In the case of Mrs D., the adhesion to ultimate and reformist ideals of Confucian wisdom was preceded by a period of personal crisis and break-down. Such an experience is somewhat exceptional among businesspeo-ple embracing Confucian ideals. In fact, for the vast majority, we already underscored that Confucianism was rather a complement to their profes-sional striving or a fulfillment rather than a refuge in the wake of personal crisis. For some, reading Confucian classics and taking part in confer-ences organized by famous universities represent crowning achievements of a life of business success and the fulfillment of a need for intellectual stimulation and aspiration for less materialistic values. For others, it is also an opportunity to display one's cultural and social capital. However, in the course of fieldwork we also encountered other examples of crisis and ruptures that reflect "the varieties of religious experiences" leading to the Confucian way.

One of those examples is somewhat parallel to that of Mrs. D., while displaying interesting differences in the process of "conversion to" or embrace of Confucianism. An entrepreneur in the city of Taiyuan, Shanxi, Mrs G., a self-made woman with an extravert personality, also turned to Confucianism after an initial traumatic experience in the business world:

---

2 What could be called in a Weberian way Mrs D.'s *intramundane askesis* or inner-worldly asceticism (*innerweltliche Askese*) aims at refashioning society and not simply at confirming a possible religious charisma. Confucianism becomes for her, as for many activists, a project of social reform. Max Weber, *Wirtschaft und Gesellschaft* (Tübingen: Mohr Siebeck, 1980), 328–329.

From 1997 to 2004, I was involved in business activities. I opened a hotel. It was a dirty industry, exclusively oriented toward money. We had to do things in contradiction with our most basic principles. This was exhausting and we only thought about money. I lost a lot and then I stopped.[3]

During almost three years, Mrs G. felt confused and adrift. She decided to stop working and gave birth to a child. In 2007, friends who were members of a local society for the study of Confucianism invited her to a conference. She found the audience's fervor striking and met people who would afterwards influence her deeply. For instance, there was the case of an elderly woman who talked to her about Buddhism but also about Confucian culture:

I was really moved. I could recognize in her words things I really believed in.[4]

Those things recollected—and that had been for long obscured in the swirl of business life—were Confucian values, to which she had been exposed since her childhood, though not in an intellectualized and systematic way.

People of my generation primarily heard critiques against traditional culture. But my grandmother and my parents are the products of such culture. They are ordinary peasants (*putong nongmin* 普通農民) and my grandmother is even illiterate. However, she had a lot of wisdom (*hen you zhihui* 很有智慧). They transmitted Confucian values to me: Trust (*xin* 信), sincerity (*cheng* 誠), and the sense of filial piety (*xiao* 孝).[5]

Advised by her friends in *minjian* Confucian circles, and despite the perplexity of her husband, she gradually identified a new professional niche: The promotion in society of reinvented Confucian rites of passage.

---

3 Interview, Taiyuan, 2010.

4 Interview, Taiyuan, 2010.

5 Interview, Taiyuan, 2010.

Like Mrs D.'s case, the conversion of Mrs. G. took place in a context of chaos, when unfortunate youth experiences generated a cognitive need and a quest for meaning. However, despite superficial similarities, these two patterns of "conversion" also present significant differences and point to the diversity of experiences leading to Confucian religiosity.

Mrs. D.'s conversion is somehow the outcome of an intellectual and experimental process that led her from "superstitions"—about which she says hardly anything—to Buddhist faith before turning to Confucianism. To some extent, she tried a variety of alternative "spiritual solutions" before meeting a master and then embracing Confucianism. This type of journey, facilitated by the fact that religious faith in China is generally not exclusive, is anything but scarce. We mentioned earlier the case of the Pinghe academy in Zhuhai that offered a sort of community life to a little group of adepts, as well as an "activity hub" to a larger number of sympathizers. The founder and director, a successful businessman, also committed himself to Confucianism after a period of time spent in America during which he embraced the Bahá'í faith. Another example of a multifaceted "spiritual quest" is that of Mr. W. in *sishu* 3 (see chapters 2 and 3): His discovery of Confucianism had been preceded first by a genuine faith in Marxism and its dialectical materialism, and then by a deep interest in Christianity. There is an obvious dimension of *bricolage* in all these itineraries that also certainly results from a recent broadening of the "offer" on the Chinese religious market.[6]

Contrary to Mrs. D., to the director of the Pinghe academy, and to Mr. W., Mrs. G., the revivalist of passage rites, had a much less erratic and much more linear journey. It provides an insight into how a person grown up in a socialist and atheistic environment, without any special attraction toward religions, could finally commit herself to forms of Confucianism. As we see below, she spontaneously associates religion with superstition and does not see anything religious either in her approach or in her ritual activities. Mrs. D.'s and Mrs. G.'s embrace of Confucianism ensued from very different types of experiences that are nevertheless classic cases in the sociological literature on conversions. In brief, whereas the itinerary of Mrs. D. consisted of a relatively quick succession of experiences and changes, that of Mrs. G. was slow and progressive. Nearly three years

---

6 This familiar phenomenon has been studied elsewhere, for example in Western Europe: see Danièle Hervieu-Léger, *Le pèlerin et le converti. La religion en mouvement* (Paris: Champs, Flammarion, 1999), 42–53.

elapsed between the end of her business activity in the hotel industry and her participation in the activities of the local Confucian society. During this relatively long phase, it was as if Mrs. G. had been somewhat temporizing, thus offering a vivid contrast with the unceasing spiritual quest of Mrs. D. However, one can assume that the long period of exit from her previous life prepared her to be receptive to the words of the Buddhist adept who introduced her to Confucianism. In fact, it is precisely this encounter that appears to be, in Mrs. G.'s narrative, the critical event paving the way for her "conversion." This encounter actually marked the beginning of a second phase of slow reappropriation of traditional Confucian values that, two years later, she would put at the very center of both a professional and existential project[7].

The Role of Buddhism

It is necessary to emphasize here the particular role of Buddhism in these conversion itineraries. Mrs. G.'s interest in Confucianism was stirred up by a Buddhist devotee who insisted on the fact that "there are no great differences between the two traditions."[8] In the case of Mrs. D., this "Buddhist stratum" of her experience was not negated but amplified and reoriented toward Confucian teaching. It was therefore important for her to reaffirm the common spirit that is at the root of the two teachings, while emphasizing the superiority of the Confucian perspective:

> One should not exaggerate the differences between the Way of the Bodhisattva (*pusa* 菩薩) and that of the Sage. Those are different words to designate a same thing. The two teachings are rooted in real life. When one becomes a Bodhisattva, what else but real life can be the focus of one's attention? The point is not only to care for the self, to escape from vicissitudes of human existence (*fannao* 煩惱), to look for a Western paradise (*xitian* 西天). That's the same with Confucianism. Of course, some only study it for themselves

---

7 To some extent, Mrs. G.'s journey also raises classic issues of Chinese thought, such as—whether in Buddhism or in Song and Ming Confucianism—the understanding of self-transformation as a gradual process (*jian* 漸, *jianmo* 漸磨) or, to the contrary, as a sudden experience (*dun* 頓, *dunwu* 頓悟).

8 Interview, Taiyuan, 2010.

(*weile geren* 為了個人) or for academic reasons (*xueshu* 學術).
That's the attitude of petty persons (*xiaoren* 小人), they are not real
Confucians. One cannot withdraw from society.

One finds in this attitude a mix of very ancient elements and more
contemporary concerns. There is no need to trace the dialectic of tension
and proximity that the two teachings have maintained since at least the
Song dynasty, and one also knows how pivotal the role of Buddhism was
for the attempts to articulate a modern Confucian philosophy during the
twentieth century. At a time when Confucian institutions were gradually
dismantled, many scholars considered Buddhism the only possible coun-
terweight to Western hegemony: They appreciated both the sophistication
of its speculative constructions and its charitable enterprises addressing
people's needs. Occasionally this supposedly nonviolent doctrine could
also encourage nationalist mobilization, in the name of the Mahayanist
virtue of compassion applied to the community of citizens.[9] It was also
possible to find in Buddhism answers to existential crises generated by
social transformation that were not contradictory with a Confucian social
commitment.

Mrs. D.'s recurrent references to Liang Shuming provide some insights
into the importance respectively ascribed to Confucian and Buddhist teachings in popular movements of cultural reconstruction over one century. In
this book, so far, it has been rather Liang's Confucian commitment that
has been emphasized. Suffice it to recall his projects of traditional academy
and rural reconstruction during the 1930s. We noticed how *minjian* revivalists such as Pang Fei (Yidan xuetang's director) and Mr. F. (*sishu* 1) have
been inspired by his example. However, Confucianism was for Liang simply the outward materialization of inner convictions: Fundamentally, he
embraced Buddhism in 1912 after an existential crisis, followed by an awakening to the relevance of the salvation message of Yogâcâra Buddhism in
the tragic context of the modern world. His decision to turn to worldly
commitments in 1916 was less a conversion to Confucianism than a realization that Confucian morals were the only recourse in a failed society. In
1966, after his house had been ransacked by Red guards, he still found the

---

9 See Chan Sin-wai, *Buddhism in Late Ch'ing Political Thought* (Hong Kong: Chinese
University Press, 1985). Regarding the importance of Buddhism on one of the major figures
of contemporary Confucian philosophy, see Jason Clower, *The Unlikely Buddhologist: Tiantai
Buddhism in Mou Zongsan's New Confucianism* (Boston, MA, and Leiden: Brill, 2010).

fortitude to write that both teachings still permeated his life.[10] His public reappearance in the 1980s and the many interviews he gave make it now possible for recent scholarship to get a more comprehensive understanding of his complex itinerary: Thus, described as the "Last Confucian" by Guy Alitto, he became the "Hidden Buddhist" for Thierry Meynard.

But beyond his personal experience, Liang Shuming also represents, in his direct opposition to Buddhist reformer Taixu (太虚), a possible way of combining both teachings: Traces of such a divergence can still be found today in Taiwan and in Mainland China. If Liang Shuming refused the intramundane option defended by Taixu in his "Buddhism for human life" (*rensheng fojiao* 人生佛教 or *renjian fojiao* 人間佛教), it was due to his refusal to allow that the Buddhist message be bowdlerized. In fact, the latter remained for him the only authentic religion likely to propose to mankind a path toward ultimate liberation. This intransigence explains the specific mission he ascribed to Confucianism in the realms of morals, society, and politics. Chapter 10 provides an opportunity to contrast the situation in Mainland China with powerful religious groups developing in democratic Taiwan that directly or indirectly inherit Taixu's spirit about the charitable and social mission of Buddhism.[11]

At any rate, the situation of the 2000s provides additional reasons for exploring this deliberate proximity or even alliance between Buddhism and Confucianism in Mainland China. It can be illustrated by many examples. Internet sites or publications promoting Confucian classics are often monitored by Buddhist adepts. Some Buddhist temples open Confucian classics reading classes: We mentioned earlier the example of Guangzhou's Guangxiao temple and the organization of reading sessions of the *Dizigui*. The same situation can be observed in other contexts: Ji Zhe's fieldwork reveals similar patterns in Liaoning province (Anshan temple 安山寺 in Dalian, and Dabei temple 大悲古寺 in Haicheng)[12] and examples could

---

10 "I converted to Confucianism because Buddhism is an other-wordly religion, and does not coincide with the human world. But I have still kept Buddhism in my heart. I have never changed on this": Liang Shuming 梁漱溟, "Foru yitong lun," 佛儒異同論 [About the Similarities in Differences between Buddhism and Confucianism], in *Liang Shuming quanji* 梁漱溟全集 [The Complete Works of Liang Shuming], vol. 7, 152–169 (Jinan: Shandong renmin chubanshe, 2005).

11 See in particular Thierry Meynard, *The Religious Philosophy of Liang Shuming: The Hidden Buddhist* (Leiden and Boston, MA: Brill, 2010), 127–146.

12 Ji Zhe, "Making a Virtue of Piety: *Dizigui* and the Emergence of a Buddhist Discourse Society," paper presented at the final conference of the research project "The Confucian

FIGURE 4.1 Flag-raising ceremony in the Lujiang center (Tangchi, Anhui) opened by Buddhist monk Jingkong. Volunteers wear cloths displaying their commitment to build a "harmonious society."

© Guillaume Dutournier.

be easily multiplied. The Pure Land Buddhism organization headed by Master Jingkong 淨空法師 is certainly on the forefront of this movement, with clusters of projects burgeoning everywhere in China and focusing on basic Confucian "education-transformation" (*jiaohua* 教化), often with the support of Confucian entrepreneurs (*rushang*).[13] One of the organization's most prominent enterprises was the opening of a Cultural Education Center in Tangchi 湯池, a town located in the Lujiang district of Anhui province (Figure 4.1). With the initial support of local authorities, the target was to train hundreds of teachers to be able to promote traditional culture in society and to contribute to the construction of a "harmonious society."

Revival in Mainland China: Forms and Meanings of Confucian Piety Today," Fuzhou, December 2013 (forthcoming).

13 See Guillaume Dutournier and Ji Zhe, "Social Experimentation and 'Popular Confucianism': The Case of the Lujiang Cultural Education Centre," *China Perspectives* 2009, no. 4 (2009): 67–81. It is in this center that some of the activists leading the little reading group taking place in Taiyuan's *wenmiao* (temple of culture) had been trained (see chapter 3).

From a Buddhist perspective, there is in this alliance of the two teachings a mix of intellectual conviction and strategy: Conviction, since Buddhist proponents of Confucian texts consider that teachings should be adapted to the level of the people receiving them. This echoes a classic conception of the "ranking of teachings" (*panjiao* 判教) existing under different forms in various Buddhist schools. In other words, it makes sense for them to promote Confucian morals in society since Confucian morals constitutes the most basic level upon which it is afterwards possible to build with more speculative Buddhist sutras. Confucian texts are provisory perspectives on the truth and therefore fulfill a soteriological function.[14] Besides, they are usually not considered by Buddhists to be religious texts. One should underscore here that classics promoted by Buddhist organizations are more often than not extremely accessible texts such as the *Rules of the Disciple*, the *Classics in Three Characters* or the *Classics of Filial Piety*. Thus, the Tangchi center mentioned above relies on only the *Dizigui* (*Rules of the Disciple*) to train and discipline its hundreds of volunteers. Sometimes (but rarely) other preimperial pieces can be included in the sets of texts promoted. However, we never encountered Buddhist organizations promoting more speculative writings for instance of the Song and Ming dynasties.

More strategic considerations also need to be taken into account in order to understand why Buddhists promote Confucian teachings. It is theoretically forbidden for religions in China to proselytize outside of places of worship. The same interdiction does not apply to Confucianism, which is not considered a religion, does not have any clear status, and is generally encompassed in the vague category of culture and morals. Proposing Confucianism-related classes or activities makes it possible for Buddhist organizations to address a larger audience.[15]

---

14 Let us for instance mention that the reading of texts on Confucianism or comments on Confucian texts by Nan Huaijin, both a Buddhist and *guoxue* ("national studies") master, happened to be decisive for the involvement of many activists in the Confucian revival.

15 There is sometimes a degree of ambiguity associated with the promotion of Confucian texts by Buddhist groups. Thus, Ji Zhe shows that in Master Jingkong's organization, a quite heterodox commentary of the *Rules of the Disciple* is promoted along with the text: "Jingkong transforms the concept of parents (father and mother) in *Dizigui* into a metaphor: Every living creature is a 'parent' for a Buddhist. In this way, filial piety in Confucianism translates into Buddhist piety." But the strategic use of the *Dizigui* goes even farther. Ji shows that there is a point for lay Buddhists to differentiate themselves from the clergy and thus legitimize their action. Ji, "Making a Virtue of Piety," 9–18.

The Role of the Master

Mrs. D.'s experience raises the issue of the legitimate transmission of Confucian teachings, that is, the question of the role of the master. The discourse on this topic is not without ambiguity. In fact, Mrs. D. sometimes tends to downplay the function of the master and then puts the emphasis on the self-transformation or self-liberation dimension of Confucianism:

> When one studies Buddhism, the mistake is to be eager to leave this world. When one studies Confucianism, the mistake is to adopt the role of a master. Without rectifying this mistake, there is no possibility of studying the true teaching (*zhenzheng de xuewen* 真正的學問). The point is not to obey to the master but to follow one's own original heart/mind (*benxin* 本心). This is the greatness of Confucianism (*rujia de weida* 儒家的偉大).

As we see later when we consider the use of the term "religion," Mrs. D.'s attitude can partly be explained by a desire not to conflate Confucian *teaching* (*jiao*) with the conception of a religious institution (*zongjiao*) imported from the Christian West. In her opinion, just as one should not obey a God or a Buddha, one should not either obey a master whose role is only to facilitate one's self-transformation. Paradoxically, such a theoretical downplaying of the role of the master goes along with a practical emphasis of his importance that can take on extreme forms. Since her initial meeting with Wang Caigui, Mrs. D. remains—at least mentally—in a constant relationship with this professor. This distant connection with the Taiwanese master goes far beyond mere pieces of advice occasionally requested over the phone or the Internet:

> Our communication is brief. But each time there is a sense of togetherness (*xiangying* 相應; literally, reciprocal resonance). This can be felt in Buddhist meditation. The master has a transcendent existence (*chaoyue de cunzai* 超越的存在), he is always here . . .

This form of mediation of the master probably contributes to explain the efficacy ascribed by Mrs. D. to Confucianism. In fact, her experience of Buddhism was largely a solitary endeavor: It was alone that she was reading sutras and comments from masters whom she had never met while adopting a lifestyle that set her apart from friends and family. By contrast, it is the living involvement of a Confucian master that provides her both with a confirmation of her vocation ("you have now reached a required state—*jingjie* 境界—of self-cultivation") and with the possibility of situating herself within a lineage of masters, past and present. Asked to tell us a bit more about these masters, she mentioned Wang Yangming 王陽明 (1472–1529), Liang Shuming, Mou Zongsan, and of course Wang Caigui. It is clear that in her mind there is a continuum between the true master and the sage able to embody Confucian teaching in his life.

The reactivation of master-disciple links certainly constitutes one of the remarkable aspects of the current Confucian revival. Whereas it is far from systematic—and the case of Mrs. G. provides in that respect a clear contrast with the one of Mrs. D.—it is a frequently encountered parameter when exploring cases of "Confucian conversion." Thus, there is no doubt that for many employees of Mrs. D.'s restaurant—her Sichuanese cook, her Dongguan waiters, her accountant who arrived from Dongbei after work experience with Walmart—she really embodies the figure of the master. In fact, she really played a decisive role in decisions that they took and that sometimes gave their lives completely new directions (e.g., giving up their former jobs, starting daily readings of the classics and related "spiritual exercises," enrolling their children in *sishu*, and so on). We have often encountered similar cases in the course of fieldwork. For instance, in Shanxi province, the two leaders of *sishu* 3 formally acknowledged as their master a professor from a university located in Beijing. The phenomenon certainly remains at an initial phase but what can be observed in China during the first decade of the new century is the reemergence, in "the space of the people," of true Confucian "spiritual" lineages, although they may advocate extremely different brands of Confucianism. Thus, the spirit of Song-Ming Confucianism claimed by Mrs. D. and her employees, thanks to the double mediation of Mou Zongsan and Wang Caigui, strongly differs from other contemporary Confucian groups. For instance, we alluded above to philosopher Jiang Qing, a promoter of the so-called Gongyang 公羊 tradition that emphasizes a political and almost messianic dimension of Confucianism.[16] It is in that spirit that he himself

---

16 On this topic, see Anne Cheng, *Étude sur le confucianisme Han: L'élaboration d'une tradition exégétique sur les classiques* (Paris: IHEC, Collège de France, 1985). On Jiang Qing's political philosophy, see Daniel A. Bell, *China's New Confucianism: Politics and Everyday Life in a Changing Society* (Princeton, NJ: Princeton University Press, 2008).

trains his disciples, many of whom are now also involved in concrete revivalist projects. In sum, the varieties of Confucian "religious" experiences in today's China facilitate the retrospective creation of extremely different (and sometimes rival) spiritual lineages building their legitimacy in China's long classical history.

5

Questioning Modern Categories

THE CURRENT EMERGENCE of forms of Confucian religiosity, even if its magnitude remains for the moment limited, can be understood only within a historical context where the modern Western notion of "religion" plays a central role in the modern reconfiguration of the Chinese religious landscape. Of course, there is some sort of prehistorical phase prior to these discussions given that the encounter between imperial China and Europe between the sixteenth and eighteenth centuries had already raised the issue of the religious specificity of Confucianism: The Chinese rites controversy resulting from bold interpretations of Chinese classics by Jesuit missionaries reflects the complexity and ambivalence of early contacts between China and the West. But the dramatic dimension of transformations taking place at the end of the Manchu dynasty naturally stems from the context of European imperialist undertakings and from the supremacy of Western knowledge that China felt obliged to embrace for the sake of its own survival. There is no room here to comprehensively trace back this complex history. It is enough to emphasize a few prevailing features whose impact can still be felt today.

A Teaching in Search of Categories

It is striking that the notion of "religion," previously unknown in China, was introduced along with a whole set of other categories structuring European culture and society: sciences, politics, fine arts, literature, philosophy—each of these concepts acquiring its full meaning in relation to the others. This whole range of concepts was introduced within a remarkably short period of time, more often than not thanks to the mediation of Meiji Japan. It required a wholesale reorganization of China's social and cultural order, which also meant the destruction and reinvention of entire compartments of Chinese civilization. Taking the risk of oversimplification, it is possible to reconstruct—in a logical rather than a chronological way since steps of this evolution overlap—the different phases of the confrontation between Confucian heritage and the new category of religion.

The first period is characterized by a strong resistance against the neologism *zongjiao* 宗教 (religion) that reflects the European notion of an exclusive "organized religion." Such a resistance stems from an attachment to a rather inclusive native category of *jiao* 教 (teaching). In this confrontation—and this point is not always emphasized—it is not Western religion in general that was imported and discussed in China, but the modern category of religion that is itself the product of an increasingly secularized European society. Whereas during the eighteenth century Emperor Yongzheng 雍正 (1678–1735), facing missionary enterprises, believed that he could still situate Confucianism and Christian monotheism within the Chinese category of teaching or *jiao* (with a "Chinese *jiao*" versus a "Western *jiao*"), the declining Manchu empire at the turn of the twentieth century was challenged by a set of Western institutions, whether churches and religious sects, universities, or parties and political movements, that were both differentiated and relatively autonomous in their own spheres of value. The ancient Confucian "teaching" that encompassed in a ritualistic spirit conceptions of cosmic and political orders as well as prescriptions of adequate ethical and social behavior had to face a much more limited institutional framework: The European religious subsystem that had been restructured within a social context characterized by secularization and democracy.

By the end of the empire, there was a growing distinction between what could be defined as "knowledge" and "teaching" (*jiao*) per se. In a context of the rising influence of Western science and technology, *jiao* acquired a much more restrictive meaning that primarily focused on pivotal values of the Chinese tradition.[1] In this respect, the very last years of the imperial period briefly witnessed differentiated appreciations of the relevance of

---

1 An illustration of this situation can be found in the proposal of Wang Zhao—though he was an adversary of Kang Youwei—to establish already in 1898 a Ministry of the Confucian teaching (*jiaobu* 教部) that would have been different from the Ministry of Education (*jiaoyubu* 教育部). See Hsi-yuan Chen, "Confucianism Encounters Religion: The Formation of Religious Discourse and the Confucian Movement in Modern China," PhD diss., Harvard University, UMI Microform 9936192, 1999, 89.

the ancient heritage. This was particularly striking during the "new policies" era (*xin zheng* 新政) that started in 1901. Whereas the suppression of the examination system in 1905 also meant the end of a pivotal institution of Confucian cultural and political order, the primacy of Confucianism as state teaching or religion (*guojiao* 國教) was at the same time reasserted since, for the first time ever, the state cult of Confucius was promoted to a status equal to that of the great imperial cults to Heaven and Earth.

Following the establishment of the republic in 1911, proponents of an inclusive understanding of the traditional *jiao* or teaching—those who wanted to promote and "preserve the *jiao*": *baojiao* 保教—such as Kang Youwei 康有為 (1858–1927) faced a new situation. A certain degree of ambiguity had still been possible when Kang's disciple Liang Qichao 梁啟超 (1873–1929) was in his Japanese exile, defending the reformist project of his mentor, promoted to the rank of a new Confucian Luther. Thus, it has been demonstrated that for a short while Liang, who introduced into China the Japanese neologism *shukyô* (宗教) in order to translate the term "religion," could use this new category while endowing it with the more ancient and comprehensive meaning of "teaching" (*jiao*). His point was not so much to underscore the would-be religiosity of Kang Youwei but rather to justify an overall reformulation of Confucianism that would for him consist of a full-fledged intramundane project (based on egalitarianism, progressivism, altruism, etc.).[2] But this ambiguity could not hold for long. The reason was not only the deepening of both the intellectual debate[3] and the understanding of religion as a Western category but also the advent of a new political order. After the revolution, the elaboration of a republican constitution demanded that the issue of the future status of Confucianism in China be addressed in precise *legal* terms: Was this doctrine likely or not to become a national religion (*guojiao* 國教)? Answering this question required discussing the compatibility of the notion with the imported modern idea of religious freedom. These constitutional debates took a somewhat chaotic turn due to political events and could do no more than generate some sort of compromise that would afterwards be

---

2 Chen, "Confucianism Encounters Religion," 62.

3 From 1902 onwards Liang refused to consider Confucius a religious figure. On his complex evolution vis-à-vis the notion of religion, see Marianne Bastid-Bruguière, "Liang Qichao yu zongjiao wenti梁啟超與宗教問題" [Liang Qichao and the Religious Issue], in *Liang Qichao, Mingzhi Riben, Xifang* 梁啟超, 明治日本, 西方 [Liang Qichao, Meiji Japan, and the West], ed. Hazama Naoki, 400–457 (Beijing: Shehui kexue wenxian chubanshe, 2001).

challenged by the most radical secularization introduced by the nationalist and communist parties.[4]

It is at the beginning of the republican era that the term *Kongjiao* 孔教—already used at the end of the empire—began to designate what can literally be called a "Confucian religion" or, more literally, "the religion of Confucius." Ironically, the Western invention of the notion of "Confucianism" fashioned by nineteenth-century Western scholars according to the model of universal religions created by Jesus or Mohammed finally became a reality on Chinese soil. Founded in 1912, the Association for Confucian Religion (Kongjiaohui 孔教會) developed quickly during the first years of the republic under the leadership of Kang Youwei's disciple Chen Huanzhang 陳煥章 (1880–1933): Two years after its establishment, 132 branches had been opened in China and abroad.[5] In that respect, it is possible to speak about a relation of mimetic rivalry with Christian protestant practices: The new Association for Confucian Religion proposed weekly services to members duly registered as "believers" (*jiaotu* 教徒), designed liturgical garbs, defined sets of symbols and specific religious ceremonies, and so on.[6]

From this period onwards, affirming the possibility of a Confucian religion within the Chinese political space entailed answering three questions that would reappear in different terms much later at the beginning of the twenty-first century. How is it possible to combine an aspiration for a national religion and the necessary religious freedom? To what extent could a Confucianism-inspired national religion endanger the unity of the

---

4 Far from validating the proposal of advocates of Confucianism as a state religion (*guojiao*), Article 11 of the 1923 constitution indicates only in vague terms that "citizens of the Republic of China have the freedom to worship Confucius or to profess any religion; This freedom shall not be restricted except in accordance with the law." Chen, "Confucianism Encounters Religion," 187.

5 On Chen Huanzhang, see Nicolas Zufferey, "Chen Huanzhang et l'invention d'une religion confucianiste au début de l'époque républicaine," in *Le nouvel âge de Confucius*, ed. Flora Blanchon and Rang-Ri Park-Barjot, 173–188 (Paris: Presses Universitaires de Paris-Sorbonne, 2007), and on the overall context see Vincent Goossaert, "Les mutations de la religion confucianiste, 1898–1937," ibid., 163–172.

6 Gan Chunsong emphasizes the influence that Christianity had on the development and transformation of "local religions" and more particularly Confucianism. He also provides elements on the organization of this Confucian religion. Gan Chunsong 干春松, "Cong Kang Youwei dao Chen Huanzhang 從康有為到陳煥章" [From Kang Youwei to Chen Huanzhang], in *Rujia, rujiao yu zhongguo zhidu ziyuan* 儒家,儒教與中國制度資源 [Confucianism, Confucian Religion, and Resources of the Chinese System], ed. Gan Chunsong 干春松 (Nanchang; Jiangxi chuban jituan, 2007), 35ff, 75–76.

nation, considering the existence of religions that are specific to non-Han populations (Tibetan Buddhism, Islam)? Finally, what kind of places of worship could fill the void after the destruction or the transformation of key Confucian institutions such as temples of Confucius (Kongmiao 孔廟, *wenmiao* 文廟) or traditional academies? It is necessary to add a few words about this last point since it is linked to what could be called a "scholarly prejudice" whose effects were felt throughout the twentieth century.

One of the main concerns of the advocates of a Confucian religion in the 1910s and 1920s was to know whether Chinese masses would join the movement. Is this not something rather paradoxical considering centuries of influence of imperial Confucianism?[7] In fact, the anxiety of these elites grew along with a nostalgia for bygone institutions—primarily Confucius temples and academies—in which former *shidafu* 士大夫 rooted their legitimate leadership over society. Some of them saw their sociological status gradually change within the new republican space: They became politicians, intellectuals, or university professors and tended to pay less attention to the wide realm of popular practices in lineages or local cults. Some lost sight of the vitality of the rituals practiced in ancestral halls (*citang* 祠堂) where classical ritual texts kept on being reinterpreted by the most educated members of local communities.[8] This growing detachment of increasingly urban elites from kinship-based practices prevailing in rural communities was reinforced by a deep-rooted suspicion about popular beliefs traditionally considered to be heretical and, after the neologism was introduced, "superstitious." This "scholarly prejudice," however, should not be overemphasized. There was certainly a variety of attitudes vis-à-vis practices that had for long been shared under the empire even though they were increasingly considered "popular ones" (*minjian*). And recent research also provides a clear confirmation that modernizing elites of the republican period were far from living in a disenchanted world.[9] In

---

7 Yan Fu noticed the lack of influence of Confucianism on ordinary people: "Yan Fu noted that 'most females and children know about the ideas of heaven, hell, Buddha and Yama' but none of them has ever heard the names of any of Confucius' disciples"; Chen, "Confucianism Encounters Religion," 185.

8 It would be necessary to await the emergence of another intellectual community, the brilliant Chinese school of sociology and anthropology of the 1930s and 1940s, to ascribe again some form of coherence to the whole universe of beliefs and practices of the Chinese population—beyond modern policies and its labels such as "beliefs," "religion," "superstition," etc.

9 Condemnation of popular practices was not shared by all. For some scholars, the aspiration for social and moral reform was not incompatible with a whole set of practices—including

any case, the new Confucian religion committed itself to regaining control of and restructuring the "de-confucianized" rural world so as to protect it from the proselytizing of Christian churches and sects particularly aggressive in their educative and charitable undertakings.[10]

The members of the Association for Confucian Religion maintained with redemptive societies of the republican era a relationship of both competition and complementarity. Competition, since all these associations were organized according to the same "modern" model and were eager to attract the maximum number of believers; complementarity, since recent scholarship also shows that there was a large degree of permeability and overlapping between all these various groups. Thus, one of the important redemptive societies of this period, the Society for Universal Morality (Wanguo daode-hui) was created in 1921 by Jiang Shoufeng 江壽峰 (1875–1926), an active member of the Association for Confucian Religion and Kang Youwei was appointed its president. Other societies, such as the Society for the Study of Morals (Daode xueshe 道德學社), established in 1916 by Duan Zhengyuan 段正元 (1864–1940), also committed themselves to promote "the Great Way of Confucius." In 1916, Duan explained that "because religion (shengxue 聖學, the study of the sacred) is declining, no one knows any longer what morality means." In fact, some of the Confucianism-inspired redemptive societies overtly committed themselves to the promotion of morality rather than to more explicitly religious doctrines.[11]

---

spirit writing—that a more rationalistic perspective could have condemned as superstitious. Such a tension at the very heart of modernity was recently emphasized in a number of recent research projects. See for instance: Paul Katz, "Wang Yiting and the Enchantment of Chinese Modernity," paper given at the conference of Groupe Sociétés, Religions, Laïcités, Paris, October 2011; David Ownby, "Politique et religion dans la Chine du XXe siècle: Le cas de Li Yujie," paper given at the University Paris-Diderot, October 2012.

10 Chen Hsi-yuan also underscores that Chen Huanzhang's program was taking into account the youth, the workers and merchants, women, and villages. Chen, "Confucianism Encounters Religion," 223–224. These kinds of ambitions can also be found in the ranks of Confucian activists in today's China.

11 On all these points and on a general perspective over redemptive societies, see Ownby, "Redemptive Societies in China's Long Twentieth Century," esp. 16–19. We have already mentioned that redemptive societies were many and the category broad. Whereas the use of this category certainly constitutes a landmark in our understanding of the religious landscape of the republican era (and even later), it nevertheless raises a number of difficulties due to the variety of organizations it encompasses. Apart from redemptive societies primarily promoting a Confucianism-inspired ethics, many were also characterized by their syncretism and millenarian eschatology. For detailed discussions on these matters, see Ownby, Falun Gong and the Future of China, 23–44; Palmer, "Chinese Redemptive Societies and Salvationist Religions," 21–71.

In sum, this second period was characterized by a full affirmation of a Confucian religion fashioned according to the Christian West. However, it happened to be a relative failure even though one also needs to take into account the parallel expansion of some of the redemptive societies. Besides, the 1920s also saw a second Western category gain considerable momentum in China, that of science (*kexue* 科學). It was under the influence of this new rising paradigm that the new intelligentsia began to reevaluate the country's cultural legacy.[12] A debate initiated by the journal *New Youth* (*Xin Qingnian* 新青年)—a main publication of the participants in the May 4th Movement—resulted in the promotion of the idea that religion, being incompatible with the scientific ideal, should be considered illegitimate in future Chinese society. Religious Confucianism was included in this condemnation of religions. In 1930, the Association for Confucian Religion could no longer really attract elites and Chen Huanzhang chose to leave Mainland China to go to Hong Kong: His undertaking had there a legacy that is not without a link with some of the phenomena that can be today observed. In any case, as Zheng Jiadong 鄭家棟 notices, most of the publications of specialists of Confucianism no longer considered it a "religion," and this lasted at least until around 1950.[13] Some more secular terminology was generally used to refer to Confucianism in scholarly publications: Confucian "school" (*rujia* 儒家) or Confucian learning (*ruxue* 儒學) were emphasized at the expense of the religious dimension.

This polemical and antireligious context emphasizing the importance of science would facilitate the emergence of a third period marked by the supremacy of the category of "philosophy" (*zhexue* 哲學). Already from the end of the empire, a number of famous scholars such as Wang Guowei 王國維 (1877–1927) followed the example of Meiji Japan and people like Inoue Tetsujirô 井上哲次郎 (1855–1944) and acknowledged that "philosophy" was probably the most relevant Western category to encompass the body of scholarship associated with the Confucian tradition. The rise of modern universities in China, the increase of academic exchanges with Europe and the United States, and the engagement with

---

12 Danny Wynn Ye Kwok, *Scientism in Chinese Thought: 1900–1950* (New Haven, CT: Yale University Press, 1965).

13 On this point see Zheng Jiadong 鄭家棟, "Rujia sixiang de zongjiaoxing wenti 儒家思想的宗教性問題" [The Issue of the Religious Dimension of Confucian Thought], in *Dangdai xinruxue lunheng* 當代新儒學論衡 [Essays on Contemporary Neo-Confucianism], 171–233 (Taipei: Guiguan, 1995).

prominent philosophical systems elaborated in the West contributed to a sort of golden age of Chinese philosophy whose most prestigious representative was maybe Feng Youlan 馮友蘭 (1895–1990), able to conceptually systematize the Confucian teaching but also to trace back its history and developments. However, the climax of this period of "philosophical Confucianism" and high-flying theorization probably took place after 1949 on the periphery of the Chinese world (Hong Kong, Taiwan) with people of the intellectual caliber of Mou Zongsan. It was only much later—that is, at the turn of the twenty-first century—that one began to measure the impoverishment of the meaning of the ancient Confucian "teaching" disconnected from practices and mainly reduced to an object of intellectual investigation taking place in a philosophy department.

The Maoist era generated a virulent anti-Confucianism that reached its most convulsive stage during the Cultural Revolution: A veil of amnesia shrouded the complexity of the modern evolution of Confucianism. When acknowledged at all, Confucius was simply referred to as an educator (*jiaoyujia* 教育家). In the post-Maoist period it would become necessary for the historians of Confucianism to trace back these three phases of the contemporary fate of Confucianism: The resistance of an all-embracing conception of a *jiao* encompassing the most diverse dimensions of human experience; the temptation of an "ecclesial destiny" of a specifically religious Confucianism; and finally, what could be called the position of "philosophical withdrawal" of a tradition claiming to be able to systematize and encapsulate in abstract philosophical propositions (*rujia zhexue* 儒家哲學) an ideal of wisdom while remaining faithful to its spirit.

Questioning Twentieth-Century Categorization

From the 1980s onwards, Confucianism gradually acquired a new visibility. However, there was not much left of the traditional concept of comprehensive teaching or *jiao* after three decades of radical criticism. It resurfaced in a fragmented way, primarily reappropriated by erudite enterprises of the academic world. Although the reform and opening policy made it possible to get an insight into the developments of Confucianism that took place outside Mainland China—and especially in Hong Kong and Taiwan—the reconstruction work carried out by philosophers, literature specialists, and historians remained largely confined to the intellectual production of academia. In particular, it remained severed from the social movements that began at that time to take place in the countryside, where one could locally observe a gradual—though formally illegal—revival of ritual practices centered on ancestral halls and local communities.

Thus, it was with much surprise that at the beginning of the 1990s, in the wake of the events that took place on Tiananmen Square, Qian Hang 錢杭, a young Shanghainese anthropologist, rediscovered the vitality of lineage practices in Southern China. He was then sent by the Shanghai Academy of Social Sciences to carry out a survey on the persistence of "feudal customs" generating social disorder—such as *xiedou* 械鬥, the traditional vendetta existing between lineage groups. Qian also reported on the productive dimension of debates between lineage elderly and local cadres gathering in ancestral halls (*citang* 祠堂) so as to tackle daily problems that the applicable socialist legislation could not solve. One of the issues discussed was for instance the use and property of the *citang*: Did they belong to the inhabitants of a village or to the descendants of a common ancestor? Qian Hang's point was that conflict solving was all the more peaceful and reasonable when traditional culture remained lively. However these practices, which constituted remnants of an ancient "popular Confucianism," remained largely anthropological curiosities, and urban scholars hardly considered them interesting. In their explorations of Confucianism, most of them preferred to focus on textual analysis and discuss values and concepts inherited from the cultural tradition.[14]

The first decade of the new century created the possibility of a broader cross-fertilization of different dimensions of Chinese society due to economic growth, increase in social mobility, and development of new means of communication. Rising fluidity in exchanges, both material and intellectual, triggered a reexamination of received categories of thought. Institutionalized categories that constrained remnants of the Confucian legacy ceased to be taken for granted, and even began to be challenged. This relative weakening of received categories could be observed both at the summit and at the grassroots level of society. On the one hand, the legitimacy of disciplinary compartmentalization was questioned by certain members of the academic elite: For instance, they posited that such

---

14 Qian Hang 錢杭 and Xie Weiyang 谢维扬, *Chuantong yu zhuanxing: Jiangxi Taihe nongcun zongzu xintai* 傳統與轉型：江西泰和農村宗族形態 [Tradition and Transformation: Lineage Structures in the Countryside of the Taihe Area, Jiangxi Province] (Shanghai: Shanghai shehui kexueyuan chubanshe, 1995). On this situation see: Thoraval, "Anthropologist and the Question of the 'Visibility'," 65–73.

a division of knowledge damaged the internal coherence and meaning of ancient "national studies" (*guoxue*). We already mentioned the discussions that took place in 2002 at Renmin University. They emphasized the negative effects of a scientific specialization modeled according to Western standards that made it difficult for specialized students to analyze and understand texts that would need to be approached from a cross-disciplinary perspective in literature, history, and philosophy.[15] On the other hand, grassroots Confucian movements also express themselves in a plurality of forms and languages: Often, they hardly fit with traditional academic classifications.

Today, the reinvention of forms of Confucian religiosity sometimes goes along with an open rejection of the very category of religion. From the previous chapter we remember the case of Mrs. G., the young woman from Taiyuan who gradually embraced Confucianism. Her "conversion" actually translated into a total reorientation of her professional career since she committed herself to the promotion of ritual activities (*liyi huodong* 禮儀活動) in society. Her first project carried out in 2010 was the organization of a rite of passage to adulthood (*chengren li* 成人禮) in Taiyuan's Confucius temple. In a "modernizing spirit," the symbolic capping ceremony (*guanli* 冠禮) for boys and hair-pinning ceremony (*jili* 笄禮) for girls had been replaced by a single rite proposed to all youths aged eighteen:[16]

> The point is not to return to the past (*fugu* 復古). Before, women could not wear a cap and the temple was the preserve of the men. Now, everyone wears the same garb.[17]

Mrs. G. now contemplates an expansion of her activities: Far from limiting herself to these rites of passage to adulthood, she also intends to organize wedding and funeral rites. As for liturgies, she underscores that she relies on "experts" (*zhuanjia* 專家), for instance descendents of Confucius famous for their self-cultivation and moral virtues (*you xiuyang, you daode* 有修養,有道德): "We are not doing this carelessly (*bu shi suibian de* 不是隨便的)." Her project is presented as the logical consequence of the influence of Confucianism in her new life:

---

15 See chapter 2.

16 The rite's name is *hanfu chengren li* 漢服成人禮 (rite of passage to adulthood in Han garb).

17 Interview, Taiyuan, 2010.

I wanted to do something so that people (*laobaixing* 老百姓) rediscover the spirit of traditional culture . . . and they apply afterwards
this spirit in their real life (*shenghuohua* 生活化). All the important
rites in people's lives are nowadays borrowed from the West. I have
nothing against these rites but we also need Chinese rites.[18]

Mrs. G. expects some rapid growth of her activities as well as some
media coverage. Confident that her business experience will be helpful
for her new projects, she intends to fully commit herself to the Confucian
cause: "There are three million people living in Taiyuan. Gathering a few
hundred of them for activities in the *wenmiao*—even if these activities are
regular—will not enable us to massively promote classical culture and
Confucianism."[19] But how does she define the ritual activities she is organizing, taking into account that their function overlaps with traditional
functions of religious specialists? To what extent might these activities be
defined as religious ones?

Confucian culture is not a religion and Confucius kept himself away
from spirits and ghosts. I don't want to have anything to do with
religion. Our activities need to have an objective and rational foundation (*hen keguan de, hen kexue de* 很客觀的,很科學的) and it is out
of the question to start to pray (*baibai* 拜拜). . . . Spirits and demons,
this is not the culture of the Communist Party (*gongchandang wenhua* 共產黨文化). We need rites that can be officially approved.[20]

This attitude of Mrs. G. provides an illustration of a double trend that
could regularly be observed in the course of fieldwork. First, there is often
some reluctance at the grassroots level to refer to the category of religion
in order to characterize Confucianism-inspired activity. We have already

---

18 Interview, Taiyuan, 2010.

19 Interview, Taiyuan, 2010. The first rite of passage to adulthood organized by
Mrs. G. received the attention of the local media and especially of a Taiyuan educational
television channel. The economic model of these activities still needs to prove that it might
be enduring. Mrs. G. intends to identify entrepreneurs who might support her. She mentions that she initially invested without earning anything. Her activities, though closely intertwined with her new "Confucian faith" are nevertheless not devoid of economic objectives.
Her undertaking is too recent and it is not possible so far to clearly analyze the articulation
between business interest and Confucian commitment.

20 Interview, Taiyuan, 2010.

underscored that this Western category generated ambiguities in theoretical discourses. Therefore, it is not surprising to encounter similar ambivalences in the current revival of practices. Thus, whereas Mrs. G.'s rejection of religion is extremely clear, it is also possible to meet activists involved in ritual reconstruction enterprises that are largely similar to Mrs. G.'s (e.g., activists reinventing rituals of weddings and funerals) but who insist on the religious dimension of their projects.[21] In sum, very similar Confucian activities can be carried out in the name of religion or, on the contrary, in frontal opposition to religion.

The attitude of Mrs. G. also reflects the problems at stake with categories imposed by socialist experience in China. For her, as for many Confucian activists who were raised in a highly secularized environment, the very word "religion" remains largely synonymous with "superstition" and its negative dimensions. To some extent, it is the paradigmatic impact of other imported categories—superstition and science—that now replaces for them any reflection on the religious: Mrs. G. wants to organize "rational" activities that she describes as *hen kexue de* (literally, *very scientific*). If we chose to adopt the vocabulary of sociologists of the "religious economy" school, we could posit that the possibility of a nonreligious definition of Confucianism certainly offers some competitive advantages on the spiritual market in order to attract a new audience.

Be that as it may, these fluid references to "religion" may be better understood if they are contrasted with some unexpected uses of other imported categories, namely "philosophy" and "science." In each case, it should be pointed out that discussing categories is not only important because of their classificatory role, but also because of their *performative* function. The role of categories is not simply to sort the content of a preexisting Confucian doctrine: They actively affect and modify the reality they qualify. Therefore, tackling Confucianism as "religion," "philosophy," or "knowledge" also transforms it into as many different and not necessary compatible dimensions. Categorization interests us because it is synonymous with practice and a demand for institutions.

Elsewhere, we have discussed the problems or even the aporias generated during the twentieth century by the creation of a "Confucian philosophy" fashioned according to standards of the European philosophical institution. The

---

21 One could for instance compare the enterprise of Mrs. G. with the much more explicitly religious project carried out by Mr. Zhou Beichen (see chapter 6).

creation by contemporary neo-Confucians like Mou Zongsan of remarkable philosophical enterprises carried out in universities went along with an intellectualization of the ancient teaching. The latter was formerly transmitted in academies. In the realm of self-cultivation, it appealed both to body and mind. However, in the contemporary period it became severed from its symbolic and physical bases: Spiritual or ritual exercises were replaced by systems of thought elaborated in a relation of mimetic rivalry with speculative and modern European philosophy. Whereas the self-transformation ideal of sagehood remained at the horizon of the new Confucian philosophy, this ideal could less and less be practically implemented. Transformed into a pure philosophical enterprise conducted in a Western-style institution, the neo-Confucian message of wisdom became increasingly stripped of its cultural and anthropological conditions of possibility.[22] During the twentieth century, this transformation of Confucianism was opposed by scholars who remained faithful to the ideals of the ancient academies, such as Ma Yifu or, to a lesser extent, Liang Shuming, and we could go as far as to mention a true Confucian "antiphilosophy." Starting with the 2000s, the "philosophical paradigm" was increasingly questioned and even challenged within the Chinese philosophical institution.

However, the observation of various "popular" movements leaves room for unexpected developments taking place out of the academic institution. Suffice it to give here some quick examples. We remember the situation of Mrs. D. and her Shenzhen restaurant. In her missionary enterprise, she does not limit herself to the promotion of classical texts or to pieces of advice given by her master. On her bookshelves, one would also find most of the work of Mou Zongsan that she has tried to systematically read in spite of her lack of philosophical training. In fact, her relation to these texts is no longer the one of a student reading the work of a famous professor:

> Master Mou is a sage (*shengxian* 聖賢), not a scholar (*xuezhe* 學者).
> He shows a way for the whole of humanity (*renlei de fangxiang* 人類的方向) . . .

Aware of her insertion within an illustrious spiritual and intellectual lineage that can be traced back to the Song dynasty or, beyond, to the sages of ancient China, she links her study of texts as hard as *Constitutive*

---

22 On these points, see Joël Thoraval, "Sur la transformation de la pensée néo-confucéenne en discours philosophique moderne," 91–119.

Heart/Mind and Nature (*Xinti yu xingti* 心體與性體) to her own practice of
self-transformation and proselytizing. It has been a rather strange experience for the authors of this book, who previously wrote on Mou Zongsan's
thought, to be confronted with a popular and unconventional interpretation of writings supposed to epitomize the most philosophical brand of
contemporary Confucianism, with all its body of speculative propositions
borrowed from Anglo-Saxon logic and Kantian philosophy. To some extent,
what this experience makes plain is the possibility of nonphilosophical reading of highly philosophical texts. In spite of its abstract dimension of a "pure
metaphysics," Mou's work carries for Mrs. D. and others a radical and inspirational message of wisdom building upon insights of the neo-Confucian
"school of the heart/mind" (*xinxue* 心學) and Tiantai Buddhism-inspired
categories. As such, it leaves the way for unexpected appropriations sharing
hardly anything with academic standards.

This example is far from being unique. Let us now mention the case
of Mr. L., a man in his thirties living in Jiangsu province and who could
be considered a "*minjian* scholar" due to his erudition, although he never
joined the academic world. We met Mr. L. in Shandong province where he
had joined a group of Confucian activists encountered on the Internet who
planned to celebrate together Confucius's birthday. Committed to a popular
revival of Confucianism, Mr. L. was originally a "self-trained Confucian,"
though he would later deepen his understanding of the Confucian tradition after he met Luo Yijun 羅義俊, a well-known Shanghainese scholar
and disciple of Mou Zongsan.[23] Mr. L. regularly participates in Jiangsu in
Wang Caigui's classics reading enterprise and he encourages the teachers
to read Mou Zongsan's work. He emphasizes the intimate relationship
between text learning and self-cultivation exercises:

> When one reads Mou Zongsan, it is necessary to associate read-
> ing with self-cultivation (*gongfu* 功夫 or 工夫). One should not
> read him in the way many professors do, that is, in a unilateral
> way. You cannot read Mou in the way you read Kant. Besides, Mou
> Zongsan uses Kant but his thought is in perfect accordance with
> neo-Confucianism of the Song and Ming periods.[24]

23 Luo Yijun managed to go to Hong Kong at the end of Mou Zongsan's life (who passed
away in 1995) and to be "officially recognized as a disciple" (personal communication, 1997).
On Luo Yijun, see Makeham, *Lost Soul*, 252–254.

24 Interview, Qufu, 2007.

He does not hesitate to criticize famous Taiwanese scholars specialized in the philosophy of Mou Zongsan: "These professors no longer understand him because of the Anglo-Saxon influence on the Chinese educational system." He deliberately maintains some distance from academic activities. His focus lies in self-transformation, popular education, and ritual practice.

These examples illustrate how categories such as "philosophy" become increasingly fluid and flexible in this new social space claiming some allegiance to Confucianism. Though their importance should not be over-emphasized, these phenomena demonstrate how changes can occur in different directions: Whereas the transformation of Confucian thought into "philosophy" seemed to be the unique way of modernizing it during the twentieth century, other possibilities now exist and the "philosophical" spirit can transform or retransform itself in a "religious" spirit and practice.

Furthermore, there are other options for the new emerging Confucianism to define its relations to imported and institutionalized categorizations. Whereas philosophy—or to some extent, religion—could appear for a while to offer to Confucianism a position of refuge during the republican era and later in Taiwan and Hong Kong, the category of "science" has also undergone unexpected transformations.

The specificity of the case that we are now going to discuss is an attempt to root Confucianism in a scientific or metascientific vision of the world. To a large extent, this attempt echoes a situation that was particularly blatant during the *"qigong* fever" studied by David Palmer.[25] It stems from the convergence of three sets of factors: First, the weight of a conception of official science that was previously dominated by ideology; second, the rediscovery—within a chaotic context—of remnants of knowledge, beliefs, and practices associated with traditional culture; third, the rise of a new cultural nationalism stirred up by a confrontation with the West, real or imaginary, in the context of globalization. Whereas in cases studied above, the aspiration to a self-realization or redemption of the world could take place thanks to the reappropriation of philosophical texts, we now introduce a situation where the most advanced physics is the starting point for

---

25 Grounded in traditional bodily techniques, groups that developed in communist China under the label *qigong* took therapeutic and religious turns before being identified as a political threat. A strong emphasis was put on its scientific dimension, and scientists such as the famous specialist of atomic energy Qian Xuesen 錢學森 identified in *qigong* signs of a scientific revolution that would constitute China's invaluable contribution to modern science. See David A. Palmer, *Qigong Fever: Body, Science, and Utopia in China* (New York: Columbia University Press, 2007), 102–135.

recalling the wisdom of ancient sages: It is not beyond but within science that Confucianism's ultimate "religious" vocation will be asserted.

Born into a family of workers, thirty-seven-year-old Mr. S. studied physics at Beijing University and never stopped pondering over a problem that official ideology could never solve: How could great physicists believe in the existence of God? What is this dimension of reality that existing science appears unable to account for? Looking for answers to these questions, he decided to spend some time in the United States after his studies, but this stay did not match his expectations. He came back to China and met in Beijing a scholar who specialized in forest management and who spent most of his spare time on a commentary of Confucian classics. This meeting was decisive: Mr. S. began to discover Confucian classics up to the point where he was convinced that he had found a method to address and solve the questions he was concerned with. The method was based on a reinterpretation of Confucian classics that completely differed from prevailing academic comments. The prerequisite was to rethink together the foundations of Confucianism and the latest development of physics in order to identify a common inspiration.

When we met him, he was wanting to open an academy, as a consequence of his studies. Since then it does not seem to have materialized into anything substantial, but it was named Junde shuyuan 俊德書院 (Academy of Eminent Virtue) and was introduced on websites in the following way:

> Since the second part of the twentieth century, humanity has faced new and serious problems that enabled people to become aware of the shortcomings and defaults of Western knowledge. It is now possible to realize that the mainstream of Chinese civilization—that is, Confucianism—provides extremely useful resources to compensate for these insufficiencies.[26]

In order to highlight these resources, Mr. S. distinguished between three main directions of Confucianism, basing himself on the famous "eight propositions" (*ba mu* 八目) of the *Great Learning* (*Daxue*) that discuss a continuum linking cultivation of the self, regulation of one's family,

---

26 The Junde shuyuan's website was www.judesy.com. At the time of writing, the site is no longer active. The Confucian revival movement undergoes a permanent reconfiguration with projects that emerge, develop, fail, or transform themselves in something else.

governance of the country, up to the pacification of the world.[27] According to Mr. S., these propositions unveil: (1) A "realistic Confucianism" oriented toward things (*wuxing ruxue* 物性儒學) and aimed at increasing knowledge; (2) a "moral" Confucianism oriented toward the heart/mind and our innate nature (*xinxing ruxue* 心性儒學) and paving the way for ethics and religion; and finally (3) a "communitarian Confucianism" (*qunxing ruxue* 群性儒學) focusing on the group and facilitating harmony in the world. It is the "realistic" orientation that should serve as a cornerstone of a reconstruction of Confucianism. Its scientific dimension is acknowledged, even though "things" (*wu* 物) discussed are not simply material things but also relations between material things and human beings. Thus, the "examination of things" (*gewu* 格物) evoked in the *Great Learning* points to experimental study of phenomena; "Extension of knowledge" (*zhizhi* 致知) reflects a concern for scientific and ontological enquiry. As for "the authentic character ascribed to intentions" (*chengyi* 誠意), it refers to the attitude of the scholar, attached to both critical thinking and objective rigor in his scientific approach.[28] The self-transformation endeavor emphasized in the *Great Learning* seems here to be reduced to an exclusively realistic and scientific dimension. However, the science alluded to is of the most peculiar kind, as stated by Mr. S.:

> Confucianism oriented toward things (*wuxing* 物性) has a spirit similar to that of Ilya Prigogine's new physics. It is already a science of complexity (*fuza kexue* 複雜科學). Such an approach is not the standard approach of ordinary science. It already exists in the spirit of Chinese medicine when the latter takes into account the yin, the yang, and the five elements (*yinyang wuxing* 陰陽五行). Such a Confucianism is already post-Newtonian, in the way discussed by Prigogine.[29]

---

27 It suffices to quote a famous excerpt of the *Great Learning* (translated by James Legge): "The ancients who wished to illustrate illustrious virtue throughout the kingdom, first ordered well their States. Wishing to order well their States, they first regulated their families. Wishing to regulate their families, they first cultivated their persons. Wishing to cultivate their persons, they first rectified their hearts. Wishing to rectify their hearts, they first sought to be sincere in their thoughts. Wishing to be sincere in their thoughts, they first extended to the utmost their knowledge. Such extension of knowledge lay in the investigation of things."

28 See the website http://www.tianya.cn/publicforum/content/no100/1/20099.shtml, April 30, 2006.

29 Interview, Shenzhen, 2006.

The emphasis on the interactions between Man and nature, on holism, and on the challenge of complexity is supposed to render this Confucianism capable of responding to the most concrete needs of humanity:

> It enables the respect of the environment without reducing production. It encourages a type of architecture and city planning that takes sustainable development into account.[30]

The small network of activists that formed out of these ideas in 2006 encompasses people who studied exact and natural sciences, economics, and law. However, it does not endeavor to attract philosophy students supposed to be interested in speculations of little use. The proselytizing of this small activist cell is primarily practical: The target is to disseminate ideas about this supreme form of knowledge to professionals with social responsibilities. The almost millenarian perspective advocated here does not rely on a text-inspired wisdom but rather on a brand of Confucianism turned into a sort of superscience capable of responding to humanity's future needs: "The Junde academy is grounded in a Confucianism oriented toward things. It promotes a teaching using contemporary language and terminology and takes into account cognitive structures of our contemporaries. It aims at training talents with a broad generalist perspective in the field of management and organization. It wants to contribute to the interpenetration of Western and Eastern civilizations with the goal of reactivating the forgotten wisdom of ancient sages and establishing the great peace for future generations."[31]

Mr. S.'s project obviously grounds its legitimacy in two different sources: An allegiance to scientific rationality and a fidelity of an almost sectarian type toward a master "who knows more," "who is introduced into influential circles," "who developed a sophisticated thought that needs to be studied and promoted." It is unlikely that this brand of "scientologist" Confucianism will develop significantly in the future. However, it provides a vivid illustration of the fluidity of the categories applied to

---

30 Interview, Shenzhen, 2006.

31 Website of Junde shuyuan. Confucianism as a science of complexity was recently theorized by Mr. S.'s master, Professor Zhang Xiangping, in *Jingdian, fuza kexue: Zhouli Lunyu Daxue Zhongyong de tuili yu yinyong* 經典複雜科學：周易論語大學中庸的推理和應用 [The Complex Science of the Classics: Application and Inferences from the *Book of Changes*, the *Analects*, the *Great Learning*, and the *Zhongyong*] (Beijing: Zhongguo sheke, 2013).

the Confucian legacy today, a fluidity that informs popular movements in a variety of different directions.

From Fluidity to Dissolution of Modern Categories: The Utopian Perspective

Some of the utopian dimensions of the Confucian revival can be understood as the outcome and imaginary prolongations of the ongoing questioning of categories and institutions. This is for instance the case of the project of well-known Peking University professor Zhang Xianglong 張祥龍, the author of a comparative study on Daoism and Heidegger. His journey as a Confucian revivalist led him from an initial call for university reform to utopian explorations severed from academia.

Originally, Zhang Xianglong was one of the participants in a critical reflection on the intrinsic limits of a modern institution such as the philosophy department of a university. Aware of the reductionist dimension of the application of a neologism such as "philosophy" (*zhexue*) when it comes to the description of the essence of traditional Chinese thought, he proposed to replace this category by the one of *daoshuxue* 道術學, that is, the "study of the arts of the Way." The ambition was to combine several complementary disciplinary fields and recover the spirit of the "six arts" (*liu shu*) of ancient China. This proposal generated a debate whose outcome both emphasized the legitimacy of the issues raised and outlined the aporias inherent in this project: Indeed, it did not systematically take into account the anthropological and historical characteristics of the academic space established by the modern university system.[32]

To some extent, Zhang's project is the logical consequence of a fundamental dissatisfaction about modern categories and institutions. Given, on the one hand, that Confucianism cannot be reduced to an academic disciplinary field, a political ideology, or an institutionalized religion and, on the other hand, that its quintessence can flourish only in daily life, within

---

32 See Zhang, " 'Zhexue' de houguo yu fencun—Du Ruile 'Ruxue jingyan yu zhexue huayu' yiwen duhou gan gan 哲學的後果與分寸—杜瑞樂'儒學經驗與哲學話語'一文讀後感" [Consequences and Standards of Philosophy: Impression after Reading Thoraval's *Confucian Experience and Philosophical Discourses*], *Zhongguo xueshu* 15 (2003): 242–259, and Joël Thoraval's answer: Du, "Zhongguo xiandai zhexue tizhi de 'yaosu' zuoyong—huiying Zhang Xianglong de jige yijian 中國現代哲學體系的要素作用—回應張祥龍的幾個意見" [The Role of "Pharmakon" of the Modern Philosophical Institution in China—A Few Remarks in Response to Zhang Xianglong), *Zhongguo xueshu* 中國學術 16 (2004): 255–266.

an organic space that would recover knowledge and practices inherited from tradition, is it not tempting to figure out the possibility of reestablishing such a space within the modern world? This question brought about the project, stunning at first, to set up—with the hypothetical agreement of the authorities—an "area of protection of Confucian culture" (*rujia wenhua baohuqu* 儒家文化保護區), which was originally conceived as per the model of the "natural parks" (*ziran baohu qu* 自然保護區) and inspired by the observation in the United States of the Amish community. In fact, the latter epitomizes the possibility of a preindustrial way of life within a modern society. This veritable "reservation" would gather a population large enough to be autonomous and to gradually recover the basic features of a dreamed "Confucian way of life": the fundamental role of kinship and lineages, refusal of modern technology, self-governance under the leadership of an elite of scholars and sages, and so on.[33] Despite heavy irony and fierce criticism from scholarly circles this project keeps on being promoted and defended by Zhang with a mix of visionary inspiration and logical precision characteristic of genuine utopian thinkers. There is no room to develop this further here. Suffice it to underline that this project is a result of a double rejection: Rejection of a Confucian revival that would be engineered from the top to serve ideological purposes; and rejection of a grassroots Confucianism that would rely on only popular initiatives. Zhang believes that the latter would only unveil fragments of the tradition without paving the way for a true communal cohesion.[34]

In sum, the refusal of categories and institutions introduced during the twentieth century leads here to a radical proposal and switch: Starting with a mere Confucianism-inspired critique of current Chinese society, Zhang's project finally translates into the invention of an imaginary Confucian society located on the margins of the current system and envisioned as a possible resource for facing the gloomy future of human kind.

---

33 Zhang Xianglong 張祥龍, "Jianli 'rujia wenhua baohuqu' yiweizhe shenme? 建立儒家文化保護區意味着甚麼" [What Is the Meaning of the Construction of a Protection Zone for Confucian Culture?], in *Rujia, rujiao yu zhongguo zhidu ziyuan*, 儒家,儒教與中國制度資源 [Confucianism, Confucian Religion, and Resources of the Chinese System], ed. Gan Chunsong 干春松, 162–169 (Nanchang; Jiangxi chuban jituan, 2007).

34 Interview, Beijing, 2006.

6

The Quest for a Recognition of Confucian Religion

THE CLAIM FOR a religious dimension of Confucianism is nowadays one of the features sometimes encountered in "the space of the people." However, there is little room for a development of that dimension without some degree of recognition or toleration by the authorities. Therefore, the 2000s witnessed the reemergence of a number of debates from the republican era that focused on the relations between religion and politics in a country partly secularized after the dismantlement of the former Confucian *jiao* and the end of its pervading domination in China.

What status could be ascribed to Confucian religion in a post-Maoist era? Four options are examined in this chapter:

(1) Confucianism can be institutionalized as a religion like any other religion recognized by the state.
(2) It can occupy a central position, as it is in Taiwan, within syncretistic religious movements that are still forbidden in Mainland China and that are now lobbying to be legalized.
(3) Confucianism can be ascribed a prevailing position in the religious landscape if it is turned into a "national teaching" or a "state religion."
(4) It can be reinterpreted as a modern "civil religion" according to a model that was conceived within a very different American context.

The first two solutions reflect already existing situations, even though they mainly materialized outside or on the margins of Mainland China. The other two, however, are primarily claims even though their importance should not be understated in the context of a growing Chinese nationalism. We introduce here the rationale behind these four options while keeping in mind the problem of their compatibility with a democratic and pluralistic state.

Unus Inter Pares: *The Emergence of a Sixth Religion?*

Let us first recall that current Chinese regulations recognize only five religions, namely Buddhism, Daoism, Islam, Catholicism, and Christian Protestantism. The promoters of the recognition by the Chinese authorities of Confucianism as a legal religion enjoying the same privileges as the others build on situations existing elsewhere, especially in Southeast Asia and in Hong Kong.

In Indonesia, the ethnically Chinese population has set up Confucian organizations of a religious type for around a century in what was the former Dutch colonial system. After independence, the relations between communities of Chinese origin and the new nationalist authorities were volatile, shifting from tolerance to persecution. The official ideology of *pancasila*—despite the affirmation of the belief in one single God—enabled for a while the recognition of Confucianism as one of the six official religions before the repressive policies of President Suharto: Confucian believers could only either dissimulate or convert themselves. However, after the election in 1999 of President Wahid, a Confucian religion could be recomposed and strengthened: Under the authority of an administrative organ—the MATAKIN—it now has its own churches (around one hundred places of worship), its clergy, and its official rites and ceremonies.[1]

---

1 An Association for Confucian Religion (Khong Kauw Hwee or Kongjiaohui 孔教會) was created in Indonesia in 1918. On the recognition in 1965 in independent Indonesia of a Confucian religion largely because of state ideology, see Yao Yingzhong, "Who is a Confucian Today? A Critical Reflection on the Issues Concerning Confucian Identity in Modern Times," *Journal of Contemporary Religion* 16, no. 3 (2001): 322–324; Heriyanto Yang, "The History and Legal Position of Confucianism in Post-Independence Indonesia," *Marburg Journal of Religion* 10, no. 1 (August 2005), http://archiv.ub.uni-marburg.de/mjr/pdf/2005/yang2005.pdf. Religious Confucianism that developed in Indonesia focusing on the cult of Confucius can be considered a new religion, where Heaven is the sovereign and Confucius a prophet (*nabi*). Chee-Beng Tang compares the situation with the one existing in Malaysia: "Chinese Religion in Malaysia; A General Overview," *Asian Folklore Studies* 42, no. 2 (1983): 217–252. On the issue of Confucian religion at the turn of the twentieth century in Singapore and Malaysia, see Yan Qinghuang 颜清湟, "1899–1911 nian Xinjiapo he Malaiya de kongjiao fuxing yundong 年新加坡和馬來亞的孔教復興運動" [The Movement of Revival of the Confucian Religion in Singapore and Malaysia in 1899–1911], *Haiwai huarenshi yanjiu 海外華人史研究* [Research on the History of Overseas Chinese], 249–255 (Singapore: Xinjiapo yazhou yanjiu xuehui, 1992).

It is also in a colonial context and before the 1997 handover to China that the recognition of Confucianism as a religion took place in Hong Kong. The nature of the religious Confucianism that developed on the margins of the mainland is of course specific, especially due to colonialism and its necessary arrangements with prevailing religions. However, for many Confucian advocates the doctrinal content of this religious Confucianism is less important than the institutional recognition by the state.

The role played by Confucianism in Hong Kong is particularly significant for three sets of factors. First, the type of Confucianism currently existing in the Special Administrative Region is in a way the prolongation in a new context of one of the possible fates of contemporary Confucianism that emerged during the republican era and that could be coined its "ecclesial temptation." In fact, if Confucianism is today one of the six official religions, it is thanks to the Confucian Academy (Kongjiao xueyuan 孔教學院) created by Chen Huanzhang after he came to Hong Kong in 1930 and one of the avatars of the Association for Confucian Religion (Kongjiaohui) discussed in chapter 5.

The activities of the Confucian Academy in Hong Kong provide some good evidence of Confucianism's ability to turn into a religious organization like the others. Not only is it involved in ritual and charitable activities, but it also plays an educative role by controlling several primary and middle schools, in which it promotes a "religious" Confucian education (Figure 6.1). Besides, the Confucian Academy also plays a political role: In the same way as the five other official religions, its representatives take part in the election of the chief executive of the Hong Kong government. Under the leadership of Dr. Tang Enjia—a Hong Kongese tycoon who made a fortune in industrial painting and introduces himself as a Confucian entrepreneur or *rushang* 儒商[2]—the academy gained a new visibility and started to organize large-scale gatherings to celebrate Confucius's birthday. Thus, in 2007 it orchestrated a massive event by renting the Hong Kong stadium for a large ritual ceremony also attended by representatives of other religions. This event was enough of an attraction that one of the authors of

---

2 The impressive activism of Tang Enjia in China and throughout the world translates in a huge number of speeches collected in a series of volumes: *Tang Enjia zun Kong zhi lü* 湯恩佳尊孔之旅 [Confucian Itinerary of Tang Enjia] (Hong Kong: Xianggang kongjiao xueyuan rongyu chuban, 2004).

FIGURE 6.1 A school controlled by the Confucian Academy in Hong Kong.
© Sébastien Billioud.

this study ran into Mainland Confucian activists previously encountered at
other ceremonies in Shandong province (Figures 6.2–6.6).[3]

The role of this academy is even more important considering the
relative influence it exerts in Mainland China. Its activities take a variety
of forms: Renovation of Confucius temples, erection all over the country of massive Confucius statues (400 as of July 2013), construction of
"Confucian hospitals," sponsorship of Confucian academic activities,

---

3 Field observation, Hong Kong, 2007. Although newspapers of the day after the event
claimed that there were 40,000 participants, this figure is probably overestimated since
the stadium was not full. This being said, the magnitude of the event remained impressive.
Among the other major projects of the Confucian Academy, let us mention the construction of a Confucius memorial (*Kongzi jinian tang*) that would constitute "the Hong Kong
base of a further dissemination of Confucian religion and Confucianism." At the time we
write these lines, we have been told that a new Confucius temple is being built in Hong
Kong in the vicinity of the Hong Kong Huang Daxian (Wong Tai-sin) temple. The Confucian
Academy proselytizing also encounters strong resistances. In 2010, with the support of both
the pro-Beijing party and the other institutionalized religions, the Confucian Academy presented a request asking the government "to promote Confucianism and to turn Confucius's
birthday into a bank holiday." This was refused by the Legislative Council due to possible
controversies if the Easter vacations had to be shortened by a day to compensate. *Ming Pao
Daily*, January 8, 2010.

FIGURE 6.2 Confucius ceremonies in Hong Kong, 2007. On the board is written: "I love my China, I sing the praises of the Motherland."
© Sébastien Billioud.

support of popular activists' projects, and so on. Behind these actions, four main goals are asserted, in the hope that Confucianism might again permeate daily life: Obtaining the status of religion for Confucianism in China; establishing Confucius's birthday as a national holiday; introducing courses on Confucianism in school curricula; and setting up in all cities, big or small, Confucius study halls (Kongsheng jiaotang 孔聖教堂) or Confucian youth organizations (Kongjiao qingnianhui 孔教青年會).[4]

Two major and complementary preoccupations can be identified in the words and writings of the leaders of the academy. In a spirit that could be traced back to Kang Youwei, proselytizing is deemed necessary as a means to contain the formidable development of Christianity. Buddhism and Daoism are considered incapable of reining in this threat and Chinese authorities, themselves concerned about this situation, are considered objective allies.[5]

---

4 All these points are discussed on the website of the Confucian Academy. See http://www. confucianacademy.com/index_mainnn.html, visited on November 1, 2006.

5 Interview with Tang Enjia, Hong Kong, January 2008, and Paris, July 2013.

FIGURE 6.3 Confucius' birthday ceremony combined with the ten-year celebration of the handover. Hong Kong stadium, 2007.

© Sébastien Billioud.

FIGURE 6.4 Confucius's birthday celebration, Queen Elizabeth Stadium, Hong Kong, 2008.

© Sébastien Billioud.

FIGURE 6.5 Tang Enjia (Tong Yun-kai), president of the Confucian Academy.
© Sébastien Billioud.

This anxiety about Christianity is itself rooted in the determination to reassert the role of Confucianism in the fabric of the national spirit. In fact, the literature published by the academy reflects a patriotism that echoes very well, and even appropriates, the ideological discourse prevailing in Mainland China.[6] Whereas requested bank holidays should provide "the opportunity to reflect upon the meaning of our country's culture," Confucian religion is considered able to fulfil the need for "strengthening unity and national cohesion" (*qianghua minzu de tuanjie yu ningjuli* 強化民族的團結與凝聚力). Confucian teaching is the best possible solution for the promotion of the "spiritual civilization" endorsed by the authorities in order to accompany the "material civilization" facilitated by the new capitalist development, whether political, economic, or technical.

---

6 On this point see the leaflet distributed during the 2007 ceremony co-celebrating the birthday of Confucius and the ten years since the handover, and more specifically Tang Enjia's speech: *Kong li erwuwuba nian jikong dadian* 孔曆2558年祭孔大典 [Great Ceremony to Honor Confucius in the Year 2558 of the Confucian Calendar], 5–7.

FIGURE 6.6 Awards for a competition of moral stories writing. Celebration of Confucius' birthday, Hong Kong, 2008.
© Sébastien Billioud.

The ambition to structure Confucianism as a religious organization in the spirit of Chen Huanzhang's Confucian Association has been revived today in Mainland China, with a recent project aiming at developing a national network of Confucian places of worship or "Halls of the Sage" (Kongshengtang 孔聖堂, literally "Halls of the Sage Confucius").[7] Such a project benefits from the financial support of Hong Kong Confucian Academy and from companies whose top executives are somewhat linked to this organization. However, it is not an initiative directly launched by the Confucian Academy. In fact, Mr. Zhou Beichen (see Box 6.1 and Figure 6.7), the initiator of this undertaking, is primarily a disciple of philosopher Jiang Qing to whom we alluded above.

By the end of the 2000s, the Kongshengtang was both a real existing project and an experimental model aiming at developing a network of Confucian churches throughout the country.

---

7 Some elements discussed here were originally introduced in Sébastien Billioud, "Carrying the Confucian Torch to the Masses: The Challenge of Structuring the Confucian Revival in the People's Republic of China," *Oriens Extremus* 49 (2010): 201–224.

BOX 6.1

In the Steps of Chen Huanzhang: Mr. Zhou Beichen

Born in 1965 in Guizhou province, Mr. Zhou Beichen is the initiator of the Kongshengtang project. After studying at Guizhou National University, he accumulated some work experience in various fields, including journalism, publishing, and teaching. His intellectual itinerary is quite representative of that of many "intellectual-activists." In the 1980s, he was primarily interested in the West and in philosophy. At the beginning of the 1990s, he read the work of many "contemporary neo-Confucians" published within the framework of a research program carried out with state support. It was also during this decade that Mr. Zhou heard about the work of Jiang Qing on the Gongyang 公羊 school of Confucianism. He was especially fascinated by Jiang's concrete ideas about political Confucianism—or, in traditional vocabulary, about the "outside Kingship" 外王—that contrasted strikingly with the metaphysical speculations of neo-Confucians. Several meetings with Jiang changed his life and in 1996 he established with Jiang the Yangming Academy (Yangming jingshe) in the Guizhou mountains. From 1996 to 2003 he settled down in Shenzhen, made a living with business activities while preparing his Kongshengtang project, which officially started in 2009.

FIGURE 6.7 M. Zhou Beichen.

FIGURE 6.8 Media coverage of ceremonies organized by the Kongshengtang to honor Confucius.

The first Confucius hall was inaugurated in 2009 in Shenzhen's Donghu park within a building that has nothing special distinguishing it from the others. This hall constitutes for Mr. Zhou the template of a new type of Confucian worship place (*daochang* 道場). Physically, it includes a large room with an altar, a representation of the sage, and an incense burner. It is primarily used for rituals, practice of traditional music, and classics reading courses. We were told in 2010—that is, around one year after the start of the activities—that around three thousand persons regularly attended activities.[8] The premises also contain offices and a meeting room. A massive Confucius statue offered by Tang Enjia and a company named Sanhe stands in front of the building. There is enough space here to organize ceremonies such as the one that takes place each year to celebrate Confucius (Figure 6.8). In 2010, the Kongshengtang was officially registered as a nongovernmental organization affiliated with another structure based in Qufu, Shandong.[9] It

8 Interview, Shenzhen, January 2010 (uncorroborated figure).

9 This structure is the Qufu rujia wenhua lianhehui (Federation of Confucian Culture of Qufu city), of which Mr. Zhou is also the director.

maintains close relations with local authorities and their representatives are invited to (and participate in) some of the activities.[10] Moreover, high-ranking dignitaries of the State Administration of Religious Affairs (SARA), located in Beijing, also attended the 2009 Confucius ceremonies and praised the legacy of the sage. The organization openly publicizes the religious nature of its activities (even though the reference to a *jiao*, teaching, rather than *zongjiao*, religion, keeps some degree of ambiguity). Therefore, it is striking to see how easily they can be performed even if the existing legal framework theoretically does not make this possible.

The Kongshengtang has a double mission: Educating and promoting Confucian rites and ceremonies. In the years ahead, Mr. Zhou expects a broad national development of his organization and one of his main concerns is of course to identify some reliable and long-term financial resources. In 2010, he was still largely depending on the support of sponsors.[11] In order to change this situation he designed a so-called "sustainable development model" (*ziyang moshi* 滋養模式) also termed in the media "the Shenzhen model" (深圳模式).[12] The basic philosophy is to promote a number of lucrative activities, among which would be wedding and funeral rites as well as training sessions for the implementation of a "Confucian corporate culture" in companies.[13] However, the ultimate goal of the Kongshengtang is not profit and it also proposes a

---

10 Additional fieldwork would be necessary to get a deeper understanding of the relations between the Kongshengtang and local authorities. It is difficult to tell at that point whether the representatives attending the ceremonies are present in their official capacities, for private reasons or both.

11 Among the sponsors, the Sanhe group (Sanhe guoji jituan 三和國際集團) currently finances the wage of the four members of the permanent staff of the Kongshengtang. The president of the Sanhe company is also the vice-president of Hong Kong Confucian Academy. See gw.samwo.com/About/Index.html. Mr. Zhou aims at opening around thirty Kongshengtang across the country in the 2010s and also works on other projects: The inauguration of a "holy Chinese mountain" (Zhonghua shengshan 中華聖山) in Shenzhen and the creation of a "Confucian religion seminary" (rujiao daxue 儒教大學). Interview, Shenzhen, 2010. In a context where implementing Confucianism-inspired activities still requires overcoming many obstacles, one can wonder whether Mr. Zhou is not extremely optimistic in his plans. In any case, the situation and expansion of the Kongshengtang do not seem to have changed substantially between 2010 and 2013.

12 See for instance: "Chuangli minzu chuantong wenhua fuxing de Shenzhen moshi 創立民族傳統文化復興的深圳模式" [The Shenzhen model of institutionalization of the revival of traditional national culture], *Shenzhen Shangbao* 深圳商報, October 13, 2009, A4.

13 Interview, Shenzhen, 2010.

number of activities—ritualistic, educational, or musical—that are free
of charge.

Given the current state of the Chinese regulatory framework regarding
religion, the Kongshengtang intends to be a transitory instrument to promote a Confucian religiosity that would coexist with other spiritual traditions despite its unclear legal status for the time being. However, Mr. Zhou
has other ambitions and also hopes that Confucianism will become in the
future China's state religion. Before discussing such a scenario—which
brings us to virtual projects—we now turn to another current development of Confucianism in China: Its appropriation by syncretistic religious
movements.

Appropriation of Confucianism
by Redemptive Societies

In chapter 1, we mentioned the importance of "redemptive societies,"
a group of organizations promoting religion and/or morals during the
republican era. The communist victory in 1949 and a series of political campaigns launched at the beginning of the 1950s and targeting
"feudal superstitions" or "secret societies and reactionary cults" stopped
the expansion of redemptive societies in the mainland. It is therefore
at the periphery—in Taiwan, Hong Kong, and among overseas Chinese
communities—that these organizations could continue their activities.
If we are interested here in redemptive societies, it is primarily because
of the central role they often ascribe to Confucianism even though they
generally claim a syncretistic religious legacy. These societies constitute
one of the new bodies attributed in the modern era to the "wandering
soul" of a Confucianism uprooted from its traditional institutions and
practices. Let us by the same token emphasize the limits of the "wandering soul" simile. A more precise exploration of the situation would
rather point to metamorphoses of a Confucianism reincarnated in many
different bodies or avatars quite different from classical institutions.
These redemptive societies are also important since there is now evidence that some of them are coming back in Mainland China and relate
to Confucianism to promote their activities. Of course, the existing legal
framework does not make it possible for them to exist officially and current developments largely take place in an underground way. However, it
is not impossible to imagine that the Chinese regulatory framework concerning religions might undergo some significant changes in the future

considering that it is today totally unable to take into account the diversity of religious phenomena developing in China. We briefly introduce here the situation of the Way of Pervading Unity, or Yiguandao 一貫道, one of the most remarkable and dynamic of these redemptive societies, sometimes also encapsulated within the sociological label of "new religious movement."[14]

The Way of Pervading Unity is a religious organization that positions itself within a *daotong* 道統 (lineage in the transmission of the Way) that can be traced back to the dawn of Chinese civilization and encompasses most of its tutelary figures. Emperors and legendary figures such as Fuxi, Yu the Great, Shennong, the Yellow Emperor, Yao, Shun or the Duke of Zhou, sages and masters such as Laozi and Confucius, famous Buddhists such as Boddhidharma and Huineng are all supposed to have been former patriarchs of the Yiguandao. More reliable historical evidence suggests that the term Yiguandao (which directly alludes to the *Analects* of Confucius 4:15) appeared at the end of the nineteenth century.

As for its ideology, the Way of Pervading Unity is characterized by its millenarian eschatology and its syncretism. It advocates a cyclical conception of the universe: Time is structured in 129,600 year-long *kalpas* (cycles) that are themselves divided in segments of 10,800 years. These cycles start with the origin of the universe to end up with its destruction. In places of worship where Billioud carried out most of his anthropological work, such a cosmology was directly associated with Shao Yong 邵雍 (1012–1077), a major Song-dynasty thinker.[15] However, beyond religious movements, such a cyclical vision of time can also be found in literary works. It is for instance introduced at the very beginning of the famous Ming-dynasty novel *A Journey to the West* (*Xiyouji* 西遊記). In the current *kalpa*, we are

---

14 The elements discussed here are based on Billioud's ongoing research. See: "Le rôle de l'éducation dans le projet salvateur du Yiguandao"; "Qi Jia 齊家: The Great Learning Ideal of Family Regulation in a Contemporary Syncretistic Context" in *Lectures et usages de la Grande Étude (Chine, Corée, Japon)*, ed. Anne Cheng, Collège de France. Paris: 2015 (forthcoming); "Yiguandao's Patriarch Zhang Tianran (1889–1947): Hagiography, Deification and Production of Charisma in a Modern Religious Organization," in *The Making of Saints in Modern and Contemporary China: Profiles in Religious Leadership*, ed. Vincent Goossaert, Ji Zhe, and David Ownby (New York: Oxford University Press, in preparation); "Les devenirs contemporains du confucianisme dans le monde chinois," thesis for the habilitation to supervise Ph.D. dissertations, Paris, 2012, 53–106.

15 Interviews in a Hong Kong *fotang* (literally "Buddha hall": the name given to Yiguandao places of worship), 2010. The reference to Shao Yong was explicit and documented with a Yiguandao publication. However, it remains difficult to assess to what extent it is widely shared within the Yiguandao.

supposed to be in a phase of human history called the "White Yang era" (*baiyang qi* 白陽期). This phase is dramatic and characterized by all sorts of disasters (of which current tsunamis, floods, nuclear accidents, and so on, are considered good examples) stemming from human flaws and sins and that constitute signs of a coming apocalypse.[16] At the same time, the hope of salvation also exists: It is possible to escape from an unceasing cycle of reincarnations by embracing the Way unveiled by the Yiguandao. Escaping from the cycle of reincarnations means joining after one's death the Eternal Mother (*wusheng laomu* 無生老母)—supreme deity of the movement—in its paradise. The Eternal Mother is the personification of the Way (*Dao* 道) or of the principle that pervades everything (*li* 理).[17]

It is precisely a distinction between the Way (*Dao*) and particular teachings (*jiao*: Confucianism, Buddhism, Daoism, Islam, Christianity) that constitutes the cornerstone of Yiguandao's syncretism (Figure 6.9). The *Dao* is considered to be the source of the five teachings and, in return, each of the five teachings constitutes a practical path of self-cultivation toward the *Dao*. Thus, the Yiguandao integrates the five teachings in that they are supposed to serve a higher truth. This being said, the cosmology briefly introduced above and this syncretistic spirit do not account for the Yiguandao's claim to be "primarily Confucian" (*yi ru wei zong* 以儒為宗). In order to consider this question, one needs to pay attention to a gradual "confucianization" at work within the Yiguandao. It is possible to identify three steps of such a process.

The first step relates mainly to theoretical or "theological" dimensions of the Yiguandao doctrine. The movement's fifteenth patriarch, Wang Jueyi 王覺一 (1821–1884), theorized a number of cosmological elements and drew some inspiration from neo-Confucian texts of the Song-Ming tradition that he commented upon. One could go as far as to speak about an appropriation of "mainstream Confucianism" (*zhuliu ruxue* 主流儒學) by "popular Confucianism" (*minjian rujiao* 民間儒教).[18] Today, the Yiguandao

---

16 This coming apocalypse can be understood as the end of the current *kalpa*.

17 The veneration of the eternal mother is a cult that can be found in many sectarian movements since the Ming dynasty. On this topic see Zheng Zhiming 鄭志明, *Wusheng laomu xinyang niyuan* 無生老母信仰溯源 [Genealogy of the Faith in the Eternal Mother] (Taipei: Wen shi zhe chubanshe, 1985).

18 On this topic see Chung Yun-ying's work and more particularly *Qing mo min chu minjian rujiao dui zhuliu ruxue de xishou yu zhuanhua* 清末民初民間儒家對主流儒學的吸收與轉化 [Appropriation and Transformation of Mainstream Confucianism by Popular Religious Confucianism at the End of the Empire and at the Beginning of the Republican Era] (Taipei: Taida chubanshe, 2008).

FIGURE 6.9 A Yiguandao altar in Taipei. In front, a statue of Confucius.
© Sébastien Billioud.

still largely refers to a constellation of notions inherited from neo-
Confucianism whose importance can easily be felt within the organization. Billioud remembers well that the first time he met the leader of one
of the major branches of the Yiguandao the first question this leader asked
him was how much he knew about Song and Ming Confucianism.[19]

The second step of this confucianization process can be traced back
to the latest and probably last patriarch of the movement, Zhang Tianran
張天然 (1889–1947, became patriarch in 1930), who introduced some
major doctrinal and practical reforms within the organization.[20] Joining
the Yiguandao today still requires a process of initiation. The access to
initiation was originally extremely difficult and limited to a little elite
of religious virtuosi. Zhang's "revolution" consisted in opening initiation to all. The justification for this radical doctrinal change was that in

19 Interview with the Elderly Initiator Han (Han *lao dianchuanshi*), Head of the Fayi branch,
Hong Kong, 2010.

20 For a detailed portrait of Zhang Tianran see Billioud, "Yiguandao's Patriarch Zhang
Tianran."

the ultimate phase of human history—the White Yang period alluded to above—salvation should be offered to the largest possible number of people. A formula sums up this turn: Whereas, formerly, "self-cultivation was a precondition for initiation" (*xian xiu hou de* 先修後得), the new situation enabled an "initiation prior to self-cultivation" (*xian de hou xiu* 先得後修).[21] However, while initiation is a prerequisite for salvation, it is not sufficient, and self-cultivation is absolutely necessary, although it can now take place afterwards.[22] With this doctrinal change, everyone is entitled to expect salvation both of the self and of others by practicing Confucian ethical precepts (*gangchang lunli* 綱常倫理) starting within one's family. The ambition of the Yiguandao is nothing less than "a revival of an authentic Confucianism" (*zhenru fuxing* 真儒復興).[23]

The third step of the confucianization process is more recent. For a long period of time, the Yiguandao remained forbidden in Taiwan. It was legalized in 1987 and now often claims to be the island's third religion. Recent research emphasizes the growing importance of Confucian texts as the foundation of self-cultivation in the Yiguandao, as well as its strategy of disseminating Confucian classics in society (Figure 6.10).[24]

In Hong Kong and Macao temples, where many believers from Mainland China come to be trained, the organization emphasizes the importance of Confucianism for self-cultivation but also to attract new adepts.[25] At the same time, the Yiguandao opened a dialogue with Chinese

---

21 See Song Guangyu 宋光宇, *Tiandao chuandeng, Yiguandao yu xiandai shehui* 天道傳燈，一貫道與現代社會 [Transmission of the Torch of the Heavenly Way: Yiguandao and Contemporary Chinese Society] (Taipei: Zhengyi shanshu chubanshe, 1996), 48–49. The Chinese term corresponding more or less to "initiation" is actually *qiu dao* 求道, which literally means "ask for the way." The word *de* 得 refers here to the idea of "obtaining the Way." On the initiation process, see David Jordan and Daniel Overmyer, *The Flying Phoenix: Aspects of Chinese Sectarianism in Taiwan* (Princeton, NJ: Princeton University Press, 1986), 300–302.

22 The Yiguandao being a decentralized organization, this is not always true throughout all branches (we thank Philip Clart for emphasizing this point). However, this was what could be observed everywhere by Billioud in the course of his fieldwork within the Fayi chongde branch.

23 Song, *Tiandao chuandeng*, 49–50.

24 Christian Jochim, "Popular Lay Sects and Confucianism," in *The People and the Dao, New Studies in Chinese Religions in Honour of Daniel L. Overmyer*, ed. Philip Clart and Paul Crowe (Sankt Augustin: Monumenta Serica, 2009), 88. Jochim analyzes the period 1981–1995, but it seems that this trend continues until today.

25 Billioud, "Le rôle de l'éducation dans le projet salvateur du Yiguandao."

FIGURE 6.10 Large classics reading ceremony organized by the Yiguandao in Taizhong (Taiwan), 2009.

© Sébastien Billioud.

authorities who sent for the first time in 2009 a delegation of scholars and officials from SARA in order to investigate the situation of the movement in Taiwan. Other exchanges followed, including the publication in China of a Yiguandao text on filial piety.[26] Yiguandao's development in Mainland China—where it has been prosecuted since the foundation of the PRC—nowadays largely takes place in an underground way.[27] However, the organization's ambition and lobbying efforts aim of course at being legalized. The current context is to some extent favorable considering that Chinese authorities in their eagerness to contain the rise of Christian churches are rather sympathetic to indigenous traditions and values. This being said, it is unlikely that an official return of Yiguandao in Mainland China will take place any time soon. In any case, the Yiguandao and other redemptive societies offer a pattern of institutionalization of elements of

26 Billioud, "Le rôle de l'éducation dans le projet salvateur du Yiguandao"; "Les devenirs contemporains du confucianisme dans le monde chinois"; "*Qi Jia.*"

27 These points are developed in Billioud's forthcoming monograph *Reclaiming the Wilderness: Contemporary Dynamics of the Yiguandao.*

Confucian religiosity that already translates in very practical terms. It is now time to turn to more virtual projects focusing on the would-be status of religious Confucianism.

Toward Hegemony: Confucianism as a State Religion?

The recognition of an official Confucian religion that would benefit from the same status as other denominations or the legalization of syncretistic cults claiming a Confucian identity raise the issue of the broadening of the "religious offer" in China, as well as that of the freedom of belief that is, in principle, guaranteed by the constitution. However, other debates also crystallize on Confucianism. They focus on its specificities compared to other religious traditions and on the fact that its core values are supposed to be widely shared by Chinese people and compatible with other religious commitments. These debates fuel hegemonic claims and the contested idea that Confucianism shall be recognized to have a specific status in China. In a modern context where religion no longer serves in principle as the foundation of society, the underlying question nevertheless remains the one of the "theologico-political" or of the "politico-religious." It constitutes the horizon of our reflection and will be more thoroughly discussed in chapter 10.

Let us for the moment turn back to Mr. Zhou Beichen's project of establishing a "Confucius hall." His current goal is to develop his organization beside other existing denominations, though with a different status. However, Mr. Zhou also expects things to turn differently in the long run. He posits that the possibility of a religious reform (*zongjiao gaige* 宗教改革) in the vein of what was contemplated by Kang Youwei and his disciple Chen Huanzhang remains a necessity.[28] In the same spirit as Chen's, he promotes a reform that would combine "unification and pluralism" (*yitong duoyuan* 一統多元): Pluralism, since people should be given the choice to practice the religion they want; but also unification, since China is supposed to have a "mainstream tradition" (*zhuliu chuantong* 主流傳統), this being of course Confucianism, considered a "spiritual abode" (精神家園) of the Chinese people.[29]

---

28 Interview, Shenzhen, 2010. This paragraph builds on Billioud, "Carrying the Confucian Torch to the People," 211–212.

29 Interview, Shenzhen, 2010. For Chen Huanzhang, "Confucianism is to the people what water is to the fish" and a state religion is for him perfectly compatible with religious

Therefore, Mr. Zhou thinks that Confucianism should be promoted to the rank of state religion (*guojiao* 國教). For him, such a situation would remain perfectly compatible with the freedom of belief and would in no way mean a return to the ancient "unity of the political and the religious" (*zheng jiao he yi* 政教合一). He encapsulates his thought in a formula: What is necessary is "an integration of governance and teaching[30] with a separation of powers between the sacred and the secular" (*zhi jiao yi ti, sheng su fen quan* 治教一體,聖俗分權). Within such a framework, the "sage king" (in other words, the Confucian church) "will be endowed with the power to educate" (*shengwang ling jiaoquan* 聖王領教權), whereas "the secular king will dispose of the power to govern" (*suwang ling zhiquan* 俗王領治權).[31] Mr. Zhou insists that his intention is not to return to a unity of the religious and the political and he acknowledges that some institutional differentiation is unavoidable. However, as many other Confucian revivalists, he ultimately remains opposed to another dimension of modernity: Pluralism in the realm of values. Thus, the limit of his understanding of religious pluralism is that, in his system, beliefs that would be authorized (in the name of religious freedom) would nevertheless have to be a compatible with Confucianism. These issues are by no means new and were extensively discussed during the 1910s when the inclusion in the constitution of Confucianism as a "state religion" was at stake.[32] For Mr. Zhou, Confucius halls are just transitory instruments that should disappear in the long run if Confucianism is elevated to the level of a state religion institutionalized through a nationwide organization supported by the authorities.

Beyond the specific project of Mr. Zhou, the possibility of a Confucianism promoted as a state teaching or religion—the Chinese expression *guojiao* enables some degree of ambiguity—is now a widely shared paradigm

---

freedom. See Liu Yi, "Confucianism, Christianity and Religious Freedom," in *Confucianism and Spiritual Traditions in Modern China and Beyond*, ed. Fenggang Yang and Joseph Tamney (Leiden and Boston, MA: Brill, 2012), 253.

30 *Jiao* has here the meaning of *jiaohua* (education-transformation) and not of religion. On all these points, see the book written by Mr. Zhou to theorize his own action: Zhou Beichen 周北辰, *Rujiao yaoyi* 儒教要義 [The Essentials about the Confucian Religion] (Hong Kong: Zhongguo guoji wenhua, 2009), 133, for the present discussion.

31 Zhou, *Rujiao yaoyi*, 135.

32 Liu's "Confucianism, Christianity and Religious Freedom" offers a very good overview of these debates and underscores the central role of Christians in the opposition to a Confucian state religion. This is helpful to put in perspective the current anxiety of many Confucian activists vis-à-vis a "Christian threat."

in radical conservative circles. The case of Kang Xiaoguang 康曉光 is
of a particular interest given the frankness with which this professor of
Renmin University—who used to be a member of Zhu Rongji's brains
trust—expresses his ideas:[33]

> Is it not a scandal that in China Confucianism no longer owns
> any place of worship whereas protestant churches are established
> everywhere? Is it normal that Confucius temples are abandoned or
> only open to tourists? Shouldn't the state involve itself in favor of
> what constitutes the fundamental teaching of the Chinese nation?[34]

It is, however, clear that his main concern is much less the vitality
of a properly religious or spiritual Confucianism than an identification
of the most effective means to reach, with the support of the government, two complementary goals. The first one is disseminating within
the country a "convincing ideology." The idea is to prevent a segment of
the population undergoing social and economic hardship from joining
subversive organizations such as the Falungong. The second goal is to
strengthen a brand of cultural nationalism deemed necessary in the context of the current globalization.[35] In a book titled *Benevolent Government*
(*renzheng* 仁政): *The Third Way of Chinese Political Development*, in
which he opposes both the old Marxist orthodoxy and Western liberalism, Kang emphasizes the following points. The doctrine or teaching
(*jiao*) that needs to be promoted is indissolubly political and religious.
The sociocultural order that should be implemented corresponds to a
"quasi-religious system" (*zhun zongjiao tixi* 准宗教體系), since it is necessary to return to an ancient pattern intertwining the political and the
religious (*zhengjiao heyi* 政教合一). Teaching and governing should not
be separated. Whereas the interpretation of the notion of *jiao*—teaching
or religion?—might appear ambiguous in some of his writings, he
also insists on the necessity of a properly religious development of
Confucianism:

---

33 For a portrait of Kang Xiaoguang, see David Ownby, "Kang Xiaoguang: Social Science,
Civil Society, and Confucian Religion," *China Perspectives* 4 (2009): 101–111.

34 Interview, Beijing, 2006.

35 Ownby, "Kang Xiaoguang," 112–116.

Confucian teaching needs to permeate daily life. It must become the religion (*zongjiao*) of the entire nation. In reality, it is only by becoming the religion of the whole nation that it can permeate daily life.[36]

The state plays a central role in such an undertaking: It must "support the Confucian teaching (*rujiao* 儒教) and ascribe to it the status of national teaching (*guojiao* 國教)."[37]

Kang's conception, despite its references to an ancient terminology, clearly opposes imperial tradition: In a striking difference with Zhou Beichen's project, what unifies the diffusion of teaching and political practice is no longer ritualism but a modern ideology, and whereas it is not devoid of ceremonial aspects, it remains primarily inspired by instrumental rationality. One can underline here the difference with "popular (*minjian*) movements" often suspicious of official (*guanfang* 官方) initiatives. Confucianism is for Kang a top-down enterprise: It is introduced as the future "religion of the people" in order to serve the totalizing action of state power controlling politics, education, and culture.

Other writings by Kang leave no doubt about the primarily political orientation that drives this "quasi-religious" enterprise. In a text entitled "Principles of Cultural Nationalism" it is clearly indicated that "the transformation of Confucian teaching in national teaching" aims at contributing to China's cultural renaissance and rise as a great power on the world scene. Referring to Kang Youwei, he highlights the fact that "Confucianism was never simply a school of thought: It fulfilled an education or transformation (*jiaohua*) function as the religion of all the people." Explicitly introduced as an all-encompassing ideology, cultural nationalism must perform three tasks: Promote and order cultural heritage (*zhengli guogu* 整理國故), mobilize society (*shehui dongyuan* 社會動員), and recreate a system or a new set of institutions (*zhiduhua* 制度化). A new specifically trained elite would play a mediating role between state initiatives and grassroots movements that need to be both encouraged and controlled.[38] Such a radical position

---

36 Kang, *Renzheng, Zhongguo zhengzhi fazhan de di san jiao daolu*, 191.

37 Ibid.

38 Kang Xiaoguang, *Dangdai Zhongguo dalu wenhua minzuzhuyi yundong yanjiu* 當代中國大陸文化民族主義運動研究 [Research on the Movement of Cultural Nationalism in Today's China] (Singapore: Global, 2008), 234–238. On Kang Xiaoguang's idea of an "alliance of elites" (*jingying lianmeng*), see Sébastien Billioud, De l'art de dissiper les nuages, réflexions à partir de la théorie politique de Thomas Metzger," *Études chinoises* 26 (2007): 210–216.

generates strong reactions in scholarly circles and while some ideologues are somewhat sympathetic, official discourse maintains a cautious distance from such a radicalism that may turn into a source of instability.[39]

A Future "Civil Religion"?

It can be interesting to show the existence in current debates of some sort of intermediary position between mere religious pluralism and the temptation of a hegemonic religious ideology. Since the beginning of the new century, various discussions on the possibility of a Chinese "civil religion" reflect the influence of Western experiences of the "theologico-political" but also the difficulties or aporias of a would-be institutionalization of Confucianism in a nondemocratic context.

Chen Ming, the founder of the journal *Yuandao*, became famous in the second half of the 1990s for his defense of a "mainland contemporary Confucianism" (*dalu de xinrujia* 大陸的新儒家), critical about the metaphysical spirit of the generation of philosophers who took refuge in Taiwan and Hong Kong (Mou Zongsan, Tang Junyi, etc.). Close to philosopher Li Zehou—both are actually natives of Hunan province—and interested like him in pragmatism, Chen was always suspicious of the production of all-encompassing philosophical systems and advocated a practical, social, and popular role for contemporary Confucianism.[40] However, it is only gradually that he became interested in the possible religious status of Confucianism in a post-Maoist society and that he began to refer to the American civil religion model.

Thus for Chen Ming "civil religion (*gongmin zongjiao* 公民宗教) is not only one of the possible brands of a Confucian renaissance: It is the way by which this renaissance can become accomplished." The reference is borrowed from a well-known study by sociologist Robert Bellah about civil religion in America. Bellah bases himself on the many references to God in presidential speeches and in American public life, despite the secularism officially spelled out in the First Amendment of the US Constitution:

39 Billioud, "Confucianism, 'Cultural Tradition' and Official Discourses at the Start of the New Century."

40 Chen Ming 陳明, "Bianhou 編後" [Postface], *Yuandao* 原道 5 (1999): 465–466. See also Thoraval, "La tentation pragmatiste dans la Chine contemporaine."

Considering the separation of church and state, how is a president justified in using the word "God" at all? The answer is that the separation of church and state has not denied the political realm a religious dimension. Although matters of personal religious belief, worship and association are considered to be strictly private affairs, there are, at the same time, certain common elements of religious orientation that the great majority of Americans share. These have played a crucial role in the development of American institutions and still provide a religious dimension for the whole fabric of American life, including the political sphere. This public religious dimension is expressed in a set of beliefs, symbols and rituals that I am calling the American civil religion.[41]

If the idea of a civil religion is so attractive for Chen Ming, it is because it echoes his own pragmatic and popular orientation as opposed to more abstract and dogmatic ones:

Mou Zongsan's understanding of Confucianism as a "perfect teaching" seems too driven by emotions. Jiang Qing's idea, according to which China should be a Confucian state uniting the political and the religious, is too simple. As for Kang Xiaoguang's program of turning Confucianism into a state religion, it is hardly applicable. To the contrary, civil religion is oriented toward society, at the grassroots level: It is compatible with freedom, democracy, and the constitution and it can contribute to their proper regulation.[42]

More precisely, for Chen Ming the concept of civil religion makes it possible to solve two problems, theoretical and practical.

The well-known theoretical problem is the unsuitability of the Western notion of religion:

While it is true that calling Confucianism a religion generates deep theoretical problems, seeing it as a civil religion involves fewer

41 Robert N. Bellah, "Civil Religion in America," in *Beyond Belief, Essays on Religion in a Post-traditionalist World* (Berkeley: University of California Press, 1970), 171.

42 Chen Ming 陳明, "Rujia gongmin zongjiao shuo 儒家公民宗教說" [On Confucianism as a Civil Religion], website of the Pinghe Academy 平和書院, http://www.pinghesy.com/data/2007/1016/article_1594.

difficulties. If we don't rigidly link the concept of civil religion to the situation of American society and if we don't stick too tightly to the modern understanding of "civil"—that is, if we understand it broadly as a "common space" (*gonggongxing* 公共性)—then, it is no exaggeration to posit that China is the country in which civil religion was the most accomplished.[43]

It is possible to find in Confucian lore the would-be equivalents of the figures, places, or sacred rituals that fuel civil religion and that Bellah introduces in the context of American history. For Chen Ming, a modern civil religion would enable the formalization and rationalization of these symbols within the "life of the state" (*guojia shenghuo* 國家生活).

As for the practical problem that could be solved thanks to the concept of civil religion, it is that of institutionalization: Confucianism, in fact, entails "the structural characteristic to be able on the one hand to communicate with popular beliefs and on the other hand to be linked to political institutions." Since the demise of the empire, it has been confined to the "space of the people" (*minjian*). Although this is probably a weakness, such a situation also has an advantage: The future civil religion could nourish itself through those vibrant elements rather than through ideological discourses disconnected from the lives of the people.[44] Thus this new concept could work as a mediating force between popular Confucianism and a new hoped-for modern political regime.[45]

These kinds of debates on the future of Confucianism as a possible civil religion generate at least three kinds of difficulties. The first one is the application to the Chinese context of conceptions that are deeply embedded in American historical experience and that reflect only one of

---

43 Ibid.

44 Ibid.

45 The idea of a Confucianism-based Chinese civil religion is also supported by some Christian intellectuals. Thus, for sociologist Yang Fenggang such a project would make it possible both to guarantee religious pluralism following an American model and to promote Chinese culture. But such a support for a civil religion seems to go along with some degree of Christianization of the Confucian teaching, for instance when the emphasis is put on the transcendent dimension of Heaven or on its will. Yang Fenggang 楊鳳崗, "Duiyu rujiao zhi wei jiao de shehuixue sikao 對於儒教之為教的社會學思考" [Sociological Reflections about Confucianism as a Religion], 2005. https://www.purdue.edu/crcs/wpcontent/uploads/2014/08/ConfucianismArticles.pdf.

the possible articulations of the political and the religious.[46] Robert Bellah was in fact the first to insist on the necessarily critical stance that should be observed vis-à-vis the concept of civil religion in the United States. The danger would be to see it degenerate into a kind of "national idolatry" tantamount to some form of "American Shintoism."[47]

The second difficulty stems from Chen Ming's appreciation that Confucianism remains rooted "in the space of the people." Of course, this situation exists and the rediscovery and popular reappropriation of Confucianism are precisely the topic of this book. However, one cannot overemphasize the importance of this trend. The process currently at work remains uncertain and despite all the dreams mobilizing the many activists encountered in the course of our fieldwork it is difficult to say that Confucianism is currently so widely embraced that it can easily become a civil religion. Confucianism's return coexists with both a symmetrical phenomenon of aversion and the indifference of a large part of the population. Without sufficient popular support the idea of a civil religion established with state support might pave the way for a mere political instrumentalization of Confucianism. To some extent, such a fate was the one of the New Life Movement in the middle of the 1930s or of the Movement of Renaissance of Traditional Culture in Taiwan at the end of the 1960s and beginning of the 1970s.[48]

The third difficulty associated with Chen's project is linked to the vagueness of the concept of civil religion when it is applied to premodern situations. From this point of view, one can probably lament that the late Bellah himself proposed to apply the notion to the type of Confucianism promoted by the Manchu elite of the Qing dynasty in order to serve the empire's political unity.[49] This strange anachronism indeed served the interests of Chinese advocates of a national Confucianism. A loose use

---

46 See for instance Marcel Gauchet's remarks (based on Bellah's work) in *La religion dans la démocratie* (Paris: Gallimard, 1998), 69.

47 Bellah, "Civil Religion in America," 168.

48 On these points see Sébastien Billioud, "Revival of Confucianism in the Sphere of the Mores and Reactivation of the Civil Religion Debate in China," in *Confucianism: A Habit of the Heart*, ed. P. J. Ivanhoe and Sungmoon Kim, (New York: State University of New York Press, 2015, forthcoming).

49 Robert N. Bellah, "Gongmin zongjiao yu shehui chongtu 公民宗教與社會衝突" [Civil Religion and Social Conflicts], *Ershiyi shiji* 二十一世紀 [Twenty-First Century] 12 (March 31, 2003), http://www.cuhk.edu.hk/ics/21c/supplem/essay/9501079g.htm.

of the concept can only encourage the feeling of a fictional continuity with the imperial past and hinder the reflection on a consubstantial link between civil religion and the idea of a society of citizens. It is difficult to conflate civil religion with a traditional state religion: Doesn't its significance precisely stem from the fact that it is the modern outcome of a democratic context where political legitimacy is no longer derived from God or Heaven but from the people?[50]

Beyond the concrete policies that they may foster, the different perspectives that have been introduced in this chapter—Confucianism as a specific religion, as a dimension of a syncretistic faith, as a state or a civil religion—are interesting in that they highlight the difficulties faced by various institutionalization attempts. These difficulties are further complicated by the fact that they result not only from specificities of the Chinese cultural tradition but also from the uncertainties regarding China's future as a political community in its relations with the Western democratic model.

Conclusion

What conclusions can be reached after this brief examination of current religious developments within the Confucian revival movement?

One should not overemphasize its importance, considering the multifaceted religious reconfiguration that is currently taking place in the PRC and that translates into the rapid rise of all kinds of denominations: Buddhism, Christianity, new sectarian movements, popular religion, and so on. One should also recall that religious brands of Confucianism also meet various kinds of opposition both outside and within Confucian circles.

Ultimately, appreciating the future vitality of this phenomenon requires taking into account two main tensions. First, there is a sort of ill-defined intermediary space between, on the one hand, the force of spiritual quests expressing a desire for religion without necessarily materializing in actual practices; and, on the other hand, the reality of practices, communal and individual, that are still scattered and looking for an institutional setting. The creativity of movements currently active unfolds in this intermediary

---

50 On the links between democracy and civil religion see Ji Zhe 汲喆, "Lun gongmin zongjiao 論公民宗教" [On Civil Religion]. *Shehuixue yanjiu* 社會學研究 [Sociological Research] 1 (2011): 1–14.

space, between the imaginary and the real. Second, there is an unresolved tension between an aspiration toward official institutional recognition and a claim to the autonomous existence of a Confucian teaching whose value is reflected in people's beliefs rather than state-sponsored projects. The role of the state is a sensitive and difficult issue due to the twists and turns of the last century's political history.

It is for this reason that an appreciation of the possible developments of religious Confucianism also requires one to take into account a form of mediation that could traditionally link individual feelings and collective behaviors, as well as political authority and popular practices. What we are alluding to, of course, are rites (*li* 禮) that have always been essential to the various expressions of Confucianism. Is a Confucianism-inspired modern neoritualism possible? It is now time, in the third part of this book, to turn to this question.

PART III

Lijiao *(禮教)*

Between Rites and Politics

During the first decade of the new century the most obvious expressions of a popular Confucian revival can be observed in the continuum between education, self-cultivation, and religion that has been so far the focus of our attention. However, politics is another realm where the reference to Confucianism is a critical issue and for at least two obvious reasons: On the one hand, it traditionally played a pivotal role in shaping the "imperial ideology"; on the other hand, some contemporary official discourses are not devoid of Confucian-sounding references, which raises new questions about a possible ideological reconfiguration.[1]

The category of ritual or of the "teaching of rites" (*lijiao*) is crucial for Confucianism. It is around ceremonies and official sacrifices that the theologico-political foundation of state power used to be celebrated in Imperial China. In that context, it is legitimate to question the reasons behind the return of prominent ceremonies supported by the authorities in order to celebrate tutelary figures of Chinese civilization.

This issue will be tackled here with a case study of the ceremonies organized each year at the end of September in the city of Qufu (Shandong province) to celebrate Confucius's birthday. After a historical retrospective of the history of the Confucius cult (chapter 7) we introduce a very factual description of a number of events that took place during the 2007 "Confucius festival" in order to emphasize its various facets (chapter 8). On this basis, it is possible to explore the multiple uses of the

---

1 For an analysis of contemporary official discourses, see Billioud, "Confucianism, 'Cultural Tradition' and Official Discourses."

figure of Confucius (chapter 9). More broadly, the issue at stake becomes the possibility of a new post-Maoist ritualism in a space where the Chinese state looking for new forms of legitimacy and popular Confucian movements jostle and negotiate with each other. Finally, chapter 10 introduces a broader comparative perspective with the Taiwanese case and analyzes the links between current state rituals and ancient cosmology.

7

The Confucius Cult:
Historical Retrospective

UNDERSTANDING THE MEANING of contemporary ceremonies honoring Confucius requires delving back into history. Our retrospective overview will be limited to a brief introduction of the history of the cult and of the special circumstances of the city of Qufu across three periods: The empire, the republic and Maoist China, and finally new developments since the beginning of the reform and opening policy.

The Cult of Confucius during the Imperial Period: A Brief Overview

During the imperial era, the cult of Confucius changed significantly from one period to another and was celebrated by different groups of people. We will primarily focus here on the state cult while also quickly mentioning literati cults that could in specific circumstances be dissociated from the state cult as well as popular ceremonies.

Chinese state cults evolved throughout history and providing an accurate diachronic overview of their situation is difficult. From the Tang dynasty to almost the end of the empire, the cult of Confucius was hierarchically considered to be of an intermediary rank (*zhong si* 中祀, literally "middle sacrifice"). This status was different from the one of "grand sacrifices" (*da si* 大祀) honoring Heaven, Earth, the spirits of Land-and-Grain, imperial ancestors, and spirits of former emperors and that were at the very heart of the empire's political symbolism. It was ranked on the same level as sacrifices offered to emperors of previous dynasties, to the Sun,

the Moon, Shennong 神農—the god of agriculture. A lower level of sacrifices honored various deities such as the god of war (Guandi),[1] the god of
fire (huoshen 火神), or the dragon god (longshen 龍神), and so on. Whereas
grand sacrifices were the prerogative of the emperor, celebrating the state cult
of Confucius was the duty of scholar-officials and ceremonies took place in
Confucius or Culture temples (Kongmiao 孔廟, wenmiao 文廟) throughout
the country.[2]

In the same way as what was done for Daoist deities or deities of the
popular pantheon, emperors also granted honorific and nobility titles to
Confucius.[3] On him was bestowed the title of duke (gong 公) during the Han
dynasty and he was made "king of propagation of culture" (Wenxuan wang
文宣王) in 739 by Tang emperor Xuanzong.[4] He was briefly elevated to the
rank of emperor (di 帝) during the Tangut Xia kingdom (1032–1227),[5] a promotion that other emperors such as Zhengzong (Song dynasty) had contemplated before.[6] If they finally decided not to grant this title, it is primarily
because this would have hindered the political function of the cult: Confucius
had to be celebrated by scholar-officials representative of the good ritual
order in temples and schools across the country—and this would have no
longer been possible had an emperor title been bestowed, thus requiring an

---

1 Cults of Guandi and Wenchang were elevated to the rank of middle sacrifices in the middle
of the nineteenth century.

2 For a chart of the various imperial sacrifices, see Stephen Feuchtwang, "School-Temple
and City God", in The City in Late Imperial China, ed. G. W. Skinner (Stanford, CA: Stanford
University Press, 1977), 586–587; Ya-Pei Kuo, "Redeploying Confucius," in Chinese Religiosities,
Afflictions of Modernity and State Formation, ed. Mayfair Mei-Hui Yang (Berkeley: University
of California Press, 2008), 67, 76–77.

3 On the different dimensions of the figure of Confucius and the titles bestowed on him see
the volume dedicated to Confucius in the modern gazetteer of Shandong province: Shandong
sheng zhi (71) Kongzi guli zhi 山東省志 (71) 孔子故里志 [Local Gazetteer of Shandong
Province, vol. 71, Gazetteer of the Native Land of Confucius] (Beijing: Zhonghua shuju,
1994), 15–70, 95–96. See also: John K. Shryock, The Origin and Development of the State
Cult of Confucius (New York and London: Century, 1932); Thomas A. Wilson, "Sacrifice and
Imperial Cult of Confucius," History of Religions 41, no. 3 (2002): 251–287, and "Ritualizing
Confucius/Kongzi," in On Sacred Grounds: Culture, Society, Politics and the Formation of the
State Cult of Confucius, ed. Thomas A. Wilson, 43–94 (Cambridge, MA: Harvard University
Press, 2003).

4 Julia K. Murray, "Idols in the Temple: Icons and the Cult of Confucius," Journal of Asian
Studies 68, no. 2 (2009): 378–379. Wilson, "Ritualizing Confucius/Kongzi," 51.

5 Wilson, "Ritualizing Confucius/Kongzi," 53.

6 Murray, "Idols in the Temple," 379.

elevation to the status of "grand sacrifice."[7] But even if Confucius was not appointed emperor, Murray notes that changes in his icon's attributes "visually upgraded the 'uncrowned king' to an emperor," at least during some of the reigns of the Song, Jin, and Ming dynasties.[8]

Apart from nobility titles granted to him, Confucius was called a sage (*sheng* 聖). During the Song dynasty the sage was for a period of time also considered "dark" (*xuansheng* 玄聖) due to would-be supernatural powers. But the most common epithet for around a millennium has probably been "Ultimate sage" (*zhisheng* 至聖).[9] The year 1530 was a turning point in the relation of the throne to Confucius as a symbol. Ming-dynasty emperor Jiating required that icons of Confucius be withdrawn from the temples and that Confucius's presence be materialized only by his tablet.[10] Furthermore, all canonized Confucian sages, including Confucius, had their nobility titles withdrawn. Finally, Confucius was awarded a new title of "Ultimate Sage and First Master" (*zhi sheng xian shi* 至聖先師).[11]

Beyond the necessary liturgical adjustments these titles incur, they are important because they also imply a set of different meanings ascribed to Confucius as a cultural symbol. For many scholar-officials, celebrating Confucius in front of his tablet in his capacity as Ultimate Sage and First Master rather than as a king was a means to prevent the development of popular cults: such cults would have identified Confucius with other ennobled deities whose spirits were traditionally supposed to descend in icons positioned on temples altars in order to be venerated. Of course, the state sacrifice of Confucius was also directed toward the Sage's spirit supposed to be present during the ceremony. However, what was primarily honored

---

7 Wilson, "Sacrifice and Imperial Cult of Confucius," 268.

8 Murray, "Idols in the Temple," 379. Murray indicates for instance that Confucius's wooden tablet could be replaced by a jade scepter or that the number of strings of jade on his crown or of emblems on his robe could be increased. More generally, Murray provides a fascinating analysis of the representations of Confucius.

9 Ibid. On the sanctification process of Confucius, see also Li Dongjun 李冬君, *Kongzi shenghua yu ruzhe geming* 孔子聖化與儒者革命 [Sanctification of Confucius and Revolution of the Confucians] (Beijing: Zhongguo renmin daxue chubanshe, 2004).

10 The same policy applied to all the Confucian sages canonized in temples.

11 Murray, "Idols in the Temple," 385. This title continued to be used later on, although other epithets could complement it. Thus, Confucius was appointed in 1645 and 1657 "Great Accomplisher, Ultimate Sage, Propagator of Culture, First Master"; Wilson, "Ritualizing Confucius/Kongzi,"57.

178   PART III: LIJIAO

through Confucius was the greatness of the Way and its transmission.[12] In other words, the rite was celebrating both a vision of the universe permeating imperial ideology and, thanks to the figure of the Master, the mediating role of *jiaohua* for the implementation of such an ideology.

Apart from the state cult that was celebrated in temples and official schools or academies at specific dates and according to precise rules, Confucius could also be celebrated simply as a kind of patron saint of the scholar officials and as a symbol of their collective identity. These celebrations also took place in academies whose dual character has been underscored by Ya-Pei Kuo: At the end of the empire, academies were both emblematic institutions independent from the imperial system of education and "co-opted components" in such a system. It is precisely the coexistence of these two dimensions that was reflected in the two different kinds of cults honoring Confucius in the same ritual space.[13] But apart from these elitist circles Confucius was also honored during the Ming and Qing dynasties in charitable and community schools or in traditional *sishu*.[14] However, this popular cult was always tightly linked to education and Confucius never enjoyed the same popularity as figures such as Guan Gong (Guandi) or Wenchang.

In 1906, at the very end of the empire, the state cult of Confucius was elevated to the unprecedented dignity of "grand sacrifice." In two detailed studies, Ya-Pei Kuo carefully analyzes this situation and demonstrates that it cannot be understood simply as the ultimate attempt of a tottering dynasty to reinvigorate its power by relying on a past ideology.[15] Rather, this striking ritual change anticipated a major evolution of the political function played by the Confucius cult, a cult that was then supposed to express the cultural unity of the nation. This change needs to be understood both within the context and as an extension of regulations already enacted during the previous years (1902, 1904). Those regulations underscored the importance of performing the Confucius cult in schools, including in

12 See Kuo Ya-Pei, " 'The Emperor and the People in One Body': The Worship of Confucius and Ritual Planning in the Xinzheng Reforms, 1902–1911," *Modern China* 35, no. 2 (2009): 132, and Murray, "Idols in the Temple," 382–383.

13 Kuo, "The Emperor and the People in One Body," 127–128. For rites in schools, see also Christian Meyer, *Ritendiskussionen am Hof der nördlichen Song-Dynastie (1034–1093)* (Sankt Augustin: Monumenta Serica Monograph Series LVIII, 2008), 349–354.

14 Kuo, "The Emperor and the People in One Body," 129.

15 Ibid.; Kuo, "Redeploying Confucius." This paragraph is based on Kuo's research.

modern institutions, but they also put an end to the dual system according to which state sacrifices were separated from ordinary ceremonies in terms of calendar and organization. With the reforms, students could take part in the state cult that was formerly the preserve of scholar-officials and orchestrated according to a liturgy giving a prevailing role to the head of the local government. Moreover, the role of the main celebrant having been suppressed, the rite ended up being performed jointly by the whole community of participants, united in front of the sage.[16] In such a context, the elevation of the cult to the dignity of "grand sacrifice" seems all the more paradoxical: Aren't grand sacrifices the privilege of the emperor? In fact, this true ritual revolution sanctioned the "unity of the sovereign and the people in one body" (*junmin yi ti* 君民一體). It was the cultural and political unity of the nation that was honored in that way by the emperor and the people. This symbol is all the more striking in that such a unity, celebrated around "the Ultimate Sage and First Master" Confucius, blatantly contrasts with the racial community promoted by anti-Manchu revolutionaries claiming a filiation to the Yellow Emperor (Huangdi), ancestor of the Han nation.[17]

The Holy City of Qufu

The "holy city" (*shengcheng* 聖城) of Qufu is located at the very heart of the Lu country, in today's Shandong province. It is the place where Confucius was born and buried, and it occupies a particular space both in the geography of Confucianism and in Chinese history. Apart from the Confucius temple (Kongmiao), the second-largest sanctuary in China after the Forbidden City, the residence of Confucius's descendants (Kongfu 孔府), and the cemetery (Konglin 孔林)—where more than 100,000 of those descendants are buried—are also located in this city. Emperors used to occasionally go to Qufu to celebrate Confucius's cult or sent representatives to attend the ceremonies.[18] Qufu certainly never enjoyed a status

---

16 Kuo, "The Emperor and the People in One Body," 143.

17 Ibid., 137–138; Térence Billeter, *L'Empereur jaune* (Paris: Les Indes savantes, 2007), 134–135. The anthropological context of the contrast between Confucius and the Yellow Emperor is discussed in chapter 10.

18 The gazetteer of Shandong province underlines that throughout history twelve emperors went personally to Qufu to celebrate Confucius's cult (twenty times altogether). *Shandong sheng zhi*, 96–98. From the Tang dynasty onwards, temples dedicated to Confucius (Kongmiao or *wenmiao*) were erected throughout the country. Shryock, *Origin and Development of the*

equivalent to Mecca's or Jerusalem's—even though the comparison is sometimes made today. Nevertheless, the place always remained highly symbolic for an imperial order that turned Confucianism into a state ideology.

It is not possible to evoke Qufu during the empire without saying a few words about the Kong lineage. The city is in fact the lineage's cradle, even though the vicissitudes of Chinese history obliged some of the lineage branches to settle elsewhere. Thus, facing the Jin (1115–1234) invasion, the Yansheng Duke 衍生公 (a title given to the first living descendant of Confucius in direct line) had to withdraw with Song loyalists to the south of China and to settle in Quzhou 衢州, Zhejiang province. Since the invaders decided to honor his younger brother with the same title, China happened to have during that period two Yansheng Dukes.[19] In that way, the Jin invaders initiated a classic pattern of imperial history: Dynasties never ceased to support financially Qufu's Confucius temples and to grant privileges (tax exemptions, official responsibilities) to the Kong lineage on the loyalty of which they could always count. It has been underscored that "this transaction symbolized and simultaneously proved their right to the Mandate of Heaven."[20] Thus, the Kong lineage could always enjoy the benefits of a very specific status in China: It could always rely on a particular social capital and maintain its privileges without having to go through China's meritocratic system. Besides official ceremonies, Kong lineage members also honored their ancestors—including ancestors earlier than Confucius—in a specially dedicated hall (jiamiao 家廟). This lineage cult exerted some influence on the state cult in the course of a complex cross-fertilization process.[21]

State Cult of Confucius, 134–135; Wilson, "Ritualizing Confucius/Kongzi," 72. Wilson mentions that these temples could be found in the capital, in provincial capitals and in county seats: Thomas A. Wilson, ed., On Sacred Ground: Culture, Society, Politics and the Formation of the State Cult of Confucius (Cambridge, MA: Harvard University Press, 2003), 2–3.

19 Abigail Lamberton, "The Kongs of Qufu," in On Sacred Grounds, ed. Wilson, 315. Wang, Nanzongjikong 南宗祭孔 [The Confucius Cult of the Southern Lineage] (Hangzhou: Zhejiang renmin chubanshe, 2008). Another branch of the lineage settled down in Gansu province, not far from Lanzhou. See Jun Jing, The Temple of Memories: History, Power and Morality in a Chinese Village (Stanford, CA: Stanford University Press, 1996).

20 Lamberton, "Kongs of Qufu," 328.

21 This situation is studied in details in Thomas A. Wilson, "The Ritual Formation of Confucian Orthodoxy and the Descendants of the Sage," Journal of Asian Studies 55, no. 3 (1996): 559–584. Wilson evokes an "uneasy convergence" between the state cult and the cult rendered by the descendants (559).

"Deritualization" under the Republic and Maoism

It is possible to consider that a period of Confucian "deritualization" started with the demise of the empire even if the Confucius cult would be episodically perpetuated under different forms (official ceremonies, commemorations in temples and schools, cults in the framework of societies independent from the state, and so on). It is difficult, however, to get a clear overview of the situation due to the fragmentation of political power and the political instability in republican China.

Yuan Shikai, who became president in 1912, asserted the necessity of honoring Confucius both in schools and during official ceremonies in which he took part, but he also emphasized that these ceremonies were totally devoid of a religious dimension. This position needs to be understood within the context of his ambition to reintroduce monarchy and find sources of political legitimacy. One can assume that it was out of a similar concern that he adopted some measures to keep on granting to the Kong lineage its former imperial privileges.[22] More generally, Gan Chunsong underlines that during the period 1912–27, a similar legitimacy concern led warlords such as Zhang Zuolin 張作霖 (1875–1928) in his Manchurian fiefdom to honor Confucius.[23] Warlords were often very much involved in the project to constitutionally establish Confucianism as China's state religion.[24] The Confucius cult took at that period of time a variety of different forms.

Apart from official ceremonies in temples and schools, the sage was also celebrated in modern societies fashioned according to the Christian model: This was the case of Chen Huanzhang's Association for Confucian Religion[25] and of several redemptive societies. The latter proliferated

---

22 Chen, "Confucianism Encounters Religion," 167–169. On the privileges granted to the Kong lineage, see Liu, "Confucianism, Christianity, and Religious Freedom," 257.

23 Gan Chunsong 干春松, *Zhiduhua rujia yu qi jieti* 制度化儒家及其解體 [Institutionalized Confucianism and Its Dismantling] (Beijing: Zhongguo renmin daxue chubanshe, 2003), 327–335, and more specifically 328–329. In 1927, Zhang Zuoling decided to organize Confucian ceremonies.

24 Gan, *Zhiduhua rujia yu qi jieti*, 327–335. The involvement of warlords in the project of a state religion needs to be contrasted with the attitude of Yuan Shikai, who cautiously avoided taking part in these debates. Chen, "Confucianism Encounters Religion," 167–169.

25 Chen, "Confucianism Encounters Religion," 225–228.

during the so-called Beiyang period (1912–1928), making the most of the
support of political elites at the highest level.[26] Thus, the Society for the
Purification of the Heart (Xixinshe 洗心社) that developed in Shanxi province at the beginning of the 1920s was strongly supported by one of the
prominent warlords of the time, Yan Xishan 閻錫山, who actively promoted Confucianism in the territories under his control. For instance,
weekly cults were organized that included sermons and incense offerings
in front of Confucius's tablet.[27] The same Yan Xishan was also a founding
member of the Society for Universal Morality (Wanguo daodehui), one
of the main redemptive societies with a strong Confucian bias that we
discussed above. Prominent members of the society also included Kang
Youwei and Kong Decheng 孔德成 (1920–2008), Confucius's first descendant in direct line, and Wang Fengyi, whose teachings are now promoted
in China by the Yidan xuetang (see chapters 2 and 3).

In 1927 and 1928, the nationalist army took Nanjing and Peking, thus
opening a new chapter of republican history. In 1928, Cai Yuanpei, who
was minister of education, required that all administrative units in his
jurisdiction stop celebrating spring and autumn cults of Confucius.[28] In
temples where Confucius's tablets were kept, instructions were given
to proceed with "commemorations"(*jinian* 紀念) instead of sacrifices
(*si* 祀)—thus generating some amount of ambiguity. However, these measures were fiercely criticized by former scholar-officials of the late Qing
dynasty and of the Beiyang period employed in the new governmental
institutions.[29] Launched in 1934, the New Life Movement initiated a new
ceremonial largely based on the celebration of "national heroes." Nedostup
underscores that the Confucius celebrations that were staged from 1935
onwards focused on the sage as a leader of national Chinese culture. His

---

26 For instance, the Society of the Common Good (Tongshanshe 同善社) benefited from
the patronage of Duan Qirui 段祺瑞 (1865–1936), chief executive of the republic between
1924 and 1926, and from the support of General Cao Kun 曹錕 (1862–1938), who was president of the republic between 1923 and 1924. See Ownby, "Redemptive Societies in China's
Long Twentieth Century." Examples could easily be multiplied.

27 Gillin, "Portrait of a Warlord," 299–302; Palmer and Goossaert, *Religious Question in
Modern China*, 95.

28 Nedostup, *Superstitious Regimes*, 263, 375n58. It seems that cults carried out in schools
were perpetuated each spring and autumn without discontinuity between 1912 and 1928, a
situation that differs from the grand ceremonies carried out in temples. Additional research
would be necessary to corroborate this claim.

29 Ibid., 266–267.

portrait was put on a table below the one of Sun Yat-sen that hung on the wall, and if a song honoring Confucius was sung, this took place only after the Guomindang hymn.[30] Confucius cults also kept being performed in territories directly controlled by warlords such as He Jian in Hunan province or Chen Jitang in Guangdong.

However, Chinese nationalists and conservatives were not the only ones trying to use Confucius in an instrumental way. At the same period of time, in Japan, an original synthesis between Confucianism and Shintoism was operating: In contrast with republican China, which was largely deemed anti-Confucian, Japan tightly integrated the Confucian tradition into the "national constitution" (*kokutai*). From the end of the 1920s, ceremonies honoring Confucius increasingly took the form of a "national cult" (*kokusai*) celebrated by Shinto priests in the presence of the highest political leaders. Attempts were made to promote this new state ideology in Manchuria and northern China after it was occupied by Japanese troops.[31]

After 1949, China's division obviously had an impact on Confucian ceremonies. The latter were abandoned on the mainland but were perpetuated in Taiwan, especially during the Movement of Renaissance of Traditional Culture (*Zhonghua wenhua fixing yundong* 中華文化復興運動) that was launched at the same time as the Cultural Revolution in the PRC. This movement was monitored by the Guomindang and aimed at promoting—besides party ideology (Sun Yat-sen's triple principles of the people, etc.)—a number of Confucian values in society. Two programs entitled "What Citizens Should Know about Daily Life" (*guomin shenghuo xu zhi*) and "Models of Rites and Ceremonies for the Citizens" (*guomin liyi fanli*) were implemented in order to mobilize the masses. In a spirit that was close to that of the New Life Movement, their objective was to moralize, discipline, and ritualize daily life in its tiniest details. It is in this context that temples and ceremonies honoring the "Great Accomplisher,

---

30 Ibid., 270–271.

31 Warren Smith, *Confucianism in Modern Japan: A Study of Conservatism in Japanese Intellectual History* (Tokyo: Hokuseido, 1973), 135–145. On the situation in Manchuria and China, see pp. 183–228. For a comparison between these practices and recent official support to Confucian ceremonies in China, see Nakajima Takahiro 中島隆博, "Senzen Nihon to gendai Chûgoku no Jukyô fukkô ni kan suru ôdanteki kenkyû 戦前日本と現代中国の儒教復興に関する横断的研究" [Transversal Research on the Confucian Revival in Japan and Contemporary China], in *Zhongguo chuantong wenhua zai dangdai zhongguo de juese* 中國傳統文化在當代中國的角色 [The Role of Traditional Chinese Culture in Contemporary China], edited by Nakajima Takahiro, 213–234 (Tokyo: University of Tokyo Center for Philosophy Booklet 5).

Ultimate Sage, First Master Confucius" (*Dacheng zhisheng xianshi Kongzi*) were reformed. Ceremonies continued up to the present time.[32]

In sum, after the demise of the empire the force of the symbolic and political reference to Confucius that crystallized in his cult never totally disappeared. However, due to historical circumstances the recourse to Confucius as a symbol was limited to specific territories and political configurations. The loss of impetus of the Movement of Renaissance of Traditional Culture in Taiwan more or less coincided with the reemergence of a possible space for a symbolic reappropriation of Confucianism in the PRC starting in the 1980s. But before turning to this point, it is necessary to briefly evoke the situation in Qufu during a large part of the twentieth century.

Qufu during the Republican and Maoist Eras

The modern gazetteer published by local authorities makes it possible to trace the rough history of the cults during the republican era and to get an overview of the situation under Mao. After the end of the empire, the Confucius cult in the "holy city" of Qufu lost its continuity and was affected by the vicissitudes of Chinese history. Apart from ceremonies carried out by various societies, including the Association for Confucian Religion, official cults were celebrated on several occasions at the beginning of the republic as per instructions given by the Peking authorities (Figures 7.1, 7.2,).[33] In the context of the beginning of the New Life

---

32 Minakuchi Takuju 水口拓寿, "Chûka bunka no fukkô to shite no Kôshibyô kaikaku, 1968–70-nenno Taihoku Kôshibyôwoshôtentoshite中華文化の復興としての孔子廟を改革, 1968–70 年の台北孔子廟を焦点として" [The Reform of the Confucius Temple as an Expression of the Renaissance of Chinese Culture: The Case of Taipei's Confucius Temple in 1968–70], in *Zhongguo chuantong wenhua zai dangdai zhongguo de juese* 中國傳統文化在當代中國的角色 [The Role of Traditional Chinese Culture in Contemporary China], 235–253 (Tokyo: University of Tokyo Center for Philosophy Booklet 5). Confucius's title is close to the one granted at the beginning of the Qing dynasty and simplified afterwards. On the Movement of Renaissance of Traditional Culture, see Paul Katz, "Religion and State in Post-War Taiwan," *China Quarterly* 174 (2003): 395–412, especially 402; Lin Guoxian (Kuo-hsien) 林果顯, *Zhongguo wenhua fuxing yundong tuixing weiyuanhui zhi yanjiu* 中華文化復興運動推行委員會之研究 [Research on the Committee in Charge of Implementing the Movement of Renaissance of Traditional Chinese Culture] (Taipei: Daoxiang, 2005).

33 In 1914, Yuan Shikai gave instructions to perform again the Confucius cult throughout the country. It is not indicated in the gazetteer whether he personally attended the 1914 ceremony. A celebration involving the president (*da zongtong*) heading a delegation of around one hundred civil servants is anyway mentioned. *Shandong shen zhi*, 48. Rites are also mentioned for 1921 and 1925. It is possibly the 1925 cult that Franz Xaver Biallas describes in his *Konfuzius und sein Kult* (Beijing and Leipzig: Pekinger Verlag, 1928). The book offers

FIGURE 7.1 Masters of ceremony for a cult to Confucius in Qufu, probably in 1925.

FIGURE 7.2 Preparation for a cult to Confucius in Qufu, probably in 1925.

FIGURE 7.3 Some PLA representatives attended the 1946 commemoration of Confucius's birth.

Movement (1934), a large ceremony was organized by the Nanjing nationalist government to celebrate Confucius's birthday and enjoyed some significant degree of media coverage. In 1938, Japanese troops took Qufu. The nationalist government had withdrawn in Chongqing and had been replaced in Nanjing in 1940 by the collaborationist government of Wang Jingwei 汪精衛 (1883–1944). The gazetteer mentions cults for 1942 and 1943 in the presence of high-ranking officials. In 1945 communist troops arrived in Qufu and a grand commemoration of Confucius took place the year after (Figure 7.3). It was still, in principle, a period of united front between the Guomindang and communist troops. The year 1947 is the last one for which we find traces of a commemoration in the gazetteer. Chiang Kai-shek, who had then returned to Nanjing, sent an envoy to assist the main Confucius descendant—Kong Decheng—during the ceremony (Figure 7.4). In 1948, the People's Liberation Army arrived in Qufu, thus marking the beginning of a new era.[34]

---

an interesting description of things seen and some information about the liturgy. In 1928, Chiang Kai-shek went to Qufu but this was for a mere visit of the place and he just met Confucius's descendant Kong Decheng.

34 This paragraph builds on *Shandong sheng zhi*, 48–55. See also Kong Fanyin 孔繁銀, *Yansheng Gong fu jian wen* 衍聖公府見聞 [Things Seen and Heard at the Mansion of the Yansheng Duke] (Jinan: Qi Lu shushe, 1992), 139–201. The author mentions cults for the years 1919, 1940, and 1947 and provides each time some detailed information about the organization of the ceremony and the liturgy.

FIGURE 7.4 The Yansheng Duke, Kong Decheng, participated in the 1947 ceremonies in Qufu.

From the end of the empire to the arrival of the communists in power, when Qufu was in a territory controlled by extremely different political regimes (Beiyang, Guomindang, Wang Jingwei, united front), official ceremonies honoring Confucius continued to be organized. They were neither necessarily regular nor of equal importance. Moreover, in the changing circumstances of this troubled period of Chinese history these ceremonies responded to a variety of different objectives. However, they all contributed to ascribe to the ruling regimes a moral and symbolical authority—or, if we borrow Duara's terms, a timeless identity and authenticity.[35]

After 1949, the organization of large ceremonies honoring Confucius seems to have stopped in Qufu.[36] High-ranking leaders traveling to Qufu sometimes visited "cultural relics" or even allocated financial resources

---

35 Duara, *Sovereignty and Authenticity*, 30–33.

36 There is no mention of any cult whatsoever in the gazetteer of Shandong province, *Shandong sheng zhi*. However, this does not mean that it is possible to exclude the possibility of a local cult that could have taken place during the very first years of the PRC (as for

FIGURE 7.5 Destruction of the ancient Confucius statue during the Cultural Revolution. The character on the trunk indicates "No.1 big bastard!"

for their preservation but there is no mention of a cult.[37] At the beginning of the Cultural Revolution, Qufu became a paroxysmal example of the anti-Confucian wave that swept the whole of China. In 1966, red guards, both local and from Beijing, were encouraged by the most radical wing within the party to denounce and "destroy the Kong family shop" (*dadao Kongjia dian* 打倒孔家店). In November of the same year violent and systematic destructions took place: Statues were pulled down or had their heads destroyed, stelae were smashed and books burned. The statue of Confucius was paraded in the city and thrown in a bonfire (Figure 7.5).

Huangdi, the Yellow Emperor). Thus, Sang Ye and Geremie Barmé briefly allude to ceremonies that took place in 1962 in Qufu; see "Commemorating Confucius in 1966–67: The Fate of the Confucius Temple, the Kong Mansion and Kong Cemetery. 孔庙、孔府、孔林," *China Heritage Quarterly* 20 (2009), http://www.chinaheritagequarterly.org/scholarship. php?searchterm=020_confucius.inc&issue=020

37 It is mentioned that a show took place in 1957 in the Confucius temple and that a documentary film was also projected. A study program on dances and music linked to the Confucius cult was also carried out. The temple seemed to turn into a museum.

With the authorization of Chen Boda, "tombs of the first three Kongs and the last three kongs" (Confucius, his sons, and grandsons, as well as the three last generations of the Kong lineage) were opened and plundered. Unearthed coffins of recently dead ancestors were opened and corpses pulled out. A few ones were even stripped and hung from a tree.[38]

In sum, during the Maoist era Qufu lost the symbolic dimension it had been endowed with for centuries. The situation only began to change with the reform and opening policy that began in 1978.

Reform, Opening and the Return of Confucius

The ongoing reappropriation of fragments of traditional culture since the beginning of the reform and opening policy gradually created the conditions of possibility of a new Confucian ritualism. We have already discussed in this book various dimensions of the popular reappropriation of references to Confucianism. To some extent, Confucius plays today the role of a floating signifier: Whereas many still simply view him as an educator (*jiaoyu-jia* 教育家) or a thinker (*sixiangjia* 思想家),[39] others consider that he is a sage and a master, and in some cases even enshrine him as a god in the big pantheon of popular religion. Finally, for some activists he is a political guide or an "uncrowned king." The changing attitude of the authorities toward traditional culture in the last three decades was instrumental in that it enabled the rediscovery of traditional culture and Confucianism by offering a favorable sociopolitical context for the development of indigenous cultural resources.

As far as ceremonies are concerned, 2006 was certainly a landmark with the establishment of what is being officially coined "state cults" (*guo ji* 國祭). The primary context was not religious but linked to heritage preservation. In a long list of 518 traditions or customs that the State Council recognizes as belonging to the "nontangible heritage of national importance"—and

---

38 On these events see Sang and Barmé, "Commemorating Confucius in 1966–67" and Wang Liang, "The Confucius Temple Tragedy of the Cultural Revolution," in *On Sacred Grounds*, ed. Wilson, 376–396. The gazetteer does not tell much about the period of the Cultural Revolution and there is nothing about the years 1967, 1968, 1969, 1971, 1972, 1975, and 1976.

39 The terms "educator" and "thinker" are the ones that are nowadays normally found in official texts. The evolution is striking compared with the way Confucius was described a few decades ago during the Cultural Revolution. In leaflets collected in Qufu and published during the Cultural Revolution he is condemned as "fierce advocate of the slavery system" or as "the great master of the proponents of a counterrevolutionary restoration."

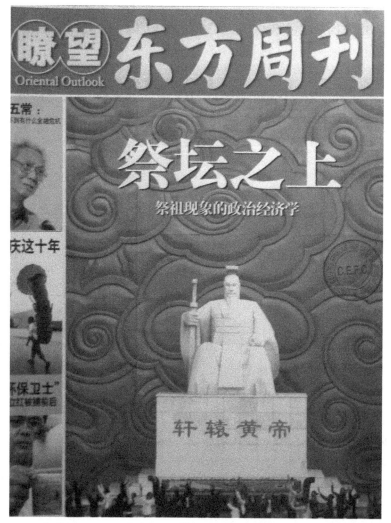

FIGURE 7.6 Cover page of the weekly magazine *Oriental Outlook* (*Liaowang Dongfang Zhoukan*). The title says: "On the sacrificial space: The political economy of the phenomenon of ancestors cult." The cover page shows dances being performed in front of Huangdi, the Yellow Emperor.

that ranges from traditional techniques to artistic practices of ethnic minorities—eight celebrations are included under the ambiguous category of "sacrificial rites" (*jidian* 祭典). These ceremonies are primarily organized to honor tutelary figures of Chinese civilization such as Emperor Yandi 炎帝 (in Yanling, Hunan), Emperor Huangdi 黄帝 (in Huangling, Shaanxi; Figure 7.6), Fuxi 伏羲 (in Tianshui, Gansu and Huaoyang, Henan), Nüwa 女娲 (in She, Hubei), and Yu the Great 大禹 (in Shaoxing, Zhejiang). But they also include two historical figures: Confucius (in Qufu) and Genghis Khan 成吉思汗 (in Ordos, Inner Mongolia). This list also encompasses Mazu 媽祖, a deity of popular religion (in Putian, Fujian).[40]

Attention should be paid to the label ascribed to these ceremonies: Contrary to what could be noted about Confucian ceremonies in Republican China, these new rites are described as "sacrificial rites" (*jidian* 祭典) and not merely as "commemorations" (*jinian* 紀念). Only field observation would make it possible to understand, in each case, to what extent this vocabulary depicts the celebration of things sacred or simply points to memorial gatherings. But beyond economic and touristic motivations that definitely play here a pivotal role, the mobilization of ritual specialists and high dignitaries of the regime also ascribes to these "cults" a dimension that is both political and "quasi-religious."[41] This twofold dimension is even reinforced by the fact that these ceremonies are not simply oriented toward inner China, but more generally toward the outside, that is, toward the great community of overseas Chinese and "Taiwanese compatriots," who actually often visit China to attend these cults.[42] Thus, these ceremonies tend to sacralize not only the state (or the nation-state as was largely the case in republican China), but more largely the *zuguo* 祖國, that is, the land of the ancestors, or the *shenzhou* 神州, the sacred land whose frontiers are potentially larger than those of the PRC.

In sum, state ceremonies honoring Confucius need to be understood within the more general context of a reinvented ritual and symbolic apparatus that is not limited to Confucianism but also encompasses mythical and tutelary figures, heroes venerated by national minorities such as Ghengis Khan, or popular deities: It is somewhat paradoxical to even see Mazu appearing in

---

40 See the First List promulgated by the State Council concerning Intangible Cultural Heritage, in 2006: http://www.gov.cn/zwgk/2006-06/02/content_297946.htm. Relevant items are nos. 480–487. About ceremonies honoring the Yellow Emperor, see Billeter, *L'Empereur jaune*. Regarding ceremonies honoring Yu the Great, see Sang Ye and Geremie Barmé, "The Great Yu/Da Yu 大禹: A Temple 禹廟 and a Tomb 禹陵," *China Heritage Quarterly* 20 (2009), http://www.chinaheritagequarterly.org/scholarship.php?searchterm=020_great_yu.inc&issue=020; and http://chinaheritagenewsletter.anu.edu.au/articles.php?searchterm=009_deluge.inc&issue=009 consulted on September 19, 2013.

41 Geremie R. Barmé and Sang Ye, "Research Notes: National Commemorative Ceremonies," *China Heritage Quarterly* 20 (2009), http://www.chinaheritagequarterly.org/scholarship.php?searchterm=020_intro_national_ceremonies.inc&issue=020.

42 On this point see Billeter, *L'Empereur jaune*, 363–394.

this list since popular religion, supposed to be "feudal and superstitious," is theoretically forbidden—even though it is practically tolerated.

In such a novel context, what can be said about the situation in Qufu?

Back to Qufu

The gazetteer of Shandong province, *Shandong sheng zhi*, provides useful pieces of information to trace the genealogy of the large ceremonies taking place today in Qufu. At the end of the 1970s, local authorities started to relate again to Confucius in a positive way through academic activities and exhibitions. At the same time some heritage preservation work was carried out in the so-called three Kongs (*san Kong* 三孔): The temple of Confucius (Kongmiao), his mansion (Kongfu), and the cemetery where Confucius and many members of the Kong lineage were buried (Konglin). In 1984, a Confucius Foundation (Kongzi jijinhui 孔子基金會) was established, headed by Gu Mu, a member of the State Council, and at the same time, a yearly tourist program called "Travel to Confucius's homeland on the occasion of his birthday" was inaugurated.[43] The tourism administration obviously played a pivotal role in the revitalization of ceremonies honoring Confucius.[44] The tourist program included not only visits to the site but also a performance of ancient ritual dances.

In 1989, this program was abandoned and replaced with a Confucius festival (Kongzi wenhua jie 孔子文化節) that today constitutes the framework of activities that we will expound in the next chapter. One year later, the festival acquired an "international" dimension (*guoji Kongzi wenhua jie* 國際孔子文化節) and gained the support of UNESCO. At the same time, the Confucius Foundation multiplied its activities in Qufu sometimes in partnership with entities such as the Singapore-based Institute of East Asian Philosophies that played an important role in the 1980s. The Confucian revival in a space broadly defined as "cultural China" was then promoted by Sino-American philosopher Tu Wei-ming.[45] The foundation also invited

---

43 *Shandong sheng zhi*, 657–658. The goals of this operation seem to have been purely touristic.

44 The tourism administration initiated the ceremonies with the support of the heritage preservation administration; Yan Hongliang and Bill Bramwell, "Cultural Tourism, Ceremony and the State in China," *Annals of Tourism Research* 35, no. 4 (2008): 974.

45 Tu Wei-ming, *Confucian Ethics Today: The Singapore Challenge* (Singapore: Federal Publications, 1984). For an overall picture see Makeham, *Lost Soul*, 21–41.

to Qufu Singapore's prime minister, Lee Kwan Yew, one of the major advocates of "Asian values" on the world stage. Gradually, the nature of the festival changed in the course of a negotiated process between central and local authorities.[46] Local authorities, at the end of the 1980s, expected to revive some ceremonies rather than a mere show and their main objective was then to boost tourism. Their application for the organization of ceremonies was however not approved: Central authorities did not want to leave any room for potential manifestations of Confucian religiosity. It is only gradually that the situation could change. From 1993 onwards, a public tribute of local officials and representatives of the Kong lineage started to take place. But it was in 2005, more than a decade later, that the ceremony acquired a new dimension with the participation of central government representatives and, later on, the inscription on the aforementioned list of "state cults." In sum, whereas after the Maoist period the initial interest for Confucius in Qufu was mainly motivated by tourism or academic research, the situation changed in the 1980s and 1990s, and all the more so in the first decade of the new century, with the return of an additional political and symbolical dimensions associated to the cults.

This political and symbolical dimension is precisely at stake in the project to establish in the Qufu area a "symbolic city of Chinese culture" (*Zhonghua wenhua biaozhi cheng* 中華文化標誌城), which some people have dubbed the "holy city of oriental culture" (*dongfang wenhua shencheng* 東方文化神誠), "common spiritual sanctuary of the Chinese nation" (*Zhonghua minzu gong you jingshen jiayuan* 中華民族共有精神家園), or even "cultural vice-capital" (*wenhua fudu* 文化副都).[47] This massive project—the figure of thirty billion yuan investment was circulating before the financial crisis of the end of the 2000s—initiated by local authorities and endorsed in 2008 at the central level, consists in creating a national symbolic space in an area that encompasses Qufu, Zoucheng 鄒城 (the native place of Mencius), and the Mountain of the Nine Dragons (*jiulongshan* 九龍山), located between these two spots (Figures 7.7, 7.8).[48]

---

46 The explanations that follow on the negotiations between local and central authorities for the organization of a cult in Qufu are based on Yan and Bramwell, "Cultural Tourism, Ceremony and the State in China," 980–984.

47 These different names can be found on the official website of the project (www.ccsc.gov. cn) and in declarations of people that took part in its blueprint.

48 The project was the object of very prominent media coverage during the 2008 session of the Chinese People's Political Consultative Conference (CPPCC) and generated fierce

FIGURE 7.7 The prospect of massive investment (thirty billion yuan) in the establishment of a "symbolic city of Chinese culture" hit the headlines, as can be seen here on the cover page of *Zhongguo xinwen zhoukan* [China Newsweek] 364 (October 2008).

Obviously, the project has a strong Confucian flavor or, more broadly, a pronounced flavor of traditional culture, even though it is not conceived as restricted to these dimensions. More generally, it is supposed to serve three main functions. First, it would be used as a space of presentation

---

controversy. It was originally a local initiative (probably linked to local economic development perspectives). However, it subsequently received the support of the country's top leaders—the website explicitly mentions the support of Hu Jintao and Wen Jiabao—and its implementation has been authorized by the National Commission for Development and

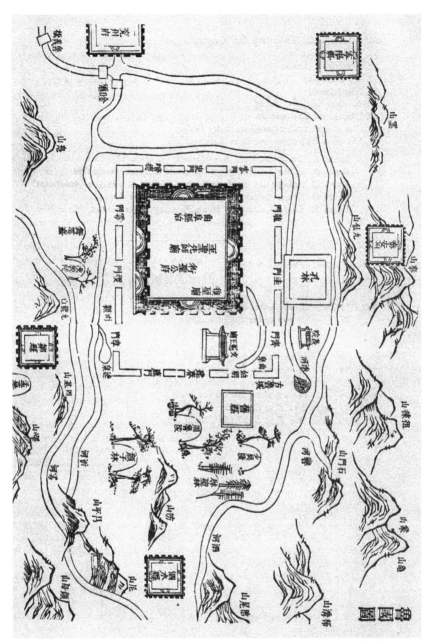

FIGURE 7.8 Ancient map of the kingdom of Lu in Shandong province and of the area where the "symbolic city of Chinese culture" may be established.

(*zhanshi gongneng* 展示功能) of Chinese culture and civilization through renovated sites and museums. Second, the area at the heart of the project would constitute a space of commemoration (*jiinian gongneng* 紀念功能) of ancestors, ancient sages, philosophers, heroes, and martyrs, thanks to the construction of a sort of pantheon, among other plans. Third, the project should also contribute to moral uplift and the edification of the people (*dehua gongneng* 德化功能).[49] The days have truly passed when Chairman Mao praised Qufu mainly for the outstanding production results of its agricultural cooperative.[50] The controversy stirred up by the project has been fierce and seems to have affected its implementation.[51] However, it is still clearly encompassed in Shandong province's Twelfth Five-Year-Plan[52] and operations on a number of construction sites have already started. This is for instance the case of a large Confucius Museum (Kongzi bowuguan 孔子博物館) which should, together with the "holy territory of Nishan" (Nishan shenjing 尼山神境) and the "Experimentation Center of Confucian

---

Reforms (NDRC). For more details on the project, see the above-mentioned website, as well as *Zhongguo xinwen zhoukan* 中國新聞週刊 [China Newsweek], March 24, 2008, 27–39 (special feature); *Liaowang dongfang zhoukan* [Oriental Outlook], April 10, 2008, 89–91; *Nanfang Zhoumou* [Southern Weekend], April 10, 2008, section D21–22.

49 *Chinese Cultural Symbolic City*, February 27, 2008, http://www.ccsc.gov.cn/qwfb/200802/t20080227_3221728.html.

50 Mao Zedong evoked Qufu in a speech delivered in 1955, but mainly to invite the visitor, beyond his tour of the temple and cemetery, to also visit the agricultural cooperative whose results were deemed outstanding: "Socialism is infinitely worthier than Confucian classics." See Xu Quanxing 許全興, *Mao Zedong yu* Kongfuzi 毛澤東與孔夫子 [Mao Zedong and Confucius] (Beijing: Renmin chubanshe, 2003), 324.

51 During the annual session of the CPPCC in March 2008 in Beijing, the representatives of this institution's Shandong provincial committee asked for funding from the central government. Such an initiative generated fierce reactions, and two petitions by members of the CPPCC opposed this project of constructing a symbolic city. The polemic and arguments of both sides have been largely discussed in the press and on the Internet. Among the main arguments of those opposing the project we have: (1) The huge cost of a project that is not considered a priority (however, the figure of thirty billion yuan has never been confirmed) and the question of the legitimacy of central funding for that kind of project; (2) the fact that a project with such a symbolic ambition has never been discussed by the National People's Congress (NPC) and CPPCC; (3) that the recommendations of experts from the Academy of Social Sciences and other scholars (several reports have been written) have replaced any real scientific debate; (4) that the project neither represents the whole of traditional culture nor reflects the diversity of nationalities that make up the country; (5) that the symbolic dimension of a city is the product of time and not an artificial construction. On these points, see the aforementioned documents.

52 *Chinese Cultural Symbolic City*, August 15, 2012, http://www.ccsc.gov.cn/qwfb/201208/t20120815_7337571.html.

Thought of the Headquarters of the Confucius Institutes,"[53] constitute "the three new sanctuaries of Confucius" (*xin san Kong* 新三孔). There is naturally a direct reference here to the traditional "three sanctuaries" (*san Kong*) evoked above.[54] In any case, the "holy city" (compared to Mecca or Jerusalem on the website of the project[55]) at least crystallizes all the ambiguities of the current rediscovery of traditional culture and Confucianism: Local imperatives of economic development that may be fueled by tourism; display of some sort of "authenticity" and identity by upper-level authorities (including central government officials); and a "creative" appropriation by the population of fragments of its past and of its tradition. This complex situation constitutes the background of the events that we are now going to describe.

---

53 *Kongzi xueyuan zongbu rujia sixiang tiyan zhongxin* 孔子學院總部儒家思想體驗中心. The experimentation center was inaugurated in September 2014: *China News*, September 29, 2008, http://www.chinanews.com/cul/2014/09-28/6639554.shtml.

54 *Chinese Cultural Symbolic City*, February 28, 2012, http://www.ccsc.gov.cn/xmtj/201202/t20120228_6955288.html.

55 *Chinese Cultural Symbolic City*, February 23, 2008, http://www.ccsc.gov.cn/qwfb/200802/t20080223_3216137.html.

8

Qufu, 2007

QUFU, CONFUCIUS FESTIVAL, September 26 to October 4, 2007. Organized on the occasion of the celebration of the 2,558th birthday of the sage, a series of events provide some fascinating clues about what could be termed the "Confucius phenomenon" of the 2000s. In this primarily descriptive chapter, we first introduce the involvement of the authorities at different levels and then examine a number of grassroots initiatives carried out in the name of Confucius.

The Variety of Top-down Initiatives

September 27, 2007: A bus heads quickly across the city of Qufu, escorted by a couple of police cars, lights flashing. On this rainy autumn morning, traffic is blocked in the center of Qufu in order to enable delegates of the World Confucian Conference (*Shijie ruxue dahui* 世界儒學大會), taking place just before the Confucius Festival, to access the city's official research organization on Confucianism, the Kongzi yanjiuyuan. It is in this monumental group of buildings that the inaugural session of the conference is going to take place. Organized by the PRC's Ministry of Culture and by Shandong provincial government, this event is supposed to become a new gathering place for global research on Confucianism (Figures 8.1 and 8.2). The group of invited participants is heterogeneous, a mixture of scholars and activists of different backgrounds, stature, and geographical horizons. Most of them are Chinese, or of Chinese descent, from the mainland or the diaspora. Around twenty foreigners are also invited, among whom are many Koreans. All these participants have arrived the day before, welcomed with a banquet hosted by the vice-governor of Shandong province.

FIGURE 8.1 Inaugural session of the World Confucian Conference in Qufu, 27 September 2007.
© Sébastien Billioud.

The inaugural meeting takes place in a large amphitheater and has a solemn character: Martial music, flowers, and grand speeches. The generality of the latter is commensurate with the ranks of the persons delivering the speeches. The governor of Shandong province discusses in a vague way Confucius's contribution to the idea of harmony, the global diffusion of Chinese culture, and the need to adapt Confucianism to the present era. The speech of the representative of the Ministry of Culture is very much in the same vein.[1] At a lower level, the official spokesman for Jining (Qufu's "mother prefecture") praises both traditional culture and Confucianism as tools of national cohesion (*ningjuli* 凝聚力), as well as their contribution to economic and tourism development. With the speech of the representative of Qufu's Kongzi yanjiuyuan there is a switch toward a much more activist position: Confucianism needs to be studied (*yanjiu* 研究), developed (*fazhan* 發展), and disseminated (*puji* 普及) among the masses

---

1 At the time that the inaugural meeting took place, a number of high-ranking personalities from the central government (including the deputy ministers of culture and education) were in town. They attended the inauguration ceremony of the festival in the stadium, but not the activities of the conference.

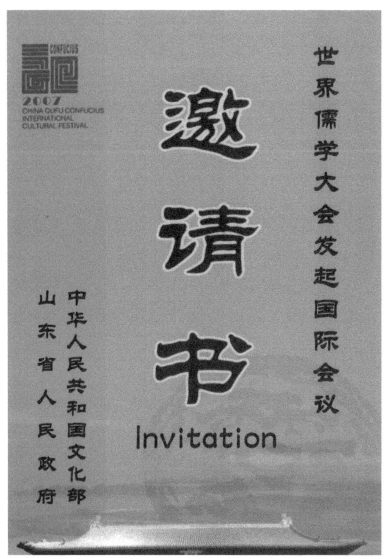

FIGURE 8.2 Invitation to the "International meeting of preparation of the first World's Confucian conference." Organizing institutions—the PRC's Ministry of culture and the provincial government of Shandong province—are explicitly mentioned.

through textbooks and so on. The efforts of the government are praised, in an allusion to the Eleventh Five-Year Plan that underscores the importance of traditional culture,[2] but the need for further measures is emphasized. A few famous scholars, such as philosopher Cheng Chung-ying and

---

2 See Billioud, "Confucianism, 'Cultural Tradition' and Official Discourses," 50–65.

historian Zhang Liwen, also deliver speeches, though with different flavors, pleading for a tolerant and humanist Confucianism.

The inaugural meeting culminates in the public reading of both the declaration of the World Confucian Conference and the draft of the charter regulating this conference in the future. Notable among the main points of these documents is that this conference will take place yearly with the funding of both the Ministry of Culture and the Shandong provincial authorities.[3] It will support the worldwide promotion of the study of Confucianism, the diffusion of the "excellent Chinese traditional culture,"[4] and the setting up of a "worldwide network of Confucian studies."[5] The declaration, full of good intentions (turning Confucianism into a useful spiritual resource in a world devastated by extreme exploitation of natural resources, moral crisis, etc.),[6] also reflects a tension between the affirmation of the universal dimension of Confucianism and its "usefulness" to the country in an ideological form.[7] These public speeches are followed in the afternoon by "working groups" aiming more or less—but not without difficulty—at approving the documents (charter, inaugural declaration) presented during the morning session and thus expressing the participants' approval of the whole project.[8]

The conference constitutes the first of the main activities conducted during the Confucius cultural festival, addressing a specific audience of

---

3 Shijie ruxue dahui faqi guoji huiyi 世界儒學大會發起國際會議, *Shijie ruxue dahui zhangcheng (cao'an)* 世界儒學大會章程 (草案) [(Draft) Charter of the World Confucian Conference], September 27, 2007, article 5.

4 Ibid., article 3.

5 Ibid., article 8.1.

6 Shijie ruxue dahui faqi guoji huiyi 世界儒學大會發起國際會議, *Shijie ruxue dahui faqi xuanyan (cao'an)* 世界儒學大會發起宣言 (草案) [Opening Declaration of the World Confucian Conference], September 27, 2007 (hereafter, "Opening Declaration"), paragraph 2.

7 There are a number of awkward formulas in the English version of the declaration, such as: "[Confucianism] encourages sacrifice for the nation and the spirit of selflessness." "Opening Declaration," paragraph 5. The declaration is largely in the vein of discourses of the 1980s on Asian values: It emphasizes the role of Confucianism in the economic growth of Southeast Asian countries and, more generally, its contribution to making a country "rich and strong" (*fuqiang* 富強); "Opening Declaration," paragraph 4.

8 Lively discussions took place within the working groups. Fierce critiques were formulated, reflecting some degree of disharmony within what was supposed to be a manifestation of "democratic unanimity." Ironically, a Japanese participant pointed out, to the surprise of the Chinese audience, that a few expressions used in the opening declaration were for him clearly reminiscent of formulas propagated by the Japanese occupying power in the 1930s, exalting the virtue of sacrifice in the name of the ancient "Kingly Way" (*Wangdao*).

scholars and activists. The second round of activities, on the other hand, is directed toward the masses.

Qufu Stadium, September 27, in the Evening

In a most chaotic fashion, a dense crowd flocks to the gates to attend the inauguration ceremony of the International Confucius Festival. High-ranking officials are many.[9] Both the benches and the central space are packed with an audience of thousands (possibly tens of thousands) of all ages and backgrounds (Figure 8.3). In one of the stands, people can be seen carrying pictures of Yu Dan, the media icon for many of those rediscovering traditional texts at that time. Impressive

FIGURE 8.3 Confucius Festival in Qufu Stadium, September 2007.
© Sébastien Billioud.

9 Noteworthy attendees of the inauguration ceremony include the vice-president of the CPPCC, Luo Haocai; two members of the standing committee of the NPC, Lin Zhaosu and Zeng Xianzi; the deputy minister of culture, Zhou Heping, and of education, Li Weihong; the deputy director of the National Bureau of Tourism, Wang Zhifa; and the president of Tsinghua University, Gu Binglin. See *Qi Lu wanbao* 齊魯晚報 [Evening newspaper of the Qi and Lu areas], September 28, 2007, A3.

towers provide a backdrop and large screens have been installed to enable people to follow the show, while television teams take their place on scaffolding. Sponsors of the event include a local Confucius wine company (*Kongfujia jiu* 孔夫家酒), whose banner advertisement are displayed above the stands. Projectors illuminate the scene and in the background three large characters twinkle in the night: *Zhonghua qing* 中華情.

Zhonghua qing: that is the theme of this inaugural evening of the festival. The expression is less common than *guoqing* 國情, which refers to the intrinsic circumstances of the country. It is an expression of Chineseness, the fundamental character of China understood as an entity that goes beyond frontiers (overseas Chinese are also encompassed, and maybe even all those linked to China by blood or culture). It also includes ethnic minorities. But *Zhonghua qing* is not simply the particular theme of a popular event to honor Confucius in Qufu. It is above all a popular television program of the CCTV4 channel (international Chinese-language channel of China's central television), entitled in English *Our Chinese Heart* (Figure 8.4).[10] The objective is to organize giant broadcasted shows—accessible both in China and internationally via the CCTV4 network. Displaying a variety of different modes of artistic expression (music and songs, theater, dance, etc.), they include artists of different origins: Mainland Chinese, Hong Kongese, Taiwanese, and foreign (with large numbers of Asian artists or artists from the overseas Chinese community). Each show is different and adapted to the context in which it is organized. Thus, in Qufu the content of the program (speeches, performances, scenography, etc.) is adapted to reflect the theme of the Confucius Festival.[11] But shows can be organized focusing on extremely different themes. The common point is that they address an audience that goes beyond Mainland Chinese and also encompasses overseas Chinese communities (the motto of the program is "Where there are people of Chinese descent, there is *Zhonghua qing*!"). All the TV shows also praise some form of "Chineseness."[12] Thus,

---

10 See the website of the program: http://cctv.cntv.cn/lm/zhonghuaqing/index.shtml.

11 The broadcast of the Qufu show (dated April 19, 2010) can be watched online: http://news.cntv.cn/program/zhongguoqing/20100419/104111.shtml.

12 Sometimes it is not simply Chineseness that is praised but directly China. See for instance the television show that was dedicated to the commemoration of the thirty years of reform and opening (*Jinin gaige kaifang 30 nian tebie jiemu*): http://news.cntv.cn/program/zhongguoqing/20100419/104343.shtml.

FIGURE 8.4 Program of the CCTV show, *Zhonghua qing*.

they can be linked to the issue of China's so-called soft power that was precisely becoming a focus point in 2007 within official discourses of the country's top leaders.[13]

In Qufu, lasting slightly more than two hours, the show features a mix of choreography inspired by the past, contemporary pop music and allusions to and praise of Confucius and traditional Chinese culture. The program is organized around three themes epitomizing this "Confucian Chineseness:" The idea of a community, respect for differences, and the dream of a grand world unity that finds its symbolic crystallization in the 2008 Olympic Games in Beijing.[14] Throughout the program, a triple dimension of Chinese culture is put to the fore: Local (the community of Chinese people, even when they are "scattered across the four seas"), regional (the sinicized world, harmonious beyond its differences, under the benevolent influence of Confucius), and global (through the reactivation of an ancient utopia of world unity or *Datong*, literally 'Great Unity'). The program benefits from a sophisticated scenography. During the performance, symbols of Chinese civilization (dragons, the "hundred families" surnames, the Great Wall, characters on rice paper, etc.) are projected on gigantic screens while huge balloons with the names of Confucius, Mencius, and disciples Zengzi and Yanhui rise slowly over the stadium (Figure 8.5). It is under these tutelary figures that Mina, a suggestively garbed young female Korean singer, offers a frenzied pop song to the enthusiastic crowd (Figure 8.6). The fervor of the audience, already increasing during the previous performances, reaches a climax at that moment, contrasting with the relative apathy of a large part of the audience during the sermons on China and its 5,000-year-old culture.

---

13 Nye mentions that: "In his keynote speech to the Seventeenth National Congress of the Communist Party of China, on October 15, 2007, President Hu Jintao stated that the CPC must 'enhance culture as part of the soft power of our country... a factor of growing significance in the competition in overall national strength.'" Joseph Nye, *The Future of Power* (New York: Public Affairs, 2011), 88.

14 The titles of the three parts of the program are noteworthy: (1) *Tong gen yi mai, si hai gong yang* 同根一脈,四海共仰, "Common roots, a single lineage. The four corners of the world share a same faith (in our culture)"; (2) *Xingtan chun yu, he er bu tong* 杏壇春雨,和而不同, "Spring rain on the almond platform [the place in the Confucius temple where the master used to teach], live in harmony while respecting differences"; (3) *Ren wen ao yun, sheng shi da tong* 人文奧運,盛世大同, "Humanist Olympic Games, the great unity of a flourishing world."

FIGURE 8.5 Confucius Festival in Qufu Stadium. Names of Confucius and two of his disciples as well as the name of Mencius can be read on the balloons rising slowly over the stadium. One can also distinguish the three twinkling characters: *Zhonghua qing*.

© Sébastien Billioud.

FIGURE 8.6 Big show in Qufu stadium, 27 September 2007.

© Sébastien Billioud.

Temple of Confucius, September 28

The grand ceremony honoring Confucius (*ji Kong da dian* 祭孔大典) that is about to take place this morning is supposed to constitute the climax of the festival. In the early morning, official guests gather on the street of the Way of Spirits (*shen dao* 神道) just outside the old town of Qufu, they line up and head toward the temple. In front of the old wall, they attend a small ceremony known as "lighting the holy fire of Chinese culture" (*zhonghua wenhua shenghuo* 中華文化聖火) (Figure 8.7). On the threshold of the temple, the procession merges with another large crowd and descends into confusion. The ceremony about to take place follows an early reading of the *Analects* of Confucius in the temple by one thousand young people (Figure 8.8).[15] At the heart of the temple, before the Hall of the Great Accomplisher (*Da cheng dian*), the chaos ceases in front of a line of PLA soldiers in "civil uniforms" (white shirts, black ties) (Figure 8.9). Alongside the terrace and behind the soldiers, a cohort of young readers of the *Analects* prepares to celebrate Confucius in his capacity of "Ancient Master" (*xianshi* 先師).

The ceremony itself is very simple. The delegations of guests (among them a CPPCC vice-president, Shandong provincial party secretary, Yu Dan, delegations of overseas Chinese, etc.) invited to honor Confucius are waiting at the foot of the terrace. When instructed, they walk up the stairs one after the other and head toward the altar. Then, for each group of delegates, PLA soldiers display floral offerings before the altar (Figure 8.10). Afterwards, the delegates walk to the floral displays to ritually arrange them and fix their ribbons. They step back (three steps) and bow three times (*san jugong* 三鞠躬) before the statue of the Master.[16] Such extremely simple offerings contrast strikingly with the complex preparation, liturgy, and animal sacrifices offered to Confucius in imperial China and even up into the contemporary era in Taiwan.[17] During the ceremony a few excerpts of

---

15 *Qi Lu wanbao*, September 28, 2007, A3.

16 Field observations and instructions given to the participants before the ceremony: *2007 jikong dadian xu zhi* (Things to know before the ceremony).

17 For the imperial era, see Wilson, "Sacrifice and the Imperial Cult of Confucius." For a first-hand testimony regarding the liturgy of ceremonies carried out during the republican period, see Biallas, *Konfuzius und sein Kult*, 100–115. On Taiwan, see Joseph S. C. Lam, "Musical Confucianism: The Case of *Jikong yuewu*," in *On Sacred Grounds: Culture, Society, Politics and the Formation of the State Cult of Confucius*, ed. Thomas A. Wilson (Cambridge, MA: Harvard University Press, 2003), 168.

FIGURE 8.7 The ceremony known as "lighting the holy fire of Chinese culture."
© Sébastien Billioud.

FIGURE 8.8 Around one thousand young people attended the early reading of Confucian classics prior to the Kongmiao ceremony.
© Sébastien Billioud.

FIGURE 8.9 Ceremony in the Kongmiao. In the first row, PLA soldiers in "civilian uniforms;" Behind them, readers of the *Analects* of Confucius; In the back, dancers and officials offering baskets of flowers.

© Sébastien Billioud.

FIGURE 8.10 PLA soldiers presenting and displaying offerings.

© Sébastien Billioud.

the *Analects* are also declaimed and a ceremonial address (*jiwen* 祭文) is read by a representative of the people's government of Shandong province.[18] Surprisingly, it consisted of eight-character-long verses (two times two characters echoing each other) celebrating "Confucius, the Ancestor of Chinese culture" (*Zhonghua wenhua xianzu Kongzi* 中華文化先祖孔子). Historically, this title does not seem to have been bestowed and contrasts strikingly both with the title of "Ancient Master" displayed on the temple and with the title of "Great Thinker and Educator of Ancient China" that appeared on the official invitation of the World Confucian Conference. This diversity of titles provides some good evidence of the extent to which Confucius has now become a most ambivalent signifier. Four main themes emerge out of this somewhat arcane prayer:

(1) A brief (supposedly) poetic and hagiographic portrait of Confucius:

> *In Shandong province, bordering on the sea,*
> *In the south of Mount Tai shone a star.*[19]
> *[The Sage was] born on an auspicious day,*
> *Drums resonated, music raised in the air.*
> *Celebrated by the song of the Yellow river*
> *Straight and vigorous, a pine tree grew on Mount Tai . . .*

(2) The idea of a continuum between China, a broader Chineseness encompassing overseas Chinese, and a world community interested in the "universality of Chinese values":

> *Our compatriots stem from a same matrix,*
> *Our roots are intertwined, our veins communicate.*
> *In Asia, in Africa, in Europe, in America,*
> *One hundred schools bear the name of Confucius.*
> *The Olympic Games*
> *Joyfully arrive at our capital city.*
> *To the whole world,*
> *We are awe-inspiring.*
> *The great unity is not a mere dream*
> *The whole world shares a common feeling . . .*

---

18 *Shandong shen renmin renfu daibiaozhang.*

19 Kuixing 奎星.

(3) The celebration of a number of classical Confucian values that can also be "harmonized" with official slogans:

> *Heaven, Earth and Human beings are in harmony*
> *All beings flourish*
> *Let us go along with the times*
> *Everything transforms and appears harmoniously*
> *When Heaven is in harmony, rains nurture all.*
> *When Earth is in harmony, myriads of beings flourish.*
> *When the family is in harmony, its activities thrive.*
> *When the country is in harmony, stability prevails.*
> *The gentleman has some empathy for the others,*
> *In harmony with them, he nevertheless respects their differences.*
> *Loyalty and filial piety are the supreme good*
> *[and the basis of] self-cultivation, family regulation,*
> *government of the people, pacification of the world.*
> *When virtue is used to govern people,*
> *Good energy prevails and the wind is pure . . .*

(4) The celebration of China's emergence as a "great country" (*da guo*) or a cultural realm (*huaxia* 華夏) that goes beyond the nation-state:

> *A great country emerges,*
> *Strengthening itself constantly.*
> *Now rising,*
> *China is regenerated.*

The completion of the offerings by all the delegations is followed by ritual dances performed by a professional dancing troop in Ming dynasty garb (Figure 8.11).[20] It is worth emphasizing here that in the traditional ceremonies to honor Confucius, dances and music were often performed by the scholars-literati themselves and often by novices.[21] The ceremony ends in complete pandemonium as the terrace is

---

20 On costumes see Lam, "Musical Confucianism," 156–164. The comparison between the illustrations provided by Lam and the costumes of the dancers in 2007 suggests that the model used today is of Ming inspiration. The same troop performed a few days later at ceremonies in the Hong Kong stadium.

21 Wilson, "Sacrifice and the Imperial Cult of Confucius," 266–270.

FIGURE 8.11 Ritual dances
© Sébastien Billioud.

FIGURE 8.12 After the main ceremony, another ceremony takes place for representatives of the Kong lineage.
© Sébastien Billioud.

opened to the public and to groups of tourists ritually snapping away at the altar and at each other. A while later, a shorter cult is organized by members of the Kong lineage to honor Confucius as their ancestor (Figure 8.12).

Grassroots Confucianism and Confucian Ceremonies

A few days after the official festival, a series of much more discreet events took place in Qufu. These no longer highlighted the national or international dimension of the event but a rather local dimension largely ignored by most of the media. From October 2 to October 4, 2007, ritual ceremonies were organized in the temple of Mencius in the nearby city of Zoucheng (birthplace of Mencius) and in the Confucius temple in the sanctuary of Nishan. Around the same time, a local association for the promotion of ancient ritualistic culture and music was inaugurated in Qufu.

Although they did not enjoy extensive coverage, these events provide an insight into the way *minjian* Confucianism has to deal with local authorities in order to create a space for its activities.

On the first day, a lunch gathers in the city of Zoucheng a group of activists coming from different places in China in order to honor Mencius. Mr. Y, the master of ceremonies is a native of Qufu where he works as an electrical technician in a local company. Gradually, he has become the head of both a real and an online network of people from relatively modest backgrounds interested for a variety of reasons in the revival of Confucian traditional culture. Among them are company employees, local administrative cadres and clerks, craftsmen, primary school teachers, intellectuals who never entered academia, and so on. In the present case, the participants include a few cadres, employees, and teachers, as well as a group of young female students from Shaanxi province Normal University who came as a group along with their professors. After the lunch, everyone dresses in Ming garb, which includes wooden tablets and, for the men, the cap of the scholar-literati. After some preliminary excitement and confusion, the atmosphere becomes more solemn and participants start to exchange about how to behave and prepare themselves for the ritual. They line up in two columns, male participants in the front and start a procession that walks in through the streets of

FIGURE 8.13 *Minjian* Confucians in Zoucheng's Mencius temple.
© Sébastien Billioud.

Zoucheng, heading toward the famous temple dedicated to Mencius, the Yashengmiao (Figure 8.13).[22]

The temple is well preserved and relatively protected from the invasions of tourist crowds. Established during the Song dynasty, it offers an atmosphere of quiet and beauty that contributes to the dignity and the solemnity of the ceremony. The column of participants enters into the temple, passing by a billboard of Hu Jintao's era featuring "The socialist concept of honor and disgrace" (*barong bachi* 八榮八恥) (Figure 8.14).[23]

---

22 Let us recall that there are in Zoucheng, as in Qufu for Confucius, three main spaces dedicated to Mencius: The temple, the mansion, and the cemetery.

23 It is in the context of the promotion of morals that the campaign of the "Eight honors, eight disgraces" was launched in 2006. The reference to the idea of shame was understood by many Confucian activists as a direct reference to classical morals. The eight honors and eight disgraces (or shames) are: (1) It is honorable to love the motherland; it is shameful to harm it; (2) it is honorable to serve the people; it is shameful to do disservice; (3) it is honorable to follow science; it is shameful to remain ignorant; (4) it is honorable to be diligent; it is shameful to be indolent and lazy; (5) it is honorable to be united and help each other; it is shameful to affect the others and strive for one's benefit; (6) it is honorable to be honest and trustworthy; it is shameful to give up morals for the sake of one's benefits; (7) it is honorable to be disciplined and law-abiding; it is shameful to be chaotic and lawless; (8) it is honorable to live frugally and struggle hard; it is shameful to wallow in luxuries and pleasures.

FIGURE **8.14** The eight socialist glories and disgraces.
© Sébastien Billioud.

They gather on the terrace before the main building (the Yashengdian), where they are joined by a few local people. Four of five people perform most of the liturgy, while the role of the other participants is mainly to bow down, kneel down, or kowtow as required.

On the terrace, a table is used both for ritual ablutions and the preparation of alcohol offerings in ancient-style tripods. Incense is also burned in incense burners. The ritual is quite simple: It consists of a series of ritual gestures (bowing down, kneeling down, kowtowing), offerings of wine and silk inside the temple, kneeling to read out a ritual document (*jiwen* 祭文: the document is not burned in Zoucheng as it will be a few days later in Nishan), and another series of ritual gestures. In his capacity

FIGURE 8.15 *Minjian* ceremony in the Mencius temple.
© Sébastien Billioud.

as master of ceremonies, Mr. Y. plays a central role, declaiming with a deep and confident voice all the ritual formulae. The whole process lasts little more than an hour (Figure 8.15).

After the end of the ceremony, the atmosphere becomes joyful. Some of the girls attending the event in Ming garb enjoy themselves trying to perform "traditional dances" and all the participants visit afterwards the remains in and around the temple. The day ends with a meeting in the ancient mansion of the Meng lineage (Mengfu), nowadays used as educational premises (among other structures, by a local branch of Renmin University's institute for national studies, or *guoxueyuan*). An evening class of classics reading for children is organized by a group of elderly people.

The day after, another ritual ceremony is organized in Confucius's sanctuary of Nishan, supposed to be the birthplace of the sage and located around thirty kilometers south of Qufu. The whole process is comparable with the one that took place in Zoucheng's Mencius temple (Figures 8.16–8.18).

It is a ceremony of another type that takes place the next day in the conference room of a hotel, celebrating the founding of the Holy City Society for the Promotion of Ritual Culture and Music" (*Shengcheng liyue wenhua cujinhui* 聖城禮樂文化促進會). Some of the main participants of

FIGURE 8.16 *Minjian* ceremony in Confucius temple, Nishan, 2007.
© Sébastien Billioud.

FIGURE 8.17 Reading of a prayer (*jiwen*), Confucius temple, Nishan, 2007.
© Sébastien Billioud.

FIGURE 8.18 Burning the prayer (*jiwen*), Confucius temple, Nishan, 2007.
© Sébastien Billioud.

the Mencius temple ritual ceremonies are here, but in a completely different micropolitical context.

Around sixty people take part in the meeting, the objective of which
is to officially establish the society and appoint its board of directors
(Figures 8.19 and 8.20). The setting and the sequence of events have
been carefully prepared. A large portrait of Confucius hangs on the rear
wall, behind a long table set on the stage. Traditional music opens the
ceremony while three categories of people seat themselves facing the
assembly: Local representatives of Jining district and the city of Qufu
(culture, tourism, and education bureaux), members of the Kong lineage (descendents of Confucius), and Confucian educators and activists
acquiring some form of legitimacy through this ceremony.

The ceremony starts with three ritual bows (*san jugong*) in front of
Confucius's picture and the reading of a "decision" praising the "historical" creation of the society. In his capacity as still-provisional vice-president
of the society, Mr. Y., the electrical technician who acted as master of

FIGURE 8.19 Ceremony celebrating the founding of the Holy City Society for the Promotion of Ritual Culture and Music.
© Sébastien Billioud.

FIGURE 8.20 Members of the Society for the Promotion of Ritual Culture and Music.
© Sébastien Billioud.

ceremonies the day before, gives an overview of the mission of the society: Handing down the rites of Confucius and Mencius, promoting "popular education" (*minjian jiaoyu* 民間教育) (giving assistance to local schools, free lessons on the classics, calligraphy, moral education), organizing activities related to classical culture for children and events promoting the "Confucian six arts," disseminating information on classical culture and Confucianism, encouraging the movement of rediscovery of traditional dress (*hanfu yundong* 漢服運動), reviving traditional festivals, among others. A few guests from other provinces are then welcomed and an old carpenter is given the opportunity to evoke with exaltation the homeland of Confucius and the coming Olympic Games.

The process of appointing the directors of the society takes place afterwards: A list prepared in advance is submitted to the—obviously unanimous—approval of the participants. Names and titles are in some cases accompanied by the designation "descendant of Confucius" (*Kongzi de houyi* 孔子的後裔). The president-elect, Mr. Kong Deban, is a member of the standing committee of the consultative assembly (*zhengxie* 政協) of Jining. In his speech he praises the "harmonious socialist society" promoted by Hu Jintao, the function of "education-transformation" (*jiaohua*) provided by rites and music, and the role that Chinese culture will increasingly play in the world. This particular ceremony is put in the larger context of a true renaissance of Chinese civilization (*wenming fuxing* 文明復興). Among the interventions, the most sophisticated is a discourse from a teacher from Xi'an, who argues for a new role for ritualism today: It is better, he says, "to evoke a real civilization of the rite rather than a simple culture. Civilization expresses the difference between humanity and animality that was defined very early in China." Many quotes from the classics (especially the *Liji* and the *Zhouli*) are referenced to show how a series of wrong interpretations, from the May 4th Movement to the Cultural Revolution, simply misunderstood the meaning of ritualism, treating it as nothing more than a "feudal practice." "Cultural renaissance," the Xi'an teacher posits, "cannot simply rely on law, it also needs to rely on rites." And this implies the promotion of a different relationship between scholars (*xuezhe*) and society:

> An increasing number of scholars now realize that Confucianism is not only knowledge; it cannot be separated from society. Confucians can no longer be these "wandering souls." The renaissance of knowledge in China is no longer a new phenomenon. But the renaissance

that is needed today is the renaissance of Chinese culture, and its prerequisite is the renaissance of rites!

The ceremony ends with the presentation of a calligraphy evoking the Confucian virtue of "benevolence" (*ren* 仁), and the final speech concludes by emphasizing the importance of ritual and music in the field of moral transformation.

Now that the sequence of events that took place in the context of the 2007 Confucius cultural festival is introduced, the next chapter attempts to analyze how a post-Maoist ritual Confucianism nowadays emerges between popular initiatives and ideological enterprises.

9

The Use and Abuse of Confucius

THE OBSERVATION OF these few days of ceremonies at a specific location with a long historical relation to Confucianism provides an additional perspective on the various meanings the figure of Confucius has taken in Chinese society today. Most of all, an analysis of the Confucius cultural festival contributes to the discussion of the following questions: How is a post-Maoist Confucianism possible? More precisely, how can an official enterprise not devoid of ideological dimension coexist with a number of local initiatives that claim to be "popular"? What kinds of relationships (coexistence, coordination, tension) can be identified between these two types of discourses and practices? How is it possible within such a context to articulate a post-Maoist ethos inspired by Confucianism and claiming a Confucian identity?

From Cosmic Rituals to Ideological Ceremonials: Celebrating a Confucius Devoid of Confucianism

The first portion of the events described above was the result of official initiatives. The authorities at different levels (national, provincial, local) organized various gatherings in the Confucius Research Institute, in the modern stadium of Qufu, and in the ancient Confucius temple. Each time, they targeted specific audiences: academic circles, the masses, the regime's new elite (political and economic). Not surprisingly, the series of events reflects two characteristics of Chinese society: Its ideological background and the increasing merchandizing of culture. The ideological agenda intertwines here with the economic needs of local authorities, for which cultural heritage and tourism revenue constitute important trump cards for local development.

An essential aspect is probably the following: If one considers that ritual lies at the heart of Confucian tradition, the aforementioned gatherings unveil fundamental performative contradictions. In other words, while these official ceremonies and gatherings claim to celebrate the sage, it is as if the figure of Confucius were cut off from Confucianism. If Confucian rituals demand an internal (*nei* 內) participation in the ceremony in a spirit of both respect and harmonization of emotions,[1] which fragments of this ancient conception of ritual still survive in planned activities seemingly characterized by a pure instrumental rationality?

The influence of a post-Maoist habitus is manifested differently in the three spots where official gatherings take place. In the Qufu stadium, the figure of Confucius is referred to in various ways, from slogans to commercials, but the event tends to turn into a gigantic show and party for the masses. It is only by borrowing a number of forms usually found in political rallies (speeches, symbols, enthusiasm from a minority of activists) that the cultural and ideological dimensions of the event are emphasized and that collective feelings may be channeled in a direction that is not pure entertainment. Moreover, the media coverage being even more important than the event itself, one may wonder what remains of the nonentertainment dimension of the show when it is broadcasted to the wider worldwide audience of the CCTV program *Our Chinese Heart* (*Zhonghua qing*). At the Confucius Research Institute where the inaugural conference takes place, the contrast is striking between the message of harmony and openness professed in the manifesto and the rigid bureaucratic procedures aimed at the manufacturing of consensus. However, it is of course the official events taking place in the ancient Kongmiao that epitomize the tension between the habitus of the organizers and the ancient ritual spirit that those ceremonies were theoretically meant to celebrate and express.

Let us highlight a number of features of such a tension, a tension that generates, as mentioned earlier, a performative contradiction characteristic of rites devoid of ritual spirit. First, and most blatantly, the ceremony was characterized by the imposing presence of the state apparatus in the form of policemen and PLA soldiers (in civil uniforms: white shirt, black tie, and so on). In that respect, one could emphasize that ceremonies performed in Qufu to honor Confucius are normally only civil (*wen* 文) in

---

1 Let us recall the historical association of the notion of *li* (rites) with that of *qing* 情 (emotions).

nature. Granted, the harmonious combination of the martial (*wu* 武) and the civil is a classical theme of Chinese cosmology. Suffice it to mention the existence in China of *wenwu miao* 文武廟, that is, civil and martial temples. Nonetheless, the rigidity of the PLA soldiers and of the young readers chanting quotations from the *Lunyu* transformed into slogans created, in the present case, an atmosphere hardly compatible with reverence. Moreover, it was a very heterogeneous population that gathered at the temple with a variety of motivations: Officials and their many guests, organizers from local institutions, troops of professional dancers, journalists, visitors, foreign tourists, and so on. This mix of rigidity in the organization and heterogeneity of the public's expectations combined with an overall ignorance regarding these rites and their ancient meaning.[2] It has often been noted that rituals do not primarily aim at promoting sets of precise beliefs and that they often leave enough room for a diversity of interpretations. But one usually underscores the necessary existence of a "minimal consent."[3] What is particularly striking in the present case is that this minimal consent hardly seemed to exist. The audience was largely in a position of exteriority vis-à-vis the cult that it attended and, to the outside observer, it was as if the main collective ritual were reduced to raising high one's camera and taking pictures.

The Emergence of a New Minjian *Ritualism*

Taking into account the outward and instrumental dimension of these official events, it is possible to contrast them with newly observed attitudes in the activities initiated by popular (*minjian*) Confucian activists.

Both in the Mencius temple and in the Confucius sanctuary of Mount Nishan one encountered a similar circle of activists eager to go some distance with the "Confucius Festival," while considering it excessively political and commercial and lacking any direct relationship with the tradition they embrace. A true ritualism, though simple in its forms, makes it possible to gather a group of supporters who share their ideals and commitment to a Confucian revival.

---

2 This remark does not apply to the rites performed after the official ceremony by a delegation of the Kong lineage.

3 Catherine Bell, *Ritual Theory, Ritual Practice* (New York and Oxford: Oxford University Press, 1992), 182–187.

The rituals at Zoucheng (Mencius's temple) and Nishan do not originate with decisions by the state apparatus but with the desires of people, more often than not from modest backgrounds. It is helpful to provide some examples of their specific itineraries in order to understand why and how a vague interest in the revival of the tradition translates into concrete practices borrowed from such a tradition. The case of one of the main organizers of the *minjian* activities, Mr. Y., enables us to better understand the gradual transition process between an imaginary dimension of Confucianism and its living reality.

Mr. Y., who was born in 1969 in Qufu and is now an electrical technician, insists that his interest in Confucianism is not the product of an encounter with someone or with an outside doctrine:

> Contrary to many intellectuals who have only recently realized the importance of Confucianism, I encountered it during my childhood. At that time, the temple of Confucius was silent and deserted, but it was for me the best of playgrounds. I also frequently enjoyed wandering across Konglin, the "forest" that constitutes the large cemetery of Confucius's descendants. I was impregnated with this atmosphere and have always had a feeling of closeness with the culture of Qufu. When I entered secondary school I was interested in history and preferred to read books related to the classics despite the opposition of my teachers.[4]

Mr. Y. experienced very early, at an age when he was not really able to understand the meaning of such an emotional state, a feeling of belonging to a civilization with an infinitely valuable past but which had somehow become ossified due to all the attacks, destruction, and waves of censorship it had suffered. It was entirely by his own initiative that he attempted in the 1980s to translate his vague intuitions into more explicit values. This individual quest took the form of solitary study of texts and the daily writing, starting from the 1990s, of a personal diary used as a tool of moral self-cultivation (*xinxing riji* 心性日記). These reflections and his understanding of the situation of Confucianism in Chinese society would later be introduced in a little booklet titled *Engaging with Confucianism* and that he would distribute free of charge in activist

4 Interview, Qufu, March 2007.

circles.⁵ Far from being an academic writing, this short text is introduced as the contribution of a student or disciple of Confucianism (*rujia xuezi* 儒家學子) who explains why his "belief" matters, whether for himself or for society at large. In fact, the intellectual and spiritual itinerary of Mr. Y goes far beyond a mere personal quest. He is extremely pessimistic about the situation of Chinese society (spiritual vacuum, bankruptcy of the educational system in the realm of values, social injustice, etc.) and identifies Confucianism as the solution to what he primarily understands as a cultural problem. Therefore, he encourages all those sharing with him a "similar faith" to introduce it to the others: "It is not simply a matter of self-cultivation and expression of virtuous power. It is necessary to strive to promote the Way (*chuan Dao* 傳道), to work hard to regenerate the people (*zuo xinmin* 作新民), or, in other ways, to guide society to establish harmony, transform the destiny of an ignorant and backward mankind, and implement an everlasting peace."⁶ While he benefits from the support of both his family and a group of friends in Qufu, it is thanks to his clever utilization of the Internet that he has managed to set up a local and nationwide network of Confucian sympathizers and activists.

In 2004, he built with his wife a virtual online "academy," the *Zhusi shuyuan*, in reference to Confucius's study hall on the Sihe River. He considered that this website would serve as a tool for the promotion of classical texts, the establishment of a small group sharing an interest in Confucianism, and the organization of ritual ceremonies within the "space of the people" (*minjian*).⁷

> We started to organize ritual ceremonies in 2004. These cults (*jisi huodong* 祭祀活動) could take place in the Kongmiao. In accordance with tradition and contrary to the official festival, we honor Confucius twice a year, in spring and in autumn. Once we had 270 believers (*xinyangzhe* 信仰者). People establish contact with

---

5 Yan Ping 炎平, *Zoujin ruxue* 走進儒學 [Advancing into Confucianism] (Qufu: Qufu shengcheng liyue wenhua cujinhui).

6 Yan, *Zoujin ruxue*, 49. Among the original ideas advocated in this booklet is the necessity for each Confucian to participate in his life in two pilgrimages to the holy city of Qufu. Mr. Y thinks that Confucianism should become an official religion but without being limited to this dimension.

7 On Mr. Y.'s activism, see the report in Kang Xiaoguang's *Dangdai Zhongguo dalu wenhua minzuzhuyi yundong yanjiu*, 104–110.

each other on an individual basis. When they are fond of these rites, they contact each other and organize themselves. They are people from a variety of different backgrounds, not scholars . . .[8]

On the basis of rituals observed in 2007 in the temple of Mencius and in Nishan, one can only highlight how the spirit of these ceremonies differs from that of the official festival in the Confucius temple. The small group collectively performing the rites is here made up of individuals from different backgrounds who probably have very different imaginary representations of Confucianism. But one has to acknowledge the existence of a true ritual community. First, the overall atmosphere of these ceremonies is both solemn and devoid of rigidity. Since the participants' historical and practical knowledge of these rituals varies, it is Mr. Y. who takes the role of ritual master. He is the central figure of these ceremonies, due both to the respect attached to his long-standing dedication to Confucianism and to his longer experience with the rites. However, he is not a ritual specialist, if this category applies to someone who has been initiated within a clearly codified ritual tradition. It is indeed a striking feature of the current Confucian revival to see many activists rediscover or reinvent, mostly through ancient texts, the rituals associated with Confucian ceremonies. In the present case, the performance of each phase of the ritual generates brief discussions between the main participants: They raise concrete questions about appropriate gestures and the positioning of the masters of ceremonies outside and within the temple, the way of presenting offerings or the proper transition between different steps of the ceremony.[9] In fact, such a ritual practice actually paves the way for self-transformation, both at the level of the individual and at the level of the group. Since none of the participants is an expert, the whole group is engaged in a mutual self-learning process, the physical impact of which is genuinely impressive. The ceremony that started in a friendly and joyful atmosphere gradually acquires a real solemnity. The original awkwardness of gestures and

---

8 Interview, Qufu, March 2007.

9 It is difficult here not to think of and mention the *Analects*, 3–15: "The Master on entering the Grand Ancestral Hall asked questions about everything. Someone remarked: 'Who said this son of a man from the Zou village knows about observing ritual propriety (*li* 禮)? On entering the Grand Ancestral Hall he asks questions about everything.' When Confucius heard of this, he said: 'to do so is itself observing ritual propriety.'" (Ames and Rosemont, *Analects of Confucius*, 85–86).

postures progressively turns into a collective attitude of reverence (*jing* 敬). In other words, bodies that only a short time ago reflected the daily habits of technicians, primary school teachers, craftsmen, or minor cadres undergo a radical transformation through the very performance in which they are engaged. Movements become slower and increasingly fluid, a transformation especially obvious during the offerings to Mencius or when a *jiwen* (prayer) is read and punctuated by interjections uttered by Mr. Y. with a calm, loud voice. Linking the individualities, a single ritual body takes shape, through which ritual efficiency is attained.

The solemn beauty of the places where these rites took place, as well as the feeling of facing the ancient sages, contributed to an atmosphere of reverence far from the noise and the exteriority of official ceremonies. Other attempts by the same group to nurture a ritual spirit translated into the organization of the "first cantonal banquet rite and second archery rite of the holy city." Although these kinds of rites are extensively described in the *Book of Ceremonies and Rites* (*Yi li*)[10] they provided in our case the opportunity of a gathering somewhat more relaxed than temple cults. The spirit of the archery rite was supposed to be inspired by a short passage of the *Analects*.[11] It took place in a park with the advice of a craftsman specialized in the production of ancient-style bows who had come especially for the event. In the evening, a dozen men in Ming garb and wearing scholar-literati caps made way for each other in front of the targets and awkwardly shot a few arrows before inviting the young ladies attending the event to do the same.

Some of the activists attending the event were well aware of the different function played by rites: Beyond the mere regulation of relationships between men and spirits or gods, they also understand that rites aim at promoting virtues of civility within society. However the banquet and the archery session were less successful than the temple cults. It seems that these "popular Confucians" had reached the limits of their ritualistic dreams. While places such as the Yashengmiao or Nishan, endowed with the prestige of a long religious history, seemed to offer proper conditions

---

10 Along with the *Zhou li* (周禮, *The Rites of Zhou*) and the *Li ji* (禮記, *Book of Rites*), the *Yi li* (儀禮) is one of the three main books (*san li* 三禮) of ancient China introducing rites and ceremonies.

11 *Analects* 3–7: "The Master said: 'Exemplary persons (*junzi* 君子) are not competitive, except where they have to be in the archery ceremony. Greeting and making way for each other, the archers ascend the hall, and returning they drink a salute. Even in contesting, they are exemplary persons.'" (Ames and Rosemont, *Analects of Confucius*, 83).

for the realization of convincing rites, the other attempts to ritualize human relations hardly produced anything more than parodies of rituals or a vain nostalgia toward fragments of Confucian heritage.

While the rituals do not all work in the same way and with a similar efficacy, what are we to learn from these events taken as a whole? We know that the participants come from various provinces in order to celebrate together Confucius in Qufu. Besides, they have extremely different sociocultural and socioprofessional backgrounds. Many would hardly have had a chance to meet in other contexts. The relationships established on the Internet before the ceremonies already enabled a number of exchanges and the emergence of a small "virtual" group sharing the same interests. But the Qufu gatherings, by extracting everyone for a while from his daily life, also made it possible to create for a limited and "liminal" period of time, a little ritual community. This "communitas," after the week spent together, will loosen itself due to the distance separating its members, but it will not disappear.[12] On the contrary, the motivation and commitment of the activists is reinforced after this collective experience and they keep in touch before gathering again for new celebrations. In the course of fieldwork we would encounter again in completely different contexts some of the people we met in Qufu and who were ready at any time to dress in Ming garb—the liturgical dress of these new "Confucian priests"—in order to honor Confucius throughout the country. Whereas this new group of "ritual specialists" remains limited in size—it probably does not encompass more than a few thousand people in the whole country—its emergence nevertheless paves the ground for a ritual reconstruction of Confucianism. In a way that echoes our previous discussions on *sishu* education, dreams of small cells of activists generate concrete and creative projects that might well give birth in the future to much more massive developments.

Interactions between "Popular" and "Official" Confucianism

In spite of the contrasts highlighted above, one cannot simply oppose popular (*minjian*) and official (*guanfang*) Confucianism. These two denominations rather constitute two extremities of a continuum within which many different attitudes are possible.

---

12 Victor Turner, *Drama, Fields and Metaphors: Symbolic Action in Human Society* (Ithaca, NY, and London: Cornell University Press, 1974), 23–59 and especially 45.

In China, at the start of the new century, there is no doubt that numerous spaces could be termed "equivocal": Actors pursuing distinct strategies, if not contradictory ones, are nevertheless able to interact by relying on a similar discourse and comparable behavioral codes. It is only by exploring specific contexts that one may determine whether the people involved tacitly accept the polysemy of symbols they refer to or whether they deliberately use a dual language.

At that point, one may point out that this "strategic equivocality" can be understood within a more general framework of transaction and negotiation on cults, myths, and symbols between different players (authorities, local or central; various social groups). Such a framework can be traced back to the imperial era and is somehow being perpetuated under a new guise in the post-Maoist period. In his work on Guandi, the god of war, Prasenjit Duara introduces the concept of "superscription" to discuss how rival versions of a myth may "jostle, negotiate and compete for position" without, however, erasing each other.[13] Michael Szonyi, in his study of the cult of the five emperors in late imperial China, shows that official efforts to standardize the gods and impose a model of superscription may fail when facing the resilience of local cultures capable of producing the illusion of compliance with state-sanctioned discourses and policies.[14] As will be discussed below, the equivocality observed in our contemporary Confucian context somehow echoes these various analyses of intertwined layers of meaning and discourse.

This equivocality originates neither with the authorities nor at the grassroots level: it is widely shared across most of the behaviors, and probably makes it possible to characterize as a whole the post-Maoist ethos of popular Confucianism today. But this was, after all, to be expected. It would have been indeed surprising not to find in activists' circles traces of several decades of communist rhetoric and the molding of minds and bodies. Let us here illustrate this point.

A thirty-seven-year-old cadre came from Shaanxi province in order to join the popular activities organized by Mr. Y. A party member and at the same time one of the itinerant Confucian militants supporting revivalist

13 Prasenjit Duara, "Superscribing Symbols: The Myth of Guandi, Chinese God of War," *Journal of Asian Studies* 47, no. 4 (1988): 778–795.

14 Michael Szonyi, "The Illusion of Standardizing the Gods: The Cult of the Five Emperors in Late Imperial China," *Journal of Asian Studies* 56, no. 1 (1997): 113–135.

efforts wherever they take place, Mr. G. retains through his attire, attitude, and language the image of the cadre he has always been. However, his embrace of Confucian ideals (in the way he understands them) has the character of a true conversion. "I have decided," he says, "to fully dedicate myself to a Confucian research society in my province and to launch a website to go with it." He adds, jokingly: "In a way, I have remained a professional revolutionary!"

Indeed, Mr. G. devotes to his cause all his proselytizing energy, as well as apparently very good organizational skills. Following the example of his daughter, who joined classics reading classes, he has himself learned the Four Books by rote, using first a local method and then the pedagogy of Taiwanese educator Wang Caigui. He is now able to recite Confucius's *Analects* or the *Mencius* with the same quick and uniform voice.

During the Mencius ritual, he put a yellow scarf around his neck but did not dress in Ming garb. Somehow, he took the role of the person in charge of public relations, dealing with the few visitors who joined the ceremony on site and inviting some of them to pay tribute to Confucius through a rudimentary ceremony. He also attended the inaugural meeting of the local Society for the Promotion of Ritual Culture and Music described in chapter 8. On that occasion, he delivered a prepared speech during which he read with fervor a number of phrases in classical Chinese. His rhetoric and body language looked very much like those of a propaganda specialist indulging his own convictions.[15]

The organization of the ceremony for the foundation of the Society for the Promotion of Ritual Culture and Music and the presence of representatives of local authorities (education, tourism, culture) illustrates that a network of activists such as Mr. Y., appointed vice-president of the society, needs some recognition through an institutional process. The keynote speech of the ceremony thoroughly echoed official rhetoric and ideology:

> Distinguished leaders and comrades:
> The creation of the Society for the Promotion of Ritual Culture and Music of the holy city of Qufu has a special historical significance.

---

15 When asked about the compatibility of his Confucian commitment with his fidelity to the Chinese Communist Party (CCP), he was not embarrassed at all: "Are not the goals the same? The idea has always been to reach the Great Unity (*Datong*), but basing ourselves on a more advanced material basis. In any case, there is no need to always have rigid definitions. The party has been able to rectify its practice." Interview, Shanxi Province, 2010.

According to *The Book of Rites* (*Liji*), there is nothing that transcends music's ability to improve morals and transform habits, and nothing that transcends the ability of rites to ensure the equanimity of the king and the good government of the people.[16] This ritual culture was a unique creation of the ancestors of the Chinese nation to express their entry into civilization. Its main social function lies in its dimension of education-transformation (*jiaohua*). Rooted in the life of the nation, serving the development of society, it is a system that unites transformation of the self, regulation of the country, and harmonization of the world. The society that we are founding today will rely on rites and music to encourage people to respond to the commands of the Way, whether through their inner life or in their outward behavior, and thereby shape an ideal life based on harmony. We must strive to promote the great traditional culture of the land of Confucius and the great renaissance of Chinese culture!

At this meeting, attended by both Confucian activists and local authorities, some amount of "concession" to official rhetoric and ideology obviously illustrates the aforementioned equivocality that permeates the spaces where Confucianism develops today. A formal consensus enables the creation of the association even though the objectives of the various participants are not necessarily the same. *Minjian* activists have no problem integrating the official vulgate for the sake of negotiating a space for their activities, but this acknowledgment in no case means that they are not at the same time relatively autonomous. An analysis of the situation that would overemphasize the instrumental strategy of the authorities might in the end overlook its very limited impact. An obvious relation of domination prevails during the inaugural ceremony of the local association: An official who does not take part in popular rites is appointed president, official speeches convey a set of usual empty political formulas, the configuration of the meeting is imbued with socialist habitus, and so on. However, such a situation coexists with an opposite relation of appropriation by the activists of their right to carry out and develop their activities. Furthermore, the president of the association, Mr. Kong Deban, as well as some other board directors, is also a member of the Confucius lineage. In other words, if one raises the "instrumentalization" issue, it is certainly not

---

16 The reference here is actually not to the *Liji*, but to the *Xiaojing* (*Classic of Filial Piety*).

unequivocal: Is it primarily the authorities that instrumentalize Confucian activists or do representatives of the Confucian lineage also use their own official positions to facilitate initiatives to honor their ancestor?

This question is all the more relevant considering that since the implementation of the reform and opening policy China has undergone a gradual revival of traditional lineages whose political importance appears today more clearly. Some activists see this trend as a promising factor for future developments of Confucianism. In a very classical way, the lineage revival sometimes translates into the reestablishment of formal attributes of lineages (ancestor temples or *citang* 祠堂, genealogies or *jiapu* 家譜, cemeteries, etc.) and the remolding of many activities, including ritual ones.[17] Besides, it also takes the form of informal relations of solidarity that never completely ceased to exist even during the Maoist era.[18] Among many such phenomena, recent surveys show that lineages are often able to exert some political influence at the local level by imposing their candidates at the time of village elections. A national survey even posits that the influence of lineages could play a role in 40 percent of the elections, and one encounters the case of local organizations of the CCP transformed into "lineage clubs."[19] In the Qufu case it is most likely that the way lineage and local political institutions are intertwined is beneficial to *minjian* Confucianism and makes it possible to overcome reluctance that may exist vis-à-vis activities endowed with a strong religious dimension.

---

17 Within a large literature, see for instance the recent attempt to modernize and promote wedding ceremonies within the lineage of Zhu Xi: Margaret Mih Tillman and Hoyt Cleveland Tillman, "A Joyful Union: The Modernization of the Zhu Xi Family Wedding Ceremony," *Oriens Extremus* 49 (2010): 115–142. The current revival of lineages in Guangdong province is discussed by Chen Bisheng 陳壁生, "Chaoshan minjian de rujiao fuxing. Yi Chaoyang Xiaoshi citang 'Sixutang' wei li 潮汕民間的儒教復興。以潮陽蕭氏祠堂'四序堂'為例" [The Popular Revival of the Confucian Teaching in Chaoshan: The Case of Ancestral Temples of the Xiao Lineage in Chaoshan], paper presented at the conference of the research project "The Confucian Revival in Mainland China, Forms and Meanings of Confucian Piety Today," Tokyo University, 2010; and Chen, "Li zai gujin zhijian—chengshi citang jisi de fuxing 禮在古今之間—城市祠堂祭祀的復興" [Rites between the Ancient and Contemporary Periods: The Revival of Sacrifices in Ancestors Temples in Cities], paper presented at the final conference of the research project "The Confucian Revival in Mainland China: Forms and Meanings of Confucian Piety Today," Fuzhou, December 2013; Chen focuses on the new institutionalization of ancestral halls (*citang*), on the transformation of their functions, and on the modernization of cults. For a survey of the situation in Jiangxi province see Qian Hang and Xie Weiyang, *Chuantong yu zhuanxing*.

18 Szonyi, "Lineages and the Making of Contemporary China," 9–14.

19 Ibid., 16–17. Lily Tsai, basing herself on the situation in 300 villages located in four provinces, links the supply of public goods with lineage organizations. Tsai, *Accountability without*

Beyond the analysis of the power relationships at work during the opening ceremony of the local society and the exploration of the links between patrilineal kinship and local politics, one needs to emphasize that claiming a *"minjian* spirit" is no empty word. A close observation makes it possible to notice a number of features that reflect the relative autonomy of these "popular" movements.

First, one often encounters in circles of activists a very strong awareness that their commitment to a Confucian ideal anchored in history goes far beyond the current political circumstances and necessary concessions to the prevailing ideology. Such an awareness is often reinforced by the conviction that the decisive strength that will make a future "Confucian revival" possible will not primarily come from the elites or from power holders but from the people themselves. The ritual prayer addressed to Mencius during the temple ceremony discussed above provides an illustration of such a point, since it was read in the name of a community of so-called *minjian xuezhe* 民間學者: Coming from the "space of the people," these self-made scholars and itinerant activists are organizing themselves according to their own rules, and are not striving for any academic or official recognition beyond what might facilitate their activities.

The shared awareness of a mission to fulfil has developed within a number of networks that often start locally and then expand to other circles through the extraordinary dynamism of Internet communication. Instrumental in the creation of a new kind of "fellowship of the Way,"[20] the Internet makes it possible to attract people from extremely different horizons and backgrounds who are eager to join each other to share values and practices, be they social, educational, or religious. A clear example of the efficiency of these networks is given by the presence, during the foundation ceremony of the Qufu ritualistic society, of an activist encountered by the authors of this study in Zhuhai and involved in a local autonomous "academy."[21] Financed with private funds,

---

Democracy: Solidarity and Public Goods Provisions in Rural China (Cambridge: Cambridge University Press, 2007) (quoted by Szonyi, 17–18). Pan Hongli emphasizes the role of associations of elderly citizens (*laorenhui* 老人會) in the reactivation of lineages in Southern Fujian; Pan Hongli, "The Old Folk's Associations and Lineage Revival in Contemporary Villages of Southern Fujian Province," in *Southern Fujian: Reproduction of Traditions in Post-Mao China,* ed. Tan Chee-Beng, 69–96 (Hong Kong: Chinese University Press, 2006).

20 The expression is borrowed from Tillman who originally used it in a Song-dynasty context. Hoyt Cleveland Tillman, *Confucian Discourse and Chu Hsi's Ascendency* (Honolulu: University of Hawaii Press, 1992), 2–4.

21 Similar cases have also been encountered in other locations.

this academy promoted a semicommunitarian life and was oriented toward educative and social work. However, this *minjian* identity is in no way a closed universe and activists are ready to engage with the "elites"—whether scholarly or political—but not without caution. Thus, it is possible to have good relations with scholarly circles, but the latter are considered partners and not masters. In the same way, activists try to develop close relations with local cadres known for their sympathy to their cause while sharing the conviction that the most important work remains proselytizing "within the space of the people."

Second, it is essential to note that while Confucian activists are obliged to look for some degree of institutionalization in order to develop their activities, such an institutionalization takes place locally and at their own initiative. In this respect, the situation resembles the reactivation of myriad popular religion temples that are technically illegal, since they are not associated with one of the five religions officially recognized on the mainland. Analyzing a number of ethnographic surveys carried out in temples located in various parts of the country, David Palmer confirms how temples often manage to diffuse anticipated tensions with local authorities and negotiate a proper space for their activities.[22]

Described by an observer in the framework of a semiofficial sociological survey, the Qufu example is particularly clear regarding the developments of relations between Mr. Y. and the authorities:

> The various departments of local government, when considering Mr. Y. and his project of a society, have switched from their original attitude of nonunderstanding and nonintervention toward a more open attitude that has gradually turned into relative support. . . . Local cadres came little by little to acknowledge the value of ritual activities (*jisi* 祭祀) and finally accepted their principle. Thus, the department of tourism granted them some facilities.[23]

As can be seen by analyzing the sequence of events taking place during the association's opening ceremony, it is the activists—probably with the

---

22 David A. Palmer, "Religiosity and Social Movements in China, Divisions and Multiplications," in *Social Movements in China and Hong Kong, The Expansion of Protest Space*, ed. Gilles Guiheux and Khun Eng Kuah-Pearce, 265–273 (Amsterdam: Amsterdam University Press, 2009). Palmer also notes that "a recurring picture emerges in several of these studies, of a constant 'tug-of-war' over the uses and appropriations of public spaces" (265).

23 Kang, *Dangdai Zhongguo dalu wenhua minzuzhuyi yundong yanjiu*, 109.

support of the Kong lineage—who are actually providing local cadres (some of them supportive, but ignorant of the historical context of these rituals) with the discourse and "traditional references" that enable them to gradually legalize and institutionalize these *minjian* activities. In Qufu, this small group is very much aware of its role of initiator and recreator of a tradition that was forgotten for a long period of time; and its members are proud that their commitment led to a Confucian ritual being organized at Mount Nishan in 2007, "for the first time since 1949."

The elements discussed above provide some insight into the complex nature of the relations between the state and nonofficial groups claiming a Confucian identity. In previous chapters, we noticed on various occasions that popular Confucianism could not be analyzed within the rigid framework of an opposition between the authorities and grassroots activists. Apart from completely autonomous undertakings we also encountered numerous cases of Confucianism being promoted by individuals holding positions in the state apparatus even though their action was not carried out in the name of the state. Such a situation can be observed in a variety of different provinces, from Guangdong to Shanxi, from Anhui to Beijing municipality. In institutions carrying out occasional activities somewhat linked to Confucianism a relative indistinctiveness between officials and activists seems sometimes to prevail. To some extent, this is reminiscent of the "*qigong* fever." The latter was described by Palmer as a movement that could develop itself thanks to the intertwinement of networks within which one could hardly distinguish state representatives from popular groups.

However, it is necessary to go beyond institutional considerations to focus on the agency of the actors involved: They are creative in the initiatives they take and they manage to develop new spaces of interaction between individuals with extremely different social backgrounds (official or not) in order to promote a specific agenda. In that respect, we have seen the flexibility and imagination of Qufu's activists that translated into an array of innovative and multifaceted activities. It is noteworthy that their activities are not limited to the human and social realm and that they may also extend to relations with invisible entities—gods, spirits, ancestors—in the course of ritual ceremonies. From this perspective and notwithstanding the aforementioned negotiation process with the authorities, it seems that a different logic is at work behind *minjian* practices than the one prevailing in the Confucius cult organized by the authorities during the festival. But is it nevertheless possible to distinguish easily between an "instrumental rationality" of the state and a "value-rationality" (*Wertrationalität*) of social movements that would relegate political considerations to a secondary position compared to their ultimate commitments? Both types of ceremonies—official and rather "secular," popular and rather "religious"—nevertheless relate to a shared cultural background.

Therefore, it is now time to turn to the broader issue of the link between the religious and the political without dissociating contemporary Confucian enterprises from the anthropological background that they share with Chinese culture in general. In the last chapter, a comparative perspective will be introduced with the case of official ceremonies that are carried out in Taiwan. The focus will be put on the way state cults are articulated with an ancient cosmology that also permeates popular practices discussed throughout this book. The contrast between China and Taiwan provides clues about the extent to which the "political" and the "religious" are articulated in different territories of the "sinicized world." By the same token, it illuminates how the relations between the state, the sage, and the people also differ on the two shores of the Taiwan Strait.

10

Between Religious Ritual and Political Ceremonial

COSMOLOGY AND NATIONAL STATE

WITHIN A GLOBAL historical trend that no longer locates political legitimacy in a transcendent order but in the people and their sovereignty, it is often posited that nation states end up generating new forms of sacredness. Such a general question has been discussed since the origin of the sociological tradition but must be addressed in specific ways within a Chinese context. While it is not difficult to identify in twentieth-century China phenomena seemingly comparable with the ones that took place in the West—suffice it to mention "nation building," the rise of a "citizenship," or "secularization"—one cannot overlook the fact that new practices and institutions were gradually asserted within a cultural background that remained extremely different from Western ones. Of course, considering the magnitude of the changes, hybridizations, and sometimes chaos that took place in China during the last century it is necessary to be cautious when facing cultural interpretations of history. But such a legitimate caution should not prevent us from questioning the possible perpetuation of fundamental schemes borrowed from an ancient cosmology that impacted action and thought for centuries. It is all the more necessary to proceed in that way when one takes into account, beyond ideological and institutional transformations, what philosopher Claude Lefort termed "the political," that is, "generative principles" structuring the organization of a world where "political and religious forms" always remain to some extent intertwined.[1]

---

1 Claude Lefort, "Permanence du théologico-politique?" in *Essais sur le Politique, XIXe–XXe siècles* (Paris: Editions du Seuil, 1986), 300.

In this book we have often encountered multiple ambiguities associated with the notion of "Confucianism." This cannot be explained merely by the complexity of the phenomena under study. These ambiguities also result from an anthropological context where, despite their now long history in China, imported Western categories cannot apply without loss. What we face is less "the religious" or "the political" than specific forms of a "politico-religious" reality. It is precisely this "politico-religious" issue that we now need to tackle by casting a light on the relation between, on the one hand, what is often acknowledged to be a new brand of Chinese nationalism, and, on the other hand, what is understood under the label "Confucianism." To address this issue, our approach will not be to delve into ideological discourses but rather to start with the observation of cults and ceremonies.

Let us start with a mere symptom. In 2012, after attending a conference on geostrategic issues organized by Chinese military authorities, Christopher Ford, a member of an American conservative think-tank, returned to his country convinced that it was neither the lack of information on both sides nor mere prejudices that was generating a growing distrust between the two countries. Rather, due to a better understanding of each other, unbridgeable differences had become increasingly blatant. The new "harmonious world" that Chinese authorities foresaw as the foundation of a new international order sounded to him like an attempt to reestablish a link with an ancient tradition. In his reports, he quoted philosopher Zhao Tingyang 趙汀陽, who attempts to rethink a "world-system" inspired by the antique All-under-Heaven (*tianxia*) tradition; international relations theorist Yan Xuetong 閻學通, for whom a future Chinese hegemony needs to revive the good government of the Heavenly Way (*Wang Dao*) of the Warring States period;[2] and political theory specialist Yu Keping 俞可平, who advocates a restoration of an "ancient Chinese dream." Ford was struck by the pervasive emphasis on continuity in the course of all the discussions about the legitimacy of a new world order. This continuity primarily translates into the negation of any gap between Chinese domestic politics and schemes of a future global governance: "Harmonious world," Yu Keping even posits, "is nothing else

---

2 See Zhao Tingyang 趙汀陽, *Tianxia Tixi: Shijie zhidu zhexue daolun daolun* 天下體系：世界制度哲學導論 [The Tianxia System: Philosophical Introduction to a World Institution] (Nanjing: Jiangsu Jiaoyu Chubanshe, 2005), and Yan Xuetong, *Ancient Chinese Thought, Modern Chinese Power* (Princeton, NJ: Princeton University Press, 2011).

but the natural *extension* of China's domestic policy of building a harmonious society."[3] To some extent, one finds here the spirit of gradualism of the ancient Confucian text *The Great Learning* (Daxue), where harmonization starts with the moral self (to be cultivated: *xiu shen* 修身), to expand afterwards in the direction of the family (to be regulated: *qi jia* 齊家), the state (to be ruled: *zhi guo* 治國), and finally the universe (to be pacified: *ping tianxia* 平天下). In Ford's opinion, the "new" concept of "harmony" is imbued with authoritarianism and hegemonic aspirations: In our information age, it works as the projection of an ancient self-centered moralism thanks to which "the emerging Chinese superpower hungers to control other peoples' narratives of China."[4]

There are two ways of analyzing these new Chinese discourses. One option is to understand them as by-products of ideological instrumentalization by a state apparatus that revives an ancient symbolism within the framework of a mimetic competition between previous and rising *hegemons*. The second option does not negate but complements the first with an exploration of practical orientations or recurrent schemes of thought that are left unexplained by such a perspective. These schemes are less visible in ideological discourses than in practical actions and behaviors. They can be observed in the course of fieldwork, especially when ordinary citizens engaged in moral or religious enterprises interact both with scholars and local representatives of the authorities.

Let us recall a few basic elements about the ancient cosmology that we believe need to be considered. It should be emphasized that such a cosmology should in no case be understood as some sort of pervasive and unchanging tradition that would provide an interpretive key for all phenomena encountered on the field. Rather, it is a backdrop that needs to be

---

3 See Yu Keping, *Democracy Is a Good Thing: Essays on Politics, Society, and Culture in Contemporary China* (Washington, DC: Brookings Institution, 2009), and, for the quote, Yu, "Hexie shijie linian xia de Zhongguo waijiao 和諧世界理念下的中國外交" [China's Approach of International Relations Within the Conceptual Context of a Harmonious World], China.com, April 24, 2007 (http://www.china.com.cn/policy/zhuanti/hxsh/txt/2007-04/24/content_8162037.htm) (our emphasis): Foreign policy is the extension (*yanshen* 延伸) of domestic policy, harmonious world and harmonious society are in a relationship of continuity (*lianxu* 連續), etc.

4 Christopher Ford, "Information-based Arms Control and Sino-American Trust," Washington, DC: Hudson Institute, December 18, 2012, http://www.hudson.org/content/researchattachments/attachment/1085/ford--armscontrolsino-americantrustdec2012.pdf; and: "Sinocentrism for the Information Age, Comments on the 4th Xiangshan Forum (2013)," *New Paradigms Forum*, January 2013, http://www.newparadigmsforum.com/NPFtestsite/?p=1498.

cautiously taken into account so as to discuss in a given context the possible degree of perpetuation and relevance of an anthropological legacy within today's creative narratives and social practices.

The basic assumption of this cosmology is that the universe is one and encompasses the dead and the living, gods and men, the human and the nonhuman. However, this unique and single universe entails polarity. Two poles that could be called, by convention, "the visible" and the "invisible" reflect the *yang* ("luminous") and *yin* ("dark") dimensions of the universe. They are contiguous and perpetually interacting with each other. We are not discussing here a new form of dualism disguised under exotic terms and reflecting a classical form of opposition (at least in some Western traditions) between a "this-worldly" universe and an "other-worldly" one. In fact, there is no absolute discontinuity, and a prevailing feature of this cosmology is what we could term its "continuism."

A consequence of this worldview is that there is not separation between sociopolitical and cosmic spheres. Within what we maybe improperly call religion there is no definitive interruption between the world of the living and that of the dead who became gods, ancestors, or spirits. Moreover, there is no unbridgeable gap between the human and the nonhuman. If we take any being or entity (a god, an immortal, a man, an animal, a plant, a stone . . .), a number of similar categories ("matter-energy" or *qi* 氣, "agents or elements" *xing* 行, etc. . . .) make it possible to arrange what elsewhere would be classified as material, psychic, or spiritual. In the Chinese world, it is not difficult for anthropologists or historians to recognize both in the popular and literati culture, elements of what French anthropologist Descola coined an "analogist" ontology, in contrast with the "naturalism" prevailing in modern Europe. Contrary to the naturalist opposition between a physicality shared by all beings ("nature") and an interiority ("culture") that would constitute human being's exclusive feature, analogical identification associates myriads of beings, whether human or not, so that "they are distributed in chains of pairings that bring the material and the immaterial together at every level in the respective scales of the microcosm and the macrocosm."[5]

---

5 Philippe Descola, *Beyond Nature and Culture*, trans. Janet Lloyd (Chicago: Chicago University Press, 2013), 207. This interpretation needs to take into account not two but four distinct "ontologies," which Descola terms naturalism, animism, totemism, and analogism. One of the benefits of this set of tools is that it makes it possible to go beyond binary comparatism (such as China versus the West) by comparing operating schemes or patterns that can be observed across cultures as diverse as China, pre-Colombian Mexico, Brahmanic India, or Mande-Voltaic Africa. Descola notices that in analogist ontologies, where cosmos and society are coextensive, "another way of imparting order and meaning to a world full

It might seem surprising to use here notions inherited from a Chinese cosmology that may sound ancient and abstract. However, fieldwork provides some evidence that they often enable more relevant descriptions of behaviors and actions than general categories of political or religious sociology. But recourse to indigenous notions also requires extreme caution and constant questioning. The insights such notions provide should not encourage distorted interpretations of phenomena that are also sometimes clearly the result of recent factors devoid of links with ancient patterns of thought.

Keeping in mind the possible perpetuation, transformation, or complete disappearance of this ancient symbolic and practical universe, we are now going to discuss the links between Confucian tradition and nationalism as a modern ideology. More specifically, we shall focus on the following question: Through and beyond the relation between "the sage and the people" that could be observed in the course of fieldwork, how is it possible to analyze the state's participation in cults whose nature seems to be ambiguous, between politics and religion?

A century after the dismantling of the imperial order and its cosmic kingship, two types of discontinuity have been amplified: The first one opposes China and the rest of the world; the second one the society of human beings and the invisible realm. Modern state cults reflect this double opposition. On the one hand, they need to emphasize the specificity of the nation located within a broad and diverse international community; on the other hand, their organization requires defining whether the celebration of tutelary figures of Chinese civilization may be only a political metaphor or whether it maintains some links with the ancient "continuism" mentioned above. We will explore these two dimensions—Which cult for which nation? Which new relationships with the realm of the invisible?—before introducing a comparative perspective with the Taiwanese situation. Taking into account the politico-religious experience that strongly developed in democratic Taiwan makes it possible to underscore the

---

of singularities is to distribute these into great inclusive structures that stretch between two poles" (218), but also "to systematize these straggling chains of meanings into ordered and interdependent sets that for the most part are designed to be effective practically: ways to cope with misfortune, the orientation of buildings, calendars, predestination... compatibility of marriage patterns, good government—everything is connected in a web so dense and so charged with consequences that it becomes impossible to tell whether it is man who reflects the universe or the universe that takes man as its model" (217–218).

specificities of the situation in the PRC and to ponder over possible alternative scenarios.

Continuism and Discontinuities

As was well noted by Christopher Ford, it is possible to identify in scholarly and ideological discourses at the start of the new century some sort of nostalgia for a well-organized universe building on ancient forms of legitimacy. These discourses often work as a reaction against the chaotic effects of globalization and international competition. Jiang Qing's Confucianism underscores, for instance, that, beyond democratic legitimacy, Heaven (*tian*) and history also provide alternative forms of political legitimacy. For philosopher Zhao Tingyang, the ancient *tianxia* (All-under-Heaven) thought is a possible direction for a failed world "incapable of thinking itself politically as a world": It is necessary to broaden our perspective, beyond the national and the international, so as to think the world globally. In this context, it is critical to reestablish an institutional continuity that would link grassroots communities, ultimately, to world governance. In fact, a political institution is deemed adequate when it aims at reducing "conflicts and incompatibility of the political levels from the world to states and families so as to create a 'political *continuum*' by which one political level could be structurally mapped onto the others."[6] To some extent, such a perspective could be considered the modern echo of an idealized imperial order, both overarching and highly hierarchic. However, the continuity of such an institutional order was definitely broken a century ago, leaving room for a smaller and problematic community, that of the *minzu* 民族 or nation.[7]

Which Cult for Which Nation? China and All-under-Heaven

What can the observation of cults, such as the ones carried out in Qufu, tell us about the various—and sometimes incompatible—conceptions of the "Chinese nation"?

---

6 Zhao Tingyang, "A Political World Philosophy in Terms of All-under-Heaven (Tian-xia)" *Diogenes* 221 (2009): 17 (emphasis is ours).

7 See Wang Gung-wu, *Renewal: The Chinese State and the New Global History* (Hong Kong: Chinese University Press, 2013).

During the twentieth century, the secular state kept sporadically organizing two major cults to tutelary figures associated with China's ancient
symbolic universe. The first is the cult of Huangdi, the Yellow Emperor, in
Huangling, Shaanxi province, and the second is the cult of Confucius in
Qufu. As mentioned in chapter 7, those were not in imperial times "great
sacrifices," such as those honoring Heaven or the ancestors of the reigning dynasty. On the ruins of the ancient ritual order, the republic appropriated two "middle sacrifices" that it transformed to serve the national
community. When they were carried out, it was generally at the provincial
level, and central authorities, whether nationalist or communist, usually
only sent delegates.

During the twentieth century, the fate of these two cults was sometimes similar but sometimes also clearly differentiated. Such a contrast
precisely enables a better insight into the modern project of nation building. Risking oversimplification, it is possible to roughly identify four successive phases. (1) By the end of the imperial period, the first generation of
nationalists had already appropriated the figure of the Yellow Emperor in
opposition not only to the Manchus but also to a brand of Confucianism
understood as a feudal and despotic ideology. Following Yuan Shikai's
restoration attempts, the young republican state was therefore much less
eager to celebrate Confucius, even though China's fragmentation and the
control of warlords over large portions of the territory make it difficult to
have a comprehensive overview of the situation.[8] (2) From 1934 to 1935
(with the New Life Movement) and following the full-fledged Japanese
invasion in 1937, Chiang Kai-shek promoted the cults of both the Yellow
Emperor and Confucius. (3) In Maoist China, the party-state continued to
honor the Yellow Emperor until 1963, occasionally as "the ancestor of the
nation's workers." But the Confucius cult stopped after 1949 and Qufu
underwent a tragic episode during the Cultural Revolution. (4) The reform
and opening policy gradually recreated proper conditions for a reactivation
of both ceremonials with a participation of central government representatives (starting in 1985 for the Yellow Emperor and in 2005 for Confucius).

Such a brief chronology reveals that over a century primarily marked by
nationalism the Yellow Emperor cult was performed with more continuity
than the Confucius cult. But the latter was somewhat more controversial,

---

8 The Qufu gazetteer mentions for instance a 1925 cult to honor Confucius. The initiative was taken by warlord Zhang Zongchang 張宗昌, who was closely associated with
Duan Qirui.

strongly promoted by some and radically rejected by others. In any case, these two figures make it possible to introduce and differentiate between two ideal types of national identity.

In 1908, at the end of the empire, members of the Chinese United League (Tongmenghui), which was established in Japan by Sun Yat-sen, secretly went to Huangling. Their objective was to symbolically appeal to the Yellow Emperor against the despotic rule of the Manchu dynasty and to call for a "national republican system." They venerated the legendary emperor as the ancestor of the Han people oppressed by a foreign race. Thus, the first brand of Chinese nationalism was anchored in this reference to the ancestral: The new Han nation was conceived according to a kinship model and the political imagination of the time envisioned a vast lineage encompassing "sons and grandsons of Emperors Yandi and Huangdi" (*Yan Huang zisun* 炎黃子孫).[9] This national model, based on an extended conception of kinship, prevailed over a long period of time. It was reflected in various ways, for instance when the new international order compelled China to take the new notion of "nationality" into account in its legal system. Thus, it is remarkable that from 1909 to 1980 Chinese nationality laws were essentially based on the right of blood (*jus sanguinis*). All descendants of Chinese ancestors, even though they could be living outside the national territory, were considered Chinese nationals. Practically, overseas Chinese (*huaqiao* 華僑) in Southeast Asia or even further in the West were *de jure* Chinese. The situation remained the same during the republican and the Maoist eras until a new nationality law passed in 1980 at the start of the reform, and opening policy put an end to a long diplomatic imbroglio.[10] But this legal change and the introduction of a right of the soil (*jus soli*) did not necessarily terminate all the lived representations of the "descendants of the Yellow Emperor." Neither did they prevent the party-state from maintaining some amount of ambiguity in its relations with foreign nationals of Chinese descent.

The kinship model, however, was only one of the symbolic patterns of national identity. In 1934, the reappropriation by the nationalist government of the Confucius cult followed a period of "deritualization,"

9 For a global perspective on the Yellow Emperor cult see Billeter, *L'Empereur jaune.*

10 About the historical context see Wang Gung-wu, *Community and Nation* (Sydney: Allen and Unwin, 1993). About legal aspects, see Dan Shao, "Chinese by Definition: Nationality Law, Jus Sanguinis and State Succession, 1909–1980," *Twentieth-Century China* 35 (2009): 4–28.

or even of "denationalization," if we consider how the Japanese used the figure of the sage. Such a reappropriation also implied a conception of the nation that, without being incompatible with the previous one, nevertheless had its own features. With the figure of the "Educator" or "First Master" culture became the focus, culture understood as a source of pride and maybe also of coherence for the nation. Therefore, the modern state reprocessed ancient ethics into forms of social morals likely to discipline the entire body of the nation. "Confucian" values appropriated by republican ideology, from filial piety to loyalty toward the ruler were supposed to permeate the whole regenerated nation, from the top to the bottom of society, from the center to the periphery. Thus, compared with the Huangling cult, Qufu no longer celebrates the vertical conception of an ideal community grounded in lines of descent and race, but the horizontal conception of a community united around the propagation of cultural practices. It is much less piety toward the founding ancestors than "education-transformation"—that is, the ancient *jiaohua* turned into propaganda—that becomes instrumental in aggregating members of the new nation-state. Using political science concepts, one could speak about an ethnic brand of nationalism being complemented or corrected by a cultural one.

However, the 2000s also revealed the somewhat artificial nature of such an opposition. As it was clearly demonstrated by Terence Billeter, Chinese authorities were perfectly aware of the difficulty of celebrating the alleged ancestor of a race within a multiethnic nation. Therefore, they encouraged scholarly and ideological initiatives aiming at transforming the Yellow Emperor into a mere cultural hero that could be accepted by the whole nation. Similarly, it is as if the distinctive features of Confucius and his teaching had been diluted into a much broader and much more vague discourse about "civilization." Thus, these two figures, who used to be well contrasted in the past, today belong to some sort of highly amorphous category coined by the state "traditional Chinese culture."

In a way, these two figures also reflect potential tensions at work within Chinese nationalism. In particular, mythical narratives about the Yellow Emperor or Confucius make it difficult to circumscribe—or to contribute to circumscribing—an exclusive political community. The vertical continuity of kinship encompasses descendants of the Yellow Emperor far beyond China's frontiers, from the Philippines to Malaysia and beyond. As for the civilizing ideal associated with Confucius, it is supposed to permeate a "Confucian Asia" if not the rest of the world. This is the reason why Chinese nationalism needed and still needs to complement myths with history: It is around ceremonials dedicated to historical characters such as Sun Yat-sen, Chiang Kai-shek, or Mao Zedong that the necessary geopolitical and military dimension of the nation can be periodically asserted.

In order to get a better insight into these two state cults of Chinese nationalism we now need to take into account the second rupture that has for already a century marked China's ancient political cosmology. To the modern discontinuity between the new nation and the rest of the world, one also needs to add a second discontinuity that seems to separate today the visible and invisible dimensions of the universe.

The Visible and the Invisible: Introduction to an Overall Context

The question could be raised in a simple way: Are the cults sponsored today by central authorities of an exclusively political nature or do they encompass what is generally called in the West "religion"? To some extent, the formulation of such a question might point to an application in China of the well-known problematic of "secularization." Without necessarily refusing to use this category we believe that it is somehow inadequate for analyzing the complexity of circumstances that can be observed empirically.[11] Before turning more specifically to the cults (next section) we come back first to the traditional continuity between the visible and the invisible and its fate in contemporary contexts.

It is necessary to briefly recall that a century ago, what we term here "continuism" was the natural paradigm permeating the official duties of scholar-officials. Whether at the top of the state apparatus or at the local level, scholar-officials were at the same time administrators, priests, and judges. Within the prevailing cosmology, although the emperor was the unique mediator between men and Heaven, local scholar-officials were nevertheless the partners, in the "luminous world" of deities incorporated within an invisible hierarchy. At the time he was appointed to his new position, the scholar-official in charge of a district was supposed to address the City God (Chenghuangshen 城隍神) with whom he would

---

11 For a critical analysis of the relationships between sociology of secularization and Chinese culture, see for instance Michael Szonyi, "Secularization, Theories and the Study of Chinese Religions," *Social Compass* 56 (2009): 312–327.

maintain ritual relations in the course of his administrative duties.[12] Early
on, foreign observers and scholars already underscored the existence of
an invisible replication of the worldly political order—Hegel mentioned
China's "invisible officials"[13]—but the metaphors used to depict it (e.g.,
mimetism, reflection) remained somewhat static and failed to pinpoint
the most important element, that is, the continuity of interactions within
a same and single world.

Of this continuity or "continuism" it is possible to give here another
example based on Paul Katz's *Divine Justice*.[14] Katz coins the expression
"Chinese judicial continuum" to describe a phenomenon encountered in
imperial China but also in contemporary Taiwanese society. This continuum links what would elsewhere belong to the political, the judiciary, or
the religious. It translates for example into a complementary settlement
of conflicts by human courts (where judgments are passed by officials)
and recourse to temples (where judgments are passed by gods). What is
being addressed in temples is not only the *post mortem* fate of souls and
possible retributions depending on one's merits or demerits. Temples also
play a role within the overall justice apparatus in the visible world. Thus,
in today's Taiwan, ordinary people keep on going to temples—especially
to City God temples—so as to carry out ancient judicial rituals (e.g.,
oath-making rituals to demonstrate one's innocence, sometimes featuring
the beheading of a chicken, in order to express "one's willingness to suffer
the fate of the unfortunate fowl in the event of perjury"; indictment rituals by people who feel they have been wronged by officials; and so on[15]).
Officials also participate in these kinds of rituals: Prosecutors, policemen,
and politicians also appeal to the invisible realm and its gods to ensure
that they will be fortunate in their enterprises within the visible world.

---

12 See for instance chapter 24 of Huang Liuhong (黃六鴻)'s *Fuhui quanshu* 福惠全書
(Complete Work on Happiness and Generosity) (1694); Angela Zito, "City Gods and Their
Magistrates," in *Religions of China in Practice*, ed. Donald S. Lopez, 72–81 (Princeton,
NJ: Princeton University Press, 1996).

13 Gods are "invisible civil-servants (*die unsichtbaren Beamten*) in the natural world, in the
same way as scholar-officials in the conscious world (*die bewußte Welt*)." Hegel, *Vorlesungen
über die Philosophie der Religion* (Hamburg: Felix Meiner, 1985), vol. 1, 204.

14 Paul Katz, *Divine Justice: Religion and the Development of Chinese Culture* (London and
New York: Routledge, 2008).

15 Katz, *Divine Justice*, chapter 3, and more specifically p. 74; chapter 4 and chapter 7 about
judicial ritual in today's Taiwan.

The intensity and the meaning of the interactions between the realm of the luminous (the visible) and that of the dark (the invisible) always varied according to location, time, and the actors involved. Besides, it must also be stressed, that, by definition, "continuism" does not associate things deemed identical, but distinct. Therefore, continuity is established only thanks to mental schemes or practical actions that connect *different* dimensions and entities (visible, invisible) of the same universe. In what has now become a classical essay, Arthur Wolf underlined the analogy between social and "suprasocial" roles in each realm: He underscored that the way Chinese people considered gods, ancestors, and ghosts reflected the way they thought of officials, parents, and outsiders.[16] But it is still necessary to explain the specificities of these entities: After all, why should one invoke the entities of the dark or invisible realm if they are nothing but the reflection of the luminous one? It is sometimes emphasized that such a reflection is not without deformation and therefore has a specific function.[17] For example, Emily Ahern insists on the complementarity between what the invisible dimension can provide and resources offered by the political community. In mundane life, when facing wrongdoings, unfair judgments, or corruption of local officials, one may need to appeal for justice to higher and supposedly more impartial and disinterested authorities. In temples, however, there is a direct and unrestricted access to the hierarchy of invisible judges.[18] Another related issue is the degree of popular favor associated with temples compared to tribunals and its correlation with the degree of popular legitimacy ascribed to political authorities. Paul Katz raises the issue in the following way: If recourse to "divine justice" were to be proportional to the degree of despotism of a political regime, wouldn't it have been normal to see the importance of these rituals decrease in Taiwan after the end of martial law and the implementation of a more independent and transparent legal system? However, observation does not seem

---

16 Arthur P. Wolf, "Gods, Ghosts and Ancestors," in *Religion and Ritual in Chinese Society*, ed. Arthur P. Wolf, 131–182 (Stanford, CA: Stanford University Press, 1974).

17 In discussions about Buddhist pictures of hell disseminated in society, a phenomenon of *distorting mimesis* has been underscored: these representations would not point to real judicial practices but to representations of representations, taking place for instance on Chinese opera stages. See Timothy Brook, Jérôme Bourgon, and Gregory Blue, *Death by a Thousand Cuts* (Cambridge, MA: Harvard University Press, 2008), 145–151. However, these analogical associations only make sense within an overarching continuum.

18 Emilie Ahern, *Chinese Rituals and Politics* (Cambridge: Cambridge University Press, 1981), 96–104.

to corroborate such a hypothesis: Plaintiffs still often go to divine courts, even though temple specialists also encourage them to have recourse to mundane justice. In sum, the development of a judiciary continuum in Taiwan translates into "a joint increase of legitimacy in *all* its dimensions," from mundane courts to the judgment of invisible entities.[19]

In other words, the type of functionalist questioning about respective roles or functions of the visible or invisible dimensions of the world here reaches its limits. Of course, taking these imperial and Taiwanese situations as references, the extent to which such a continuum might still be relevant in Mainland China remains an open question, a question that we specifically intend to address with a comparison between state ceremonies. But in any case, when it comes to exploring religious, judicial, or political backgrounds of the phenomena at stake here, taking into account China's "continuist" cosmological background is certainly as fruitful as building upon a sociology of secularization that would emphasize the autonomy of value spheres or processes of functional specialization.[20] Let us now turn back to the more specific issue of Confucian ceremonies.

Ritual and Ceremonial

It might in fact be convenient to distinguish between two poles in the spectrum of various ceremonies honoring Confucius: They could be termed here "ceremonial" and "ritual."

The official *ceremonial* is an intransitive performance totally confined to the realm of the "visible." No concrete result is expected from any interaction whatsoever with spiritual entities. The performative dimension of the ceremony involves only those human beings gathering for a commemoration, the celebration of a given narrative or that of a political community. As for *ritual*, its nature is different. It is supposed to be a form of transitive action that establishes some continuity with invisible entities.

---

19 Katz, *Divine Justice*, 182–183, emphasis is ours. This could be compared with the degree of skepticism toward the judiciary subsystem in itself: There would be some sort of recurrent "incapacity of the courts system to acquire a full-fledged legitimacy in the eyes of the Chinese people" (81).

20 In a similar vein, Paul Katz explains in an interview that the judiciary continuum "calls into question the rather narrow definition of law and legal history that prevails in the field today based on the Western secular humanist perspective, which never really held in China anyway." http://www.taipeitimes.com/News/feat/archives/2010/10/15/2003485407 visited on December 5, 2012.

In other words, political ceremonials crystallize on recollections of absent entities and celebration of symbols whereas rituals generate some forms of "copresence": humans and nonhumans are interacting in the course of a reciprocal exchange, and spirits (*shen*), though invisible, remain as present as the human celebrants invoking them. Hence the specific performativity that is associated with rituals, since they are much more than commemorations of the past or self-celebrations of a community. What is being expected is nothing less than a transformation that renews and revitalizes the relation between the two dimensions (visible and invisible) of the same universe. Whereas contemporary political ceremonials epitomize a radical rupture in the ancient continuity between tangible and intangible beings, rituals reestablish or reassert such a continuity.[21]

There is no doubt that the gradual construction of a modern nation-state in China coincided with a strong and systematic tendency to radically break with previous worldviews. In her study about rituals reform and the implementation of political ceremonials by Guomindang and nationalist authorities, Nedostup emphasizes rightly their "secular" ambitions. As was already mentioned, the cults honoring Confucius and China's national heroes that were restored in the 1930s and 1940s were understood as "commemorations" (*jinian* 紀念) rather than "sacrifices" (*si* 祀).[22] Whether in Nanjing or in Chongqing, the precedence of nationalist ideology and the figure of Sun Yat-sen over the ancient symbolism honoring Confucius was conspicuous. Either in funerals or in state-sponsored commemorations of tutelary figures and heroes, mere remembrance was in principle the only way to relate to those who had passed away.[23]

---

21 Such an appreciation of rituals can be accessible only to an anthropology that does not perceive the essence of ritual as a mere corruption of thought (through the performing of gestures and the manipulation of objects) and thought as only understandable thanks to structural oppositions at work within myths. For Lévi-Strauss, who embraces such a dismissive perspective, rituals become "a bastardization of thought, brought about by the constraints of life" and represent a "desperate, and inevitably unsuccessful, attempt to re-establish the continuity of lived experience." See Claude Lévi-Strauss, *Mythologiques IV: L'Homme nu* (Paris: Plon, 1971), 603 (translated by John Weightman and Doreen Weightman, *The Naked Man* [Chicago: University of Chicago Press, 1990], 675). For a critical approach of this highly intellectualistic understanding of ritual, see Maurice Godelier, *Claude Lévi-Strauss* (Paris: Seuil, 2013), 436–453.

22 Nedostup, *Superstitious Regimes*, 266.

23 For an analysis of state reforms regarding funerals see Vincent Goossaert and Fang Ling, "Les réformes funéraires et la politique religieuse de l'État chinois, 1900–2008" *Archives des sciences sociales des religions* 144 (2008): 51–73.

However, state control over ancient practices and worldviews could certainly not be overarching. In some provinces ancient ceremonies were perpetuated in Confucius temples. Resistance to radical modernization also took place within the nationalist state apparatus. Moreover, whereas the 1934 Confucius ceremonial organized in Nanjing reflected a modernizing and secular ambition, the cult that was organized the same year in Qufu in the presence of representatives of ministries and parliament displayed sacrifices and invocations to spirits.[24]

What about the situation today? Let us recall that during our 2007 fieldwork in Shandong province we observed two kinds of parallel events. The ceremonial organized by the authorities in Qufu offered a clear contrast with rituals reappropriated and reinvented by grassroots activists in Zoucheng and Nishan. But the contrast between these two ends of the spectrum becomes more relevant for an overall reflection about the link between the religious and the political if we compare sets of practices that all benefit from official sponsorship. Thus, the official Qufu ceremonial can also be compared with the situation of the Tainan Confucius temple in Taiwan and its ritual, such as it has been for instance observed and presented by Thomas Wilson.[25]

Pivotal for this comparison is the following issue: Who interacts with whom and in what kind of relationship? Both in Qufu and in Tainan, people attending the events include officials (respectively from Shandong province or Tainan city), members of the academic community, guests, and visitors. In Taiwan, some of the personalities are also celebrants, whose titles and roles are clearly defined. During the ceremony that starts at dawn, ritual specialists, schoolchildren, and members of the society organizing the event turn into a single rite-performing body. In Qufu, the situation is very different: It is not in the temple building, but on the front platform of the Dachengdian that the "show" takes place, involving an array of different actors under the command of a master of ceremonies.

---

24 See Li Junling 李俊領, "Kangzhan shiqi Guomindang yu Nanjing guomin zhengfu dui Kongzi de jisi dianli 抗戰時期國民黨與南京國民政府對孔子的祭祀典禮" [Offering Rites to Confucius Carried out by the Guomindang and the Nationalist Government during the War against Japan], *Shehui kexue pinglun* 社會科學評論 4 (2008): 45–62.

25 For the Tainan ceremonies, see: (1) the videos posted and commented by Thomas Wilson during the 1998 ritual: *Autumnal Sacrifice to Confucius: A Study of Confucianism's Sacrificial Tradition*, http://www.academics.hamilton.edu/asian_studies/home/autumnalsacrifice/index.html; and (2) Michael Nylan and Thomas A. Wilson, *Lives of Confucius* (New York: Doubleday, 2010).

Although it is possible to posit that in both cases we have ceremonies honoring Confucius, such a way of presenting the situation and assimilating these two events is also somewhat misleading. In Tainan, the Confucius tablet materializes his actual presence and he is also associated with a community of disciples and worthies whose tablets are positioned on separate altars. The community also includes scholar-officials of more recent dynasties. Thus, beyond the very person of Confucius, offerings are also made to a broader spiritual lineage with which well-learned participants to the ceremony can also identify themselves. In Qufu, however, the name of Confucius is that of an icon whose public eulogy largely exalts the nation and its culture. Confucius remains an isolated figure detached from the set of ritual references with which he was traditionally associated. Furthermore, the meanings of these two ceremonies remain basically different. The ceremonial of communist authorities remains largely in the same vein as the secular project of nationalist authorities. In fact, Qufu in the 2000s and Nanjing in the 1930s present clear similarities: Gestures and discourses are officially controlled so that their real meaning is linked to the necessities of the "visible world." In 2013, as in 2007, the eulogy to Confucius in Qufu remains addressed to his spirit (*shenling* 神靈). However, we face the mere commemoration of a dead figure. Confucius is absent and no communication with him is contemplated. Ceremonies are actually addressed to the living, attending the event either directly or only indirectly through modern media technology.

The Tainan ceremony offers a sharp contrast with Qufu. Perpetuating around two thousand years of history, the essence of this rite is to be a sacrifice. The tradition of bloody sacrifices is actually kept alive, even though animal flesh is brought to the temple before the start of the ritual.[26] According to a predetermined order, successive offerings of incense, silk, and wine are also made to the spirit of Confucius and those associated with him by kinship or learning. It is necessary here to emphasize that the spirit alluded to is not simply a metaphor. As is the case during rituals honoring various gods, the ceremony starts with a rite of "welcoming spirits" (*ying shen* 迎神). Spirits were already attracted into the temple by "the smell of blood and fur." They are considered to be present in the

---

26 On the properly sacrificial nature of this ritual and its differences with the Indian model of sacrifices, see Wilson, "Sacrifice and the Imperial Cult of Confucius," 251–287. On the importance of sacrificing animals and sharing flesh among the celebrants, see Jean Lévi, *Histoire et sacrifice en Chine ancienne* (Nanterre: Société d'ethnologie, 2007).

temple before being sent back in the course of a symmetrical rite (*song shen* 送神). Between these two phases of the ritual, a space of communication is opened between the visible and invisible dimensions of the universe. In order to be received by spirits, offerings such as silk or texts are burnt in a dedicated furnace.

Such a ritual does not merely enable an exchange between human beings and spirits, but also a temporary "copresence." In the past, bodies used to be prepared by fasting and meditating. As underscored by Wilson, the range of adequate attitudes and emotions for a sacrifice to Confucius was not different from those requested for the more familiar cult to the ancestors. Basically, filial respect was extended to the various categories of spirits honored in a cult.[27] And this was also the case for Confucius and his worthies.

These examples illustrate the two poles—taken as ideal types—of a continuum. Between the "political" ceremonial and the "religious" ritual, the twentieth century offered a whole spectrum of possibilities.[28] The ultimate problem for us here is to understand to what extent and in which contexts these possibilities might materialize in today's China.

Continuism: Potentiality and Actuality

Should we posit that, offering a vivid contrast with imperial and Taiwanese examples, China is today much more "secularized"? Or, at least, that ceremonials associated with the figure of Confucius are nowadays downscaled to a mere visible dimension? The answer is probably positive if we simply consider state-sponsored ceremonies honoring Confucius in the PRC. However, taking into account the multiple dimensions of what we term "popular Confucianism" might help to illuminate this issue from a broader perspective.

For a long time, a similar "continuist" logic was applied to various dimensions of experience, both personal and social. By the time of secular

---

27 Nylan and Wilson, *Lives of Confucius*, 144–148.

28 One could add here that in some circumstances these ceremonies also reflected the influence of Japanese state cults that could be performed in Manchukuo or in colonial Taiwan. See Nakajima Takahiro 中島隆博, "Civil Spirituality and the Female Element in Confucian Piety Today: The Activities of Confucian Temples in Qufu, Taipei and Changchun," paper presented at the final conference of the research project "The Confucian Revival in Mainland China: Forms and Meanings of Confucian Piety Today," Fuzhou, December 2013.

radicalization under Maoism, "macroscopic institutions" of the ancient universe, either social or political, had ceased to exist. The ancient ritualistic dimension of political institutions was abolished and replaced by a new state apparatus and a "materialist" ideology. However, the microcosmic bases of experience did not necessarily die out. Continuity between material and intangible realms—or, at least, between realms that could be perceived as such from a modern perspective—could be maintained or reestablished through individual or even community practices: bodily practices, reappropriation of sacred writings, relationship to dead ancestors, invention of new cults, and so on.

We have already emphasized the importance of the body when exploring the so-called anti-intellectualistic dimension of grassroots Confucian movements. The body is not simply the vehicle of a personal appropriation of ancient teachings, it is also the vessel through which connections between the visible and invisible dimensions of a shared universe are created and maintained. Grassroots Confucians involved in rituals in Mencius and Confucius temples (Zoucheng, Nishan) did not simply communicate with the spirits by means of offerings and the burning of writings. They also attempted to transform their mental and bodily attitudes in order to enable a successful ritual performance. These kinds of bodily practices can also be understood more broadly as challenging naturalistic conceptions of the body carried by forms of scientism and political control that have been prevailing in modern and contemporary China. From this perspective, bodies cannot be reduced to their mere psychical and physical expressions. They contribute to a broader transformative power reflecting cosmic dynamism.[29]

Palmer's work on contemporary *qigong* movements offers an interesting analogy with what we observe in Confucian circles. In modern times, and often with state support, ancient practices of *qi*/energy cultivation were uprooted from their ancient symbolic contexts and turned into mere technologies of the body.[30] This was also largely the case with "Chinese medicine" that was simplified, standardized, and promoted in specialized institutions. The result was the creation of a sort of hybrid knowledge that problematically attempted to import and appropriate the "objective criteria

---

29 On the various dimensions of the body, see Catherine Despeux, "Le corps, champ spatio-temporel, souche d'identité," *L'Homme* 137 (1996): 87–118.

30 For an overall perspective see David A. Palmer, "The Body: Health, Nation, and Transcendence," in *Chinese Religious Life*, ed. David A. Palmer, Glen Shive, and Philip Wickeri, 87–106 (New York: Oxford University Press, 2011).

and standards" of Western biomedicines. At the same time, a number of traditional texts or sections of those texts were either abandoned (for being nonscientific) or reinterpreted in a purely naturalistic way.[31] However, in recent decades, reductionist approaches toward ancient *qigong* or medical traditions became increasingly challenged, as if they could be only partial and provisional. In the 1990s, new developments of *qigong* practices turned the bodies into vehicles of salvation. Palmer describes the religious turn of *qigong* therapy that, facing the opposition of the authorities, became also endowed with a political dimension.[32] Those developments are not mere signs of a return to the past, but they epitomize a creative process that generates new discourses and practices partially borrowed from a much more ancient grammar.

In the course of our fieldwork, we would encounter comparable behaviors among the advocates of popular Confucianism. Suffice it to recall the existence of scores of Confucian groups involved in all kinds of Classics reading activities. Personal and group experiences were for them in a continuity that could occasionally also take a cosmic dimension. To some extent, the case of the Shenzhen businesswoman who "converted" to Confucianism, discussed in chapter 4, belongs to the same kind of experiences. She was reading speculative texts of philosopher Mou Zongsan as if they had been the crystallization of an ultimate wisdom transmitted from generation to generation by masters whose presence could be felt even at a distance. Indeed, modern Confucian philosophy is in the same situation as the official "traditional Chinese medicine": They were both institutionalized during the twentieth century as the result of a new paradigm that severed them from the ancient continuist ontology.[33] Today, what is at stake is not simply to reestablish some forms of continuity between theory and practice but to emphasize that various dimensions of experience, that is, the "material" and the "spiritual," can no longer be dissociated.

The point is not, to borrow terms frequently encountered, to add some "transcendence" to an "immanence" but to observe the reemergence of

31 Elisabeth Hsu, *The Transmission of Chinese Medicine* (Cambridge: Cambridge University Press, 1999).

32 Palmer, *Qigong Fever*. Ownby, *Falungong and the Future of China*.

33 On the analogy between the fates of "traditional Chinese medicine" and "modern Confucian philosophy" see Joël Thoraval, "Confucian Experience and Philosophical Discourse," in *Culture and Social Transformation in Reform Era China*, ed. Cao Tian Yu, Zhong Xueping, and Liao Kebin, 138–146 (Leiden and Boston, MA: Brill, 2010).

experiences that could never be reduced to or limited by such a dualism. Incidentally, this might also help us to better understand why the very category of "religion" is also sometimes rejected. We previously mentioned the explicit reluctance of organizers of rites of passage carried out in Taiyuan's *wenmiao* to assimilate these rites to any possible form of religion. Such a position could of course result from an anxiety linked to the legal regulation of religious activities (and from the fact that Confucianism is not officially a religion). But the refusal of such a category might also mean, at least intuitively for the activists, the refusal of a framework putting too many constraints on the type of experience they live. Indeed, the problem with the category of religion, such as it is officially understood in the PRC (that is, stemming from Western paradigms), is precisely that it threatens to sever the ancient continuity between the visible and the invisible. In other words, with its implicit overemphasis on transcendence (as a means to fight against "superstitions") it introduces a rupture in a perspective that, at the grassroots level, primarily remains "continuist." But the development of "macroscopic dimensions" of ritual experience that starts with the body does not need to translate into anything religious (strictly understood): It primarily points to the possibility of a passage to another regimen of activity or a superior degree of empowerment of the self. Such a possibility is nothing but the actualization of the ancient continuist cosmology that remains a potentiality even in a contemporary context. Depending on concrete political circumstances it can be either encouraged or deterred in individual or community life.

The probability of this potentiality translating into real activities is not always the same. Sometimes, it remains almost nonexistent. But when the potentiality materializes, one realizes that it has little to do with ideology or abstract notions. Rather, it consists in sets of very practical dispositions that operate both in the everydayness of one's life (e.g., when cultivation of the self turns into self-transformation) and in more specific contexts, whether ritualistic, therapeutic, aesthetic, divinatory, and so on (when cultivation of the self turns into mastery of a specific art). Besides, due to the various scales associated with continuist or analogist ontology,[34] practices perpetuated at a microcosmic level (the individual and his family) abide by similar principles to those that used to permeate practices carried out at a macrocosmic level (the social and political community). Depending on

---

34 Descola, *Beyond Nature and Culture*, 207, quoted above.

historical circumstances, there is more or less room for the deployment of each set of practices.

One does not need to experience personally the formalism of ancestors' cult to be perfectly aware of the enduring relationships between the living and the dead. They constitute together the domestic community. However, the magnitude of this interaction between visible and invisible realms may vary. When the founder of a Confucian academy in Zhuhai in the 2000s (see chapter 2) decides a decade later to reorient his Confucian activism by focusing on his lineage and "*citang* culture" that, in his own words, "constitute China's true religion," he is applying in the field of kinship an inspiration that remains faithful to "continuist ontology."[35]

Thus, it is important to emphasize that when the "continuist inspiration" is given enough room to translate into concrete enterprises it cannot be easily understood with usual and "modern" or Western dualist concepts and categories. The European debate on secularization is deeply dependent on such a "dualist framework" that for instance opposes the spiritual and the material or the sacred and the secular. But it hardly fits with conceptions and practices in which visible and invisible dimensions of the universe remain in constant interaction.

The passage from microcosmic practices to macrocosmic ones remains always a possibility. However, in the realm of political life it is nowadays hindered in the PRC. The opposition discussed above between "religious ritual" and "political ceremonial" already provides an illustration of such a tension. A deeper comparison with the Taiwanese case will make it possible both to get a better insight into the specificities of the situation in the PRC and to ponder over future possible developments.

Taiwan and Mainland China: Contrasted Fates of "Continuism"

During the first phase of this discussion we have emphasized the two types of discontinuities that the collapse of the ancient politico-religious order gave birth to. The first one was an opposition—or, at least, a clear differentiation—between the new Chinese nation and the world since nationalist ideology put an end to the ancient ideal of a universal empire. The second discontinuity, linked to the emergence of new secular

---

35 See the epilogue.

techniques of knowledge and governance, was an attempt to sever and iso-late from each other the visible and invisible dimensions of the universe. Our analysis of state cults organized by both nationalist and communist authorities underscored the reality but also the limits of these new dis-continuities. One cannot deny that the ancient analogist and continuist ontology has been deeply broken in its macrocosmic dimension. However, microcosmic potential still exists and occasionally paves the way for new reconfigurations at both a personal and a collective level.

Delving further in the situation of democratic Taiwan might help to cast a new light on the relations between the political and the religious in an open and pluralistic society that, at least to some extent, still remains shaped by this continuist ontology. The problem of the nation generates specific difficulties in the island. Three conflicting projects jostle and com-pete with each other: The nation understood in the vein of the nationalistic heritage of the Guomindang; the possibility—for many the threat—of an assimilation to the communist model; and finally, the ambiguous quest for a new and specifically Taiwanese identity. The symbolic and religious background of these discussions and projects is itself particularly com-plex. Since the end of martial law in 1987 we face a "religious renaissance" with broad social impacts. At the same time, the new situation is also characterized by the powerful developments of transnational religious or quasi-religious movements.

In order to explore the relations between what we termed "political ceremonials" and "religious rituals" in Taiwan one possible approach would have been to keep on exploring ceremonies honoring Confucius (*ji Kong*) in the island's temples of culture (*wenmiao*) and especially in Taipei's Confucius temple. Another option would have been to analyze expressions of "popular religion," for instance the Mazu cult.[36] In both cases, officials of various importance attend the events to which they ascribe a political dimension. However, our main concern primarily focuses on the relations between "the sage and the people." Whereas in the first case, the figure of Confucius is pivotal, the popular dimension of the event remains somewhat limited. In the second case, cults of local dei-ties certainly provide opportunities for large gatherings, but the Confucian reference is much less obvious. Therefore, we shall turn to another type

36 On the political dimension of the Mazu cult in Taiwan see Kuo Cheng-Tian, *Religion and Democracy in Taiwan* (New York: State University of New York Press, 2008), 79–85.

of event that brings us to the core of some of the Taiwanese paradoxes and offers stimulating comparisons with the situation in the PRC.

Commemoration and Sacrifices: Introduction to a Hybrid Ceremony

The question is plain: How is it possible for a mass gathering taking place in central Taipei on March 6, 2011, to celebrate a supreme deity, Heaven, and at the same time to commemorate in the most solemn way the hundredth birthday of the Republic of China? How can one analyze the fact that in front of 20,000 persons, the highest authorities of the state, including President Ma Yingjiu (Ma Ying-jeou) and the leaders of many religious organizations, could participate to such a hybrid ceremony?

If one considers the vast ritualistic heritage of the empire, let us recall that twentieth-century Chinese nationalism attempted to turn only two "middle sacrifices" into significant national ceremonies: the ancient sacrifices to Confucius and the Yellow Emperor. The possibility of the republican state appropriating Heaven worship, a former privilege of the emperor, was never considered a serious option. Through this solemn sacrifice that took place during the winter solstice, the emperor was asserting the centrality of his cosmic role as a mediator between Heaven and the human world.[37] The last time this sacrifice was organized in Beijing was in 1914 in the Temple of Heaven. The initiative was President Yuan Shikai's and the event took place briefly before his failed attempt to restore monarchy. When Qing dynasty's last emperor Pu Yi became in 1934 emperor of the state of Manchukuo (a Japanese protectorate), a modest altar of Heaven was erected in the new capital (Mukden, today's Changchun) in order to carry out the imperial rite.[38] However, the republican form of the state,

---

37 On the origins of this important cult and on the changes that took place during the Han dynasty, see Léon Vandermeersch, *Wangdao ou la Voie royale*, vol. 2 (Paris: EFEO, 1980); Marianne Bujard, *Le Sacrifice au Ciel dans la Chine ancienne* (Paris: EFEO, 2000). On the situation at the end of the empire, see Marianne Bastid-Bruguière, "Sacrifices d'Etat et légimité à la fin des Qing," *T'oung Pao* 83 (1997): 162–273.

38 From 1940 onwards this Chinese rite became incorporated in Japan's State Shintoism and subordinated to the compulsory cult of goddess Amateraru. See Ruoff, *Imperial Japan at Its Zenith: The Wartime Celebration of the Empire's 2,600th Anniversary* (Ithaca, NY: Cornell University Press, 2010), 60. Apart from China, this rite of Heaven worship was accomplished in three modern states: In Korea, during the Chosôn dynasty (1392–1910) when the king Kojong claimed the title of emperor (1897) and had an altar of Heaven erected, soon to be destroyed (1910) by the Japanese; in Manchukuo in the 1930s; in Vietnam when Annan

either nationalist or communist, always seemed incompatible with such a reference to cosmic legitimacy.

The 2011 ceremony was carried out in Taipei within an urban space deprived of religious nature but whose political and symbolic dimension remains complex and ambiguous. It took place on the large square facing the memorial dedicated to President Chiang Kai-shek after he passed away in 1975. The architecture of this monument has the features of some official buildings erected in China before the communists seized power. Names given to the main gates surrounding the square are supposed to illustrate Confucian values: Gate of Great Integrity, Gate of Great Loyalty, and Gate of Great Filial Piety. However, during President Chen Shui-bian's rule in the 2000s the square itself was renamed Liberty Square (*ziyou guangchang* 自由廣場). It has also been the place where many demonstrations took place in the long way that led from an authoritarian regime to the current pluralistic democracy. Thus, this composite space is the crystallization of an array of different symbols, some borrowed from the imperial tradition, others from twentieth-century anticommunist nationalism or the new Taiwanese national community. The 2011 ceremony is also difficult to characterize. Accordingly, it requires some precision in the description.

The authorities did not take the initiative of organizing such a large event. Things originated from a religious organization, the Way of Pervading Unity (Yiguandao). We already mentioned this group as one of the most important redemptive societies of the republican era (see chapter 6). Its development was far from linear. After a quick expansion in the 1930s and 1940s it was repressed both in the PRC and in the ROC. After the legalization of the movement in 1987, its membership increased and reached around 1.5 million regular adepts, which turned the organization into one of the largest religious groups of the island. One also recalls that the movement nowadays has undergone a quick expansion all over Asia and that two of its main features are its millenarianism and its syncretism.

If we consider the 2011 ceremony, the problem is to understand how its political dimension and the celebration of the hundredth anniversary of the republic could be articulated to the Yiguandao ritual.[39] Understanding

---

Emperor Bao Dai could carry out in the city of Hue the *Nam Giao* (*nanjiao*) rite at a time when the country was still under French rule.

39 See the detailed account of the ritual in the journal of the Jichu branch of the Yiguandao: "Qingzhu Zhonghua minguo jianguo yibainian yiguandao wenhua xingguo heping huguo qifu dadian 慶祝中華民國建國一百年, 一貫道文化興國和平護國祈福大典"

FIGURE 10.1 Taipei's Liberty Square, on which a massive sacrifice to Heaven was organized on March 6, 2011, in the presence of around 20,000 persons. Courtesy of Yiguandao's Yu Shan Pao Kuang temple.

this event requires us to consider how three different frameworks could fit with each other. In charge of organizing the event, the Yiguandao first delineated its own ritual time-space. In this context, it incorporated a sacrifice to Heaven that was also open to other religions and formally echoed an ancient ritual pattern. It is within this sacrificial choreography that President Ma was invited to intervene, both as a celebrant and as a head of state delivering an address to the nation.

Thousands of people were sitting in front of the large stage fit to accommodate hundreds of dancers and musicians (Figure 10.1). On the upper level, tables had been set to display fruits and other offerings. Behind, a gigantic canvas provided the symbolic backdrop for the two overlapping dimensions of the ceremony. Three huge pictures of wooden tablets of entities worshipped by the Yiguandao were painted in the center. Their unfamiliar names were written in characters which were hardly

Grand Prayer Ceremonial for Culture, National Prosperity and Peace Organized by the Yiguandao in Order to Celebrate the 100th Anniversary of the Foundation of the Republic of China], *Jichu zazhi* 基礎雜誌 268 (April 2011): 25–31. For Ma Yingjiu's speech: http://www.youtube.com/watch?v=Fqq5cXVXoS8, and http://www.president.gov.tw/Default.aspx?tabid=131&itemid=23680.

decipherable by outsiders: The Luminous Emperor Reigning over the Worlds (*Mingming shangdi zhenzai* 明明上帝真宰), the Principles of All Beings (*Wanwu ben* 萬物本), and the Spirit of the Holy Mother (*Shengmu xin* 聖母心). They can be understood as various titles evoking the Eternal Mother, supreme divinity of the movement. On each side of this huge canvas, however, a few characters pointed to the nature of the event: It was a "great prayer ceremonial (*qifu dadian* 祈福大典) for cultural rejuvenation and the peace of the country" as well as a "celebration of the hundredth anniversary of the foundation of the Republic of China."

The ceremony started with two small Yiguandao rituals: Offerings were made and Yiguandao representatives lit lamps so as to welcome deities to the altar. This opening ceremony was short and followed by modern songs and dancing performances, while guests and audience took their seats on the main square. Then, drums announced the start of the sacrifice to Heaven (*ji tian* 祭天). Several ranks of musicians and dancers took their place on the lower part of the main stage. The structure of the ritual basically echoed other sacrifices, such as those usually carried out in Confucius temples: Deities were welcomed, offerings made, and deities were solemnly sent back at the end of the ceremony. However, contrary to what traditionally happens in Confucius temples, there was no meat offering and no bloody sacrifice. Indeed, vegetarianism is one of the important dimensions of Yiguandao ideology.

Welcoming deities (*ying shen* 迎神) was a part of the ritual carried out by delegates from both Yiguandao and other religious groups, who formed a procession heading for a small altar located on the edge of the square. The master of ceremonies announced the name of the gods: First, Heaven (*Tian* or *Haotian dadi*, Great Emperor of the Vast Heaven), and afterwards, in a secondary position, gods of sun and moon, clouds and rain, wind and thunder. After a few bows and offerings of incense, the procession of celebrants accompanied the gods to the altar on the main stage.

The next step was the triple ritual of offerings (*san xianli* 三獻禮), which entailed three phases. During the first one (*chu xianli* 初獻禮), President Ma acted as a primary celebrant and was assisted by the presidents of the legislative and executive Yuan (Figure 10.2). Wearing long traditional Chinese garbs identical to those usually worn by Yiguandao celebrants[40] these three dignitaries bowed and offered incense, silk, and

---

40 This long gray Chinese garb is typically worn by Yiguandao members, including initiators, when attending all kinds of ritual ceremonies.

FIGURE 10.2 Officials take part in the ritual. From right to left: President Ma Yingjiu; Wu Dunyi 吳敦義, president of the Executive Yuan from 2009 to 2012 (the function is more or less equivalent to that of prime minister); Wang Jinping 王金平, president of the legislative Yuan (i.e., president of the parliament); Wu Boxiong 吳伯雄, former Guomindang president. Courtesy of Yiguandao's Yu Shan Pao Kuang temple.

alcohol (Figures 10.3–10.5). The offering address (zhuwen 祝文), read by an Yiguandao official, emphasized that the meaning of this ritual was to pray to Heaven for the mores and the way of the world (shidao renxin 世道人心). The second phase (ya xianli 亞 獻 禮) was carried out by representatives of religious organizations—Yiguandao, Buddhist, and Daoist delegates—and included similar offerings. Heaven was called on for the future of Taiwan. The third phase of the ritual (zhong xianli 終 獻 禮) continued in the same vein, but celebrants were elderly initiators of the Yiguandao and regional representatives of its General Association. This time, Heaven was called on for the future of each part of the world.

The ceremony's following stage was the burning of offerings (wangliao 望燎). Standing, the celebrants turned to the furnace where texts read previously as well as silk could be burnt in order to be transferred to the invisible world. The ceremony ended with the deities being solemnly sent back (songshen 送神).

It is within the triple ritual of offerings that the properly political part of the ceremony took place. After the first offerings, President Ma delivered

FIGURE 10.3 President Ma Yingjiu offers incense to Heaven. Behind him is Annette Lü (Lü Xiulian 呂秀蓮) who was vice-president of the Republic of China from 2000 to 2008, under Chen Shui-bian's presidency. Courtesy of Yiguandao's Yu Shan Pao Kuang temple.

FIGURE 10.4 Offering of silk to Heaven. Courtesy of Yiguandao's Yu Shan Pao Kuang temple.

FIGURE 10.5 Offering of alcohol to Heaven. Courtesy of Yiguandao's Yu Shan Pao Kuang temple.

FIGURE 10.6 The altar in front of which President Ma Yingjiu delivers his speech. Three big wooden tablets representing the Eternal Mother are painted. The supreme deity's presence is also manifested in the upper Yiguandao symbol that represents an inverted and rounded "mother" Chinese character (*mu* 母). Courtesy of Yiguandao's Yu Shan Pao Kuang temple.

FIGURE 10.7 President Ma Yingjiu delivering his speech. Courtesy of Yiguandao's Yu Shan Pao Kuang temple.

a commemorative speech for the hundredth anniversary of the foundation of the Republic of China (Figures 10.6, 10.7).[41] Three main points can be highlighted. First, Ma Yingjiu paid a clear tribute to the social and cultural action of the Yiguandao and did it in a way that left little doubt about the official recognition and the influence of an organization that was still forbidden three decades ago: "What is being promoted by the Yiguandao," Ma declared, "is basically Confucian thought," and "Yiguandao support to

---

41 There are slight discrepancies between the available written versions of the speech and the video of the event.

the classics reading movement was praised by every segment of society."
To some extent, the Taiwanese classics reading movement largely stirred
up by the Yiguandao echoes the situation in the PRC with the promotion
of classics reading by grassroots activists.[42] Second, Ma praised what he
considered to be pivotal Confucian values, among them "the way of filial
piety" (*xiaodao* 孝道). Third, he introduced his wishes for the new century. In his opinion, the Republic of China could play a central role in the
promotion of Chinese culture. Such a role would be facilitated by a very
favorable environment of full religious freedom.

Spirits, Nations, Political Parties

How can such an event be assessed if we both compare it to the situation
of Mainland China and keep in mind the two dimensions of our analysis, namely the degree of extension of the political community and the
degree of interaction between the visible and invisible dimensions of the
universe? Which function is being ascribed in this new Taiwanese context
to the ancient cosmology and to what extent would this form of association
between the political and the religious be possible or not in today's communist China?[43]

Before tackling this issue, it should be pointed out that such a phenomenon is to some extent overdetermined by the geopolitical situation opposing Beijing and Taibei. The legacy of history is reflected in the way the
ceremonies were carried out. In 2011, both states celebrated the hundredth
anniversary of the 1911 revolution. But whereas in Beijing Chinese president Hu Jintao primarily alluded to Sun Yat-sen, while downplaying the

---

42 One of the main actors of classics-reading promotion on the two sides of the Taiwan
Strait is Taiwanese educator Wang Caigui, whose role in the mainland has already been
introduced (see chapters 2 and 3). Wang was also instrumental in convincing the Yiguandao
to promote Confucian education.

43 An introduction to the ancient imperial sacrifice to Heaven has been organized each
year since 2004 in Beijing within the context of a "cultural week" launched by the Tiantan
park management during the spring festival. Around 200 actors play the role of the celebrants (including the emperor) and attract large audiences. No political or religious
authorities attend this event. See http://culture.gmw.cn/2014-01/30/content_10269226.
htm (updated January 30, 2014). However, the memory of the ancient ritualism generates
debates and controversies about the possibility of organizing ceremonies that would be
more meaningful than purely touristic events. Hence the question of whether a sacrifice
to Heaven in Tiantan is necessary; see http://www.youtube.com/watch?v=YL4S6mYmo3o,
visited on January 30, 2014.

foundation of the republic, the importance of the latter was emphasized by President Ma in Taiwan. In fact, a celebration of the republic could not have taken place in Beijing, where the very idea of "revolution" tends to be retrospectively associated with the 1949 "liberation"—the underlying assumption being that the People's Republic is the direct heir to the 1911 revolution. This being said, one should not forget that a large part of the Taiwanese population pays little attention to this mimetic rivalry between the two states, considering that other landmarks determine Taiwan's history, in particular 1895 (Japanese sovereignty), 1945–47 (cession to Chiang Kai-shek's regime followed by the period of "white terror"), and 1987 (the end of the martial law and beginning of the democratization process). Ma's speech that called for the people to safeguard the *guo* 國 (country) symbolically epitomized an ambiguity that remains structural. The nationalist legacy always needs to be inserted within two concentric circles, the larger one representing Chinese culture and the smaller one the Taiwanese experience: "Taiwan," Ma posits, "is the place in the sinicized world (*huaren shijie* 華人世界) where Chinese culture (*zhonghua wenhua* 中華文化) is embodied in the deepest and most thorough way." "In the coming century the Republic of China (*Zhonghua minguo* 中華民國) will play a leading role in [the promotion of] Chinese culture." However, the latter has become in Taiwan a "Chinese culture with Taiwanese characteristics" (*juyou Taiwan tese de Zhonghua wenhua* 具有台灣特色的中華文化). In sum, Taiwan patriotism seems to be assigned a cultural mission much more than a political one.

While the Chinese and Taiwanese states largely differ in terms of the historical narratives they display, another fundamental opposition also exists regarding the function that they ascribe to the "religious," even though such a dimension remains difficult to grasp due to the ambiguity of the concept in a Chinese context.

Strikingly, in the 2011 Taibei celebration it was the religious ritual that encompassed the political ceremonial, and not the other way around. The commemorative speech was delivered within a broader ritual sequence devised by the Yiguandao that took the form of a sacrifice to Heaven. One could legitimately ask about the respective roles played by the political parties and the state apparatus in such a conspicuous display of continuity between the realm of the spirits and that of the living. To what extent might such a practice be related not to the Taiwanese state itself but to a political strategy of symbol manipulation specific to a political party, namely the Guomindang? Indeed, it is true that since President Chen Shuibian (in office between 2000 and 2008) left power, his successor, President Ma, happened to be particularly active in the organization of ritual cults. His involvement was strong in the promotion of the two state cults (Confucius and the Yellow Emperor) discussed above. Thus, he was the first one to attend the Confucius cult in the Kongmiao in his capacity of head of state. Before that, it had been rather in their capacities of city mayors that Ma's predecessors had attended the ritual. Once elected, they merely sent representatives.[44] In 2009, Ma Yingjiu was also the first president since 1949 to pay a special tribute to the Yellow Emperor. Incidentally, one could underscore that such a tribute was organized in a reverse order from that of the 2011 ceremony. In 2009, the state ceremonial was the structuring framework and only encompassed a few dim elements of more ancient rituals. It did not take place in a temple but in the national sanctuary of revolutionary martyrs (*zhonglieci* 忠烈祠), where thousands of tablets of dead soldiers and civil servants are kept.[45] Offerings—incense, flowers, a written address that was not burnt—were briefly made in a rather martial way. It is clear that a variety of different ceremonies can be organized along a continuum between "religious rituals" and "political ceremonial."

All this being said, it is noteworthy that most of the controversies about Ma Yingjiu's involvement in those ceremonies did not concentrate on the relationship between the "political" and the "religious" in a supposedly secular state. Rather, they focused on a completely different problem, that is, the nonspecifically Taiwanese dimension of the symbols and references put to the fore by Ma. Thus, the ceremonial to the sanctuary of martyrs was introduced as a "remote sacrifice carried out by the central government on the tomb of the Yellow Emperor" (*zhongshu yaoji huangdi ling dianli* 中樞遙祭黃帝陵典禮). We have already mentioned that this tomb is located in Huangling, Shaanxi province. The tribute was paid to Huangdi in front of a tablet dedicated to the ancestor of the Chinese nation (*Zhonghua minzu yuanzu* 中華民族遠祖), thus reestablishing a link with the state ceremonial carried out by Guomindang authorities in the 1930s and, by the same token, the imaginary kinship link so characteristic of early Chinese nationalism. It is actually the emphasis on national

---

44 Confucius temples in Taiwan are local temples under the authority of cities or districts (*xian*). Apart from Taipei (in 2008, 2010, 2013), Ma Yingjiu also attended the sage's birthday in Tainan (2009), Taizhong (2011), and Taoyuan (2012).

45 The dead whose tablets are kept in the sanctuary are the "martyrs" of a nationalist epic that includes struggles and wars against the Manchus, the Japanese, and the communists.

symbols shared by both Beijing and Taipei governments—rather than on purely Taiwanese symbols—that was fiercely criticized in Taiwan by pro-independence supporters.

By contrast, the interaction with spirits of the invisible world did not generate any controversy and the 2011 sacrifice to Heaven actually involved officials or former officials beyond party lines. It was the state and the representatives of its institutions and not a given political force that were involved in the ritual sacrifice. Behind Ma Yingjiu, the former vice-president Annette Lü, formerly in office with Chen Shuibian, also enjoyed a place of honor in the protocol.[46]

Ancient Cosmology and the Modern State

The episodic incorporation of a political ceremonial within a ritual context is of course not sufficient in itself to infer to what extent the "political" and the "religious" remain tightly intertwined in Taiwan. Such a phenomenon must also be understood within the broader context of a pluralistic society where religious freedom is protected. On this highly complex question, we shall simply limit ourselves here to three brief observations based on a comparison between the island and the mainland.

First of all, it is not the constitution itself that may be very helpful to further assess the degree of intertwinement of the religious and the political. In fact, whether in the mainland or in Taiwan, the constitution theoretically guarantees religious freedom and assumes a clear differentiation between the realms of the religious and the political.[47] But merely exploring policies carried out to monitor religious activities is not sufficient either for our purpose. In a recent article discussing the Taiwanese situation, André

---

46 In 1987, the Yiguandao engaged in some sort of trade-off with the Guomindang authorities, offering its support in the new democratization process in exchange for its legalization. Later, things changed and supporters of the Yiguandao can now be found in both camps. On the political commitments of the Yiguandao and its links to the Democratic Progressive Party (DPP) side, see Kuo, *Religion and Democracy in Taiwan*, 66–79. During the January 2008 funerals of the leader of Yiguandao's Fayi Chongde branch, Chen Hongzhen (Chen Dagu), both Ma Yingjiu and Chen Shuibian (at that time in office) decided to attend the ceremony, though not at the same time (*China News Agency*, January 28, 2008). It seems that Chen Shuibian himself became a Yiguandao adept before the 1994 city elections (Kuo, *Religion and Democracy in Taiwan*, 77).

47 According to Article 13 of the constitution of the Republic of China, people have "the freedom to believe in a religion" (*xinyang zongjiao de ziyou* 信仰宗教的自由). The same situation applies for Article 36 of the PRC's 1982 constitution: Citizens have "freedom of religious belief" (*zongjiao xinyang de ziyou* 宗教信仰的自由).

LaLiberté underscores insightfully that little attention has been paid so far to what he calls "the influence of the cultural heritage on state-religion relations." His own work attempts to contribute to the understanding "of the state's changing attitudes towards religious affairs in Taiwan."[48] However, the exploration of both the legal context and the oppositions it generates does not make it possible to tackle another important dimension: the state apparatus itself. How do the multiple actors involved in the state machinery themselves behave vis-à-vis the realm of the invisible? One could underscore that the very idea of a "neutrality" of the Taiwanese state is much less the result of an objective observation of concrete practices than a narrative promoted by the state about itself using foreign concepts and categories. This reminds of Bourdieu's late discussions at the Collège de France: He posited that a certain "spontaneous sociology" remains entangled in the discourses of the institutions it analyzes, since "it applies in its analysis of the state a logic produced by the state." The result is that the state becomes "almost unthinkable." By adopting a functionalist approach (focusing for instance on issues of control or legitimacy), one "fails to think about what this thing called 'a state' actually is and does."[49] Would the prevailing narrative about "secularization" prevent us from grasping specific features of and differences between the European and Chinese state apparatuses? From the perspective that we adopt here, namely discussing the possible fates of "continuism," it is as if the Chinese state was understood as some sort of "outside place" (hors lieu) and as if the appropriation of ideologies and technologies of governance had completely severed it from its own historical and anthropological milieu. Examining the 2011 ceremony enables us to take into account the continuity of interactions structuring this celebration, thus making it possible to go beyond a mere functional explanation of the event and to delve into the thickness of its meanings. More generally, rather than pointing to an imaginary "neutrality" of the state that is hardly more than the consequence of the state's own narrative about its secular nature,

---

48 André Laliberté, "The Regulation of Religious Affairs in Taiwan: From State Control to Laisser-faire?" Journal of Current Chinese Affairs 38, no. 2 (2009): 54, 59.

49 Pierre Bourdieu, Sur l'État: Cours au Collège de France, 1989–1992 (Paris: Seuil, 2012), 13–19: "[une sociologie spontanée] applique à l'État une pensée d'État"; "on escamote la question de l'être et du faire de cette chose qu'on désigne comme État." Bourdieu also posits that: "There is a good chance that the very structures of consciousness, thanks to which we build the social world and this peculiar object—the State—are themselves the product of the state" ("les structures mêmes de la conscience à travers laquelle nous construisons le monde social et cet objet particulier qu'est l'État ont de bonnes chances d'être le produit de l'État") (13).

it is more appropriate to perceive an ever-changing equilibrium between forces, be they "religious," "political," or others, that never cease to share to a varying extent a common anthropological background.

The second observation is a corollary one: whereas neither Beijing nor Taipei can be considered *laïc* states, it is for opposite reasons.[50]

In Taiwan, the institutional distinction between political and religious realms is no obstacle to their intertwinement or to the interaction between the visible and invisible dimensions of experience, whether individual or collective. The regular organization of ceremonies associating state representatives and religious organizations is possible due to a social space characterized by openness and fluidity. As demonstrated by the 2011 event, there is ample room for enterprises characterized by a macrocosmic extension of one's individual lived experience.

This situation contrasts vividly with the amount of state violence prevailing in Mainland China. If the postcommunist state is not *laïc*, it is due to an official counterreligion actively promoted by the authorities. This counterreligion—inadequately called "atheism" (*wushenlun* 無神論)—somehow intends to sever the core of the state apparatus from the rest of the population. As was indicated in 2011 by a representative of the United Front department quoting Deng Xiaoping and his successors, the policy of religious freedom "naturally only applies to ordinary citizens (*gongmin* 公民), and not to Party members." The latter can in no case have a religious faith. In other words, dozens of millions of cadres holding power positions in society are theoretically deprived of part of their constitutional rights.[51] Beyond such a paradox, it is noteworthy that the concept of atheism,

---

50 "Laicity" (*laïcité*) is a particular case of secularism which, beyond the common principle of separation of church and state, considers as desirable the exclusion of religion from an officially defined public (or rather civic) space. In the French edition of this book we referred to this concept primarily because it constitutes the main entry point to reflections on secularism from a French perspective. We did not feel the need to rephrase this section here considering that comparativism is always relative to an adopted vantage point. For an attempt at comparing American and French experiences of secularism, see for example Talal Asad, "Trying to Understand French Secularism," in *Political Theologies*, ed. Hent de Vries and Lawrence L. Sullivan, 494–526 (New York: Fordham University Press, 2006).

51 See Zhu Weiqun 朱维群 (vice-president of the Standing Committee of the Central Committee's Bureau of the United Front), "Gongchandangyuan bu neng xinyang zongjiao 共產黨員不能信仰宗教" [A Communist Party Member Cannot Believe in a Religion], December 16, 2011, Zhongguo gongchandang xinwenwang (Chinese Communist Party news network), http://theory.people.com.cn/GB/16625667.html." Some more flexibility seems nevertheless to be introduced. See Xuyang Jingjing, "Religion in the Party" *Global Times*, February 27, 2014, http://www.globaltimes.cn/content/845166.shtml#.Uo1li9xGw78.

imported from both the Christian and anti-Christian West, needs to be understood in a broader way in a Chinese context, where it designates a dogmatic creed in the nonexistence of spirits (*shen*). Such a doctrine vilifies not only "constituted religions" but also "popular superstitions." In so doing, it splits ancient practices and knowledge by isolating therein a "naturalist core." A good example of this situation is the aforementioned case of traditional Chinese medicine. Due to current social transformations, this imposed dogma also translates into unavoidable performative contradictions, since a growing segment of elite members are involved in activities—cult to dead ancestors, divinatory practices, and so on—that go far beyond the restricted framework of state-sanctioned practices. These activities are tolerated as long as they remain an individual matter and do not acquire any institutional and collective dimension. Their extension is forbidden by a state apparatus careful to maintain a compartmentalization of the social space, thus hindering the fluidity of individual itineraries and the free circulation of symbols that can be observed in Taiwan.[52]

Our third observation focuses on *Tian* or Heaven, the entity for which the 2011 celebration was organized with state support. It raises the issue of the nature of the current coexistence between practical schemes that we term, by convention, "continuist" and modern trends that tend to split them or reduce their importance. If we borrow Descola's vocabulary, at stake is how to think about the articulation between behaviors determined by an ancient "analogist ontology" and those governed by Western-inspired naturalism.

---

52 We have deliberately decided not to use here the concepts of "secular religion" or "political religion" discussed by various scholars from Raymond Aron and Eric Voegelin to Marcel Gauchet and Emilio Gentile. Such a choice is linked to our wish in this monograph to remain as close as possible to the Chinese context. This is not to deny that these concepts might be helpful for a broader comparative enterprise. Within the broad array of "religions of the political," Gentile distinguishes more specifically between "political religions" and "civil religions": while a political religion is a form of sacralization of the political that has an exclusive character and is hostile to traditionally established religions, "a civil religion is a form of sacralization of a collective political entity which does not identify with the ideology of a particular political movement" and which respects religious pluralism. Gentile's distinction could give room for an original periodization of China's twentieth century: Before and after a period of "political religion" represented by Maoist totalitarianism we would have two ways of actively elaborating a "civil religion," both under the republic and since the start of the reform and opening policy. See Emilio Gentile, *Les religions de la politique, entre démocraties et totalitarismes* (Paris: Seuil, 2001), 258–259. For an overview of phenomena linked to "political religiosity" in postimperial China, see also Goossaert and Palmer, *Religious Question in Modern China*, 167–178.

Within the 2011 ceremony, *Tian*/Heaven pointed to a reality that can be understood in a variety of different and sometimes contradictory ways. For the Yiguandao organizers of the event, it was actually another name for the Eternal Mother, the divinity worshipped by the movement and supreme source of all beings. For some other participants to the ceremony, it was "Heaven," invoked as *Haotian dadi* and honored with a prayer and a sacrifice. It could also have been broadly and traditionally perceived as the supreme principle of a cosmological order.[53] Besides, beyond the plurality of meanings carried by the symbol, the ceremony provided the experience of a lived continuity between a number of instances, both visible and invisible, jointly structuring the universe. The presidential speech also emphasized, though in an abstract way, the orientation of this "great praying ceremony" supposed to express "respect of Heaven, love of the country and the people" (*jing Tian, ai guo, ai ren* 敬天, 愛國, 愛人). A Yiguandao representative mentioned different levels structuring cosmic hierarchy and encompassing human beings and the universe, as well as the effect of their harmonious order: heart or mind (*xin*), Heaven and earth, wind and rain, prosperous country, peaceful people, and so on. "Sacrifice to Heaven is the expression of respect and gratitude toward the ultimate source of all beings' destiny . . .; It translates in a practical disposition that consists in knowing Heaven by fulfilling one's heart or mind and acknowledging one's nature." Such a cosmological overview that does not put to the fore Yiguandao's most esoteric teachings is broad enough so that everyone may incorporate it or link it with their particular beliefs.

Noteworthy about the notion of *Tian*/Heaven is not that it might operate as the crystallization of some sort of unanimous *Weltanschauung* but that it enables a coexistence of potentially different behaviors and worldviews. It works as some sort of "shifter" facilitating the circulation between the analogist legacy and naturalist conceptions of modern science and governance. Celebrants' appeal for reverence of cosmic rhythms might be accepted by outsiders—far beyond the audience of the 2011 event—as a sign of respect for the environment and nature. However, such a superficial consent conceals deeper contradictions. Let us incidentally recall here that neither in China nor in Japan is "nature" an indigenous concept. Such a notion, borrowed from modern Europe's naturalism, assumes the

---

53 President Ma Yingjiu hardly expresses himself publicly about his own affiliation to a religious organization—he is a Catholic Christian—but one can imagine that his own invocation of Heaven might be endowed with a peculiar interpretation.

existence of a natural world governed by its own rules, independently from human beings' cultural order. Such a rigid separation between human and nonhuman dimensions of experience vividly contrasts with the continuum of ancient Chinese cosmology. Deemed completely new when introduced in Japan and China, the concept of nature generated plenty of discussions about its possible translation in Japanese and Chinese. In short, the common translation—自然 ziran (shizen)—required the transformation of an ancient adverbial expression ("spontaneously") into a substantive designating an entity that would be autonomous from values and institutions of human world ("nature").[54] But Tian is also one of the notions of traditional vocabulary that could point to natural reality as analyzed by science or transformed by technique. At the junction between "cosmos" and "nature," it can therefore be incorporated in discourses or in the descriptions of behaviors whose underlying rationales differ greatly.

There is a potential tension between the cosmic and the natural or between, on the one hand, the continuity of human and nonhuman realms and, on the other hand, the radical discontinuity generated by the notion of "nature." However, such a tension is somewhat less visible in Taiwan due to the utilization of a hybrid vocabulary associating ancient and modern concepts. It tends to be much more blatant in Mainland China due to the Maoist legacy. Whereas the idea of domination and manipulation of nature has been prevailing in China now for more than a century, this idea turned into an extreme form of agonistic radicalism when Mao Zedong's thought was hegemonic. It is enough here to recall the example of the Great Leap Forward when class struggle was accompanied by "a war against nature" and when violence against society went along with ravages of the natural environment.[55] From Mao's first essays up to the slogans of his political campaigns one always finds some sort of "desecrating pleasure," the pleasure of challenging and transforming Tian/Heaven. In 1917, he proclaimed: "To struggle with Heaven, the joy is boundless!" and in 1959, his poem "Return to Shaoshan" ("and we asked

---

54 See chapter 7 of Yanabu Akira, *Honyaku no shisô: "shizen" to Nature* 翻訳の思想: 自然と Nature [Thought within Translation: *shizen* and Nature] (Tokyo: Heibonsha, 1977); on the difference between Chinese *ziran* and Japanese *shizen*, see Mizoguchi Yûzô, *Chûgoku no shisô*.

55 On the specific context of the Great Leap Forward, see: Judith Shapiro, *War against Nature: Politics and the Environment in Revolutionary China* (Cambridge: Cambridge University Press, 2001), 67–93.

the sun, the moon to alter the sky...") was engraved on mountains while scores of peasants—mobilized in a military way—were engaged in massive projects with little regard for huge material and human costs.[56] *Tian* represented both Heaven, as the ultimate source of legitimization of the "feudal order," and "nature," that needed to be shaped and transformed by Marxist-Leninist superscience. This paroxysmal policy was neither carried out in the name of (objective, value-neutral) science nor in the name of properly Chinese values. Rather, it was the result of a special combination of an ideological appropriation of science (Soviet Lysenkism) and a utopian vision borrowed from an extremely limited portion of Chinese cultural tradition. This particular theoretical connection stopped when political violence diminished.

In sum, it is obvious that Chinese and Taiwanese cultural spaces display a hybrid universe associating forms of analogism and naturalism. The scholar's task is in each context to analyze the specific nature of this association. Here, it is possible to underscore that although the introduction into the Chinese world of the Western notion of "nature" (translated as *ziran* or *tian*) could affect the ancient "continuism," it could not manage to destroy it completely. Even if modern naturalism imposes its logic over whole segments of the political or technical life, it still coexists with practices generating, sometimes at limited scales, continuous interactions between human and nonhuman dimensions of experience. Echoing Robert Weller's work, it would be possible to emphasize the limits in the Chinese world of European naturalism's hegemony—whether a brand of naturalism that isolates nature to transform it (a technicist approach) or a brand that aims at preserving it (an ecologist approach). Patterns of behavior inspired by cosmological continuism continue to develop in daily practices that relate to divination, relations with dead ancestors, medicine, nutrition, and so on. These practices are no more compatible with the explanations of technoscience than with prescriptions of naturalist

---

56 *Yu tian fendou, qi le wu qiong! Yu di fendou, qi le wu qiong! Yu ren fendou, qi le wu qiong!* 與天奮鬥,其樂無窮!與地奮鬥,其樂無窮!與人奮鬥,其樂無窮! ("To struggle with Heaven (Earth and Men), the joy is boundless!"), quoted by Jiang Yihua and Roderick MacFarquhar, "Two Perspectives on Mao Zedong," in *A Critical Introduction to Mao*, ed. Timothy Cheek, 337 (Cambridge: Cambridge University Press, 2010). Reference is made to *Mao Zedong nianpu*. This fragment of the young Mao's journal seems to have been written in 1916. During a visit to his birthplace in 1959, Mao wrote a poem titled "Return to Shaoshan": "And we asked the sun, the moon to alter the sky " (*Gan jiao ri yue huan xin tian* 敢教日月換新天), See Willis Barnstone, trans., *The Poems of Mao Zedong* (Berkeley: University of California Press, 2008), 95.

ecology.[57] In brief, whereas Western-inspired modernity translated into the autonomization of certain realms to which specific laws and institutions were applied, it is also clear that this historical trend was not a farewell to deeper cultural and historical patterns.

Which Encounter between the Sage and the Masses?

A last dimension of the 2011 ceremony that we originally analyzed in order to provide a comparison with the situation in the PRC will enable us to come back to our initial question: In such a diversified context, what can be said about the encounter between the sage and the people? Or, if we attempt to be more specific: Which channels and mediations may contribute to the dissemination, on a massive scale, of supposedly "Confucian" behavioral standards? And how could the situation that we observe in Taiwan be compared with the one developing in the PRC?

Let us first point out that whereas Confucius was not the prevailing figure in the 2011 sacrifice to Heaven, he—or rather, his teaching—was nevertheless indirectly present, especially in the presidential address. Moreover, Confucius's teaching is closely intertwined with the affirmation of values traditionally associated with Heaven, ultimate source of "moral power" (de 德): As mentioned in the Zhongyong, the sage is the one who, because he is perfectly able to accomplish what he has been endowed with, is also able "to participate in the generative process of Heaven and Earth and thus to constitute a triad with both of them."[58] Moral transformation of the self and others is intrinsically linked to the macrocosmic process.

Two points tackled by President Ma Yingjiu in his speech are helpful to discuss differences between Taiwan and the mainland regarding the way Confucian teaching acquires again a truly popular dimension: First, the importance ascribed to filial piety and, second, the existence of religious mass organizations.

Ma began to posit that "the way of filial piety (xiaodao 孝道) is the root of Chinese culture." Quoting the Classic of Filial Piety (Xiaojing), he associated in a very classical way filial feeling and loyalty to the state (zhong 忠). He nevertheless downplayed the importance of the link between this pair

---

57 On these issues see Robert P. Weller, *Discovering Nature: Globalization and Environmental Culture in China and Taiwan* (Cambridge: Cambridge University Press, 2006).

58 *Analects*, VII: 22; *Zhongyong*, 7.

of notions and the traditional political order. For him, these notions are "neither feudal nor dated" and should be able to find their room within a democratic society. In the same way a son has the right to criticize his father's mistakes, the government should also listen to the people's remonstrances. Therefore, filial piety and loyalty need to be tightly associated with a sense of "righteousness" (*yi* 義).

The ancient idea of filial piety does not point to an abstract notion but to a very practical way (*dao*). Depending on historical contexts, the magnitude of its implementation varied, whether along a horizontal axis of social relations or along a vertical axis linking the living to the dead. In the purely visible realm, the way of filial piety enabled the transfer to higher hierarchical authorities of the respect one expresses toward one's own parents; At the junction between invisible and visible realms, filial piety, epitomized in the ancestors' cult, associates the living and the dead.[59] As a central pattern of traditional Chinese society, filial piety, in both its dimensions, has been fiercely attacked by reformers and revolutionaries alike, and for more than a century. It is therefore not surprising that it becomes central again for many enterprises of cultural reconstruction on both shores of the Taiwan Strait.

We have already mentioned the importance of this notion in circles of grassroots Confucian activists in Mainland China. Of course, elements of filial piety remain implicitly pregnant in society, beyond these circles, and include some level of interaction with the invisible realm, at least through the cult of dead ancestors. However, for the activists encountered during our fieldwork, the promotion of this virtue, in its social and cosmic dimensions, is often incorporated in much more explicit projects. Whether in educational or ritual enterprises, family regulation is put to the fore as the condition of possibility of a broader social transformation. For some, filial piety constitutes the practical means to reestablish a link with an ancient tradition of sagehood and get involved in new rituals. From this perspective, this practical pattern may again acquire its broadest extension within a cosmological horizon long ago defined by the Xiaojing in the following way: "Immense indeed is the greatness of filial piety!... Yes, filial piety is the constant (method) of Heaven, the righteousness of Earth, and the practical

---

59 Illustrations of the use of filial piety in the course of history can be found in Alan Chan and Soor-hoon Tan, eds., *Filial Piety in Chinese Thought and History* (London and New York: Routledge, 2004); and in Charlotte Ikels, ed., *Filial Piety: Practice and Discourse in Contemporary East Asia* (Stanford, CA: Stanford University Press, 2004).

duty of Man. Heaven and earth invariably pursue the course (that may be thus described), and the people take it as their pattern."[60] Suffice it to take the example of Yang Ruqing, educator and founder of a small Confucian academy, as well as disciple of Jiang Qing. He understands filial piety as the practical mediation space between the sage's self-transformation and further concerns about politics and the world: the Confucian ideal simply becomes for him a call for "governing All-under-heaven (*tianxia*) by the means of filial piety."[61]

Due to his emphasis on filial piety toward dead ancestors and their spirits, Yang epitomizes the position of the most "ritualistic" proponents of this virtue. An opposite attitude would be to simply take it into account when pragmatically dealing with political and social issues. Thus, the party-state now multiplies references to this virtue as a central one in "the construction of citizen morals." Suffice it to mention the recent promotion of a classical text dating from the Yuan dynasty, *The Twenty-Four Illustrations of Filial Piety*. The content has been adapted to modern times so that it can be disseminated broadly in society, from classrooms to blackboards of neighborhood committees in cities and villages.[62] It is not difficult to identify the multiple social problems that explain this recourse to a superficially confucianized utilitarianism: population ageing and family transformations, the dismantling of the ancient system of social protection, increasing mobility of the population and solitude of the elderly, moral anomy in Chinese society and the related necessity of developing moral doctrine in the youth, and so on. The law itself has been modified

---

60 *Xiaojing*, 7. (*Xiao zhi da ye. Zi yue: fu xiao, tian zhi jing ye, di zhi yi ye, min zhi xing ye. Tian di zhi jing, er min shi ze zhi, ze tian zhi ming, yin di zhi li, yi shun tianxia*. 孝之大也。子曰: 夫孝, 天之經也, 地之義也, 民之行也。天地之經, 而民是則之. 則天之明, 因地之利, 以順天下) Translated by James Legge, *Chinese Text Project*, http://ctext.org/xiao-jing.

61 According to Yang, founder of the Weihang Academy (葦杭書院), since Confucians see Heaven as their father and Earth as their mother, filial piety necessarily extends to their spirits. And such an interaction with spirits (*gui shen* 鬼神) can already be experienced in the relation to ancestors. See Yang Ruqing 楊汝清, "Yi xiao zhi Tianxia 以孝治天下" [Governing the World by the Means of Filial Piety], in *Rujia xianzheng yu Zhongguo weilai* 儒家憲政與中國未來 [Confucian Constitution and the Future of China], ed. Fan Ruiping et al., 167–178 (Shanghai: Huadong shifan daxue chubanshe, 2012).

62 See for instance: http://news.eastday.com/c/20120815/u1a6784964.html and http://money.huagu.com/cfrw/1208/150252.html (updated on August 15, 2012). In this modernized version of a Yuan-dynasty text, children are for instance encouraged, "to make sure that their parents do not lack pocket money" and "to teach their parents how to use a computer and surf the Internet."

and clearly mentions obligations toward one's elderly parents.[63] However, there is often a big gap between hopes nurtured at the grassroots level for the development of a popular Confucianism and the authoritarian temptation of a partial and superficial confucianization imposed from the top. In its ideological formalism, such a temptation might somewhat recall the enterprises of cultural reconstruction launched several times by the Guomindang between the 1930s in Mainland China and up to the 1960s and 1970s in Taiwan. However, in Taiwan the situation has changed tremendously since the end of martial law. The striking development of what has been called a "religious revolution" enabled the development of mass organizations with a mediating role for the promotion of Confucian culture. By contrast, their expansion in the PRC today remains either forbidden or at least very difficult.

It is to this phenomenon that President Ma Yingjiu was alluding in a second key excerpt of his speech. It is noteworthy that on this point his understanding of the situation is in line with more neutral sociological observations: "The Republic of China," he said, "protects religious freedom. . . . Lots of religions that originally came from China could find, after their arrival in Taiwan, a new vitality. They have increasingly orientated themselves toward the affairs of this world [*rushihua* 入世化] and developed their character of enterprises [*qiyehua* 企業化], their volunteering activities [*zhigonghua* 志工化], and their international dimension [*guojihua* 國際化]. Religions have deeply entered the life of the people and promoted social progress. This is the reason why they play in our lives a vital role." A study by sociologist Richard Madsen precisely emphasizes the importance in Taiwanese society since the end of the 1980s of new religious organizations adapting discourses of ancient Chinese traditions to the requirements of new middle classes living in urban environments.[64] First encouraged—if not obliged—to get involved in charitable activities by a state eager to limit its public expenditure in the realm of social protection, they finally expanded strongly and contributed decisively to shaping the new democratic political culture. The this-worldly orientation evoked by Ma in his speech is particularly obvious in Buddhist organizations such as the Ciji 慈濟 (Compassion and Assistance) or Foguangshan

---

63 A detailed law on the protection of senior citizens was enacted in 1996. A new 2013 text goes further and for instance includes the obligation to frequently visit one's old parents.

64 Richard Madsen, *Democracy's Dharma: Religious Renaissance and Political Development in Taiwan* (Berkeley: University of California Press, 2007).

佛光山(Buddha Light Mountain). They involve hundreds of thousands of adepts dedicated not only to self-transformation but also to social change through temples, hospitals, or modern universities. Some of the founders of this type of organization are disciples of monk Taixu 太虛, who promoted in the 1920s in China a new form of so-called "lay Buddhism." Volunteering and charitable (*zhigonghua*) work constitute one of the pivotal dimensions of these structures that are managed as efficiently as business corporations (*qiyehua*). Although movements studied by Madsen are Buddhist or Daoist (as in the case of the Xingtiangong, Enacting Heaven Temple), it is noteworthy that they foster a social ethics largely borrowed from Confucianism.[65]

Madsen does not discuss the situation of the Yiguandao. However, the organization could easily have been included as an extra case in his study. It is also one of the organizations that came from Mainland China and acquired a new vitality in Taiwan in the context of the democratization of Taiwanese society. When Ma Yingjiu praised the Yiguandao in his speech, he emphasized its Confucian dimension and its consequences: The Yiguandao contributes to a process of cultivating culture in society (*wenhua zhagen* 文化扎根) at the grassroots level. The praise of such a work echoes an ancient nationalist rhetoric that contrasted cultural promotion with the destruction that once characterized the communist side. The purpose is to clearly highlight the superiority of Taiwan when it comes to the defense and the revival of an authentic Chinese culture. But for the anthropologist or the sociologist, this political propaganda also reflects a real situation. The liberalization of Taiwanese society has enabled the revitalization and expansion within an urban population of behavioral patterns that an authoritarian political control had reduced to the mere level of abstractions. The situation is no longer characterized by ideological catchwords on social harmony or filial piety, or by the speculations of academics on the "union of man and Heaven" (or other matters). "Confucian-inspired discourses" that now emerge thanks to the new form of religious pluralism are not necessarily embraced by all and they do not necessarily claim

---

65 An integral part of the event organized by the Yiguandao on Liberty Square consisted of a "cultural exhibition," where a dozen religious organizations (including sectarian movements) were invited to display the "excellence of one hundred years of Chinese religious culture in Taiwan." Apart from global or international religions, such as Islam and Bahá'ism, representatives of Japanese movements (Tenrikyô, Tenchi seikyô) and of other "redemptive societies" also attended the event: Tiandejiao 天德教 (Teaching of the Heavenly Virtue), Tiandao 天道 (Heavenly Way), Tiandijiao 天帝教 (Teaching of Heavenly Emperor), and so on.

a Confucian identity; however, they are promoted in mass organizations and translate into efficient collective practices, themselves reflecting the reemergence, at least in a partial way, of various dimensions borrowed from the ancient "continuism."[66]

It is not surprising that "the way of filial piety" constitutes some sort of matrix out of which these new dimensions emerge. Filial piety is indeed a practice that plays a mediating role between the dead and the living and between individuals and families or communities. It is maybe more surprising, however, to observe that nonstrictly Confucian groups are instrumental in Taiwan in the promotion of behavioral patterns central to the Confucian teaching. Thus, Ciji, a Taiwanese organization set up by Zheng Yan, a Taiwan-born nun, is heavily involved in charitable activities inspired by a very Buddhist spirit of compassion. However, it is filial piety that constitutes for Ciji "the gate of good actions." The association itself operates as an enlarged family and attracts urban adepts who have sometimes settled down in cities located far away from their native places. Their participation in collective practices and events carried out by Ciji enables interactions with local kinship groups and shapes the adepts' vision of society. Madsen observes that these associations eclipse the frontier between the "public" and the "private" and influence the understanding one has about the national community: the latter looks more like a family writ large than like a nation of equal citizens.[67] New sets of relations invigorated by filial piety do not really square with the institutionalized separation between the "private" and the "public," a pair of concept that has now been widely used in China for more than a century but that only partially overlaps with other notions—in particular *gong* 公 (public but also impartial) and *si* 私 (private but also egoistic)—associated with the "continuist" legacy.[68] In any

---

66 For instance, filial piety for Yiguandao adepts can also translate into a ritual of "conversion" or "initiation" of dead ancestors. Interviews, Hong Kong, 2010.

67 Madsen, *Democracy's Dharma*, 25, 46–48.

68 The "continuist legacy" would rather oppose, along an axis that is both moral and social, two notions difficult to translate: *gong* and *si*. These distinctions are context-related and therefore entail some degree of relativism. Thus, a behavior that might be deemed "egoistic" from the perspective of the big community might simply reflect a disinterested duty toward a smaller community such as the family. One can behave in a "partial" (*si*) way in a public (*gong*) context, and, to the contrary, in an "impartial way" (*gong*) within a domestic or private group (*si*). For a classical anthropological model, see Fei Xiaotong 費孝通, *Xiangtu Zhongguo* 鄉土中國 [Earthbound China] (Beijing: Sanlian shudian, 1985), 21–28, as well as Yan Yunxiang's remarks on its contemporary interpretation: Yan Yunxiang 閻雲翔, "Chaxu geju yu Zhongguo wenhua de dengjiguan 差序格局與中國文化的等級觀" [(Fei Xiaotong's) Differential Mode of Association and Hierarchical Conceptions within Chinese Culture],

case, the Taiwanese situation strikingly demonstrates that the practice of filial piety, broadly understood, is largely intensified thanks to the action of Buddhist and Daoist organizations. This case of a "Confucianism without Confucius" can also be encountered in Mainland China, where Buddhist groups also promote a shared social ethics based on Confucianism. However, in comparison with the Taiwanese situation, these phenomena still remain much more limited. More often than not we face relatively loose groups of people rather than well-structured and legal organizations. Between, at the top, the state apparatus, and, at the bottom, grassroots initiatives there is no room yet for the same kind of religious corporations as the ones developing in Taiwan.[69]

Conclusion

In order to link the three pillars of our reflection—the Sage, the people, the state—we have used the problematic notions of religion and politics. Our aim was to suggest that within a set of cultural practices encouraged by state nationalism, some of the phenomena that can be observed can be better understood when considered within the broader context of modern discontinuities vis-à-vis an ancient cultural legacy. This legacy was not limited by frontiers of current nation-states and it tightly linked the visible and invisible dimensions of experience. The Taiwanese counterexample was primarily discussed to illustrate the variety of possible developments from what was largely a common matrix.

In this chapter as in the previous ones, the focus of our attention has not primarily been discourses but practices. Our main aim was to understand to what extent it is relevant when encountering politico-religious

---

Shehuixue yanjiu 社會學研究 [Sociological Research] 4 (2006): 201–212. The difference to be ascribed to the notions of *gong* and *si* in the Japanese and Chinese contexts has been emphasized, in an illuminating way, in the work of Mizoguchi Yūzô. See *Kô shi* 公私 [Public and Private] (Tokyo: Sanseidô, 1996), and "Zhongguo yu Riben 'Gong Si' guannian zhi bijiao 中國與日本 '公私'觀念之比較" [Comparison between the Notions of "Public" and "Private" in China and in Japan], *Ershiyi shiji* 二十一世紀 21 (1994): 85–97.

69 One remark: Some organizations, such as that of the Buddhist monk Jingkong, try to develop their activities in a more organized way but also encounter real difficulties. The Lujiang Cultural Education Center, opened in Tangchi (Anhui province) by this organization with the support of local authorities, finally had to be closed down. On this project see Guillaume Dutournier and Ji Zhe, "Social Experimentation and 'Popular Confucianism': The Case of the Lujiang Cultural Education Centre," *China Perspectives* 2009, no. 4 (2009): 67–81, as well as a few additional comments in the epilogue.

phenomena to analyze them by taking into account a "continuist" anthropological perspective. The cases explored here call for a very nuanced answer. In the PRC, "continuism" seems to be both weaker and more resilient than what one could expect. Weaker, since its macrocosmic dimension has been severely affected both by the effects of the state apparatus's "counterreligion" and by the institutional autonomization of segments of social experience, now governed by a logic that is closer to modern naturalism. More resilient, however, since continuist ontology, even if it primarily withdrew into personal and family practices, can also occasionally develop into larger collective practices linking the human and the nonhuman, as well the visible and the nonvisible. From that perspective, "popular Confucianism" is indeed just a specific expression of a much larger trend.

As for Taiwan, the specificity of its history prevents us from considering it as a possible fate for the PRC. The "religious renaissance" mentioned above follows half a century of Japanese domination that impacted both state ritualism and local religions; and half a century of largely American influences conveying alternative models about the role of religion in society. In today's circumstances, the difference between the island and the continent becomes quite clear if we consider for instance the possibility of a "civil religion" that would be commonly shared in "greater China." Let us simply recall that this concept—that Madsen contributed to developing, along with Robert Bellah—originates from a very specific American experience that is, however, also the result of a comparative analysis taking into account East Asian societies.[70] In Taiwan, Madsen identifies the gradual emergence of a specific civil religion that became possible thanks to the constitution of an open and pluralistic political space. He underscores that such a process illustrates the sometimes neglected role of religious movements in the piecemeal creation of a civic culture, according to a model that shares little with mainstream Western theories of democratization. There is no room here to enter the more general debate about the concept of "civil religion." It is sufficient to notice that it can certainly be useful to describe a Taiwanese context where the religious and the political interact

---

70 Specialists of Japan and China, respectively, Bellah and Madsen questioned the fate of the protestant tradition in the United States by comparatively taking into account two "confucianized" cultures where the ethical order did not lay in an instituted religion. As Bellah mentioned in an interview (in Chinese): "We were both particularly sensitive to what we called—in a provisory way—the mores: this pointed to the concept of *li* in the Confucian tradition, which designates an adequate behavior and also includes rites"; Bellah, "Gongming zongjiao yu shehui chongtu."

rather easily within a public sphere that is both open and fluid. By contrast, "civil religion" in Mainland China is so far primarily a catchword for a handful of activists and scholars. Such a claim reflects a desire for the institutionalization and recognition for the ancient Confucian teaching, even in a simplified form. However, both the weight of political ideology and the compartmentalized nature of the social space make it difficult to distinguish this project or dream from an enterprise of indoctrination, or from what would in the end turn out to be a state religion (*guojiao*).

The possibility of an expansion of the Confucian teaching beyond national frontiers is also a difference between continental and Taiwanese situations. Ma Yingjiu stands on solid ground when he mentions the internationalization (*guojihua*) of religious movements that originated from Mainland China and found in Taiwan the conditions of possibility for new developments. Even if they are Buddhist or sectarian, these movements also contribute more or less directly to the global promotion of Confucian values. Branches or networks opened globally by Buddhist mass organizations or the Yiguandao have no equivalent in the PRC. To some extent, there is a sort of striking contrast between the two shores of the Taiwan Strait. In Taiwan, a somewhat weaker state suffering from a problem of international legitimacy manages to find some measure of cultural and even diplomatic leverage thanks to the action of autonomous religious organizations displaying a pluralistic and ecumenical spirit.[71] By contrast, in the PRC a powerful state eager to maintain its ideological grasp on the politico-religious realm and actively looking for some form of hegemony, or, at least, counterhegemony and soft power on the international stage, manages to promote only an extremely limited and formatted version of its cultural heritage. The Confucius institutes now opened throughout the entire world are just an overt symptom of the possibility of having a "Confucius without Confucianism."[72]

---

71 Madsen, *Democracy's Dharma*, 137–39.

72 For a realistic presentation of the limits of Chinese soft power, see David Shambaugh, *China Goes Global: The Partial Power* (New York and Oxford: Oxford University Press, 2013), 207–268. On the Confucius Institutes, see Falk Hartig, "China Confucius Institutes and the Rise of China," *Journal of Chinese Political Science* 17, no. 1 (2011): 53–76; Anne-Marie Brady, "We Are All Part of the Same Family: China's Ethnic Propaganda," *Journal of Current Chinese Affairs* 41, no. 4 (2012): 172; See also the long critical article by Marshall Sahlins: "Confucius Institutes Censor Political Discussions and Restrain the Free Exchange of Ideas. Why, then, Do American Universities Sponsor them?" *Nation*, October 29, 2013, http://www.thenation.com/article/176888/china-u.

We now reach this end of this study. In the epilogue, we introduce a few brief considerations about possible developments of the grassroots Confucianism described in this book. For that purpose, we take into account a "double temporality": the temporality of always evolving social phenomena, as well as the temporality of a research project now carried out over nearly a decade.

Epilogue

ARRIVING AT THE end of this book, it is not possible to conclude and offer a definitive appreciation of the many popular enterprises dedicated to the revival of Confucianism. All in all, this social phenomenon remains still new and the process is ongoing, developing in directions sometimes difficult to anticipate. However, since we started this research in the middle of the 2000s, that is, almost a decade ago, it is possible to make the most of the temporality of our own work and to come back on some of the phenomena that we could observe. This will enable us to share here with the readers the evolution of our own judgment with time. In a still hypothetical way, we will ponder some possible evolutions of the Confucian revival: What are the new orientations of some of the projects we have attempted to follow? Which difficulties did the protagonists meet and which new ways are they now exploring? Our limited ambition in the final pages of this volume will be to briefly tackle these issues, basing ourselves on a few concrete cases.

The Double Dream of Popular Confucianism: Continuity and Autonomy

Two main kinds of aspirations emerged from the various itineraries of activists we met over the years: On the one hand, they attempted to reestablish links with ancient traditions or "lineages in the transmission of the Way" (*daotong*) by looking for threads of historical continuity challenging ruptures taken for granted or sometimes promoted by the state in educational, religious, and political realms. On the other hand, they strove to negotiate and make room for local spaces of autonomy enabling them to carry out and experiment with practical dimensions of the Confucian teaching. In retrospect, when we look at the situation from the vantage point of the 2010s, those challenges were met with unequal success.

Confucian activists endeavored first to reactivate forgotten filiations with an ancient past. We could observe the difficulty of this quest due to the interruption of ritual and doctrinal lines of transmission. However, the ambition of people with modest backgrounds to reappropriate sacrificial Confucian rites while maintaining a distance from official ceremonies provided us with the opportunity to observe a process of self-institutionalization. We encountered various attempts to reinvent rituals, for instance in Taiyuan and in Shenzhen. However, it is the 2007 *minjian* ritual in Qufu—the one we chose to describe in length in chapters 8 and 9—that was maybe the epitome of such a process. It was by looking up in ancient ritual books and through mutual teaching and learning that activists attempted to reconstruct rites endowed with an ultimately religious dimension. In Max Weber's terms, what was displayed was a *Virtuosenreligiosität* ("religiosity of virtuosi") producing its own virtuosi. These new ritual specialists, thanks to real or virtual (i.e., Internet) exchanges now manage to constitute broader networks within or even beyond China proper. Such a ritual creativity is a necessity due to the absence of masters able to perpetuate ancient rituals. However, it also goes along with a wish to reestablish intellectual and spiritual traditions. As a matter of fact, one of the striking dimensions of the current revival is the reappearance of master–disciple relationships that may also be incorporated within broader "spiritual lineages," whether real or reinvented, encompassing former dead masters. These lineages did not necessarily disappear before, but in the PRC they were limited and primarily perpetuated in the academic world after the "philosophical turn" of Confucianism.[1] In the 2000s they developed far beyond this limited framework and attracted all sorts of new activists at the grassroots level.

The search for threads of historical continuity also crystallized in education-transformation (*jiaohua*) of children. The emergence on the margins of the compulsory school system of traditional schools or *sishu*, emphasizing character shaping and memorization of classical texts,

---

[1] The situation in Taiwan was different: Even though it was the center of "philosophical Confucianism" after 1949, all kinds of "spiritual and master–disciple filiations" could also be perpetuated through the various forms of popular Confucianism existing in the island (redemptive societies, phoenix halls, etc.)

statistically represents a minor phenomenon. However, their expansion continues and the optimism of their advocates is encouraged both by the available resources and by the relative tolerance of local authorities.[2] Whereas a handful of radicals dream about a new "production of sages or saints," most activists rather expect that these thousands of children will later take over and, in their turn, not only promote Confucian teaching but also take major social responsibilities. For all, they potentially represent the future perpetuation of the aforementioned spiritual lineages.

The desire for autonomy probably generated more difficulties than the recreation of spiritual lineages. In the 2000s, the limited magnitude of collective projects aiming at recreating forms of "Confucian life" probably had various causes. Conscious self-limitation was maybe one of them. New opportunities offered by authorities involved in the promotion of fragments of "traditional culture" as well as the increasing commodification of society were also understood as possible dangers. To some extent, this remains the attitude of the leadership of the Yidan xuetang. In 2012, this organization—whose activities expanded quickly in the middle of the 2000s—seemed to be facing a number of difficulties. However, its founder was still upholding or claiming a spirit of independence, frugality, if not rusticity. He mentioned that he paid little attention to official ceremonies, academic Confucianism or even to the restoration of lineage temples (*citang*) or traditional academies (*shuyuan*). More often than not, their success requires "outside supports" likely to endanger their spirit. Given the state of dereliction of Chinese culture, suffering of the people must be the departure point of any reflection, as well as the practical horizon of action. Priority is given to action and the development, at the grassroots level and within the lowest classes of society (*shehui diceng*), of modest but autonomous enterprises carried out in a disinterested spirit of social justice and commitment to the most fragile social groups: workers, children, elderly people. Such a project of social reconstruction requires,

---

2 *Sishu* 1 (see chapters 2 and 3) provides a good illustration of this expansion. Whereas it had around 100 registered students in 2010, there were 180 two years later. Its expansion benefited from an increase in its incomes (apart from tuition fees, educational publications, and a vegetarian restaurant) and from the broad network of *guanxi* (connections) of its director. Targeting the children of the new middle class, the director is optimistic about the future and believes that "in the coming decade, this new system and the official system might be complementary." Moreover, *sishu* 1 also organizes one-week training sessions for parents, taught by Taiwanese professors. A certificate is given at the end. Field observation, Beijing, July 2012.

"within the space of the people," a "psychological and cultural revolution" based on the model of the sage's self-transformation. This commitment to serve "ordinary people" (*pingmin*) goes along with an apparent lack of interest in institutionalization and hierarchy, even though this low-profile attitude might also result from concrete difficulties encountered for the organization's development.[3]

When an autonomous project does not work as expected, another option is to give it up and reorient one's activism in a completely different direction. This was the case for the director of the Pinghe academy, a little entity that in the mid-2000s attempted to reestablish elements of collective or semicollective life in the city of Zhuhai (see chapter 2). In the 2010s, Hong Xiuping, the businessman heading the organization, lucidly came to the conclusion that the development of this enterprise had not matched his expectations. The contrast was striking between the expansion of vocational teaching institutions such as his English-language school and the relatively weak popular appeal of more traditional entities. In 2010, a presentation of his projects at the ancient Yuelu shuyuan put things in the following way:

> Hong noticed a strange phenomenon. In his English-language school, tuition fees were high but people came massively and registering was not easy. By contrast, the service of Pinghe academy was free of charge but visitors remained scarce. Therefore, he realized that the time had not come for a mass-promotion of national studies.[4]

The director of Pinghe academy decided to move from Guangdong to his birth town of Hangzhou in Zhejiang province. This new step reflected a change in his understanding of the future of Confucian education. From that period, he started to consider that two main orientations are possible for Confucian teaching institutions. The first orientation should be the result of a revival of prestigious ancient institutions such as the Yuelu shuyuan that would at the same time be adapted to take into account a

3 Interview, Beijing, 2012.

4 Yuelu shuyuan was a famous Confucian institution of the Song dynasty that now belongs to the campus of Hunan University. This presentation was made during a conference about the promotion of Confucianism that gathered cadres and scholars: http://xxhs.ee23.net/bbs/viewthread.php_?action=printable&tid=1509.

global environment. In a discussion with philosopher Jiang Qing, Hong
Xiuping posited that there is an absolute need for students registered in
these institutions to obtain degrees that would be comparable with those
of Western-style universities and provide similar opportunities to obtain
high positions within society: "Obviously, Confucianism is unlikely to
have a broad appeal [in the same way as Christianity] if it cannot attract a
large number of capable believers who can testify to its value in today's glo-
balized market economy"[5] The objective of these academies would be to
contribute to the training of the country's political elite. The second target,
educating ordinary people, is not abandoned but ascribed to small traditional schools (*sishu*). However, *sishu* should be incorporated into another
traditional institution, that of the ancestors' halls or *citang*. For Hong, lineage temples should in the future be able to support future *sishu* due to
their educational tradition and their economic basis.[6] He is himself now
involved in the revival of his own lineage in Zhejiang province. One can
notice here clearly how the failure to create an autonomous community
translates into a quest for new political, economic, and cultural resources
that radically modify the original project.

A large spectrum of different options exists between the adamant
ambition to root the Confucian revival in "the space of the people," at the
grassroots level—if possible within the less privileged segments of the
population—and the temptation to look for new economic and political
resources. Successful projects often result from paradoxical combinations
between utopian perspectives and pragmatic choices taking into account
current circumstances. The director of our *sishu* 1 (see chapters 2 and 3),
the Confucius Academy of the Four Seas, is representative of this state of
mind. His visionary spirit does not take the form of purely utopian projects dreamed of by some activists or intellectuals.[7] In 2010, he was part of
a small group of activists, cadres, and entrepreneurs who had the ambition

5 Hong Xiuping, "Rujia shuyuan de tezheng ji qianjing" and, from the same author, "The
Characteristics and Prospects of the Confucian Academy: A Commentary on Jiang Qing's
Ideas on the Confucian Academy."

6 "It is necessary to rely on lineages: With their support, schools reestablish a link with
tradition. This is a way of settling both the relation to history and the financing issue. Thus,
we somewhat have a cultural foundation in line with historical tradition." Speech in Yuelu.

7 One remembers the controversial project of establishing a "Confucian cultural reservation" (*rujia wenhua baohuqu*) proposed in 2001 by Beida Professor Zhang Xianglong (see
chapter 5). In 2013, he gave an interview to the *Nanfang Zhoumou* and appeared as convinced
as ever of the relevance of his proposal: "It is no utopia at all. Should an opportunity arrive
in the future, this would be implementable. Jews waited two or three thousand years for the

of creating in the Nishan area (Shandong province) a small territory that could, with the support of local authorities, experience a new type of governance associating local people and proponents of the Confucian ideal. This project would have been implemented within the more general and ambitious framework of the creation of a "symbolic capital of Chinese culture" (see chapter 7). Two years later, he acknowledged that such a project was not realistic due to a very practical difficulty: In the eyes of the authorities, it was not attractive enough to develop tourism, especially on an international scale. However, this failure did not undermine his passion and his energy: He now takes part in other cultural and educational enterprises within the new "touristic economy development zone" opened by the local government.[8] The initial project is not definitely abandoned but it is simply postponed, awaiting more favorable conditions. In the meantime, new opportunities are grasped, in collaboration with local authorities.

In sum, the two aforementioned aspirations of popular Confucianism— restoring ancient continuities, creating a relatively independent space for collective initiative and action—obtained some unequal results. But some new perspectives also seem to emerge in the 2010s. The Taiwanese

---

foundation of Israel. We can also wait! But what we first need is a thought that would make people realize that such a possibility exists and that would convince them. It is only with the support of a community of faith that people will be convinced to commit their lives to such an undertaking."
See: http://www.infzm.com/content/96475 visited on June 25, 2014.

8 In 2010, a small informal network that included activists, businesspeople, cadres, educators, and scholars planned to propose to the local government the creation in the Nishan area of a special zone that would be organized according to Confucianism-inspired principles: "There would be four principles: No (organized) religion; no politics; no frontiers (whether ethnic or national); no industry but only high-quality craftsmanship." The starting point was to obtain the support of both the local population and cadres by demonstrating the historical value of the project and its economic sustainability. Operations would have started afterwards with a few hundred households and a little community of intellectuals, scholars, and businesspeople who would have settled in the area. The project was emphatically differentiated from Jiang Qing's political Confucianism (deemed overambitious in its dream to change the constitution) and from Zhang Xianglong's "reservation," considered radical in its rejection of modernity. In this new zone, Internet would have been available (but with restrictions regarding the content). In 2012, one of the promoters of the project explained that its economic sustainability was not convincing enough for officials and for the local population much too aware of the touristic development potential of the area. "Our dream of a Confucian paradise (*rujia taohuayuan*) has been broken by capitalism!" mentioned one of the activists. Interviews, Beijing, June 2010 and July 2012. In 2013, Shandong provincial government considered that the establishment of a "special tourist economy zone" in the "holy land of Nishan" was a priority. See http://0537.fccs.com/news/201307/3934331.shtml, July 2, 2013.

counterexample, introduced in chapter 10, makes it possible to perceive them more clearly.

The New Potentialities of Popular Confucianism

The Taiwanese case taught us that popular expressions of Confucianism could develop on a favorable ground for two sets of intertwined reasons. First and foremost, from the end of the 1980s liberalism and pluralism of Taiwan's religious policy echoed projects of a variety of religious movements that, themselves, promoted forms of civic morals compatible with the democratic turn. Second, the new legal and political framework created proper conditions for the spectacular development of these mass organizations (Buddhist, Daoist, syncretist) emphasizing the mundane and transnational dimension of ancient teachings while implementing practical social projects such as charitable work in an increasingly professional way.

Such a situation offers a vivid contrast with the situation of popular Confucianism in the PRC. Confucian advocates face institutions and a political culture that do not make room for similar developments. Due to their lack of cohesion and resources Confucian activists achieved in the 2000s only fragmented projects that did not fulfill their desire for institutionalization. However, it might be helpful to consider the two Taiwanese orientations—first, a state more or less in tune with basic ethical views promoted by religious movements; second, the emergence of mass organizations—in order to ponder possible future developments in the PRC.

Compared to the 2000s, Confucian activists have to deal during the 2010s with a state apparatus sometimes involved at the local level in unprecedented cultural promotion projects. Whereas the political agenda sometimes underlying these developments does not necessarily overlap with targets of smaller activist cells, it nevertheless provides some room for "overlapping consensuses." At least, some sorts of authorized spaces are now created, facilitating all sorts of different projects.

One of the most spectacular recent developments is maybe the opening in 2012 in Guiyang, Guizhou province, of a "Confucius study hall" (Guiyang Kongxuetang 貴陽孔學堂). Its nature and mission must be clearly distinguished from those of Shenzhen's Hall of the Sage (Kongshentang 孔聖堂) discussed in chapter 6. Although it attempts to maintain the best possible relations with local authorities, the latter remains a purely *minjian* initiative fostering a religious project. By contrast, Guizhou provincial government launched the Guiyang project with clear *jiaohua* objectives, that is, as an enterprise of transformation and shaping of public morals: "It is not a religious hall (*miaotang* 廟堂), but a study hall."[9] The project required the construction of a massive architectural group of buildings. Its mission is to facilitate the promotion of Confucianism, through ritual and educational activities (rites of passage, wedding ceremonies), in the population as well as in the academic community. The local Communist Youth League (*gongqingtuan* 共青團) regularly takes part in the organization of its activities. One year after its opening, it is emphasized that 80,000 citizens of Guiyang attended various activities and that Hu Jintao and Xi Jinping themselves visited the premises.[10] Delegations from other provinces now come to study this initiative and some have mentioned that they would be interested in replicating the scheme.[11] Such a space might facilitate interactions between local Confucian groups and the authorities. From that perspective, it could be compared with the small Society for the Promotion of Ritual Culture and Music of the holy city of Qufu that we previously introduced (see chapter 8). However, the scale here is of a completely different magnitude.[12]

---

9 Interview with the deputy director of the Kongxuetang's management committee, Fuzhou, December 2013.

10 President Xi Jinping has expressed several times his interest in Confucianism and Chinese traditional culture. On September 24, 2014, in a speech at the Great Hall of the People during an international academic conference organized by the International Confucian League on the occasion of the celebration of Confucius' 2,565th birthday, he declared that "Chinese Communist Party members are always the faithful heirs and promoters of China's outstanding traditional culture."

11 Interviews, Fuzhou, December 2013. This case provides another illustration of a situation mentioned previously in this book, that of a progressive dissemination of Confucian ideas within the political apparatus. Here, such a dissemination takes place at the highest level since it is the provincial authorities of Guizhou province that are introducing this model to other provinces.

12 It is noteworthy that initiatives taken at the top and at the grassroots level sometimes do not have the same temporalities. Thus, in 2012 the authorities formally approved the creation of the Beijing Academy of National Studies (Beijing Guoxueyuan). The location of the academy is symbolically meaningful: In the vicinity of the Forbidden City, it is one of the temples of the ancient Sanctuary of Imperial Ancestors (Taimiao 太廟), which was turned in 1951 into a Cultural Palace of Laboring People (Laodong renmin wenhuagong). The decision of the central authorities grants to this new academy a relatively flexible status of "nonentrepreneurial work unit operated by the people" (*minban feiqiye danwei*). Such a status facilitates the implementation of projects, sometimes even with Taiwanese counterparts. This type of official initiative might anticipate future developments. However, when we visited the academy in 2012, it was still largely an empty shell. The deputy director lamented that Confucian activists such as the young volunteers of the Yidan xuetang (and others) were not very actively interacting with them. Interviews and field observation, Beijing, July 2012.

If we come back to the Taiwanese experience, it is noteworthy that the relative impartiality of the state in a democratic context succeeded a period of nationalism and authoritarianism, during which the relative distrust vis-à-vis popular religions went along with privileges granted to Christian churches, especially in the charitable and educational realms. Today, a new balance has been struck in the island to the benefit of local and Chinese religious movements, but without impeding Christian churches from participating to the multiple state–society interactions. By contrast, the "Christian issue" in the PRC may translate into common defensive interests between the state and Confucian groups. The expansion of the Christian faith, and more particularly of protestant denominations, is a source of concern and this point was recurrent in the course of our field-work interviews. A feeling of rivalry often seems to emerge and there are many Confucian activists who call for state support, believing that they could embody the bulwark China needs to contain Christianity. A recent example of such a particularly tense situation was the 2010 project to build a large Christian church (3,000 seats) in the "holy city of Qufu." Paradoxically in that case, the project was supported by local authorities. However Confucian activists rose up in arms against it throughout the country: Prominent scholars petitioned to express their opposition and Confucian websites and blogs engaged in the campaign with radical catch-words ("Qufu is not Jerusalem"; "They nail Confucius on the cross," etc.).[13] Of course, this situation is an extreme case that does not reflect the overall situation of Confucian–Christian relationships. Whether in scholarly circles or at the grassroots level there are also reports of much smoother and ecumenical interactions. Suffice it to mention the examples of studying sessions of the *Analects* taking place in Christian churches in Beijing and Changsha (Hunan province).[14] However, the expansion of Christianity is an issue for the authorities, and the instrumental use of local Chinese traditions in order to serve a broader containment policy is far from being a mere

---

13 Sun, *Confucianism as a World Religion*, 174–178.

14 About study sessions of the *Analects* initiated by Christians in Beijing and Changsha, see Xuyang Jingjing, "Confucius in Church," *Global Times*, October 9, 2012, http://www. globaltimes.cn/content/737236.shtml. Some Confucian activists are intensely involved in the Confucian–Christian dialogue and are convinced of its importance. A good example is certainly the so-called Oxford consensus, signed in August 2013 between well-known representatives of various intellectual currents who met in a symposium. It is noteworthy that apart from liberal, new left, and Confucian scholars, some Christians were also represented. See the manifesto: http://www.nfpeople.com/story_view.php?id=4824, September 17, 2013.

rhetorical question. This parameter should not be overlooked when pondering the future possible organization of Confucianism in China, between state policies and grassroots initiatives.

In any case, the situation in the PRC today makes it impossible to see the emergence of some sort of "civil religion" in the sense Madsen evokes it in Taiwan: The existence of a state "counterreligion" (atheism), even much more limited than it used to be, as well as the compartmentalization of social space, are obvious obstacles to the broader dissemination of a properly "religious Confucianism." Since the room left by the state is limited, future developments might take another direction: The promotion of Confucian values and "civil religiosity" by means of structures that are not exclusively or primarily dedicated to the promotion of Confucianism. Buddhist and syncretistic organizations might play in that respect an important role, bringing us back to trends already important during the republican era and still very significant in Taiwan.

The importance of Buddhism for the Confucian revival has been mentioned several times throughout this book. In the 2010s, this trend seemed to develop quickly. One of the organizations promoting the most actively Confucian ethics in China is probably that of Buddhist monk Jingkong. We previously mentioned that he managed to open in the 2000s—with the initial support of local authorities—a Cultural Education Center in Lujiang, Anhui province, that did not focus on Buddhist teachings but on the *Rules of the Disciple* (*Dizigui*) and the construction of a harmonious society. Even though the center was finally closed—or, rather, the scope of its activities largely reduced—it contributed to the training of hundreds, if not thousands, of activists.[15] We met some in the Taiyuan temple of literature (see chapter 5). At the start of the 2010s, the activities of this group take an even greater magnitude. Suffice it to give here a few examples: In Gansu province, one of their projects, supported by local authorities, is to create a Dizigui school (Dizi gui xuexiao 弟子規學校) and an Institute of sinology (hanxue xueyuan 漢學學院).[16] In Suzhou, Jiangsu province, an

---

15 Dutournier and Ji, "Social Experimentation and Popular Confucianism." In 2013, according to informants associated with the Jingkong group, up to 20,000 volunteers may have been on short- or long-term training periods in the center. Interview, Paris, May 2013.

16 The term "sinology" is understood in this group in a very different way than its standard meaning in the academic world. For the initiator of the Gansu project, sinology is synonymous with study and promotion of "national tradition." In such a context, sinologists, or *hanxuejia* 漢學家, are those specializing in the study of the *guoxue* tradition and who promote it as well as a classical ethos. In other words, sinology is not considered a value-neutral scientific approach. The Venerable Jingkong uses the word with the same meaning. For him, sinologists are at the forefront of a "civilizing mission" with a universal (*tianxia*) dimension.

entrepreneur and disciple of the Venerable Jingkong now includes the promotion of Confucianism and traditional values at the core of his corporate project.[17] In Qingdao, Shandong province, a large forum of Confucian entrepreneurs is also organized every year by disciples of the Buddhist monk.[18] As is always the case, organizers and activists each time need to liaise with the authorities. Once again, it is noteworthy that a number of people involved in these projects also have official positions within state structures (even though it is not state structures that initiate projects). This overlapping of roles (activist, official) contributes to the ambiguity of these projects, but also to their success. In any case, the civilizing mission promoted by Jingkong needs to be understood from the perspective of a long temporality. Therefore, short-term pragmatic accommodations with the policies and ideological projects of the authorities (including the authorities' civilizing ambition to increase the "quality of the population," *suzhi* 素質) do not present any special difficulty.

Apart from being promoted by Buddhist organizations—with an enormous impact in Taiwan and a growing one in the PRC—Confucian ethos and values are also largely disseminated by ancient "redemptive societies" the importance of which was discussed in chapter 6. During the republican era, these organizations were probably the largest promoters of Confucian values. The legal and ideological framework makes it difficult for them to develop openly in the PRC. Some of them are nevertheless extremely active again although they operate in an underground way. It is for instance reported that the Association for Universal Morality (Wanguo daodehui) carries out activities in northeast China.[19]

Especially striking is the action of the Yiguandao, which has had a major influence in Taiwanese society. Ongoing research on the movement shows that the organization is nowadays expanding quickly in China. Its goal is not simply to attract new adepts but also to negotiate a new status in

---

Western sinologists are considered to be part of such a mission. The integration of Western knowledge and scholars in a universal project reminds one of philosopher Tu Wei-ming's "cultural China" (*wenhua Zhongguo*). International sinology was also considered to be part of this cultural sphere. Interview with Master Jingkong and his following, Paris, May 2013.

17 Interview with the director of the company, Paris, May 2013.

18 We met several times participants or organizers of this forum. In 2010, we were told that the forum attracted 800 Confucian entrepreneurs (*qiyejia*). In 2013, the figure reached 1300 people. Interviews, Taiyuan 2010 and Paris 2013.

19 Luo, Qiu, and Zhou, *Cong Dongbei dao Taiwan*, 139–141.

the People's Republic.[20] Therefore, the question is whether, to what extent, and under which forms Confucian aspirations expressed "in the space of the people" could interface with the return—underground or maybe one day, legal—of Yiguandao in the PRC.

The new attitude of Chinese authorities seems to create a more favorable context for such an encounter. Since 2009, exchanges of delegations took place on both shores of the Taiwan Strait. Representatives of Yiguandao's general association, as well as branch leaders, could meet directly with Chinese officials thanks to the mediation of Taiwanese officials. The interest for the Yiguandao on the Chinese side—a novel phenomenon considering that the organization used to be considered a dangerous reactionary and feudal sect—is largely linked to the organization's influence in Taiwan (including in political circles) and to its promotion of Confucianism-inspired social morals. One of the symbols of this renewed interest is the publication in China of one of Yiguandao's texts on filial piety, though expunged from its purely religious content.[21] It is significant that among the activists mentioned in this book one of them is now in contact with this organization. One remembers the case of Mrs. D., the manager of a Shenzhen restaurant whose journey was discussed in chapter 4. Since the time of our fieldwork, her commitment to Confucianism has been enduring and she was able to get in touch with larger circles of people. In 2012, she went to a Yiguandao temple in Taizhong (Taiwan). Facing a large audience of adepts, she introduced her vision of Chinese culture, her action of promotion of classics reading in the mainland, and the importance of the ongoing cultural reconstruction process. This last, she posited, goes in the opposite direction from society's prevailing utilitarian values and therefore enables the reestablishment of a link with the highest wisdom. The speech was followed by a question-and-answer session and an exchange of experience with the participants. Indeed, the Yiguandao is massively involved in the promotion of Confucian classics, and Wang Caigui, Mrs. D's Taiwanese master, played a pivotal role in this orientation.

---

20 Billioud, "Le rôle de l'éducation dans le projet salvateur du Yiguandao"; "*Qi jia*"; "Yiguandao's Patriarch Zhang Tianran." The dynamics of the movement are discussed in a forthcoming monograph: Billioud, *Reclaiming the Wilderness*.

21 See references mentioned on footnote 20.

Relations between Confucian activists and the Yiguandao are only at a starting point and future developments are not possible to anticipate. However, it is clear that should some of the historical "redemptive societies" confirm and amplify their return in the PRC, it would have a massive impact in terms of the promotion of a Confucian ethos and relation between the sage and the people.

***

Arriving at the end of this study one realizes how diverse—and sometimes contradictory—the relations between the sage and the people have been since the start of the new century. Confucius sometimes becomes a label attached to products and projects that share little (or even nothing) with a "Confucian spirit," no matter how hard the latter might be to define. To the contrary, Confucian values may also be efficiently promoted by all kinds of groups without any ambition to cling to the figure of the sage. Between these two poles a whole range of other possibilities exists.

This book placed the emphasis on the novelty of the 2000s, which saw the emergence of a "popular (*minjian*) Confucianism." In the course of fieldwork it was possible to clearly identify a number of popular or populist aspirations that often took the form of anti-elitism, that is, of a distance at the grassroots level from both intellectual and political elites. A few years later, everything happens as if there had been some sort of gradual split between the two meanings—administrative and social—of the word *minjian*. Initially, "*minjian* Confucianism" could keep a light flavor of dissent due to the lack of legal or regulatory framework applying to Confucian or Confucianism-inspired activities. But this is decreasingly the case since the state, at the highest level, is now making room for brand new types of organization (such as the Kongxuetang) with a clearer legal status. They are granted a certain degree of autonomy while being still part of a broader parastatal configuration.

Accordingly, in 2014, when we write these lines, "popular Confucianism" could point in the PRC to two ideal types of very different projects, at least in the spirit with which they are implemented. The first one still reflects a concern for self-cultivation and, by extension, the education of ordinary people or giving assistance to the less privileged. It often emphasizes the importance of roots and rural culture. In a word, it continues to ascribe to the word *minjian* and the expression "*minjian* Confucianism" a certain emancipatory dimension. References to reformers such as Liang Shuming or to village sages such as Wang Fengyi (and, implicitly, his organization) exemplify this emerging Confucianism-inspired post-Maoist ethos. The second ideal type however, is largely devoid of the same populist and vaguely egalitarian tones. It consists of enterprises able to mobilize both economic resources of consumer society and official support that, in the end, serve the emergence of a new middle class. It is no longer a form of anti-elitism but rather an attempt, engineered by the elites themselves—whether political, economic, or intellectual—to shape model citizens and, beyond, to reproduce new elites in a complementary relationship with existing sociopolitical hierarchies.

It would be overambitious at this stage to go beyond this brief overview considering the pace at which all kinds of developments are now taking place. Looking in retrospect at the changes of our own appreciation of the Confucian revival over a decade made us realize the nature of this book. As much as an anthropological contribution to the study of the present time, it constitutes a reflection on what is already part of history: The very special circumstances of the first decade of the new century.

Bibliography

Ahern, Emilie. *Chinese Rituals and Politics*. Cambridge: Cambridge University Press, 1981.

Alitto, Guy. *The Last Confucian: Liang Shu-ming and the Chinese Dilemma of Modernity*. Berkeley: University of California Press, 1986.

Alitto, Guy. "Rural Reconstruction during the Nanking Decade: Confucian Collectivism in Shantung." *China Quarterly* 66 (1976): 213–246.

Ames, Roger T., and Henry Rosemont Jr. *The Analects of Confucius: A Philosophical Translation*. New York: Ballantine, 1998.

Asad, Talal. "Trying to Understand French Secularism." In *Political Theologies*, edited by Hent de Vries and Lawrence L. Sullivan, 494–526. New York: Fordham University Press, 2006.

Ayers, William. *Chang Chih-tung and Educational Reform in China*. Cambridge, MA: Harvard University Press, 1971.

Bai Limin. *Shaping the Ideal Child: Children and Their Primers in Late Imperial China*. Hong Kong: Chinese University Press, 2005.

Barmé, Geremie R., and Sang Ye. "Research Notes: National Commemorative Ceremonies." *China Heritage Quarterly* 20 (2009). http://www.chinaheritage-quarterly.org/scholarship.php?searchterm=020_intro_national_ceremonies.inc&issue=020.

Barnstone, Willis, (trans.). *The Poems of Mao Zedong*. Berkeley: University of California Press, 2008.

Bastid-Bruguière, Marianne. "Liang Qichao yu zongjiao wenti 梁啟超與宗教問題" [Liang Qichao and the Religious Issue]. In *Liang Qichao, Mingzhi Riben, Xifang* 梁啟超, 明治日本, 西方 [Liang Qichao, Meiji Japan, and the West], edited by Hazama Naoki, 400–457. Beijing: Shehui kexue wenxian chubanshe, 2001.

Bastid-Bruguière, Marianne. "Sacrifices d'Etat et légitimité à la fin des Qing." *T'oung Pao* 83 (1997): 162–173.

Béja, Jean-Philippe. "The Rise of National-Confucianism." *China Perspectives* 1995, no. 2 (1995): 6–12.

Bell, Catherine. *Ritual Theory, Ritual Practice*. New York and Oxford: Oxford University Press, 1992.

Bell, Daniel A. *China's New Confucianism: Politics and Everyday Life in a Changing Society*. Princeton, NJ: Princeton University Press, 2008.

Bellah, Robert N. "Civil Religion in America." In *Beyond Belief, Essays on Religion in a Post-traditionalist World*, 168–192. Berkeley: University of California Press, 1970.

Bellah, Robert N. "Gongmin zongjiao yu shehui chongtu 公民宗教與社會衝突" [Civil Religion and Social Conflicts]. *Ershiyi shiji* 二十一世紀 [Twenty-First Century] 12 (March 31, 2003). http://www.cuhk.edu.hk/ics/21c/supplem/essay/9501079g.htm.

Bergère, Marie-Claire. *Sun Yat-sen*. Paris: Fayard, 1994.

Biallas, Franz Xaver. *Konfuzius und sein Kult*. Beijing and Leipzig: Pekinger Verlag, 1928.

Billeter, Térence. *L'Empereur jaune*. Paris: Les Indes savantes, 2007.

Billioud, Sébastien. "De l'art de dissiper les nuages, réflexions à partir de la théorie politique de Thomas Metzger." *Études chinoises* 26 (2007): 191–234.

Billioud, Sébastien. "Carrying the Confucian Torch to the Masses: The Challenge of Structuring the Confucian Revival in the People's Republic of China." *Oriens Extremus* 49 (2010): 201–224.

Billioud, Sébastien. "Confucianism, 'Cultural Tradition' and Official Discourses at the Start of the New Century." *China Perspectives* 2007, no. 3 (2007): 50–65.

Billioud, Sébastien. "Confucian Revival and the Emergence of *Jiaohua* Organizations: A Case Study of the Yidan Xuetang." *Modern China* 37, no. 3 (2011): 286–314.

Billioud, Sébastien. "Les devenirs contemporains du confucianisme dans le monde chinois." Thesis for the habilitation to supervise PhD dissertations, Paris, 2012.

Billioud, Sébastien. "*Qi jia* 齊家: The Great Learning Ideal of Family Regulation in a Contemporary Syncretistic Religious Context." In *Lectures et usages de la Grande Étude (Chine, Corée, Japon)*, edited by Anne Cheng. Paris: Collège de France, 2015 (forthcoming).

Billioud, Sébastien. *Reclaiming the Wilderness: Contemporary Dynamics of the Yiguandao*. In preparation.

Billioud, Sébastien. "Revival of Confucianism in the Sphere of the Mores and Reactivation of the Civil Religion Debate in China." In *Confucianism: A Habit of the Heart*, edited by P. J. Ivanhoe and Sungmoon Kim. New York: State University of New York Press, 2015 (forthcoming).

Billioud, Sébastien. "Le rôle de l'éducation dans le projet salvateur du Yiguandao." "Religion, éducation et politique en Chine moderne," edited by Ji Zhe. Special issue, *Extrême-Orient Extrême-Occident* 33 (2011): 211–234.

Billioud, Sébastien. *Thinking through Confucian Modernity: A Study of Mou Zongsan's Moral Metaphysics*. Leiden and Boston, MA: Brill, 2012.

Billioud, Sébastien. "Yiguandao's Patriarch Zhang Tianran (1889–1947): Hagiography, Deification and Production of Charisma in a Modern Religious Organization." In *The Making of Saints in Modern and Contemporary China: Profiles in Religious Leadership*, edited by Vincent Goossaert, Ji Zhe, and David Ownby. New York: Oxford University Press, in preparation.

Billioud, Sébastien, and Joël Thoraval. "*Anshen liming* or the Religious Dimension of Confucianism." *China Perspectives* 2008, no. 3 (2008): 88–106.

Billioud, Sébastien, and Joël Thoraval. "*Jiaohua*: The Confucian Revival Today as an Educative Project." *China Perspectives* 2007, no. 4 (2007): 4–20.

Billioud, Sébastien, and Joël Thoraval. "*Lijiao*: The Return of Ceremonies Honouring Confucius in Mainland China." *China Perspectives* 2009, no. 4 (2009): 82–99.

Billioud, Sébastien, and Joël Thoraval, eds. "Regards sur le politique en Chine aujourd'hui." Special issue, *Extrême-Orient Extrême-Occident* 31 (2009).

Bourdieu, Pierre. *Sur l'État: Cours au Collège de France, 1989–1992*. Paris: Seuil, 2012.

Brady, Anne-Marie. "We Are all Part of the Same Family: China's Ethnic Propaganda." *Journal of Current Chinese Affairs* 41, no. 4 (2012): 159–181.

Brook, Timothy, Jérôme Bourgon, and Gregory Blue. *Death by a Thousand Cuts*. Cambridge, MA: Harvard University Press, 2008.

Bujard, Marianne. *Le Sacrifice au Ciel dans la Chine ancienne*. Paris: EFEO, 2000.

Camroux, David, and Jean-Luc Domenach, eds. *Imagining Asia: The Construction of an Asian Regional Identity*. London: Routledge, 1997.

Chan, Alan, and Sor-hoon Tan, eds. *Filial Piety in Chinese Thought and History*. London and New York: Routledge, 2004.

Chan Sin-wai. *Buddhism in Late Ch'ing Political Thought*. Hong Kong: Chinese University Press, 1985.

Chen Bisheng 陳壁生. "Chaoshan minjian de rujiao fuxing. Yi Chaoyang Xiaoshi citang 'Sixutang' wei li 潮汕民間的儒教復興—以潮陽蕭氏祠堂'四序堂'為例" [The Popular Revival of the Confucian Teaching in Chaoshan: The Case of Ancestral Temples of the Xiao Lineage in Chaoshan]. Paper presented at the conference of the research project "The Confucian Revival in Mainland China, Forms and Meanings of Confucian Piety Today," Tokyo University, 2010.

Chen Bisheng 陳壁生. "Li zai gujin zhijian—chengshi citang jisi de fuxing 禮在古今之間—城市祠堂祭祀的復興" [Rites between the Ancient and Contemporary Periods: The Revival of Sacrifices in Ancestors Temples in Cities]. Paper presented at the final conference of the research project "The Confucian Revival in Mainland China: Forms and Meanings of Confucian Piety Today," Fuzhou, December 2013.

Chen, Hsi-yuan. "Confucianism Encounters Religion: The Formation of Religious Discourse and the Confucian Movement in Modern China." PhD diss., Harvard University. UMI Microform 9936192, 1999.

Chen Ming 陳明. "Bianhou 編後" [Postface]. *Yuandao* 原道 5 (1999): 465–466.

Bibliography

Chen Ming 陳明. "Rujia gongmin zongjiao shuo 儒家公民宗教說" [On Confucianism as a Civil Religion]. Website of the Pinghe Academy 平和書院. http://www.ping-hesy.com/data/2007/1016/article_1594.

Chen Pingyuan 陳平原. *Daxue hewei* 大學何為 [Why the University?]. Beijing: Beijing daxue chubanshe, 2006.

Chen Rui 陳銳. *Ma Yifu yu xiandai Zhongguo* 馬一浮與現代中國 [Ma Yifu and Contemporary China]. Beijing: Zhongguo shehui kexue chubanshe, 2007.

Chen Wenyi 陳雯怡. *You guanxue dao shuyuan* 由官學到書院 [From Official Schools to Academies]. Taipei, Lianjing, 2004.

Cheng, Anne. *Entretiens de Confucius*. Paris: Points, 1981.

Cheng, Anne. *Étude sur le confucianisme Han: L'élaboration d'une tradition exégétique sur les classiques*. Paris: IHEC, Collège de France, 1985.

Cheng, Anne. *Histoire de la pensée chinoise*. Paris: Éditions du Seuil, 1997.

Cheung Chan Fai. "Tang Junyi and the Philosophy of General Education." In *Confucian Tradition and Global Education*, edited by Wm. Theodore de Bary, 9–73. Hong Kong: Chinese University Press, 2007.

Chou, Grace Ai-ling. *Confucianism, Colonialism and the Cold War: Chinese Cultural Education at Hong Kong's New Asia College*. Leiden and Boston, MA: Brill, 2011.

"Chuangli minzu chuantong wenhua fuxing de Shenzhen moshi 創立民族傳統文化復興的深圳模式" [The Shenzhen model of institutionalization of the revival of traditional national culture]. *Shenzhen Shangbao* 深圳商報, October 13, 2009, A4.

Chung Yun-ying. 鐘雲鶯, *Qing mo min chu minjian rujiao dui zhuliu ruxue de xishou yu zhuanhua* 清末民初民間儒家對主流儒學的吸收與轉化 [Appropriation and Transformation of Mainstream Confucianism by Popular Religious Confucianism at the End of the Empire and at the Beginning of the Republican Era]. Taipei: Taida chubanshe, 2008.

Ci Jiwei. "La crise morale dans la Chine post-maoïste." *Diogène* 221 (2008): 26–35.

Clart, Philip. "The Concept of Ritual in the Thought of Sima Guang." In *Perceptions of Antiquity in Chinese Civilization*, edited by Dieter Kuhn et Helga Stahl, 250–252. Heidelberg: Edition Forum, 2008.

Clart, Philip. "Confucius and the Mediums: Is There a Popular Confucianism?" *T'oung Pao* 89 (2003): 1–38.

Clower, Jason. *The Unlikely Buddhologist: Tiantai Buddhism in Mou Zongsan's New Confucianism*. Boston, MA, and Leiden: Brill, 2010.

Cui Weiping 崔衛平. "Women de zunyan zaiyu yongyou jiazhi lixiang 我們的尊嚴在於擁有價值理想" [Our Dignity Stems from the Fact that We Have an Ideal in the Realm of Values]. *Nanfang Zhoumou* 南方週末 [Southern Weekend], January 11, 2007, B14.

Dan Shao. "Chinese by Definition: Nationality Law, *Jus Sanguinis* and State Succession, 1909–1980." *Twentieth-Century China* 35 (2009): 4–28.

Deng Xinwen 鄧新文. *Ma Yifu liu yi yi xin lun yanjiu* 馬一浮六藝一心論研究 [Research on Ma Yijiu's Theory of Heart/Mind and the Six Arts]. Shanghai: Shanghai guji chubanshe, 2008.

Descola, Philippe. *Beyond Nature and Culture*. Translated by Janet Lloyd. Chicago: Chicago University Press, 2013.

Descola, Philippe. *Par delà nature et culture*. Paris: Gallimard, 2005.

Despeux, Catherine. "Le corps, champ spatio-temporel, souche d'identité." *L'Homme* 137 (1996): 87–118.

Ding Xueliang. "Institutional Amphibiousness and the Transition from Communism: The Case of China." *British Journal of Political Sciences* 23, no. 3 (1994): 293–318.

Dirlik, Arif. "The Ideological Foundations of the New Life Movement." *Journal of Asian Studies* 34, no. 4 (1975): 945–980.

Dirlik, Arif, ed. "The National Learning Revival." Special issue, *China Perspectives* 2011, no. 1 (2011).

Duara, Prasenjit. *Sovereignty and Authenticity: Manchukuo and the East Asian Modern*. Lanham, MD: Rowman and Littlefield, 2003.

Duara, Prasenjit. "Superscribing Symbols: The Myth of Guandi, Chinese God of War." *Journal of Asian Studies* 47, no. 4 (1988): 778–795.

Duléry, Fabrice. "Discours sur la culture traditionnelle à l'usage de la modernité: L'Émission Bai jia jiangtan." MA thesis, University Paris Diderot, Sorbonne Paris Cité, 2013.

Dutournier, Guillaume. "Les écoles familiales en Chine et à Taïwan: Triple regard sur un traditionalisme éducatif." In "Religion, éducation et politique en Chine moderne," edited by Ji Zhe. Special issue, *Extrême-Orient Extrême-Occident* 33 (2011): 171–210.

Dutournier, Guillaume, and Ji Zhe. "Social Experimentation and 'Popular Confucianism': The Case of the Lujiang Cultural Education Centre." *China Perspectives* 2009, no. 4 (2009): 67–81.

Fan Chen-hsiang, and Su Yung-yao. "President Exalts Yellow Emperor." *Taipei Times*, April 4, 2012. http://www.taipeitimes.com/News/front/archives/2012/04/04/2003529457.

Fei Xiaotong 費孝通. *Xiangtu Zhongguo* 鄉土中國 [Earthbound China]. Beijing: Sanlian shudian, 1985.

Feuchtwang, Stephen. "School-Temple and City God." In *The City in Late Imperial China*, edited by G. W. Skinner, 581–608. Stanford, CA: Stanford University Press, 1977.

Ford, Christopher. "Information-based Arms Control and Sino-American Trust." Washington, DC: Hudson Institute, December 18, 2012. http://www.futureofmuslimworld.com/files/publications/Ford—ArmsControlSino-AmericanTrustDec2012.pdf.

Bibliography

Ford, Christopher. "Sinocentrism for the Information Age, Comments on the 4th Xiangshan Forum." *New Paradigms Forum*, January 2013. http://www.newpara-digmsforum.com/NPFtestsite/?p=1498.

Gan Chunsong 干春松. "Cong Kang Youwei dao Chen Huanzhang 從康有為到陳煥章" [From Kang Youwei to Chen Huanzhang]. In *Rujia, rujiao yu zhongguo zhidu ziyuan* 儒家,儒教與中國制度資源 [Confucianism, Confucian Religion, and Resources of the Chinese System], edited by Gan Chunsong 干春松, 35–83. Nanchang; Jiangxi chuban jituan, 2007.

Gan Chunsong 干春松. *Zhiduhua rujia ji qi jieti* 制度化儒家及其解體 [Institutionalized Confucianism and Its Dismantling]. Beijing: Zhongguo renmin daxue chubanshe, 2003.

Gauchet, Marcel. *La religion dans la démocratie.* Paris: Gallimard, 1998.

Ge Zhaoguang 葛兆光. "Ge Zhaoguang: yao gongtong tisheng bu neng jiti chenlun 葛兆光:要共同提升,不能集體沈淪" [Ge Zhaoguang: We Need to Progress Together, We Cannot Sink Together]. *Nanfang Zhoumou* 南方週末 [Southern Weekend], March 22, 2007, 28 (interview).

Gentile, Emilio. *Les religions de la politique, entre démocraties et totalitarismes.* Paris: Seuil, 2001.

Gernet, Jacques. *Chine et christianisme, la première confrontation.* Paris: NRF Gallimard, 1991.

Gernet, Jacques. "L'éducation des premières années (du XIe au XVIIe s.)." In *Education et instruction en Chine*, edited by Christine Nguyen Tri and Catherine Despeux. Vol.1, *L'éducation élémentaire*, 6–60. Paris and Louvain: Editions Peeters, 2003.

Gernet, Jacques. *L'intelligence de la Chine: Le social et le mental.* Paris: NRF Gallimard, 1994.

Gillin, Donald G. "Portrait of a Warlord: Yen Hsi-shan in Shansi Province, 1911–1930." *Journal of Asian Studies* 19, no. 3 (1960): 289–306.

Godelier, Maurice. *Claude Lévi-Strauss.* Paris: Seuil, 2013.

Gong Pengcheng 龔鵬程, ed. *Dujing you shenme yong* 讀經有甚麼用 [What Is the Use of Reading the Classics?]. Shanghai: Shanghai renmin chubanshe, 2008.

Goossaert, Vincent. "Bureaucratie, taxation et justice: Taoïsme et construction de l'État au Jiangnan (Chine), XVIIe–XIXe siècle." *Annales Histoire, Sciences Sociales* 4 (2010): 999–1027.

Goossaert, Vincent. "L'invention des 'religions' dans la Chine moderne." In *La pensée en Chine aujourd'hui*, edited by Anne Cheng, 185–213. Paris: Gallimard, 2007.

Goossaert, Vincent. "Les mutations de la religion confucianiste, 1898–1937." In *Le nouvel âge de Confucius*, edited by Flora Blanchon and Rang-Ri Park-Barjot, 163–172. Paris: Presses Universitaires de Paris-Sorbonne, 2007.

Goossaert, Vincent, and Fang Ling. "Les réformes funéraires et la politique religieuse de l'État chinois, 1900–2008." *Archives des sciences sociales des religions* 144 (2008): 51–73.

Goossaert, Vincent, and David A. Palmer. *The Religious Question in Modern China.* Chicago and London: University of Chicago Press, 2012.

"2006 Guowuyuan guanyu gongbu diyi pi guojiaji feiwuzhi wenhua yichan minglu de tongzhi" 2006 國務院關於公佈第一批國家級非物質文化遺產名錄的通知 [Circular issued by the State Council about the first list of intangible cultural heritage items of national level importance], http://www.gov.cn/zwgk/2006-06/02/content_297946.htm.

Hartig, Falk. "China's Confucius Institutes and the Rise of China." *Journal of Chinese Political Science* 17, no. 1 (2011): 53–76.

Hegel, Georg Wilhelm Friedrich. *Vorlesungen über die Philosophie der Religion.* 2 vols. Hamburg: Felix Meiner, 1985.

Hervieu-Léger, Danièle. *Le pèlerin et le converti: La religion en mouvement.* Paris: Champs, Flammarion, 1999.

Hong Xiuping. "The Characteristics and Prospects of the Confucian Academy: A Commentary on Jiang Qing's Ideas on the Confucian Academy," in *The Renaissance of Confucianism in Contemporary China*, edited by Fan Ruiping, 185–204. Dordrecht: Springer, 2011.

Hong Xiuping 洪秀平. "Rujia shuyuan de tezheng ji qi qianjing" 儒家書院的特徵及前景 [The Characteristics and Prospects of the Confucian Academy: A Commentary on Jiang Qing's Ideas on the Confucian Academy]. In *Rujia shehui yu daotong fuxing: yu Jiang Qing duihua* 儒家社會與道統復興：與蔣慶對話 [Confucian Society and the Revival of the Transmission of the Way: A Dialogue with Jiang Qing], edited by Fan Ruiping 範瑞平, 224–244. Shanghai: Huadong shifan, daxue chubanshe, 2008.

Hsu, Elisabeth. *The Transmission of Chinese Medecine.* Cambridge: Cambridge University Press, 1999.

Huang, Philip. *Code, Custom and Legal Practice in China: The Qing and the Republic Compared.* Stanford, CA: Stanford University Press, 2001.

Huo Taohui 霍韜晦, ed. *Anshen liming yu dongxi wenhua* 安身立命與東西文化 [*Anshen liming* and Eastern and Western Cultures]. Hong Kong: Fazhu chubanshe, 1992.

Ikels, Charlotte, ed. *Filial Piety: Practice and Discourse in Contemporary East Asia.* Stanford, CA: Stanford University Press, 2004.

James, William. *The Varieties of Religious Experience.* New York: Barnes and Noble, 2004.

Jeans, Roger B. *Democracy and Socialism in Republican China: The Politics of Zhang Junmai.* Lanham, MD: Rowman and Littlefield, 1997.

Jensen, Lionel M. *Manufacturing Confucianism, Chinese Traditions and Universal Civilization.* Durham, NC, and London: Duke University Press, 1997.

Ji Zhe 汲喆. "Educating through Music: From an 'Initiation into Classical Music' for Children to Confucian 'Self-Cultivation' for University Students." *China Perspectives* 2008, no. 3 (2008): 107–117.

Ji Zhe. "Lun gongmin zongjiao 論公民宗教" [On Civil Religion]. *Shehuixue yanjiu* 社會學研究 [Sociological Research] 1 (2011): 1–14.

Ji Zhe. "Making a Virtue of Piety: *Dizigui* and the Emergence of a Buddhist Discourse Society." Paper presented at the final conference of the research project "The Confucian Revival in Mainland China: Forms and Meanings of Confucian Piety Today," Fuzhou, December 2013.

Jiang Yihua and Roderick MacFarquhar. "Two Perspectives on Mao Zedong." In *A Critical Introduction to Mao*, edited by Timothy Cheek, 332–352. Cambridge: Cambridge University Press, 2010.

Jin Guantao 金觀濤. "Dangdai Zhongguo Makesizhuyi de rujiahua 當代中國馬克思主義的儒家化" [The Confucianization of Marxism in Contemporary China]. In *Rujia fazhan de hongguan toushi* 儒家發展的宏觀透視 [Overall Perspective on the Development of Confucianism], edited by Tu Wei-ming 杜維明, 152–183. Taipei: Zhengzhong shuju, 1988.

Jochim, Christian. "Carrying Confucianism into the Modern World." In *Religion in Modern Taiwan: Tradition and Innovation in a Changing Society*, edited by Philip Clart and Charles B. Jones, 48–83. Honolulu: University of Hawaiʻi Press, 2003.

Jochim, Christian. "Popular Lay Sects and Confucianism." In *The People and the Dao, New Studies in Chinese Religions in Honour of Daniel L. Overmyer*, edited by Philip Clart and Paul Crowe, 84–107. Sankt Augustin: Monumenta Serica, 2009.

Jordan, David, and Daniel Overmyer. *The Flying Phoenix: Aspects of Chinese Sectarianism in Taiwan*. Princeton, NJ: Princeton University Press, 1986.

Jun Jing. *The Temple of Memories: History, Power and Morality in a Chinese Village*. Stanford, CA: Stanford University Press, 1996.

Kang Xiaoguang 康曉光. *Dangdai Zhongguo dalu wenhua minzuzhuyi yundong yanjiu* 當代中國大陸文化民族主義運動研究 [Research on the Movement of Cultural Nationalism in Today's China]. Singapore: Global, 2008.

Kang Xiaoguang. *Renzheng, Zhongguo zhengzhi fazhan de di san jiao daolu* 仁政：中國政治發展的第三條道路 [Benevolence-Based Politics: The Third Way of Chinese Political Development]. Singapore: Global, 2005.

Kang Xiaoguang. "A Study of the Renaissance of Traditional Confucian Culture." In *Confucianism and Spiritual Traditions in Modern China and Beyond*, edited by Fenggang Yang and Joseph Tamney, 54–56. Leiden and Boston, MA: Brill, 2012.

Katz, Paul. *Divine Justice: Religion and the Development of Chinese Legal Culture*. London and New York: Routledge, 2008.

Katz, Paul. "Religion and State in Post-war Taiwan." *China Quarterly* 174 (2003): 395–412.

Katz, Paul. "Wang Yiting and the Enchantment of Chinese Modernity." Paper given at the Conference of Groupe Sociétés, Religions, Laïcités, Paris, October 2011.

Keck, Frédéric. *Un monde grippé*. Paris: Flammarion, 2010.

Keenan, Barry. *The Dewey Experiment in China*. Cambridge, MA: Harvard University Asia Center, 1977.

Kleinman, Arthur, et al. *Deep China: The Moral Life of the Person. What Anthropology and Psychiatry Tell Us about China Today.* Berkeley: University of California Press, 2011.

Kong Fanyin 孔繁銀. *Yansheng Gong fu jian wen* 衍聖公府見聞 [Things Seen and Heard at the Mansion of the Yansheng Duke]. Jinan: Qi Lu shushe, 1992.

Koselleck, Reinhart. *Vergangene Zukunft, Zur Semantik geschichtlicher Zeiten.* Frankfurt: Suhrkamp, 1989.

Kuo, Ya-Pei. "Redeploying Confucius." In *Chinese Religiosities, Afflictions of Modernity and State Formation,* edited by Mayfair Mei-Hui Yang, 65–86. Berkeley: University of California Press, 2008.

Kuo, Ya-Pei. " 'The Emperor and the People in One Body': The Worship of Confucius and Ritual Planning in the Xinzheng Reforms, 1902–1911." *Modern China* 35, no. 2 (2009): 123–154.

Kuo, Cheng-Tian. *Religion and Democracy in Taiwan.* New York: State University of New York Press, 2008.

Kwok, Danny Wynn Ye. *Scientism in Chinese Thought: 1900–1950.* New Haven, CT: Yale University Press, 1965.

Lagerwey, John. *China: A Religious State.* Hong Kong: Hong Kong University Press, 2010.

Laliberté, André. "The Regulation of Religious Affairs in Taiwan: From State Control to *Laisser-faire?*" *Journal of Current Chinese Affairs* 38, no. 2 (2009): 53–83.

Lam, Joseph S. C. "Musical Confucianism: The Case of *Jikong yuewu.*" In *On Sacred Grounds: Culture, Society, Politics and the Formation of the State Cult of Confucius,* edited by Thomas A. Wilson, 134–172. Cambridge, MA: Harvard University Press, 2003.

Lamberton, Abigail. "The Kongs of Qufu." In *On Sacred Grounds: Culture, Society, Politics and the Formation of the State Cult of Confucius,* edited by Thomas A. Wilson, 297–332. Cambridge, MA: Harvard University Press, 2003.

Lee, Thomas H. C. (Li Hongqi). "Academies: Official Sponsorship and Suppression." In *Imperial Rulership and Cultural Change in Traditional China,* edited by Frederik P. Brandauer and Chun-chieh Huang, 117–143. Seattle: University of Washington Press, 1994.

Lee Ming-huei. *Der Konfuzianismus im modernen China.* Leipzig: Leipziger Universitätsverlag, 2001.

Lefort, Claude. "Permanence du théologico-politique." In *Essais sur le Politique, XIXe–XXe siècles,* 251–300. Paris: Editions du Seuil, 1986.

Levenson, Joseph R. *Confucian China and Its Modern Fate.* 3 vols. London: Routledge and Kegan Paul, 1965.

Lévi, Jean. *Confucius.* Paris: Pygmalion, 2002.

Lévi, Jean. *Histoire et sacrifice en Chine ancienne.* Nanterre : Société d'ethnologie, 2007.

Lévi-Strauss, Claude. *Mythologiques IV: L'Homme nu.* Paris: Plon, 1971.

Lévi-Strauss, Claude. *The Naked Man*. Translated by John Weightman and Doreen Weightman. Chicago, IL: University of Chicago Press, 1990.

Liang Shuming 梁漱溟. "Foru yitong lun" 佛儒異同論 [About the Similarities in Differences between Buddhism and Confucianism]. In *Liang Shuming quanji* 梁漱溟全集 [The Complete Works of Liang Shuming], vol. 7, 152–169. Jinan: Shandong renmin chubanshe, 2005.

Liaowang dongfang zhoukan 瞭望東方周刊 [Oriental Outlook], April 10, 2004, 79–81.

Li Caidong 李才棟. *Zhongguo shuyuan yanjiu* 中國書院研究 [Research on the Academies in China]. Nanchang: Jiangxi gaoxiao chubanshe, 2005.

Li Dongjun 李冬君. *Kongzi shenghua yu ruzhe geming* 孔子聖化與儒者革命 [Sanctification of Confucius and Revolution of the Confucians]. Beijing: Zhongguo renmin daxue chubanshe, 2004.

Li Hongqi (Thomas H. C. Lee) 李弘祺. "Shuyuan, chuantong xueshu de zhongxin 書院, 傳統學術的中心" [The *Shuyuan*, Centres of the Traditional Academic World]. In *Zhongguo wenhua de zhuancheng yu chuangxin* 中國文化的傳承與創新 [Innovation and Transmission within Chinese Culture], edited by Wang Shouchang 王守常 and Zhang Wending 張文定, 355–364. Beijing: Beijing daxue chubanshe, 2006.

Li Jing 李靜. "Geren de jingshen chengshu yu Zhongguo wenyi fuxing 個人的精神成熟與中國文藝復興" [Spiritual Maturity of the Individual and Chinese Renaissance]. *Nanfang Zhoumou* 南方週末 [Southern Weekend], January 25, 2007, B15.

Li Junling 李俊領. "Kangzhan shiqi Guomindang yu Nanjing guomin zhengfu dui Kongzi de jisi dianli 抗戰時期國民黨與南京國民政府對孔子的祭祀典禮" [Offering Rites to Confucius Carried out by the Guomindang and the Nationalist Government during the War against Japan]. *Shehui kexue pinglun* 社會科學評論 4 (2008): 45–62.

Li Zehou 李澤厚. *Makesizhuyi zai Zhongguo* 馬克思主義在中國 [Marxism in China]. Hong Kong: Mingbao chubanshe, 2006.

Li Zehou. *Nanfang Zhoumo* 南方週末 interview, 22 March 2007, 28.

Lin Anwu 林安梧. "Yinyang wuxing yu shen xin zhiliao—Yi Wang Fengyi shi'er zi xinchuan wei hexin de zhankai 陰陽五行與身心治療—以王鳳儀'十二字薪傳'為核心的展開" [Yin-Yang, Five Elements and Therapy of the Body and Mind: Developments Based on Wang Fengyi's Twelve Characters Transmission]. In *Zhongguo zongjiao yu yiyi zhiliao* 中國宗教與意義治療 [Chinese Religions and Therapies Based on the Meaning of Things], edited by Lin Anwu 林安梧, 211–241. Taipei: Mingwen shuju, 1996.

Lin Guoxian (Kuo-hsien) 林果顯. *Zhongguo wenhua fuxing yundong tuixing weiyuan-hui zhi yanjiu* 中華文化復興運動推行委員會之研究 [Research on the Committee in Charge of Implementing the Movement of Renaissance of Traditional Chinese Culture]. Taipei: Daoxiang, 2005.

Liu Dong. "The Weberian View and Confucianism." *East Asian History* 25–26 (2003): 191–217.

Liu Junning 劉軍寧. "Zhongguo, ni xuyao yi chang wenyifuxing! 中國,你需要一場文藝復興" [China, You Need a Renaissance!]. *Nanfang Zhoumou* 南方週末[Southern Weekend], December 7, 2006, B15.

Liu Yi. "Confucianism, Christianity and Religious Freedom." In *Confucianism and Spiritual Traditions in Modern China and Beyond*, edited by Fenggang Yang and Joseph Tamney, 247–276. Leiden and Boston, MA: Brill, 2012.

Luo Jiurong 羅久蓉, Qiu Huijun 丘慧君, and Zhou Weipeng 周維朋. *Cong Dongbei dao Taiwan, Wanguo daodehui xiangguan renwu fangwen jilu* 從東北到台灣—萬國道德會相關人物訪問紀錄 [From the Northeast to Taiwan: Compilation of Interviews with Figures Associated with the Wanguo Daodehui], 139–141. Taipei: Zhongyang yanjiuyuan jindaishi yanjiusuo, 2006.

Madsen, Richard. *Democracy's Dharma: Religious Renaissance and Political Development in Taiwan*. Berkeley: University of California Press, 2007.

Madsen, Richard. *Morality and Power in a Chinese Village*. Berkeley: University of California Press, 1986.

Makeham, John. *Lost Soul, "Confucianism" in Contemporary Chinese Academic Discourse*. Cambridge, MA: Harvard University Press, 2008.

Mast, Herman, III, and William G. Saywell. "The Political Ideology of Tai Chi-t'ao." *Journal of Asian Studies* 34, no. 1 (1974): 73–98.

Meyer, Christian. *Ritendiskussionen am Hof der nördlichen Song-Dynastie (1034–1093)*. Sankt Augustin: Monumenta Serica Monograph Series LVIII, 2008.

Meynard, Thierry. *The Religious Philosophy of Liang Shuming: The Hidden Buddhist*. Leiden and Boston, MA: Brill, 2010.

Minakuchi Takuju 水口拓寿. "Chûka bunka no fukkô to shite no Kôshibyô kaikaku, 1968–70-nen no Taihoku Kôshibyô wo shôten to shite 中華文化の復興としての孔子廟を改革, 1968–70 年の台北孔子廟を焦点 として" [The Reform of the Confucius Temple as an Expression of the Renaissance of Chinese Culture: The Case of Taipei's Confucius Temple in 1968–70]. In *Zhongguo chuantong wenhua zai dangdai zhongguo de juese* 中國傳統文化在當代中國的角色 [The Role of Traditional Chinese Culture in Contemporary China], edited by Nakajima Takahiro, 235–253. Tokyo: University of Tokyo Center for Philosophy Booklet 5.

Mizoguchi Yûzô 溝口雄三. *Kô shi* 公私 [Public and Private]. Tokyo: Sanseidô, 1996.

Mizoguchi Yûzô 溝口雄三. "Zhongguo yu Riben 'Gong Si' guannian zhi bijiao 中國與日本 '公私'觀念之比較" [Comparison between the Notions of "Public" and "Private" in China and in Japan]. *Ershiyi shiji* 二十一世紀 21 (1994): 85–97.

Mizoguchi Yûzô 溝口雄三 and Nakajima Mineo 中嶋嶺雄. *Jukyô runessansu wo kangaeru* 儒教ルネッサンスを考える [Reflections on the Confucian Renaissance]. Tokyo: Daishûkan shoten, 1991.

Murray, Julia K. "Idols in the Temple: Icons and the Cult of Confucius." *Journal of Asian Studies* 68, no. 2 (2009): 378–379.

Nakajima Takahiro 中島隆博. "Civil Spirituality and the Female Element in Confucian Piety Today: The Activities of Confucian Temples in Qufu, Taipei and Changchun." Paper presented at the final conference of the research project "The Confucian Revival in Mainland China: Forms and Meanings of Confucian Piety Today," Fuzhou, December 2013.

Nakajima Takahiro. "Senzen Nihon to gendai Chûgoku no Jukyô fukkô ni kan suru ôdanteki kenkyû 戦前日本と現代中国の儒教復興に関する横断的研究" [Transversal Research on the Confucian Revival in Japan and Contemporary China]. In *Zhongguo chuantong wenhua zai dangdai zhongguo de juese* 中國傳統文化在當代中國的角色 [The Role of Traditional Chinese Culture in Contemporary China], edited by Nakajima Takahiro, 213–234. Tokyo: University of Tokyo Center for Philosophy Booklet 5.

Nedostup, Rebecca. *Superstitious Regimes: Religion and the Politics of Chinese Modernity.* Cambridge, MA: Harvard University Press, 2009.

Nye, Joseph. *The Future of Power.* New York: Public Affairs, 2011.

Nylan, Michael, and Thomas A. Wilson. *Lives of Confucius.* New York: Doubleday, 2010.

Oldstone-Moore, Jennifer. "The New Life Movement of Nationalist China: Confucianism, State Authority and Moral Formation." PhD diss., University of Chicago, UMI Microform 9959107, 2000.

Ownby, David. *Falun Gong and the Future of China.* Oxford: Oxford University Press, 2008.

Ownby, David. "Kang Xiaoguang: Social Science, Civil Society, and Confucian Religion." *China Perspectives* 4 (2009): 101–111.

Ownby, David. "Politique et religion dans la Chine du XXe siècle: Le cas de Li Yujie." Paper given at the University Paris-Diderot, October 2012.

Ownby, David. "Redemptive Societies in China's Long Twentieth Century." In *The Modern Chinese Religion, 1850–Present*, edited by Vincent Goossaert. Leiden and Boston, MA: Brill, 2014 (forthcoming).

Palmer, David A. "The Body: Health, Nation, and Transcendence." In *Chinese Religious Life*, edited by David A. Palmer, Glen Shive, and Philip Wickeri, 87–106. New York: Oxford University Press, 2011.

Palmer, David A. "China's Religious *Danwei*: Institutionalizing Religion in the People's Republic." *China Perspectives* 2009, no. 4 (2009): 17–31.

Palmer, David A. "Chinese Redemptive Societies and Salvationist Religions." *Minsu Quyi* 172, no. 1 (2011): 21–71.

Palmer, David A. *Qigong Fever: Body, Science, and Utopia in China.* New York: Columbia University Press, 2007.

Palmer, David A. "Religiosity and Social Movements in China, Divisions and Multiplications." In *Social Movements in China and Hong Kong, The Expansion of Protest Space*, edited by Gilles Guiheux and Khun Eng Kuah-Pearce, 265–273. Amsterdam: Amsterdam University Press, 2009.

Pan Hongli. "The Old Folk's Associations and Lineage Revival in Contemporary Villages of Southern Fujian Province." In *Southern Fujian: Reproduction of Traditions in Post-Mao China*, edited by Tang Chee-Beng, 69–96. Hong Kong: Chinese University Press, 2006.

Pan Wei 潘維, ed. *Zhongguo moshi: jiedu renmin gongheguo de liushi nian* 中國模式，解讀人民共和國的 60年 [The Chinese Model: Decoding 60 Years (of History) of the People's Republic]. Beijing: Zhongyang bianyi, 2009.

Pepper, Suzanne. *Radicalism and Education Reform in Twentieth-Century China: The Search for an Ideal Development Model*. Cambridge: Cambridge University Press, 2000.

Peng Guoxiang 彭國翔. "Ruxue fuxing de shensi 儒學復興的慎思" [Pondering over the Confucian Revival]. *Ershiyi shiji jingji baodao* 二十一世紀經濟報道, December 18, 2006, 34–35.

Qi Lu wanbao 齊魯晚報 [Evening newspaper of the Qi and Lu areas], September 28, 2007, A3.

Qian Hang 錢杭 and Xie Weiyang 謝維揚. *Chuantong yu zhuanxing: Jiangxi Taihe nongcun zongzu xingtai* 傳統與轉型：江西泰和農村宗族形態 [Tradition and Transformation: Lineage Structures in the Countryside of the Taihe Area, Jiangxi Province]. Shanghai: Shanghai shehui kexueyuan chubanshe, 1995.

Qian Mu 錢穆. *Xin Ya yiduo* 新亞遺鐸 [Past Echoes of the Xinya Academy]. Beijing: Sanlian shudian, 2004.

Qian Mu 錢穆. *Shiyou zayi* 師友雜憶 [Remembering Teachers and Friends]. Taipei: Dongda tushugongsi, 1983.

"Qingzhu Zhonghua minguo jianguo yibainian yiguandao wen-hua xingguo heping huguo qifu dadian 慶祝中華民國建國一百年，一貫道文化興國和平護國祈福大典" Grand Prayer Ceremonial for Culture, National Prosperity and Peace Organized by the Yiguandao in Order to Celebrate the 100th Anniversary of the Foundation of the Republic of China]. *Jichu zazhi* 基礎雜誌 268 (April 2011): 25–31. http://1-kuan-tao.org.tw:443/zongsu/culture/9902/magzine_subject.asp?isession=268&iorder=29&subject, visited on January 6, 2014.

Qiu Feng 秋風. "Zhongguo xuyao wenyifuxing hai shi bie de yundong? 中國需要文藝復興還是別的運動?" [Does China Need a Renaissance or Another Movement?]. *Nanfang Zhoumou* 南方週末 [Southern Weekend], December 21, 2006, 15B.

Qiu Feng 秋風. "Zhongguo xuyao daode chongjian yu shehui jianshe yundong 中國需要道德重建與社會建設運動" [China Needs a Movement of Moral Reconstruction and Social Construction]. *Nanfang Zhoumou* 南方週末 [Southern Weekend], February 8, 2007, 15B.

Qiu Feng 秋風. "Daode chongjian, shehui jianshe yu geti zunyan 道德重建,社會建設與個體尊嚴" [Moral Reconstruction, Social Construction and Dignity of the Individual]. *Nanfang Zhoumou* 南方週末 [Southern Weekend], January 18, 2007, 29D.

Ruoff, Kenneth. *Imperial Japan at Its Zenith: The Wartime Celebration of the Empire's 2,600th Anniversary.* Ithaca, NY: Cornell University Press, 2010.

Sahlins, Marshall. "Confucius Institutes Censor Political Discussions and Restrain the Free Exchange of Ideas. Why, then, Do American Universities Sponsor them?" *Nation*, October 29, 2013. http://www.thenation.com/article/176888/china-u.

Sang Ye and Geremie Barmé. "Commemorating Confucius in 1966–67: The Fate of the Confucius Temple, the Kong Mansion and Kong Cemetery. 孔廟、孔府、孔林." *China Heritage Quarterly* 20 (2009). http://www.chinaheritagequarterly.org/scholarship.php?searchterm=020_confucius.inc&issue=020.

Sang Ye and Geremie Barmé. "The Great Yu/Da Yu 大禹: A Temple 禹廟 and a Tomb 禹陵." *China Heritage Quarterly* 20 (2009). http://www.chinaheritagequarterly.org/scholarship.php?searchterm=020_great_yu.inc&issue=020.

Schulte, Barbara. "The Chinese Dewey: Friend, Fiend, and Flagship." In *The Global Reception of John Dewey's Thought: Multiple Refractions through Time and Space*, edited by Rosa Bruno-Jofre and Jürgen Schriewer, 83–115. London: Routledge, 2012.

Shambaugh, David. *China Goes Global: The Partial Power.* New York and Oxford: Oxford University Press, 2013.

Shandong sheng zhi (71) Kongzi guli zhi 山東省志 (71) 孔子故里志 [Local Gazetteer of Shandong Province, vol. 71, Gazetteer of the Native Land of Confucius]. Beijing: Zhonghua shuju, 1994.

Shapiro, Judith. *War against Nature: Politics and the Environment in Revolutionary China.* Cambridge: Cambridge University Press, 2001.

Shijie ruxue dahui faqi guoji huiyi 世界儒學大會發起國際會議. *Shijie ruxue dahui faqi xuanyan (cao'an)* 世界儒學大會發起宣言 (草案) [Opening Declaration of the World Confucian Conference], September 27, 2007.

Shijie ruxue dahui faqi guoji huiyi 世界儒學大會發起國際會議. *Shijie ruxue dahui zhangcheng (cao'an)* 世界儒學大會章程 (草案) [(Draft) Charter of the World Confucian Conference], September 27, 2007.

Shryock, John K. *The Origin and Development of the State Cult of Confucius.* New York and London: Century, 1932.

Shu Qinfeng 舒秦峰. "Zhongguo zhen de xuyao yi chang wenyifuxing 中國真的需要一場文藝復興" [China Really Needs a Renaissance]. *Liaowang Zhoukan* 瞭望周刊, December 28, 2006, 74–76.

Smith, Warren. *Confucianism in Modern Japan: A Study in Conservatism in Japanese Intellectual History.* Tokyo: Hokuseido, 1973.

Song Guangyu 宋光宇. *Tiandao chuandeng, Yiguandao yu xiandai shehui* 天道傳燈,一貫道與現代社會 [Transmission of the Torch of the Heavenly Way: Yiguandao and Contemporary Chinese Society]. Taipei: Zhengyi shanshu chubanshe, 1996.

Song Guangyu 宋光宇. "Wang fengyi de xingli jiang bing 王鳳儀的性理講病" [Wang Fengyi's Discourse on Illness Based on [His Conceptions] of Nature and Principle]. In *Zongjiao wenhua lunwen ji* 宗教文化論文集, 214–241. Yilan: Foguang renwen shehui xueyuan, 1999.

Sun, Anna. *Confucianism as a World Religion: Contested Histories and Contemporary Realities*. Princeton, NJ: Princeton University Press, 2013.

Sun, Anna. "The Revival of Confucian Rites in Contemporary China." In *Confucianism and Spiritual Traditions in Modern China and Beyond*, edited by Fenggang Yang and Joseph Tamney, 309–328. Leiden and Boston, MA: Brill, 2012.

Szonyi, Michael. "The Illusion of Standardizing the Gods: The Cult of the Five Emperors in Late Imperial China." *Journal of Asian Studies* 56, no. 1 (1997): 113–135.

Szonyi, Michael. "Lineages and the Making of Contemporary China." Paper presented at the conference "Modern Chinese Religion: Values Systems in Transformation, 1850–Present," December 13, 2012, 9–14.

Szonyi, Michael. "Ming Fever: The Present's Past as the People's Republic Turns Sixty." *China Heritage Quarterly* 21 (March 2010). http://www.chinaheritagequarterly.org/articles.php?searchterm=021_mingfever.inc&issue=021.

Szonyi, Michael. "Secularization Theories and the Study of Chinese Religions." *Social Compass* 56 (2009): 312–327.

Tang, Chee-Beng. "Chinese Religion in Malaysia: A General Overview." *Asian Folklore Studies* 42, no. 2 (1983): 217–252.

Tang Enjia zun Kong zhi lü 湯恩佳尊孔之旅 [Confucian Itinerary of Tang Enjia]. Hong Kong: Xianggang kongjiao xueyuan rongyu chuban, 2004.

Tang Enjia 湯恩佳, *Kong li erwuwuba nian jikong dadian* 孔曆 2558 年祭孔大典 [Great Ceremony to Honor Confucius in the Year 2558 of the Confucian Calendar], 5–7 [leaflet].

Thøgersen, Stig. *A Country of Culture: 20th Century China Seen from the Village Schools of Zouping, Shandong*. Ann Arbor: University of Michigan Press, 2002.

Thøgersen, Stig. "Revisiting a Dramatic Triangle: The State, Villagers, and Social Activists in Chinese Rural Reconstruction Projects." *Journal of Current Chinese Affairs* 38, no. 4 (2009): 9–33.

Thoraval, Joël. "The Anthropologist and the Question of the 'Visibility' of Confucianism in Contemporary Chinese Society." *China Perspectives* 23 (1999): 65–73.

Thoraval, Joël. "Confucian Experience and Philosophical Discourse." In *Culture and Social Transformation in Reform Era China*, edited by Cao Tian Yu, Zhong Xueping, and Liao Kebin, 138–146. Leiden and Boston, MA: Brill, 2010.

Thoraval, Joël. "La fièvre culturelle chinoise: de la stratégie à la théorie." *Critique* nos. 507–508 (1989): 558–572.

Thoraval, Joël. "Idéal du sage, Stratégie du philosophe: Introduction à la pensée de Mou Zongsan." In Mou Zongsan, *Spécificités de la philosophie chinoise*, 7–60. Paris: Éditions du Cerf, 2003.

Thoraval, Joël. "Religion ethnique, religion lignagère: sur la tentative d' 'islamisation' d'un lignage Han de Hainan." *Études chinoises* 10, nos. 1–2 (1991): 9–75.

Thoraval, Joël. "Sur la transformation de la pensée néoconfucéenne en discours philosophique moderne: Réflexions sur quelques apories du néoconfucianisme contemporain." *Extrême-Orient, Extrême Occident* 27 (2005): 91–119.

Thoraval, Joël. "La tentation pragmatiste dans la Chine contemporaine." In *La pensée en Chine aujourd'hui*, edited by Anne Cheng, 103–134. Paris: Folio, 2007.

Thoraval, Joël. "La tradition rêvée: Réflexions sur *L'Elégie du fleuve* de Su Xiaokang." *L'Infini* 30 (1990): 146–168.

Thoraval, Joël 杜瑞樂. "Zhongguo xiandai zhexue tixi de 'yaosu' zuoyong—huiying Zhang Xianglong de jige yijian 中國現代哲學體系的要素作用—回應張祥龍的幾個意見" [The Role of "Pharmakon" of the Modern Philosophical Institution in China—A Few Remarks in Response to Zhang Xianglong). *Zhongguo xueshu* 中國學術 16 (2004): 255–266.

Tillman, Hoyt Cleveland. *Confucian Discourse and Chu Hsi's Ascendancy.* Honolulu: University of Hawai'i Press, 1992.

Tillman, Margaret Mih, and Hoyt Cleveland Tillman. "A Joyful Union: The Modernization of the Zhu Xi Family Wedding Ceremony." *Oriens Extremus* 49 (2010): 115–142.

Tsai, Lily. *Accountability without Democracy: Solidarity and Public Goods Provisions in Rural China.* Cambridge: Cambridge University Press, 2007.

Tu Wei-ming. *Confucian Ethics Today: The Singapore Challenge.* Singapore: Federal Publications, 1984.

Turner, Victor. *Dramas, Fields, and Metaphors: Symbolic Action in Human Society.* Ithaca, NY, and London: Cornell University Press, 1974.

Vandermeersch, Léon. *Wangdao ou la Voie royale*, vol. 2. Paris: EFEO, 1980.

Veg, Sebastian, ed. "Mao Today: A Political Icon for an Age of Prosperity." Special issue, *China Perspectives* 2012, no. 2 (2012).

Wang Caigui 王財貴. "Ertong jingdian songdu de jiben lilun 兒童經典誦讀基本理論" [Basic Theory of Classics Reading by Children]. In *Jingdian daodu shouce* 經典導讀手冊 [Introductory Handbook for the Reading of Classics], 4-10. Beijing: Beijing shifan daxue yinxiang chubanshe, 2005.

Wang Fengyi 王鳳儀. *Cheng ming lu* 誠明錄 [On the Brilliance of Authenticity]. Changchun: Jilin sheying chubanshe, 2003.

Wang Fengyi 王鳳儀. *Du xing lu* 篤行錄 [On a Firmly Established Practice]. Changchun: Jilin sheying chubanshe, 2003.

Wang Fengyi 王鳳儀. *Jiating lunli jiangyanlu* 家庭倫理講演錄 [On Family Morality]. Beijing: Yishu yu renwen kexue chubanshe, 2006.

Wang Gung-wu. *Community and Nation*. Sydney: Allen and Unwin, 1993.

Wang Gung-wu. *Renewal: The Chinese State and the New Global History*. Hong Kong: Chinese University Press, 2013.

Wang, Jessica Ching-Sze. *Dewey in China, to Teach and to Learn*. Albany: SUNY Press, 2007.

Wang Liang. "The Confucius Temple Tragedy of the Cultural Revolution." In *On Sacred Grounds: Culture, Society, Politics and the Formation of the State Cult of Confucius*, edited by Thomas A. Wilson, 376–396. Cambridge, MA: Harvard University Press, 2003.

Wang Xiaobing 王霄冰. *Nanzong jikong* 南宗祭孔 [The Confucius Cult of the Southern Lineage]. Hangzhou: Zhejiang renmin chubanshe, 2008.

Wang Zhensheng. "L'influence de la théorie de la reconstruction rurale de Liang Shuming dans la société chinoise actuelle." MA thesis (East Asian studies), University Paris-Diderot, 2012.

Wang Zongyu 王宗昱. "Shi rujia haishi fojia? 是儒家還是佛家?" [Confucian or Buddhist?]. *Zhongguo wenhua yu Zhongguo zhexue*, 560–565. Beijing: Dongfang chubanshe, 1986.

Weber, Max. *Wirtschaft und Gesellschaft*. Tübingen : Mohr Siebeck, 1980.

"Wenyifuxing haishi daode chongjian? 文藝復興還是道德重建?" [Renaissance or Moral Reconstruction?]. *Zhongguo xinwen zhoukan* 中國新聞週刊, January 22, 2007, 2 [op-ed].

Weller, Robert P. *Discovering Nature: Globalization and Environmental Culture in China and Taiwan*. Cambridge: Cambridge University Press, 2006.

Wilson, Thomas A., ed. *On Sacred Grounds: Culture, Society, Politics and the Formation of the State Cult of Confucius*. Cambridge, MA: Harvard University Press, 2003.

Wilson, Thomas A. "The Ritual Formation of Confucian Orthodoxy and the Descendants of the Sage." *Journal of Asian Studies* 55, no. 3 (1996): 559–584.

Wilson, Thomas A. "Ritualizing Confucius/Kongzi." In *On Sacred Grounds: Culture, Society, Politics and the Formation of the State Cult of Confucius*, edited by Thomas A. Wilson, 43–94. Cambridge, MA: Harvard University Press, 2003.

Wilson, Thomas A. "Sacrifice and the Imperial Cult of Confucius." *History of Religions* 41, no. 3 (2002): 251–287.

Wilson, Thomas A. Video of the 1998 Tainan Ritual to Honor Confucius. *Autumnal Sacrifice to Confucius: A Study of Confucianism's Sacrificial Tradition*. http://academics.hamilton.edu/asian_studies/home/autumnalsacrifice/pages/videos.html.

Wolf, Arthur P. "Gods, Ghosts and Ancestors." In *Religion and Ritual in Chinese Society*, edited by Arthur P. Wolf, 131–182. Stanford, CA: Stanford University Press, 1974.

Woodside, Alexander. "The Divorce between the Political Center and Educational Creativity in Late Imperial China." In *Education and Society in Late Imperial China, 1600–1900*, edited by Benjamin A. Elman and Alexander Woodside, 458–492. Berkeley: University of California Press, 1994.

Wu Shugang and Tong Binchang. "Liang Shuming's Rural Reconstruction and its Relevance for Building the New Socialist Countryside." *Contemporary Chinese Thought* 40, no. 3 (2009): 39–51.

Xu Quanxing 許全興. *Mao Zedong yu Kongfuzi* 毛澤東與孔夫子 [Mao Zedong and Confucius]. Beijing: Renmin chubanshe, 2003.

Xuyang Jingjing. "Confucius in Church." *Global Times*, October 9, 2012. http://www. globaltimes.cn/content/737236.shtml.

Xuyang Jingjing. "Religion in the Party." *Global Times*, February 27, 2014. http:// www.globaltimes.cn/content/845166.shtml#.Uo1l19xGw78.

Yan Hongliang and Bill Bramwell. "Cultural Tourism, Ceremony and the State in China." *Annals of Tourism Research* 35, no. 4 (2008): 969–989.

Yan Ping 炎平. *Zoujin ruxue* 走進儒學 [Advancing into Confucianism]. Qufu: Qufu shengcheng liyue wenhua cujinhui (undated and noncommercial booklet).

Yan Qinghuang 颜清湟. "1899–1911 nian Xinjiapo he Malaiya de kongjiao fuxing yundong 年新加坡和馬來亞的孔教復興運動" [The Movement of Revival of the Confucian Religion in Singapore and Malaysia in 1899–1911]. *Haiwai huarenshi yanjiu* 海外華人史研究 [Research on the History of Overseas Chinese], 249–255. Singapore: Xinjiapo yazhou yanjiu xuehui, 1992.

Yan Xuetong. *Ancient Chinese Thought, Modern Chinese Power*. Princeton, NJ: Princeton University Press, 2011.

Yan Yunxiang 閻雲翔. "Chaxu geju yu Zhongguo wenhua de dengjiguan 差序格局與中國文化的等級觀" [(Fei Xiaotong's) Differential Mode of Association and Hierarchical Conceptions within Chinese Culture]. *Shehuixue yanjiu* 社會學研究 [Sociological Research] 4 (2006): 201–212.

Yan Yunxiang. *The Individualization of Chinese Society*. London: Berg, 2009.

Yanabu Akira 柳父章. *Honyaku no shisô: "shizen" to Nature* 翻訳の思想: 自然と Nature [Thought within Translation: *shizen* and Nature]. Tokyo: Heibonsha Publishers, 1977.

Yang, Heriyanto. "The History and Legal Position of Confucianism in Post-Independence Indonesia." *Marburg Journal of Religion* 10, no. 1 (August 2005). http://archiv.ub.uni-marburg.de/mjr/pdf/2005/yang2005.pdf.

Yang Fenggang 楊鳳崗. "Duiyu rujiao zhi wei jiao de shehuixue sikao 對於儒教之為教的社會學思考" [Sociological Reflections about Confucianism as a Religion], 2005. https://www.purdue.edu/crcs/wp-content/uploads/2014/08/ConfucianismArticles.pdf.

Yang Ruqing 楊汝清. "Yi xiao zhi Tianxia 以孝治天下" [Governing the World by the Means of Filial Piety]. In *Rujia xianzheng yu Zhongguo weilai*

儒家憲政與中國未來 [Confucian Constitution and the Future of China], edited by Fan Ruiping et al., 167–178. Shanghai: Huadong shifan daxue chubanshe, 2012.

Yao Yingzhong. "Who is a Confucian Today? A Critical Reflection on the Issues Concerning Confucian Identity in Modern Times." *Journal of Contemporary Religion* 16, no. 3 (2001): 313–328.

Yidan xuetang 一耽學堂. *Xiandai yishu xuanchuan ziliao* 現代義塾宣傳資料 [Promotional Materialof Tradition-Inspired Modern Schools]. VCD published by the organization.

Yidan xuetang 一耽學堂. *Xing ming zhexue, xing li liaobing* 性命哲學,性理療病 [Philosophy of Nature and Heavenly Mandate: Curing Illness Basing Oneself on Principle and Nature]. VCD published by the organization.

Yidan xuetang 一耽學堂. *Yidan xuetang tongxun* 一耽學堂通訊 [Yidan Xuetang's Information Letter] issues 1–11 (2002–2006).

Yidan xuetang 一耽學堂. *Peiyang minzu jingshen, jiangou hexie shehui—Yidan xuetang zhongyang jingshen xuexi gangyao* 培養民族精神, 建構和諧社會,一耽學堂中央精神學習綱要 [Nurturing National Spirit, Constructing a Harmonious Society, Presentation of the Yidan Xuetang's Study of the Spirit Promoted by Chinese Central Authorities]. Unpublished material distributed by the Yidan Xuetang.

Yidan xuetang 一耽學堂. *Yidan xuetang bangongshi xinwen jianbao* 一耽學堂辦公室 新聞簡報 [Information Bulletin of the Yidan Xuetang]. Distributed through an electronic mailing list.

Yu Dan. *Le bonheur selon Confucius*. Paris: Belfond, 2009.

Yu Keping. *Democracy Is a Good Thing: Essays on Politics, Society, and Culture in Contemporary China*. Washington, DC: Brookings Institution, 2009.

Yu Keping 俞可平. "Hexie shijie linian xia de Zhongguo waijiao 和諧世界理念下的中國外交" [China's Approach of International Relations Within the Conceptual Context of a Harmonious World]. China.com, April 24, 2007. http:// www.china.com.cn/policy/zhuanti/hxsh/txt/2007-04/24/content_8162037.htm.

Yu Ying-shih 余英時. *Zhongguo jinshi zongjiao lunli yu shangren jingshen* 中國近世宗教倫理與商人精神 [Religious Intra-Mundane Ethics and the Spirits of Merchants in China]. Taipei: Lianjing, 1987.

Yu Ying-shih 余英時. "Xiandai ruxue de kunjing 現代儒學的困境" [The Predicament of Modern Confucianism]. In *Xiandai ruxue lun* 現代儒學論 [On Contemporary Confucianism], 159–164. River Edge: Global Publishing, 1996.

Zhang Qiang and Robert Weatherley. "The Rise of Republican Fever in the PRC and the Implications for CCP Legitimacy." *China Information* 27, no. 3 (November 2013): 277–300.

Zhang Xianglong 張祥龍. "'Zhexue' de houguo yu fencun—Du Ruile 'Ruxue jingyan yu zhexue huayu' yiwen duhou gan 哲學的後果與分寸—杜瑞

樂'儒學經驗與哲學話語'一文讀後感" [Consequences and Standards of Philosophy: Impression after Reading Thoraval's *Confucian Experience and Philosophical Discourses*]. *Zhongguo xueshu* 15 (2003): 242–259.

Zhang Xianglong 張祥龍. "Jianli 'rujia wenhua baohuqu' yiweizhe shenme? 建立儒家文化保護區意味着甚麼" [What Is the Meaning of the Construction of a Protection Zone for Confucian Culture?]. In *Rujia, rujiao yu zhongguo zhidu ziyuan*, 儒家,儒教與中國制度資源 [Confucianism, Confucian Religion, and Resources of the Chinese System], edited by Gan Chunsong 干春松, 162–169. Nanchang; Jiangxi chuban jituan, 2007.

Zhang Xiangping 張祥平. *Jingdian fuza kexue: Zhouyi Lunyu Daxue Zhongyong de tuili yu yingyong* 經典複雜科學:周易論語大學中庸的推理和應用 [The Complex Science of the Classics: Application and Inferences from the *Book of Changes*, the *Analects*, the *Great Learning*, and the *Zhongyong*]. Beijing: Zhongguo sheke, 2013.

Zhao Tingyang 趙汀陽. *Tianxia Tixi: Shijie zhidu zhexue daolun* 天下體系:世界制度哲學導論 [The Tianxia System: Philosophical Introduction to a World Institution]. Nanjing: Jiangsu Jiaoyu Chubanshe, 2005.

Zhao Tingyang. "A Political World Philosophy in Terms of All-Under-Heaven (Tian-xia)." *Diogenes* 221 (2009): 5–18.

Zheng Jiadong 鄭家棟. "Rujia sixiang de zongjiaoxing wenti 儒家思想的宗教性問題" [The Issue of the Religious Dimension of Confucian Thought]. In *Dangdai xin-ruxue lunheng* 當代新儒學論衡 [Essays on Contemporary Neo-Confucianism], 171–233. Taipei: Guiguan, 1995.

Zheng Yuan. "The Status of Confucianism in Modern Chinese Education, 1901–49: A Curricular Study." In *Education, Culture & Identity in Twentieth-Century China*, edited by Glen Peterson, Ruth Hayhoe, and Yonglin Lu, 193–216. Ann Arbor: University of Michigan Press, 2001.

Zheng Zhiming 鄭志明. *Wusheng laomu xinyang suyuan* 無生老母信仰溯源 [Genealogy of the Faith in the Eternal Mother]. Taipei: Wen shi zhe chubanshe, 1985.

Zhongguo xinwen zhoukan 中國新聞週刊 [China Newsweek], March 24, 2008, 27–39.

Zhou Beichen 周北辰. *Rujiao yaoyi* 儒教要義 [The Essentials about the Confucian Religion]. Hong Kong: Zhongguo guoji wenhua, 2009.

Zhu Weiqun 朱维群. "Gongchandangyuan buneng xinyang zongjiao 共產黨員不能信仰宗教" [A Communist Party Member Cannot Believe in a Religion]. December 16, 2011, Zhongguo gongchandang xinwenwang (Chinese Communist Party news network), http://theory.people.com.cn/GB/16625667.html.

Zito, Angela. *Of Body and Brush: Grand Sacrifice as Text/Performance in Eighteenth-Century China*. Chicago: University of Chicago Press, 1997.

Zito, Angela. "City Gods and Their Magistrates." In *Religions of China in Practice*, edited by Donald S. Lopez, 72–81. Princeton, NJ: Princeton University Press, 1996.

Zufferey, Nicolas. *To the Origins of Confucianism; The Ru in Pre-Qin Times and During the Early Han Dynasty.* Berne: Peter Lang, 2003.

Zufferey, Nicolas. "Chen Huanzhang et l'invention d'une religion confucianiste au début de l'époque républicaine." In *Le nouvel âge de Confucius,* edited by Flora Blanchon and Rang-Ri Park-Barjot, 173–188. Paris: Presses Universitaires de Paris-Sorbonne, 2007.

Index